TRIBE
OF HACKERS
RED TEAM

TRIBAL KNOWLEDGE FROM THE BEST IN OFFENSIVE CYBERSECURITY

MARCUS J. CAREY & JENNIFER JIN

WILEY

Published by John Wiley & Sons, Inc. Indianapolis, Indiana

Published simultaneously in Canada

ISBN: 978-1-119-64332-6
ISBN: 978-1-119-64336-4 (ebk.)
ISBN: 978-1-119-64333-3 (ebk.)

Manufactured in the United States of America

For general information on our other products and services or to obtain technical support, please contact our Customer Care Department within the U.S. at (877) 762-2974, outside the U.S. at (317) 572-3993 or fax (317) 572-4002.

Wiley publishes in a variety of print and electronic formats and by print-on-demand. Some material included with standard print versions of this book may not be included in e-books or in print-on-demand. If this book refers to media such as a CD or DVD that is not included in the version you purchased, you may download this material at http://booksupport.wiley.com. For more information about Wiley products, visit www.wiley.com.

Library of Congress Control Number: 2019945380

V10012255_071619

Contents

Acknowledgments

Tribe of Hackers would not exist without the awesome cybersecurity community and the contributors in it. I owe them tremendously for allowing me to share their perspectives on our industry.

I'd like to give a special shout-out to my wife, Mandy, for allowing me to do whatever the heck I want as far as building a business and being crazy enough to do this stuff. To Erran, Kaley, Chris, Chaya, Justin, Annie, Davian, Kai: I love you all more than the whole world!

I also want to thank Jennifer Jin for helping build the Tribe of Hackers book series and summit. She would like to thank her parents for not thinking that she's crazy for quitting pre-med.

Thanks also goes to Jennifer Aldoretta for helping me build a company that is true to our values. Shout-out to every one of the people that I've worked with over the past few years.

Thanks to Dan Mandel, Jim Minatel, and the Wiley team for believing in the whole vision.

—Marcus J. Carey

Introduction

Howdy, my name is Marcus, and I'm a hacker. You probably picked up this book to learn from the best in red teams. I'm going to start off with one of my favorite sayings: "We have two ears and one mouth so that we can listen twice as much as we speak." This quote is attributed to the Greek Stoic philosopher Epictetus. Trying to live out that wisdom is something I may never master.

When I was young, I was a know-it-all. I'd argue just to be right even when confronted with facts that definitively showed I was wrong. I was that kid in class who would raise my hand at every question, practically jumping out of the seat when a question was asked.

At some point, my parents bought an encyclopedia set, which I read from cover to cover. I read dictionaries to learn new words. I wanted to be like Einstein and Martin Luther King, Jr., rolled up into one. This behavior of wanting to know everything and believing I was the smartest person on Earth was crushed when I joined the military.

I was pretty smart and an excellent test taker, so I got into the U.S. Navy's cryptologic program. After I left basic training and arrived at my technical training command, I noticed it was swamped with nothing but really smart people.

When I arrived in Scotland for my first duty station, it was more of the same. I worked with senior noncommissioned officers and civilians who absolutely blew my mind. The old me was still there, but I eventually put my pride away and started asking more questions. I started taking the saying "There is no such thing as a dumb question" seriously.

From then on, I asked the most questions. Asking questions, and more importantly, listening to what others had to say, changed my life and learning. I still read everything I could get my hands on and kept close to the people who knew their stuff.

All my question-asking led me to a successful career in cybersecurity. My question-asking and listening was great when dealing with prospects and customers on the sales side of things. When people ask me how I got here, I tell them, "I ask more questions than anyone else."

Last year, when I started working on the original *Tribe of Hackers*, we asked more than 70 individuals in cybersecurity questions about how they started and found success. In this book, I've brought along a merry bunch of hacker friends who specialize in offensive security (aka red teaming).

Before we get started, let me quickly lay out what a red team is. A *red team* is a cybersecurity function that tests networks, applications, and systems to find vulnerabilities that may lead to compromise. Sometimes, red teams are allowed to exploit systems to validate that the vulnerability is real. Red teams also can perform physical assessments and social engineering engagements.

On the opposite side of the house, a *blue team* is responsible for monitoring networks, systems, and applications for intrusions and for making sure that the confidentiality, integrity, and availability of all assets are not affected. Nowadays, organizations are combining red and blue teams and sometimes use the term *purple team*.

To formulate questions, I reached out the cybersecurity community on Twitter to hear what they wanted to know about the most.

Marcus J. Carey ✓
@marcusjcarey

Shall we play a game?

We are working on a new book.

@TribeOfHackers Red Team Edition

Tweet a question in this thread that you'd like answered in the book.

We will feature five tweets/questions in the book from the community.

If you see a good question, like it.

12:43 PM - 12 Apr 2019

Originally, I planned on using five questions from the book, but on second thought, I decided to take more than five questions from the community. The following are the questions inspired by the response from the community, plus a few more from me.

1. How did you get your start on a red team?

 ShadowBroker @ShadowBroker218 · Apr 12
Replying to @marcusjcarey @TribeOfHackers
How did you get your start on a red team? What was it that got you that first red team job?

2. What is the best way to get a red team job?
3. How can someone gain red team skills without getting in trouble with the law?
4. Why can't we agree on what a red team is?

 **Ryan O%27Horo**
@redteamwrangler   Following ⌄

Replying to @marcusjcarey @TribeOfHackers

Why can't we agree on what Red Team is?

1:11 PM - 12 Apr 2019

5. What is one thing the rest of information security doesn't understand about being on a red team? What is the most toxic falsehood you have heard related to red, blue, or purple teams?

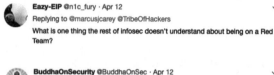

Eazy-EIP @n1c_fury · Apr 12
Replying to @marcusjcarey @TribeOfHackers
What is one thing the rest of infosec doesn't understand about being on a Red Team?

BuddhaOnSecurity @BuddhaOnSec · Apr 12
Replying to @marcusjcarey @ian_infosec @TribeOfHackers
What do you think is the single most toxic falsehood you have heard around red (and/or purple/blue) teams?

6. When should you introduce a formal red team into an organization's security program?

Accidental CISO
@AccidentalCISO

Follow

Replying to @marcusjcarey @TribeOfHackers

What is the appropriate point in the maturation of a security program to introduce a formal read team into the org?

9:37 AM - 13 Apr 2019

Isaiah Sarju @isaiahsarju · Apr 12
Replying to @marcusjcarey @TribeOfHackers
How do you know when you can use a red team?

7. How do you explain the value of red teaming to a reluctant or nontechnical client or organization?

8. What is the least bang-for-your-buck security control that you see implemented?

Integgroll
@integgroll

Follow

Replying to @marcusjcarey @TribeOfHackers

What is the least bang for your buck control you see implemented?

2:04 PM - 13 Apr 2019

9. Have you ever recommended not doing a red team engagement?

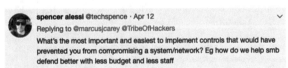

cyberphilosopher ⊕
@_4_d_4_m_

Follow ⌄

Replying to @marcusjcarey @TribeOfHackers

At what point do you recommend not doing a red team, and offer something else more suitable, even when a customer asks for one?

2:16 PM - 12 Apr 2019

10. What's the most important or easiest-to-implement control that can prevent you from compromising a system or network?

spencer alessi @techspence · Apr 12   ⌄
Replying to @marcusjcarey @TribeOfHackers
What's the most important and easiest to implement controls that would have prevented you from compromising a system/network? Eg how do we help smb defend better with less budget and less staff

11. Why do you feel it is critical to stay within the rules of engagement?

Shawn Romines
@infosecusa

Following ⌄

Replying to @marcusjcarey @TribeOfHackers

Why do you feel it is critical to stay within the rules of engagement?

3:54 PM - 12 Apr 2019

12. If you were ever busted on a penetration test or other engagement, how did you handle it?

Dann Tannher ✔ @Viss · Apr 12   ⌄
Replying to @marcusjcarey @TribeOfHackers
May I suggest a few of the phobos redteam interview questions?

- tell me story about being on a physical and getting caught

- walk me through how your malware got burned and you lost all your shells

- what was your craziest exfil

- what was your craziest 'busted' moment

13. What is the biggest ethical quandary you experienced while on an assigned objective?

 ryan @skykn0t · Apr 12
Replying to @marcusjcarey @TribeOfHackers
What was the biggest ethical quandary you experienced while accomplishing your assigned objective?

14. How does the red team work together to get the job done?

 L0KK1 @L0kk12 · Apr 12
Replying to @marcusjcarey @TribeOfHackers
Describe the team aspect of red team? How do you work together to get a job done? Including working with the blue team after? Or just some simple documentation tips?

15. What is your approach to debriefing and supporting blue teams after an operation is completed?

 SHADOWOPS | DATA PRIVACY AND SECURITY RESEARCH ... · Apr 12
Replying to @marcusjcarey @TribeOfHackers
Can you describe your approach to debriefing and supporting blue teams after an operation is completed, and why you feel this is important to all teams regardless of their role?

16. If you were to switch to the blue team, what would be your first step to better defend against attacks?

 (((Ken N.))) @Sakuracon
@K3n_5s   (Follow)

Replying to @Viss @marcusjcarey @TribeOfHackers

"If you were to be switched to blue, what would be your first three steps to better defend against attacks, and if they aren't commonly done already, why do you suppose that's the case?"

1:22 PM - 12 Apr 2019

17. What is some practical advice on writing a good report?

18. How do you ensure your program results are valuable to people who need a full narrative and context?

 Mark @markstjohn · Apr 12
Replying to @marcusjcarey @TribeOfHackers
How do you ensure your program results are valuable to people who need a full narrative and context instead of a showcase of their weaknesses vs. your skill set?

19. How do you recommend security improvements other than pointing out where it's insufficient?

> **𝓡𝓪𝓫𝓫𝓲𝓽** @ra6bit · Apr 12
> Replying to @marcusjcarey @TribeOfHackers
> What have you done to improve security other than point out where it is insufficient?

20. What nontechnical skills or attitudes do you look for when recruiting and interviewing red team members?

> **Eric Kates** @positronek · Apr 12
> Replying to @marcusjcarey @TribeOfHackers
> What is one of the most beneficial non-technical skills used for red-teaming activity?

21. What differentiates good red teamers from the pack as far as approaching a problem differently?

Chris Campbell
@obscuresec

Following

Replying to @marcusjcarey @TribeOfHackers

How does a good red teamer approach a problem differently than other types of testers?

12:45 PM - 12 Apr 2019

So, those are the 21 questions we asked 47 experts, including myself. I thought I'd chime in with my opinions to set the stage before getting to the 46 others. Hope you enjoy!

Marcus J. Carey
April 12, 2019

> "Today, open source tools dominate the red team space, making it possible for more people to get familiar and practice."

Twitter: @marcusjcarey • **Website:** https://www.linkedin.com/in/marcuscarey/

Marcus J. Carey

Marcus J. Carey is a cybersecurity community advocate and startup founder with more than 25 years of protecting government and commercial sensitive data. He started his cybersecurity career in U.S. Navy cryptology with further service in the National Security Agency (NSA).

How did you get your start on a red team?
The funny thing about my red team journey is I wasn't technically a paid red teamer until I got fired from a job and had to make ends meet. I picked up work at an East Coast consultancy doing penetration testing and product development.

I was able to gain red team skills by working at the Defense Cyber Crime Center (DC3). There I did research, taught, and did course development. Amazingly, I had access to all the red team tools that you could imagine, plus every digital forensics tool on the planet. I also had the pleasure of working with a guy named Johnny Long who was quite the hacker and red teamer himself.

I'm extremely lucky to have been in those positions to prepare me for a red team role. Today, open source tools dominate the red team space, making it possible for more people to get familiar and practice.

They say luck is when preparation meets opportunity. It sucks that I was laid off, but it was a blessing to have red team skills to pay the bills.

What is the best way to get a red team job?
It is uncommon for people to start directly into red team jobs. The best way is to have or gain a skill such as internetworking, system administration, or software engineering and start out in a blue team role. Getting into a blue team

role will allow you gain cybersecurity experience and network with people in your dream role.

You can network internally and externally from your organization at local events and regional cybersecurity conferences. There are a couple of certifications tailored to red teaming that can get you noticed by red teams looking to add some human resources.

How can someone gain red team skills without getting in trouble with the law?

I recommend downloading virtual machines and web applications that have vulnerabilities on them when trying to learn at home. There are plenty out there; just be careful and don't put them on the internet because they will be compromised in short order.

If you don't have permission from the system owners to test or run tools, you are probably violating some law. If you are trying to get into red teaming, try to exploit only the systems that you own or systems that you have explicit written permission to exploit.

Why can't we agree on what a red team is?

I think it's human nature to want to differentiate from each other, especially in a competitive environment like the cybersecurity community. What I have learned is that there are only so many ways to solve problems. Many times we end up with the same solutions to the same problems we see. We end up having different names for the same thing. The old saying "There are no new ideas under the sun" is proven right every time I talk to people trying to solve the same issues.

What is one thing the rest of information security doesn't understand about being on a red team? What is the most toxic falsehood you have heard related to red, blue, or purple teams?

There is a natural conflict between the red team and the blue team caused by a mixture of bad experiences and misunderstandings. I think the toxic bit sometimes comes from people making mistakes like taking down servers or leaving malware on endpoints. The problem is that everyone hears red team horror stories, and there isn't a lot of data that backs anything up.

When should you introduce a formal red team into an organization's security program?

I believe that everyone in information technology and software engineering should know how to build, secure, and hack anything they are in charge of. My crazy vision is everyone always threat modeling and red teaming everything they do. You don't need to have red team as your title to utilize red team skills. I always say, "Hack more. Worry less."

How do you explain the value of red teaming to a reluctant or nontechnical client or organization?

I believe the best way to do this is to explain that even though the red team has an adversarial role, internal and external red team goals are aligned in the sense that we all want to protect sensitive data and critical systems. To keep the trust over time, red teams should always avoid showing up blue teams and internal stakeholders. You can only do this by working closely as a team. It takes only one bad experience to potentially ruin these relationships.

What is the least bang-for-your-buck security control that you see implemented?

Antivirus.

Have you ever recommended not doing a red team engagement?
I certainly have. I recommend that the organization start with vulnerability management and getting policy and governance into play. I see too many organizations out there getting "penetration tested" for compliance. I put those words in quotes because organizations are typically getting a limited-scope vulnerability scan.

What's the most important or easiest-to-implement control that can prevent you from compromising a system or network?
I'm going to go with restricting administrative privileges for end users. I've seen first hand how this drastically reduces infections on a network. This simple control applies to organizations of any size. Restricting privileges is easy to implement and scale.

Why do you feel it is critical to stay within the rules of engagement?
The only difference between a good person and a bad person is that the good person follows the rules. Violating the rules of engagement breaks the trust between teams. If you violate the rules of engagement, you may be breaking the law as well.

If you were ever busted on a penetration test or other engagement, how did you handle it?
One of the most embarrassing things I ever did related to red teaming is owning a USB thumb drive with a volume name of Marcus Carey. I ended up using the thumb drive in a server, and the forensics software detected the device that had my name on it.

I'll never make that mistake again. I'm sharing this story so it doesn't happen to you. Sharing is caring!

What is the biggest ethical quandary you experienced while on an assigned objective?
The biggest ethical quandary is being intentionally deceptive in spear phishing and social engineering. This is primarily because you could cause actual harm to people and their livelihoods on the other side of the phish.

One of my mentors would always ask for a few executives to be in scope in every engagement so management couldn't blame it on their staff. He wasn't satisfied until an executive was compromised. Sometimes he'd conceal the identity of the person whom he compromised so they wouldn't get in trouble.

How does the red team work together to get the job done?
If you are working with a team, communication is the most important element. Split up work and ensure you document everything that you do on an engagement. Trust is important as well, because I've seen situations where team members lose faith in their teammates.

I recommend using collaborative tools so everyone can see what their teammates are doing. Transparency always wins. One more thing, don't be afraid to ask for help; that's what teammates are for. If your teammate is an expert at a certain thing, simply ask for help.

What is your approach to debriefing and supporting blue teams after an operation is completed?
Professionalism is the key. Since we are all human, feelings can come into play when debriefing to internal and external blue teams. Always let them know you are on the same team as far as the big mission goes. If you do it right, they will have a detailed plan for how to correct any issues you discovered.

The hard part is when you help someone and then come back in the future and find that the same issues exist. Don't get mad. Try not to get burnt out. Stay professional and try to help. You can lead a horse to water, but you can't make it drink.

If you were to switch to blue team, what would be your first step to better defend against attacks?
I'm blue team for life, but I occasionally red team. The first step to being able to defend against attacks is putting policy in place and following it. I repeat, follow it.

People don't implement policies because it feels cumbersome. Security policy should be looked at like a map. You may not be where the policy says you are, but if you don't have a map, you'll never reach your destination.

What is some practical advice on writing a good report?
My advice is to not reinvent the wheel—there are plenty of resources out there to describe vulnerabilities, exploitation, and risk scoring. Feel free to grab content from NIST, CVSS, or MITRE ATT&CK and cite them as references. Citing them as references actually boosts the credibility of your findings and report.

Use something like CVSS to help score the vulnerabilities that you find. MITRE ATT&CK is great for discussing exploitation techniques and suggested remediations. If you use those resources, the report will be easier to write for you and easier for the consumer to trust.

How do you ensure your program results are valuable to people who need a full narrative and context?
I think it's important to use something that tells both sides of the story. I like things like the MITRE ATT&CK framework and the NIST Cybersecurity Framework because they both can be used to measure your actual capabilities and skill sets. It's possible to be effective at cybersecurity without mastering all the skill sets. Pick three things and be the best at them.

The book *From Good to Great* talks about how great businesses understand what they are good at. We can apply the same thing to cybersecurity.

How do you recommend security improvements other than pointing out where it's insufficient?
I always try to find some areas where organizations are doing some things right. So, low-hanging fruits for positive reinforcement are two-factor/two-step authentication, password length, and automatic updates.

Another way to help out as a red teamer is to understand ways to fix issues, whether on a system, on a network, or in code, that build camaraderie. I've sat side by side with Unix administrators helping them issue commands to harden systems. This is especially important if you are doing internal corporate red teams. At the end of the day, you are on the same mission.

What nontechnical skills or attitudes do you look for when recruiting and interviewing red team members?
Empathy is a great skill to have when you are delivering bad news. As a red teamer, you are going to have to give some bad news every once in a while. Put yourself in the other person's shoes and don't be a jerk.

What differentiates good red teamers from the pack as far as approaching a problem differently?
I think good red teamers study and know how things work. I mentioned empathy before. A good red teamer can put themselves in the system administrator, network engineer, or software developer mind-set and solve the problems they are facing. A good red teamer is always hungry to improve their skills and help others do so as well. ■

"There's no 'right way' to become a red team member."

Twitter: @operant

David Bell

2

Dave is currently the director of the red team for General Electric (GE), where he leads engagements against strategic assets in many industries across the globe. Prior to joining GE, Dave spent 10 years with the U.S. Navy red team, where he planned, led, and executed engagements against all branches of the U.S. military, many government agencies, and even coalition partners. Dave is also a veteran of the U.S. Navy, where he spent 10 years in the intelligence and special programs communities.

How did you get your start on a red team?
I got my start in 2006 with the U.S. Navy red team as a contractor. I had just spent about six months working nights as an IDS analyst with another contracting company, and prior to that I was on active duty in the Navy, mostly in signals intelligence. I spent a lot of time leading up to my separation from the Navy studying for certifications and hacking on home-built networks. That was enough to get me in the door, where the real learning began! I spent 10 years with that team, converted to a government civilian, and was the deputy director by the time I left. I'm now the director of the red team at GE.

What is the best way to get a red team job?
This is a question I am asked quite often, and I still struggle to answer it. There's no "right way" to become a red team member. I worked with one really smart guy who at one point drove bulldozers. Having said that, demonstrating the ability to think like an attacker is critical and can't be taught. We can teach technical skills, but mind-set seems to be innate. If someone has the right

mind-set, generally my advice is to pursue applicable training and certifications and get involved in capture-the-flag (CTF) events.

Like college degrees, the certifications tell me that the candidate is committed and will follow through, and the CTF events give me an idea how they will perform as part of a team. I also suggest starting with other InfoSec jobs, such as pentesting or incident handling.

How can someone gain red team skills without getting in trouble with the law?

This really shouldn't be an issue anymore. There is a lot of training available, both online and in-person. Cloud platforms provide cost-effective learning environments, too; we no longer need to buy old gear from eBay or Craigslist to build a home lab.

Why can't we agree on what a red team is?

Coming from the U.S. military red team community, I have a pretty strong opinion on the misuse of this and other terms with military roots. It's tempting to blame industry marketing for this, but it really is a community problem. Penetration testing is a distinct and separate discipline from red teaming, and furthermore, there is a significant difference between internal red teams and consultant red teams. These differences can get quite confusing to customers who just want the best engagement they can get with the budget they have, and less principled teams might take advantage of this.

What is one thing the rest of information security doesn't understand about being on a red team? What is the most toxic falsehood you have heard related to red, blue, or purple teams?

Red team operations can be painfully boring. It's mind-numbing, detailed, analytical work, punctuated by moments of sheer elation and adrenaline. Most people only see the highlights in the debriefings or have misconceptions from Hollywood movies.

When should you introduce a formal red team into an organization's security program?

I often tell people that they don't need a red team engagement until they *think* they don't need a red team engagement. As soon as the organization feels like they understand all of the threats and have a good handle on things, it's time for a good red team to challenge those assumptions. And that first report won't be pretty.

How do you explain the value of red teaming to a reluctant or nontechnical client or organization?

Learning the business! I can't stress this enough. The red team has to understand what they are attacking in the context of the business they are supporting. Showing this understanding will go a long way toward establishing trust and true partnership with the customer.

What is the *least* bang-for-your-buck security control that you see implemented?

Vulnerability scanning. While this is an important security function, I rarely see it done correctly, especially at scale. If an organization is too large to keep an accurate asset inventory, how can they possibly expect to be able to scan all the things?

Have you ever recommended not doing a red team engagement?

Yes, quite often. I've found that while many customers are asking for a red team engagement, they're often really (unknowingly) looking for a web app test or another form of limited-scope penetration test. In these cases, I will facilitate an introduction to another team that can better meet their needs. Some may see this as "losing business," but I see it as building trust.

What's the most important or easiest-to-implement control that can prevent you from compromising a system or network?

Endpoints rarely need to be able to communicate with each other across the network. Blocking or monitoring this type of traffic should go a long way toward limiting an attacker's lateral movement. Keep in mind that the attacker is after data that will reside in a database, and so on. Lateral movement is used to locate and acquire the permissions needed to gain access to this data. Limit that movement as much as possible, and force the attackers to make mistakes.

Why do you feel it is critical to stay within the rules of engagement?

Rules of engagement (ROE) are used to define how the engagement should be conducted, the scope of the engagement, who should be contacted in case of emergency, and any other items of importance. The ROE is the primary safety net for both the red team and the customer, so if the red team were to deviate from those rules, systems could be damaged, or physically unsafe conditions could be created. Accidents can and do happen, however, so good ROE will define reporting processes for those incidents, and the red team will be completely honest about what happened.

If you were ever busted on a penetration test or other engagement, how did you handle it?

I've never done a penetration test, but I have been part of many red team engagements, including network exploitation, wireless, and even physical assessments overseas. One of my favorite stories is when my teammate and I got busted trying to convince some military personnel to let us plug in a USB thumb drive. A higher-ranking officer overheard the conversation from the next room and immediately rushed in to confront us. He was shaking with anger and informed us, "The red team did this to me last year, and you're not going to do it again!"

I had no idea what he was talking about, but knew I had two choices: I could either back down and admit I was caught, or I could maintain character and react the same way anyone else in that position would have. I chose the latter and started shouting back that I didn't appreciate accusations while I was just trying to do my job. He didn't buy it for a second, but I wasn't going to give him the satisfaction. He took us to his security officer, who informed him that our (actually fake) ID cards looked normal to him. While the first officer left the room to retrieve the encryption key for his phone (so he could call "my boss"), I explained to the security officer that we had an authorization letter in the car, and we would just grab that and be right back.

Once we got in the car, we still had to get off the base, which was nerve-wracking as well! That evening I discovered that there was a "be on (the) lookout" alert (BOLO) for me issued by the local host-nation police (no doubt the work of the angry senior officer), so I left the country shortly after. I didn't fully relax until I cleared customs in the United States.

What is the biggest ethical quandary you experienced while on an assigned objective?

Being asked to "target" specific individuals is always a little creepy. I prefer not to and will always argue against it. I have no problem targeting specific roles or positions within an organization, however, as long as there is a solid threat model justifying it. One example is that I've been asked to look at the social media profiles of executives and their families. Careful controls need to be in place, and permission given, before I will entertain tasks like this.

How does the red team work together to get the job done?

The ability to function as a cohesive team is often what separates highly effective teams from those that are not. While every team member is important, skilled, and talented, no team member is so highly skilled that they can complete an engagement without the help of their teammates. Similarly, no red team operator should ever work on an engagement alone. Either physically or virtually, another operator should be working on the same engagement so they can function as a safety/sanity check for each other.

Detailed documentation is of the utmost importance during red team engagements. The customer is paying for the information contained in the report, which is derived from detailed, disciplined logging done during the actual engagement.

What is your approach to debriefing and supporting blue teams after an operation is completed?

Debriefs should always be tailored to the audience. Defenders should get an in-depth technical report that walks them through the attack path from start to finish. Ample time for questions should be scheduled, and the red team should be prepared for any follow-up reports for key people who weren't able to attend for some reason. I also encourage the teams to be available for mini-retests or other forms of support to enable defenders to learn from the engagement.

This is a partnership, and the report should reflect that—you should state facts without ego and recognize that some people are going to be embarrassed or defensive. Be sure to also give credit where credit is due.

If you were to switch to the blue team, what would be your first step to better defend against attacks?

Prevention is preferred, but detection is a must. My first step would be to understand what data sources were available and make sure they were accessible to defenders. Many defenders have complained of data overload, but almost every engagement I've ever been part of had shown some kind of blind spot. The more data available to automation and manual queries, the more likely an attack will be detected.

What is some practical advice on writing a good report?

Stick to the facts, and paint the picture of the attack path. Don't use jargon, and provide references to CVEs or technical guides wherever possible. The report is the product you are providing; it is what the customer is paying for. Nothing else matters, so get this right every time. If there are follow-up questions, answer them promptly and accurately and make note of them for your next report.

How do you ensure your program results are valuable to people who need a full narrative and context?

This will vary with each organization, but a good way to start is to identify who the red team's true customers are. Customers are different than stakeholders, and this differentiation becomes important when trying to prioritize engagements and reports.

Once the true customers and stakeholders are identified, red team leadership should begin to tailor their communications to those individuals. Reports should be at the correct level of detail and clearly answer the inevitable "so what?" question before it is even asked. This requires learning the business and understanding how the technology your team has just assessed fits into those processes (and therefore the impact of your team's actions on the business as a whole). The business is the ultimate customer, and the business does not exist solely to run a CIRT (or a red team).

How do you recommend security improvements other than pointing out where it's insufficient?

Red teams are often asked for recommendations for security improvements, but frustratingly, the answer is almost always "it depends." Red teams provide a snapshot-in-time look at an environment. Red teams likely have no idea *why* the environment looks the way it does, but almost certainly there were decisions made at some point, for some business reason, to design and build the environment in that particular way. One way to take this into account is for the red team to sit down with the teams responsible for implementing fixes and walk through the attack path from start to finish.

This helps the network owners get a peek into the mind of the attacker, and it helps the red team understand what challenges the network owners face. Then, potential mitigations can be brainstormed and table-topped at that moment, resulting in quality recommendations that can actually be implemented. The red team can even come back at a later date and retest the environment to see whether the recommended fixes are performing as intended.

What nontechnical skills or attitudes do you look for when recruiting and interviewing red team members?

When I am talking to candidates, I am looking for positive attitudes and strong internal drive/motivation. Red teamers will often find themselves neck-deep in mind-numbing analysis, the results of which could determine the success of the engagement.

Therefore, it is important that candidates are able to motivate themselves to keep going, not lose sight of the objective, and not complain that they're "not doing cool stuff." Red team work is usually pretty boring, minus the moments of sheer adrenaline when that shell finally comes back, so candidates need to give the impression that they have the patience and determination to accomplish the mission.

What differentiates good red teamers from the pack as far as approaching a problem differently?

Good red teamers are able to think, plan, and act like an attacker. This ability is often referred to as the *attacker mind-set*, but it's more of a lifestyle than something that can just be turned on or off as needed. For example, once a good red teamer has been trained and has conducted physical engagements, that red teamer will habitually and unconsciously "case" every building they enter. They will automatically make note of the position and angle of cameras, security personnel, type and condition of locks on doors and windows, and so on, all without thinking about it. The same is true for red teamers on the keyboard: they will develop an innate ability to "feel" vulnerabilities and intuitively understand not only how to exploit them but whether they *should* exploit them in furtherance of their ultimate objectives.

This quality is difficult to identify in candidates and even harder to express in words. However, I have seen good results from having candidates demonstrate their talents in skills challenges during the last stages of the interview process. How a candidate approaches problems in a high-pressure virtual environment tells us quite a bit about whether the attacker mind-set is fully present, needs developing, or simply doesn't exist within a candidate. Not everyone can think this way, and not everyone is cut out to be on a red team, and that's okay. I've seen very smart people struggle with this aspect but then go on to build successful careers in other aspects of cybersecurity. ∎

> "As you can imagine, the best way to get a red team job is to first understand what it is that you want to do and then build a technical skill set and foundation to align with what that type of role would entail."

Twitter: @ProfBrager

Paul Brager

3

Regarded as a thought leader and expert in the cybersecurity community for more than 25 years, Paul has deep expertise evaluating, securing, and defending critical infrastructure and manufacturing assets (ICS, IoT, and IIoT). An avid speaker and researcher, Paul seeks to move the conversation forward surrounding ICS cyber and managing the threat surface.

He has provided commentary on several security-related podcasts, publications, and webinars that provided guidance and insight into strategies for critical infrastructure and manufacturing cyber defense. Paul has a passion for mentoring and guiding people of color who are aspiring to contribute to the advancement of the industry and promoting diversity within the cyber community.

How did you get your start on a red team?
My red team beginnings (much like most experiences in this space) came about from necessity. Company leadership fired a "legacy" employee who was using a Windows 95 desktop with local accounts (yes, Windows 95). At the time, it wasn't uncommon for workstations to not be part of a domain (Windows domains weren't terribly common in the mid-'90s), but there also weren't many methods of getting into a workstation if the password was lost. Novell was still king of the network operating systems, so you get the picture. Recovering a machine typically means re-installing over the top of it and hoping that you didn't step on any of the critical documents/areas or getting into it with one of many "magic boot disks" that had started to appear at the time.

These were generally Slackware-based, but you needed some "skills" to be able to get them to work without destroying the master boot record (MBR) on the target. "Hacking" those disks with predictable results became more of an art than a science, as you needed not only some Linux/BSD knowledge but also knowledge of how partitions worked within Windows. After spending countless hours building (and rebuilding) a Windows 95 test machine to get the parameters correct, I was able to successfully gain access to the Windows 95 workstation and recover valuable source code that would have cost the company months in development.

What is the best way to get a red team job?

Well, it depends—red team job doing what? Pure penetration testing? Survivability testing? Penetration testing against certain classes of assets, in other words, ICS? As you can imagine, the best way to get a red team job is to first understand what it is that you want to do and then build a technical skill set and foundation to align with what that type of role would entail. Experience is generally key here but not always—sometimes raw knowledge and demonstrated know-how are enough. Much of how you are received as a legitimate red teamer is left to the devices of those interviewing, but those who can truly recognize talent may show interest. Networking, either in person or through social media (or both), remains one of the strongest ways to get insight into available red team roles, but you may also luck out and talk to someone in a position to make a hiring decision.

How can someone gain red team skills without getting in trouble with the law?

Today, gaining red team skills without getting into legal trouble is easy. Many of the tools that one would need to practice are open source and easily downloaded; the same is true about access to many of the operating systems that would be potential targets. The world of virtualization has opened the door to the creation of virtual labs that can be destroyed and rebuilt with no impact to anyone—other than you, of course. Additionally, there are numerous hackable platforms available to test various skills and abilities (such as Hack The Box) to further hone red teaming skills. The more specialized type of practice—against ICS assets, for example—is a bit trickier, although some PLCs (the primary targets in an ICS) can be purchased on eBay. Likewise, IoT devices (such as Raspberry Pis) can be purchased inexpensively to develop skills against those.

Why can't we agree on what a red team is?

As with many things in cybersecurity, there is always an implied "it depends" when discussing what constitutes red teaming. Some believe that red teaming is just hacking; others believe that red teaming is far more robust and systematic than that. I believe that ultimately it depends on the perspective of the audience. For those in a purely corporate setting, red teaming gives a more elegant name to penetration testing with a nonmalicious purpose. It infers a sense of structure and methodology that leverages offensive security capabilities to uncover exploitable vulnerabilities. Among the hacker community, however, there may be a much looser definition being used.

What is one thing the rest of information security doesn't understand about being on a red team? What is the most toxic falsehood you have heard related to red, blue, or purple teams?

Being on a red team does not automatically make a person nefarious or malicious. Rather, what excites them within the realm of cybersecurity tends to be more the offensive capabilities. Researching and discovering exploitable vulnerabilities is both tedious and painstaking, and to be able to do so *and* articulate findings in a consumable manner is more an art than a science. While their pedigree may be hacker-made, it does not define them but legitimizes their necessity within the cybersecurity ecosystem.

Perhaps the most toxic falsehood to date that I have heard is that cybersecurity professionals completely fit within one of three buckets: red team, blue team, and purple team. This gives the perception that cybersecurity professionals are single-threaded, which simply isn't true at all. While each professional may have more of an affinity to one or the other depending on how they have matured within cybersecurity, it is functionally impossible to not consider the other buckets. Red teamers must understand how their penetration attempts could be thwarted or detected and come up with countermeasures to lessen the likelihood of that happening. Blue teamers must understand at some level the TTPs that adversaries are launching to better develop countermeasures to repel them. Most cybersecurity professional are a shade of purple, being more red or blue depending on affinity and maturity in the field.

When should you introduce a formal red team into an organization's security program?

A formal red team can be introduced into a security program at any point. The value and benefit of doing so largely depends on what is to be gained from the red team exercises. If the intent is to understand the threat surface and to what degree a program (or a part of the program) is vulnerable, then it is reasonable to engage red team services early in the program's develop phase as a tool to better frame overall risks. Similarly, formal red team engagement can be part of the overall security strategy and lifecycle to reassess the robustness of controls and the organization's ability to detect and respond.

How do you explain the value of red teaming to a reluctant or nontechnical client or organization?

Lobbying for red teaming within one's organization can be challenging, particularly if the organization's security program has not matured beyond vulnerability assessment and/or vulnerability management. Additionally, if the organization has not sufficiently invested in or implemented controls or resources, red teaming may uncover vulnerabilities that have not been budgeted for and which there are insufficient resources to address, which exacerbates the problem. My approach has always been to frame the notion of red teaming as a function of risk management/mitigation. Red teaming allows for an organization to find potentially damaging or risky holes in their security posture before bad actors exploit them, minimizing the potential impact to company reputation, customers, and shareholders. Taking this approach makes the question of whether to use red teaming a business decision, as opposed to a technical one.

What is the *least* bang-for-your-buck security control that you see implemented?

With the myriad of security products, services, and capabilities that are on the market, they all should be supporting two principal edicts: detect and respond. However, many security organizations are not staffed appropriately to consume and act on all the data that is available to them from these tools. Standalone threat intelligence tools, in my opinion, offer the least bang for the buck because they still require contextual correlation to the environment, which implicitly requires human cycles. Even with automation and orchestration between firewalls, SIEM, and IDS/IPS, correctly consuming threat intelligence requires resources—and burns cycles that may be better utilized elsewhere. The robustness of many of the more effective controls (firewalls, IDS/IPS, EPP) will generally give you the threat context that is necessary to detect and respond, without the overhead of another tool.

Have you ever recommended not doing a red team engagement?
Typically, a customer or an organization can always benefit from some form of
"red team" activity, even if it is just a light penetration test. In my consulting life,
we generally would recommend against a full-blown red team exercise if there
was significant immaturity evident within the organization's security program
or if the rules of engagement could not be settled upon to safely conduct the
red team exercise. What has been recommended in the past is a more phased
approach, going after a limited scope of targets and then gradually expanding as
the organization's security maturity increases.

**What's the most important or easiest-to-implement control that can
prevent you from compromising a system or network?**
Security awareness training can be one of the easiest and most important
controls that bolsters the overall security posture of an organization. User
behavior can be the difference between a managed threat landscape and
an unruly one, and in many instances, the end user will see incidents before
security. Educate and empower users to practice good cyber hygiene. Beyond
that, certain security controls that are cloud-based can be leveraged to offset
the capital costs of infrastructure, if that is a barrier. This is particularly true in
small to medium-sized businesses with limited staff and/or budgets.

Why do you feel it is critical to stay within the rules of engagement?
Rules of engagement are established as the outer markers for any red team/
pentesting exercise. They basically provide the top cover for activities that
may cause harm or an outage, even if unintentional. Additionally, the rules of
engagement can be your "get-out-of-jail-free" card should something truly go
sideways, as they generally include a hold harmless clause. Deviating from the
stated rules of engagement without expressed written consent of the client
could open you up to legal liability issues and be devastating to your career.

**If you were ever busted on a penetration test or other engagement,
how did you handle it?**
I had an instance where a physical penetration test was being conducted for a
client, and the sponsor had neglected to notify site security about my presence.
After gaining access to the facility through a propped-open door in the back
(repair personnel didn't want to keep badging in), I was walking through the
facility with a hard hat that I had "borrowed" from a table, and I was apprehended
by site security and the local police. To make matters worse, my contact was
unavailable when they called to confirm that I was authorized to conduct the
penetration test. After two intense hours of calling everyone that I could to get
this cleared up and the threat of charges being filed, the contact finally called
back and I was released without being arrested.

**What is the biggest ethical quandary you experienced while on an
assigned objective?**
Without question, the biggest ethical quandary I've experienced is stumbling
upon an account cache, financial records, or PII in a place where they shouldn't
be and being told by the sponsor not to disclose the details to the impacted
individuals until the penetration testing exercise was complete, which may
be over several days. For me, there are certain discoveries that take priority
and need to be acted upon immediately, particularly when it is PII or financial
information. In this case, the sponsor was attempting to prove a point to
another member of management and had virtually no regard for what had been
discovered.

How does the red team work together to get the job done?
Red teaming, as the name implies, generally involves more than one person. The coordination that is needed to engage in a penetration test against multiple targets requires clear accountability as to what is expected of each team member. Additionally, there are generally members of the team who are better at certain tasks than others—those more suited to speaking with the customer do so, those more technical stick to those roles, and so on. It is always useful to have a team of red teamers comfortable speaking with customers, as each of them (particularly in large engagements) may have to report at different times to different audiences.

What is your approach to debriefing and supporting blue teams after an operation is completed?
When I was consulting, there would be two report-outs. One would be for management and reported on the high-level activities that were conducted, what was found, and the risk concerns that had arisen from those findings. Any extraordinary findings would be enumerated within that conversation so that if any legal or other actions needed to get underway, the accountable parties could get started. The second report was the technical deep-dive; it was generally divided into finding areas, and individual small sessions were conducted with blue team designees to confirm what was in the report and walk through any questions. It was also during these sessions that follow-on remediation efforts and next steps would be discussed.

If you were to switch to the blue team, what would be your first step to better defend against attacks?
Having lived on both sides of the fence, one of the things I am always amazed about is the lack of contextual visibility—not just logs and so on, but actual visibility with context into the associated assets. Additionally, there still seems to be considerable challenge in identifying assets within the ecosystem. The introduction of IoT (IIoT in the industrial world) has exacerbated this problem. Those two areas need to be addressed from a defense-in-depth approach because you simply cannot defend what you cannot see and identify. Effective cybersecurity defense is deployed in layers so that even if attackers get past one layer of defenses, it is increasingly difficult for them to get past subsequent layers. Lastly, I would spend more time and energy on security awareness training and arming the end user with the information needed to change behavior.

What is some practical advice on writing a good report?
When writing a testing report, it is important to understand what the objective of the customer is and write the report to align with those objectives. At the end of the day, any remediation efforts are going to need to be funded, and the more the testing report can help build that case, the more likely the client is to reach back out to your entity (or you) for follow-up work. Consider what the customer would need to show management to compel them to act. Get feedback from the customer during the drafting process and incorporate it; certainly the style and tone of the report can be critical to the efforts of the security function within that organization. Seek to highlight areas where the security function performed well, followed by findings characterized by risks. Also keep in mind that the content will have to be defended, so make the language succinct and as unambiguous as possible.

How do you ensure your program results are valuable to people who need a full narrative and context?

In my experience, how value is added to the red team program varies from organization to organization, but principally it should align with the overall security program and the risk posture of the organization. The program should strive to enumerate material and exploitable vulnerabilities within a given ecosystem, understanding that all findings may not be outside of the organization's risk tolerance, whereas some may be nonnegotiable as a risk that absolutely has to be mitigated. In either case, the ability to link the red team program to some repeatable metric, such as the number of materials and exploitable vulnerabilities found, the number of successful versus unsuccessful attacks, or the number of false positives, can go a long way in legitimizing the value of the effort. Your skill set really doesn't matter if the work you are doing doesn't align with something of value to the business. Senior management isn't interested in a report showcasing how skillful and smart you are—what they *are* interested in is their overall risk exposure given what you have discovered, so frame your activities in that light.

How do you recommend security improvements other than pointing out where it's insufficient?

In any red team exercise, it is important to highlight those areas where the customer/organization did things well. For instance, if the organization has a robust patching program and it led to a smaller attack surface for the red team, be certain to acknowledge that. Remember, part of the job of a red team is to legitimize not only its skill capability but its intrinsic value as part of the security program. If the red team cannot contribute to the success of the security program to get the funding it needs, then its value is severely diminished. Conversations with blue team members should be as informative as possible, and if both teams come from the same company, it may be useful for the red team members to assist the blue team in identifying countermeasures. Be a source of expertise that is not just for hacking into systems but also for securing them—help the blue team think like hackers (assuming they aren't already).

What nontechnical skills or attitudes do you look for when recruiting and interviewing red team members?

The most important nontechnical skill any security professional can have is strong communication skills. When recruiting for red team members, there must be an air of trustworthiness and integrity within the candidate. Red teamers will have access to very sensitive knowledge about infrastructures, security controls, vulnerabilities, and so on, and that information will need to be held in the utmost of confidence. The ability to be not only technically astute but also able to explain those technical concepts to the layperson is invaluable in a red team asset.

What differentiates good red teamers from the pack as far as approaching a problem differently?

Good red teamers are not only technical hacks but also have an innate understanding of what value their activities represent to their organizations (as an employee or consultant). Good red teamers are thorough and detail-oriented and comfortable with their own skill. Good red teamers are always looking to hone their abilities and figure out ways to exploit without detection. Problem-solving can be highly methodical, or it can be serial. Regardless of the approach, a good red teamer applies the proper approach when necessary and adjusts when that approach runs into a dead end. ■

"I'm a firm believer that one should not jump directly into an offensive role without first getting a deep understanding of underlying protocols, including not only technical details but also business logic."

Twitter: @dafthack

Beau Bullock

4

Beau Bullock is a senior security analyst and penetration tester who has been with Black Hills Information Security since 2014. Beau has a multitude of security certifications and maintains his extensive skills by routinely taking training, learning as much as he can from his peers, and researching topics that he lacks knowledge in. He is constantly contributing to the InfoSec community by authoring open source tools, writing blogs, and frequently speaking at conferences and on webcasts.

How did you get your start on a red team?

I meet a lot of people who are interested in pentesting or red teaming and want to jump straight into those roles. I did not start out my career in information security on the offensive side. Being tasked with protecting a network, its users, and their data forced me to think like an attacker so I could be a better defender. I first developed an interest in offensive operations during an ethical hacking course I took while in college, but that interest did not develop into an offensive role until years later.

Working on a blue team at a hospital and then at a bank, I would consider how an adversary would get around the controls we had in place. So naturally I began performing offensive tests against our own controls to see where we were missing things. It was integral for me to learn as much as possible about every single layer of the organization. Everything from firewall rules to router configs to host-based protections to physical security to managing risk associated with one-off exceptions for C-suite members to protecting data to stopping people from getting phished—these were all opportunities for me to find where protections were lacking. Through all of this I learned what pitfalls many organizations and blue teams face day to day.

From an operational standpoint, understanding the struggles blue teams have to deal with, how networks function, and what defensive controls are possible provides a much clearer picture to the offensive operator. I pivoted to an offensive role in 2014 when I started working at Black Hills Information Security. Throughout the first few years of working there, I performed many penetration tests for various organizations. This gave me the opportunity to tune my capabilities and develop red team tactics. Within the last three years, I have been fortunate enough to be assigned formal red team engagements.

What is the best way to get a red team job?

Being on a red team takes a unique and dedicated individual who has knowledge in vastly different areas. I'm a firm believer that one should not jump directly into an offensive role without first getting a deep understanding of underlying protocols, including not only technical details but also business logic. Do you know how the business you are targeting functions day to day? Can you determine what the organization values?

Many red teams consist of multiple individuals with skills in different areas. You might see team members who can perform architecture setup, payload delivery, and/or social engineering, act as internal network specialists, and more. Before you get a job on a red team, I would recommend first developing offensive skills in multiple areas on penetration tests. The key to being a good red teamer is having the knowledge to attack an organization from many angles and the discipline to use the one method that is necessary and won't get you caught.

If you are already a pentester looking for a red team role, I would say networking is probably going to be your best bet. Go out and meet the people working on red teams and introduce yourself. Show them projects you've been working on. I see job openings posted by others on my Twitter timeline all the time.

If you are working for a company as an internal security analyst or the like and your company doesn't have an internal red team, maybe it's time to make a case for one. You might be able to build your own internal red team for your own organization and essentially create your own red team role.

How can someone gain red team skills without getting in trouble with the law?

For building skills, I am a huge advocate of participating in capture-the-flag contests. Also, jumping in on bug bounties is a good way to build web application hacking skills. Building a home lab doesn't have to be expensive and can provide you with a test platform for performing red team research without breaking laws.

> "The key to being a good red teamer is having the knowledge to attack an organization from many angles and the discipline to use the one method that is necessary and won't get you caught."

Why can't we agree on what a red team is?

I think many have a hard time understanding where a pentest stops and a red team starts. There is definitely some overlap between the two that people get hung up on. Commonly people describe red team engagements as a penetration test without restrictions. But red team engagements do have restrictions. If they didn't, then kidnapping, extortion, and blackmail would be in the rules of engagement. So since red teams are not truly unrestricted, I think people have a hard time grasping why it's different from a pentest.

What is one thing the rest of information security doesn't understand about being on a red team? What is the most toxic falsehood you have heard related to red, blue, or purple teams?

For the majority, I think they still think red teams are trying to sling exploits with Metasploit. I haven't had to use an actual software exploit in years. Configuration issues, bad passwords, and poor user awareness of phishing are typically how we get in. Once inside a network, it is 100 percent a game of credentials: pivot, dump creds, pivot, dump creds, rinse, and repeat.

I think the most toxic thing I've seen is how some blue teamers and red teamers treat each other. Many treat the other side as an adversary in a bad way. Our job as red teamers is to help the blue team get better. We should never gloat about our ops. The same goes for the blue team. I love purple team assessments where we can work collectively to make the organization better. Some of the coolest things I've found on engagements have been on purple team engagements.

When should you introduce a formal red team into an organization's security program?

Only after an organization has gone through multiple penetration tests and has done their due diligence in mitigating any of the vulnerabilities presented to them would I consider recommending a red team engagement. The most important thing to consider when deciding whether an organization is ready for a red team engagement is, can a red team get in using a vulnerability that shows up in a pentest? If so, the organization is not ready for a red team. The organization should already have an internal social engineering program to ensure its users don't submit credentials to a malicious page the red team hosts. Solid alerting and hardening of infrastructure should be in place, and I damn well better not find an exposed portal that doesn't have MFA.

How do you explain the value of red teaming to a reluctant or nontechnical client or organization?

Explaining the fact that it is a true test of their defensive capabilities usually is effective for me. I like to describe a pentest to a customer by explaining that I am going to attempt to find as many vulnerabilities as I can but will likely be very noisy. I explain that on red team engagements I may find only a few vulnerabilities but will be much less noisy and those vulnerabilities will likely be much more valuable to them, as they probably allowed me to compromise the network.

What is the *least* bang-for-your-buck security control that you see implemented?

For the most part, if you are paying for antivirus, it is the least bang-for-your-buck control. I say that because, honestly, the free Windows Defender that comes installed by default on Windows systems is actually pretty good for doing what antivirus is supposed to do.

Have you ever recommended not doing a red team engagement?

Yes, during scoping calls, if I sense that the customer hasn't done previous pentests or struggles to conceptualize what a red team is, then I might recommend something else. Definitions are huge in this industry. Without the proper definitions being agreed upon, it can be difficult to determine if by *red team* they actually mean pentest or even vulnerability scan. Laying out these definitions usually results in a customer realizing they meant a pentest instead of a red team.

What's the most important or easiest-to-implement control that can prevent you from compromising a system or network?
One of the easiest-to-implement controls that makes our lives hard as red teamers is Microsoft's Local Administrator Password Solution (LAPS). Randomizing local administrator passwords on every system makes it so that the compromise of a single local admin credential doesn't allow widespread access to every other asset in the network. Network segmentation between hosts, including client isolation so workstations can't talk to other workstations is another great control to have in place. If I can't pivot from one workstation to another, it's going to be hard for me to escalate privileges in the domain.

Even though this question asked for only one control, I would say the following are the most important things to look at locking down to prevent full domain compromise: MFA everywhere you can implement it, VPN requiring MFA and client-side certs, strong password policy (15 characters or more), strong log consolidation and alerting, application whitelisting/behavioral analytics software, strong egress filtering (allow web ports out only through an authenticated proxy with filtering in place), and user awareness to social engineering. If the organization implements those things, I'm going to have a bad day as a red teamer.

Why do you feel it is critical to stay within the rules of engagement?
Staying within the rules of engagement or not is like the difference between landing a shell on your target and landing a shell on the personal device of your target's significant other. One of these things is a highly illegal thing to do, and you might not be able to unsee what you see there.

If you were ever busted on a penetration test or other engagement, how did you handle it?
Busted? What's that?

What is the biggest ethical quandary you experienced while on an assigned objective?
One time I was tasked with performing a penetration test for a company and made my way to the CIO's system, where I found some very questionable things. I had a Meterpreter shell on the guy's system and noticed some KeePass processes running. I thought, "Cool, I'll wait for him to leave, log in, and then see if he left KeePass unlocked." Late at night after he left work for the day, I connected to his system using RDP. Sure enough, he had left KeePass open, so I now had access to a ton of creds, including some personal ones of his.

But I also noticed some other windows open on his system. First, he was using RDP to connect to another company's server outside of the target network, where he appeared to be doing some sort of "system administration." To make things stranger, he was also using RDP to connect to a personal system. This personal system had well-known tools on the desktop for performing mass spamming and other tools. At this point in the engagement, it became an ethical quandary, so I stopped the engagement. I ended up hearing from the customer later on that the CIO was let go.

How does the red team work together to get the job done?

Collaborative infrastructure across the entire operation is necessary in my opinion. To be successful during the operation, we need to be able to share shells, data, and so on, easily. On the reporting side, it's the same thing. We don't want to be working in separate documents. This creates too much work later when we want to merge them. If we can collaborate on the same document platform, it creates a much smoother reporting process.

What is your approach to debriefing and supporting blue teams after an operation is completed?

After an engagement, I like it when the organization can get all the entities involved in a meeting with me. I want the security team there as well as members of the SOC and maybe even other sysadmin-type employees. This way, those who typically don't see pentest reports now have an awareness of what can happen on the network. In turn, this helps arm them with the knowledge that they need to be diligent in protecting their own systems. I typically walk through the entire operation, from reconnaissance to initial compromise to escalation and finally data compromise.

If you were to switch to the blue team, what would be your first step to better defend against attacks?

Not switching back to the blue team. But if I did, I would first have a long discussion about budget. Knowing the budget can help you know how to best divvy it up to get the most out of it. You don't want to go blow your whole budget on the latest blinky light system that likely requires another full-time employee to even manage. There are so many free and open source options out there for securing a network, but many of those require time and effort as well. So perhaps using your budget to hire another co-worker might be the best bet. Some things I would try as soon as possible if they weren't already there would be to deploy Microsoft's LAPS, up the password policy, and deploy MFA.

What is some practical advice on writing a good report?

Take lots of notes while you are testing and essentially write the report as you move along. The worst thing you can do is fill up a notes document with screenshots but forget why you actually took them. Trust me, I know it is really hard to stop what you are doing and go write a couple sentences. Especially when you are faced with a new shell, it can be tempting to just start hacking away at it. But if you don't document, you will be regretting it later.

How do you ensure your program results are valuable to people who need a full narrative and context?

As much as possible, I try to explain what an attacker who was actually trying to do malicious things could have done. Most real attackers don't have the same deadlines as red teamers, so they are not worried about being done within a few weeks' time. They can take all the time they want. So for many organizations, being able to tie an actual threat actor's potential actions to data you provide can result in great value for them, because they understand how bad things could really be.

An important part of my red team engagements is that I'm not placing domain admin access as a primary goal. In most cases, the data I want doesn't require domain admin credentials to get it. I feel like the goal of the assessment needs to be something that the organization deems sensitive. If I can show that I've been able to compromise the CEO's desktop or maybe a database containing credit card data or plans to build a battleship and then describe how these would be useful to an attacker, most organizations seem to find value in that.

How do you recommend security improvements other than pointing out where it's insufficient?

Oftentimes I'm providing positive findings to customers to let them know where I think their controls are working. Even though something might be preventing me as an attacker, there are cases where those could still be improved. For example, maybe the organization has an exposed Outlook Web Access portal. Maybe I wasn't able to access it during the assessment, but I still might recommend that they move it to the internal network and protect it behind a VPN.

Additionally, constant testing of your controls is a must. Even though the red team engagement is over, learn and utilize some of the techniques that were used. The methodology of the tester should be outlined in the report and will typically include both successes and failures. While some of the tester's techniques might have failed during your engagement, you might find that something gets changed on your network without you knowing and now those techniques are successful. Lastly, having management support behind security improvements is critical. Policy controls that executives need to address should be provided in the report.

What nontechnical skills or attitudes do you look for when recruiting and interviewing red team members?

The hacker mind-set and creativity are the most important nontechnical character traits for a red teamer. Frequently on red team engagements they will be faced with challenges they have never seen before. Having the hacker mind-set means they will not stop when they face the unknown, but instead they will question everything and find unique and new ways to face a problem. When facing highly secured environments that utilize defense-in-depth strategies along with quality alerting and response, creativity on the red team is a must.

> "Having the hacker mind-set means they will not stop when they face the unknown, but instead they will question everything and find unique and new ways to face a problem."

What differentiates good red teamers from the pack as far as approaching a problem differently?

Most of the really good red teamers I have met specialize in some area heavily. This enables them to develop a deep understanding of a certain technology or software. Becoming a master of infrastructure setup, coding, device hacking, lock picking, or any other area will help you develop a niche skill that is useful on red team engagements. Having the ability to approach unique problems with a creative mind-set can make the difference between a successful red teamer and one who fails. ■

> "What are red team skills? When you list the skills that make someone a competent and effective attacker, you realize that those are the same skills that make someone a good server administrator, network engineer, or security practitioner."

Twitter: @obscuresec

Christopher Campbell

5 Christopher Campbell has been doing security research for many years and has a few college degrees, industry certifications, and open source project contributions. He has also found a few bugs and given a few talks at conferences. Chris is currently the red team chief for ManTech ACRE and was formerly a member of the U.S. Army red team.

How did you get your start on a red team?
The opportunity to join the U.S. Army red team was a lot more luck than anything else. I was on the receiving end of an assessment 15 years ago before I had any idea that it was a possible career field. I decided to work on making myself marketable and reaching out to members of the red team community at conferences. I received a lot of helpful advice. I would like to think that it helped, but ultimately it was just applying for positions that seemed interesting, working through the interview process, and following up after being interviewed about where I needed to focus more attention. Once I got on the team, my true journey started.

What is the best way to get a red team job?
The best way to get any job that you want is to document demonstrated competency and diligently apply. I had the opportunity to interview and have a part in hiring some really awesome red teamers, and they were all persistent throughout the process. All were honest about their skill sets during their interviews, and many asked for feedback afterward. Demonstrating passion and

a willingness to learn whatever is necessary to be successful in a task goes a long way in the hiring process.

How can someone gain red team skills without getting in trouble with the law?

This question hits at a really misunderstood topic. What are red team skills? When you list the skills that make someone a competent and effective attacker, you realize that those are the same skills that make someone a good server administrator, network engineer, or security practitioner. You can gain all the skills you need to be a good tester without ever breaking a law. Even things that seem borderline illegal can be done within virtualized environments on your own computer with free software. Ultimately, getting in trouble with the law could likely be far more detrimental to your future career aspirations than most people realize. Why risk it?

> "Ultimately, getting in trouble with the law could likely be far more detrimental to your future career aspirations than most people realize. Why risk it?"

Why can't we agree on what a red team is?

In a similar semantic shift as the word *cyber*, *red team* has lost the meaning that many still associate with it. The key distinction between a red team assessment and any other kind of test is adversarial replication. In other words, if you aren't utilizing the tactics, techniques, and procedures of an actual, documented threat actor, then it is likely you aren't conducting a red team assessment. That doesn't mean you aren't a red teamer. However, if you can't articulate which actors use which techniques, then many would have a hard time believing that you are. Red team assessments aren't better or worse than any other type of assessment, but for a long time they have been considered the sexiest. They exercise an actual defender on production networks and test policies and human responses that aren't otherwise properly evaluated. I hope that the industry is able to reclaim the old definition, but it is probably unlikely.

What is one thing the rest of information security doesn't understand about being on a red team? What is the most toxic falsehood you have heard related to red, blue, or purple teams?

One thing that people are often surprised by is the fact that I value empathy over most other traits when looking for red team members. Unfortunately, that empathy typically develops from being in the position to build, configure, develop, or defend production environments. That leads to the oft-repeated statement that being a red teamer shouldn't be your first job. Some scoff at that statement because at first glance it appears to be gatekeeping. However, being able to quickly spot where a competent professional would apply their efforts is invaluable. It allows you to quickly home in on areas where less effort or attention may be applied and rapidly gain elevated access in your target environment. In other words, empathy helps you be better at the job and also helps you deliver the hard message at the end of an engagement. People who lack empathy or are ignorant of the actual struggle of day-to-day IT work often display the toxic mentality often associated with arrogant testers, which hurts their effectiveness on the job and in delivery.

When should you introduce a formal red team into an organization's security program?

The hard truth is that most organizations, even mature ones, don't need a formal red team. The sole purpose of a red team is to exercise the defenders so that they will improve. The easy answer is when a program is mature enough to have the cycles to be exercised, it might be time for a red team. Red teams aren't easy to build from scratch, and there are plenty of qualified organizations that offer their services on a temporary basis. Start there and then use them to help build, train, and augment your team when the time comes.

How do you explain the value of red teaming to a reluctant or nontechnical client or organization?

I once had the opportunity to sit next to someone on a cross-country flight who strongly believed that there was zero business value in paying for red team assessments. It was a point of view that I was unfamiliar with, so I listened to him. In the end, our views weren't actually far from each other. The problem is that most people don't understand what the core mission of a red team is and instead compare it to other types of testing and assessment. Red teaming doesn't replace automated vulnerability assessments or penetration testing but rather complements it later in the defensive maturity of some organizations.

> "Red teams aren't for every organization, but every defender can benefit from having an adversarial mind-set."

Red teams aren't for every organization, but every defender can benefit from having an adversarial mind-set. Sometimes that is hard to envision without having a trained team demonstrate it for you. Furthermore, red teams test how all of your policies and procedures work together in the actual production environment, where there are real people. For example, I have seen environments where immediate network-blocking actions were taken with minimal inspection. A few spoofed packets allowed for a large outage and a perfect social-engineering opportunity against upset, internet-deprived users. That type of logic flaw might be hard to see on paper but is much clearer thanks to the red team.

What is the *least* bang-for-your-buck security control that you see implemented?

It is hard to name just one. I think any device that you purchase in order to secure your environment and that adds more attack surface would be my answer. Unfortunately, that includes probably half the blinking-light appliances being peddled at the booths at most security conferences. They typically have elevated credentials stored in them and have gone through minimal testing before being advertised as the answer to all your security problems. No CISO wants to see their latest security acquisition on the report, but it happens far too often.

Have you ever recommended not doing a red team engagement?

Any honest tester should have many stories like this. While on the Army red team, we didn't have the flexibility to offer different options most of the time because the engagements were mandated. Assessing the maturity of an environment is a critical step in the planning of an engagement, but it is often a tricky one. Years of internal and external penetration tests should occur long before a red team happens. This is further complicated by the wide misuse of the term *red team* throughout the industry.

What's the most important or easiest-to-implement control that can prevent you from compromising a system or network?
Something that I have mentioned a few times in conference talks is a creative practice that legitimately caught us on an engagement. The organization used log review as a punishment of sorts for almost anything in the office. If you were late to a meeting, lost a wager on last night's game, or failed to contribute to a swear jar, you earned log review time. The manager handed out logs from a different team for review every week, and they would produce a write-up on the most serious thing they found for the teams afterward. This had a few benefits. All teams knew that their logs would be reviewed and likely were more thorough as a result, and there was an obvious focus on security in all departments. Fresh and curious eyes were able to find anomalies that would have otherwise been lost in the noise, which led to the discovery of compromise without the use of any expensive security appliances. Finally, skills and knowledge were passed between the teams, which kept people engaged and, I believe, more satisfied in their work.

Why do you feel it is critical to stay within the rules of engagement?
The rules of engagement (ROE) are absolutely critical and need to be ironclad. Trust and professionalism are paramount to the ultimate success of a red team. If you violate the ROE, you have broken the trust the organization has put in the entire team. The time to question and adjust the ROE for everyone's benefit is before the engagement begins. The level of access a typical team achieves during an assessment is likely greater than that of any individual admin or IT section in the organization. That trust should never be violated.

If you were ever busted on a penetration test or other engagement, how did you handle it?
I have been busted many times during assessments and could probably write an entire book on those interactions alone. One of my favorite incidents involved signing up for a conference room through social engineering, tailgating into the building, and then joining several members of the red team while we plugged into the target's internal network. After using traditional methods of acquiring credentials, I attempted to utilize those credentials on the first interesting hostname I saw in Active Directory. We underestimated our audience, and the use of credentials over the network directly to a workstation from another workstation IP address caused an alert to prompt from their host-based security product. The warning contained my IP address, the account that I was using, and what file I was attempting to access. Unfortunately, the machine I targeted was the machine being used to project slides for a meeting that the entire IA section was attending. They jumped into action and were able to figure out where we were before I realized that I had tripped anything. We were busted, and it was all my fault. They ran into the room where we were quietly working and demanded to know who we were. Feeling responsible for the situation, I firmly told them to go get their boss so we could discuss their disturbing our work. This confused the group, but they declared that they would be right back. Afterwards, they returned to an empty conference room, and we endured a super-awkward out-brief a few days later.

What is the biggest ethical quandary you experienced while on an assigned objective?
A situation that I have encountered several times is being asked to leave out specific critical findings from a report. I imagine this is common, based on discussions with other testers. Sometimes assessments come with far greater ramifications than a tester realizes. As tests have become more normal and more organizations have publicly reported being breached, it has ideally reduced the stigma that comes with poor performance on an assessment. An experienced and properly scoped red team engagement will almost always result in a successful compromise. No one should lose their job because of it unless they are found to have violated company policies or acted unethically. The point is to train and improve the security posture of the organization and not poke people in the eye. For that reason, I am against withholding confirmed findings from a report.

How does the red team work together to get the job done?
The "team" element of red teaming is critical. No one can be an expert in everything. Having people with diverse technology backgrounds allows you to work together to accomplish the mission. Communication is important, and each member of the team should have an understanding of what the others are working on. Additionally, leadership of the team is extremely important. Each action on the network and the risk it presents of being caught or reacted to needs to be understood and analyzed. Rogue actions can be detrimental and lead to internal conflict as well as poor results. Documentation during the assessment should be everyone's responsibility, but it is my experience that rotating one person to combine the results into the report leads to better results.

What is your approach to debriefing and supporting blue teams after an operation is completed?
Every engagement is going to have required written or oral deliverables, but I have always been partial to the informal out-brief. This brief is free of managers and egos and is just a frank discussion of the things that were done with all who were involved. When it is done correctly, both sides benefit. Additionally, this is a great time to glean things that the organization did well or things the defenders would like you to emphasize for their bosses in order to secure support or funding.

If you were to switch to the blue team, what would be your first step to better defend against attacks?
I believe that the first step in defending any environment is to map it. There is almost always a discrepancy between the number of machines an organization believes they have and how many they actually have. It seems so simple, yet there are often surprises that have been either forgotten over the years or never documented. You have to figure out what is there before you can ever hope to defend it.

What is some practical advice on writing a good report?
The unfortunate reality is that the report matters more to everyone else than to the person writing it. The best reports are accurate, concise, and engaging. Accuracy comes from documenting your actions and providing evidence of

your findings and not overstating them. State the facts that your data points to. Concise writing prevents reader fatigue. If you have made it this far into my answers, you have likely discovered that I struggle with this. Figure out who on the team is good at it and have that person edit reports until everyone improves their writing style. Provide raw data and results as addendums. Finally, you want your reports to be engaging. Speak to the reader in a way that keeps them reading. Show them how much work went into the assessment and possibly inspire one of their admins to go into security.

How do you ensure your program results are valuable to people who need a full narrative and context?

The narrative is what differentiates a red team report from a pentest report, and for many it is where much of the value of a red team engagement comes from. What techniques did you use? What adversary were you emulating? Why did you choose that group over other groups? All of those questions should be answered in a red team report. The reader should learn not just what you did to them but how their environment could be realistically attacked in the future.

How do you recommend security improvements other than pointing out where it's insufficient?

It is important to understand that you don't know why decisions were made in an environment. It is so easy to recommend specific improvements without having any knowledge of business needs, which makes your recommendations potentially worthless and may actually serve to discount your findings entirely. Presenting findings with generic recommendations for how to improve their security posture is likely the best a true red team will be able to do. You need to have a better understanding of an organization's needs to make specific recommendations in a lot of cases. You just don't get that from the adversarial perspective.

What nontechnical skills or attitudes do you look for when recruiting and interviewing red team members?

Empathy and passion are what I look for. Passion keeps you learning new technologies and not becoming complacent with the same techniques you have previously used. Empathy helps you predict what people would likely not have had time to devote attention to, and it helps you write a more effective report.

What differentiates good red teamers from the pack as far as approaching a problem differently?

Good red teamers are able to quickly evaluate attack surface. All testers rely on some sort of methodology, but a red teamer doesn't need to flip every stone. They can look at an application or system and see where the quick wins or low-hanging fruit are and move on. I like to describe it as being in a dark room with one door. A typical tester will walk in every direction and will eventually find the door after touching most of the walls. A good red teamer will walk straight to the door and never touch the wall. It looks like magic, but being able to quickly identify attack surfaces is what separates a good red teamer from the rest of the pack. ∎

Twitter: @_sn0ww

Stephanie Carruthers

6

Stephanie "Snow" Carruthers is a professional liar performing social engineering as a service for her clients. Stephanie specializes in using her social engineering skills to perform a variety of assessments, including OSINT, phishing, vishing, covert entry, and red team exercises. She works with clients of all sizes from startups to Fortune 100 companies in all industries, as well as government agencies. Since 2014, Stephanie has presented and taught at numerous security conferences and private events around the world. For fun, Stephanie has earned black badges for winning the Social Engineering Capture the Flag (SECTF) at DEF CON 22 and also The Vault, a physical security competition at SAINTCON 2017. Stephanie also enjoys traveling the world to see beautiful locations and meeting new people, like Larry, who just let her into your data center.

How did you get your start on a red team?
The short answer is slowly. I started my career by specializing in social engineering and physical security by working at different organizations, including an information security consultancy and government contractor, and I even started my own business. At each of these different types of organizations, I was able to grow and learn professionally in different ways. However, I still worked hard at developing and expanding my specific skill set.

In time and as a result of networking, a red team saw value in my specialized skill set and made me an offer. I brought a specific talent and value to the team. I think a common misconception about red teamers is that they must be jacks-of-all-trades, and that is not the case at all. Having a group of talented individuals in specific areas makes for a much more talented and capable team.

What is the best way to get a red team job?

I believe this answer is two-part. First, you need to develop a specialty. There is no doubt that solid, specific talent is a requirement. As Charley Bowdre once said, "You can't be any geek off the street; gotta be handy with the steel if you know what I mean; earn your keep"!

The second part is the hard part. The best way to get a red team job is to network. The goal when networking with people is building relationships. As those relationships build, which is naturally a slow process, you must show that you can be trusted. The value of trust between red team members can't be overstated.

How can someone gain red team skills without getting in trouble with the law?

I think this question is flawed. First and foremost, when people say "red team skills," I feel like Inigo Montoya would say, "You keep using that word. I do not think it means what you think it means." Red team skills aren't anything more than working in a fast-paced team dynamic. The technical aspect of red teaming aside, you can get "red team skills" anywhere there is a fast-paced team dynamic, from McDonald's to the military. Any time you're required to work as a part instead of the whole, you're working on red team skills. In fact, you'd have to go out of your way to gain these skills in an illegal manner with so many opportunities present. It's just a matter of knowing where to look.

I'd be remiss if I didn't talk about the technical aspect, though. This is where the trouble with the law caveat in the question comes from. Twenty years ago, in 1999, this would have been a real problem. However, it's 2019. Access to labs, capture-the-flag (CTF) events, blogs, YouTube, a vibrant and social information security community, university degree programs, high school programs (CyberPatriot), college programs (Collegiate Penetration Testing Competition, National Collegiate Cyber Defense Competition, etc.), and even paid training programs exist. The resources are here in abundance. You can't go 30 seconds on YouTube without a Udemy ad trying to teach you ethical hacking. Even with the physical security portion, at the SAINTCON conference in Utah, I proudly help run the The Vault, a physical security challenge that gives attendees an opportunity to practice attacks against physical security controls such as RFID cloning, lockpicking, request-to-exit bypasses, under- and over-the-door tools, alarm systems, biometrics, and so on. With all this information present, the bar to a technical skill set has been drastically lowered as compared to 20 years ago.

Why can't we agree on what a red team is?

Spoiler alert: we can, and we have. However, there is a consumer education problem. Some in the information security industry want to do things "their way" or want to make new definitions for things to meet their abilities but add more markup to their services. This is unfortunate and contributes to the confusion of the consumer. Unfortunately, because the commercial sector doesn't usually look to the government sector, many aren't aware that the term *red team* has been defined for quite some time and is a very good definition.

In 2005 the Department of Defense released Manual 8570.01-M, which defines "red team" as

> "An independent and focused threat based effort by a multi-disciplinary, opposing force using active and passive capabilities; based on formal; time bounded tasking to expose and exploit information operations vulnerabilities of friendly forces as a means to improve readiness of U.S. units, organizations, and facilities."

In recent years, as this concept is expanded, I feel that this industry will naturally align with the 8570 definition much as PCI has helped drive the difference between *vulnerability scan* and *penetration test*.

What is one thing the rest of information security doesn't understand about being on a red team?

Hot take: being on the offensive side doesn't mean you're on a red team. There is no red side. You're confusing it with opposition forces (OPFOR). Stop saying you're red or blue—this isn't fucking gang territory, and you aren't Bloods or Crips.

Many people think that a red team is a one-person show, which isn't the case at all. A true red team has multiple team members and a lead. These team members work as a cohesive unit toward a common goal. There is no room to operate independently, which is difficult for many offensive testers as they are used to doing things their way at their pace.

> "Many people think that a red team is a one-person show, which isn't the case at all. A true red team has multiple team members and a lead."

When should you introduce a formal red team into an organization's security program?

While this is a gut feeling, it's a pretty easy one to come by. Consider how a company isn't going to get the right value they need out of a penetration test if they have never done a vulnerability assessment and also have no patch management process. An organization is ready for red team assessments once penetration tests have diminished in value.

How do you explain the value of red teaming to a reluctant or nontechnical client or organization?

I explain that the value from a red team comes from the team aspect. Typically, companies get penetration tests conducted by a single consultant who usually has a general skill set. A red team brings a group of individuals whose specific skill sets are aligned with the company's infrastructure. The idea is that just because you're on the team for this client doesn't mean you will be on the team for the next. If your background is Linux penetration testing, there is no reason why you should be on the team against a target that is a full Windows shop. On the client side, having a penetration tester skilled in Linux is a waste of their money and will provide less value. Keep in mind, I'm not saying the Linux tester is not good and couldn't learn, but we must remember that we are beholden to the client and not our pride.

Lastly, but equally important, red team engagements focus on targeted goals instead of a specific scope. Without a rigid scope, the red team can work naturally and pragmatically to attempt to achieve the goals in the best way they see fit, much as an actual attacker might.

Have you ever recommended not doing a red team engagement?
Absolutely. I've seen clients get sold on the buzzword *red team* and want one, but in reality, they still haven't fixed their critical, high, or even medium findings from their last few penetration tests.

When a client requests a red team, I try to understand how they have been performing previous security assessments and how they are handling remediating the findings. If they are still doing vulnerability scans and haven't moved to penetration testing, they aren't ready for a red team. If they are doing penetration tests and not remediating findings, they aren't ready for a red team.

What's the most important or easiest-to-implement control that can prevent you from compromising a system or network?
This isn't the answer you want but the answer you need: small and medium-sized businesses are typically solely focusing on building their business and scaling. As a result, their dollars are usually allocated to endeavors to facilitate this. The right answer is that you need a consultant. Just as most small and medium businesses outsource things such as accounting, human resources, and information technology, you need to outsource security as well. Hire a reputable consultant who can come in and look at your business holistically and consider all aspects of the business so that any recommendation keeps its impact to your business's operations and tempo to a minimum, but also helps increase your security posture. Our industry often forgets that our goal isn't to make an organization unhackable, but to help increase their security posture in a way that allows them to focus on the business's mission and vision.

Why do you feel it is critical to stay within the rules of engagement?
Elementary, my dear Watson. You must always remember the three Ls: liability, liability, liability. Staying within the rules of engagement comes down to liability. If a client has specific requests (don't target C levels, don't touch these IPs, don't go to this floor in our building, etc.), it is important to abide by those requests, no matter how irritating they may be. The last place you and your team want to be is at the receiving end of a lawsuit for breach of contract.

If you were ever busted on a penetration test or other engagement, how did you handle it?
This is a tricky one for me to answer because many times the client requests that I intentionally test until I get caught. What I mean by this is during physical security assessments, for example, I slowly escalate my methods and noise to determine at what point an employee stops to question me. These metrics have given my clients a huge understanding of how and when their employees respond. Yes, I can go in and try to be undetected (which is the goal while red teaming); however, while performing a physical assessment, why not test as much as possible? If you don't, you're doing a disservice to your client. Then, when I'm caught, my clients also get to see how their incident response process handles it. Why wouldn't you want to test every employee's detection and capabilities in a controlled manner?

However, I do have a time I was caught while not trying to be. A few years ago, I was performing a physical security assessment for a client. During the kickoff call and follow-up communication, they were acting slightly odd and continuously decreasing the scope, including shortening the assessment from three days to one. I've learned that these are usually warning signs of trouble afoot.

When I arrived on site, I was able to successfully gain access to one of their floors. I found their mailroom and proceeded to place a USB drive inside an employee's mailbox. As soon as I was leaving the room, I was stopped by an employee who said, "Oh, I found you! We were told to be on the lookout all day for you and to turn you in right away." After talking for a few minutes, I found out that the client had sent out an email to all employees saying that a female would be coming on site during the limited time window they gave me to test and to stop me immediately.

This client wanted good results and didn't want me to succeed. To achieve that, they rigged the test. However, this left me in an ethically hard spot. How was I supposed to write my report? I decided to be truthful and document in my report that the employee who stopped me explained that they were notified ahead of time and tasked with attempting to find me. To this day, that engagement was the most expensive game of corporate hide-and-seek I've ever played.

What is the biggest ethical quandary you experienced while on an assigned objective?

I had a client ask me to leave out findings from a phishing assessment. A C-level employee provided their network credentials to my malicious website, and they didn't want that information to be in the final report. On one hand, it would be an extremely easy piece of data to omit from the final report; no one would even know it was missing. On the other hand, I knew deep down that it was wrong. I ended up explaining to the client that I could not remove any findings and proceeded to deliver an honest final report.

How does the red team work together to get the job done?

My absolute favorite part of red teaming is the team aspect. I love the camaraderie that is developed during the engagement. We work together under a team lead who builds out a strict plan to execute, where everyone knows their role and target. The documentation and reporting are really just a matter of good record keeping. There isn't a team member specifically tasked with the job of the scribe. However, working with the blue team is always a learning experience. It's interesting when we do our debriefs, and they show us what they were able to catch and not catch and dive into the technical portions of some attacks. Both teams learn a lot, and it is one of the most critical elements of the engagement.

> "My absolute favorite part of red teaming is the team aspect. I love the camaraderie that is developed during the engagement."

What is your approach to debriefing and supporting blue teams after an operation is completed?

This is a question that we ask during kickoff calls with the client—to determine *what* they want. Some clients like to be very hands-on with daily calls, multiple after-engagement calls/demos with different departments, and so on, while other clients are just looking forward to the final report. It all comes down to delivering the value that the client needs from the engagement.

If you were to switch to the blue team, what would be your first step to better defend against attacks?

Don't assume. One of the biggest benefits any new hire brings to an organization is a fresh set of eyes. However, you need to capitalize on this while they are still fresh. I would personally start at the beginning, going from policies and procedures to technologies and to roles and responsibilities. I would take stock of what was present in order to determine what was missing. Things are often put in place in the blue team to meet policy need but never touched or exercised. Additionally, over time complacency sets in and things move to the wayside that should still be actively monitored.

What is some practical advice on writing a good report?

I've written, reviewed, and read others' reports, which means I've seen the good, the bad, and the ugly. I have some tips here.

Executive summary: This should be more than a single sentence (yes, I've seen that)! This section should include the high-level assessment details (who, what, when, where, and why). Additionally, this section is typically the only part of the report that is handed off to executives, so don't get too technical here.

Findings: For every finding, you need to show the steps to re-create the finding and a risk rating to help the client prioritize the order of remediation.

Recommendations: Never provide findings without recommendations.

Review: Don't forget to run spell-check. A client will start to question your work if they see grammar errors and misspellings in your report. Also, ensure your report is QA'd. Having a second set of eyes is always beneficial, no matter what. If your report comes back with red lines throughout, don't take it personally. It's not about you; it's about the client.

What nontechnical skills or attitudes do you look for when recruiting and interviewing red team members?

Hands down, soft skills. I can teach you technical skills or send you to training, but I can't teach you manners, how to be on time, how to talk to clients, how to respond to teammates, and so on. One of the most nontechnical skills used in red teaming is communication. You have to be able to communicate with both your teammates and the client to be successful.

> "I can teach you technical skills or send you to training, but I can't teach you manners, how to be on time, how to talk to clients, how to respond to teammates, and so on."

What differentiates good red teamers from the pack as far as approaching a problem differently?

A good red teamer knows where they fit into a team and how they can provide value. They also need to be outside-the-box thinkers. Often during assessments things don't always go to plan, so being able to throw out ideas with teammates to figure out the best next steps is valuable. ∎

"Passion is what drives you to continue to learn and constantly take on challenges because they are more interesting than watching your favorite Netflix show."

Twitter: @bullz3ye

Mark Clayton

7

Mark Clayton (Bullz3ye) is a red teamer, security engineer, and application developer who can't seem to choose between the three. Professionally he is a red teamer and security engineer but is always developing web and mobile applications at night. As of late, his primary focus has been on DevSecOps, where he is able to blend his security and development experience. Since a young age, Mark has been under the mentorship of a Cult of the Dead Cow (cDc) member, who showed him the ropes and taught him the security ecosystem, and he's stayed true to those lessons.

How did you get your start on a red team?

I guess you could say my path was a bit unconventional. During college, I was originally cut out to be a software developer. My primary focus was building mobile applications on the Windows Phone...because that was going to take the world by storm. I even had a track laid out for me to potentially join Microsoft after my graduation—that is, until one day during my sophomore year a close friend of mine asked me to join his Collegiate Cyber Defense Competition (CCDC) team, and that's really when it all changed for me.

About a month into training for the competition, I'm sitting at a CentOS terminal when this tattooed bald guy comes up to me and says, "You like this shit, kid?" I respond with, "Yeah, man, I'm having a blast," nervously. He then simply says, "Give me a call tonight, man; we'll chat." This man was one of the mentors for my CCDC team, but what I didn't know until later was that he was also CDC (Cult of the Dead Cow). Long story short, during the years I was about

18 to 20 years old he was my mentor. He taught me about the "old school days," talked philosophy, pushed mandatory Phrack High Council reading material, and preached that FreeBSD is God. Over those years we became good friends, and eventually he said I was ready to join his team as a junior penetration tester, with a specific focus on the web. App sec came naturally for me since I was a natural software developer, so as I grew within the company, I was able to transition into the red team as the "web kid." Ah, good times. Nowadays I just feel old, and I'm bald at 25.

What is the best way to get a red team job?

Honestly, I think that passion is everything. Passion is what drives you to continue to learn and constantly take on challenges because they are more interesting than watching your favorite Netflix show. Of course, you have to be technical, and it really helps if you know a little about everything but also a lot about one subject. Too often, people try to be the best l33t hacker and know everything about everything, until they realize exactly how vast the technical landscape is.

Understand that a red team is just that—a team. Every person plays their part and has their specialty. If you want to join a red team, I'd say double down on your specialty, stay passionate, and always be curious. I believe that this energy can be seen from across the room, and a candidate in this position will be a quick hire. You can always teach technical skills, but you can't teach, much less force passion. Also, get involved in the community and put yourself around others and soon enough you'll begin to hear about positions.

> "If you want to join a red team, I'd say double down on your specialty, stay passionate, and always be curious."

More practically, I would also say that taking the time to first be a blue teamer, system admin, software dev, or network engineer is key if it's in your cards. How else will you be able to practically understand environments both culturally and technically if you've never been on the other side? I think the best red teamers are previous blue teamers, just like red teamers make fantastic incident response folks!

How can someone gain red team skills without getting in trouble with the law?

Now I'm young, but I would say that back in the day "teetering" on the lines of the law was a given. You didn't have these massive amounts of CTF challenges, Hack The Box, vulnerable VMs, and training courses. The world was your lab, so you learned by doing...practicing on prod, baby! Today, things have changed. There is a plethora of training materials, classes, and labs to simulate real-world environments so that you can emulate the attacks all within the confines of the law.

Why can't we agree on what a red team is?

Because it sounds sexy to be part of the red team, everybody wants to call themselves that. Red teamers are seen as the grown-up versions of penetration testers. You do penetration testing for a while; then you go to the big leagues, and now you're red teaming! I've spoken to people who claim they are red teamers, and it's just a team of one within the organization. There is no "I" in team. The allure of wanting to be classified as a red team has muddied the definition to the point where any offensive consultant says they are a red teamer because it is cool to say. You have to get back to the roots of where the term comes from.

What is one thing the rest of information security doesn't understand about being on a red team? What is the most toxic falsehood you have heard related to red, blue, or purple teams?

As a red teamer, your true goal is to help the blue team and emulate attacks and scenarios, not break everything and start celebrating (in front of the blue team at least). The red team is there to help the blue team, not break the blue team's spirits and pillage villages. There is no (or shouldn't be) a red team without a blue team, even if the red team is a drop-in consultant shop. There is always an adversarial stance between the two, and it is reinforced on both ends. The blue team is mad at the red team, or the red team brags about owning the blue team. It isn't about who wins; it's about training together to make the organization's security posture stronger as a whole.

When should you introduce a formal red team into an organization's security program?

When you can actionably digest the results of the red team's findings. If your security program is immature and you don't do any threat modeling, letting a red team loose throughout your environment will tell you what you already know—that your security program needs work. First take the time to understand your environment, your security controls, and your potential pitfalls. Once that happens, you can start to bring in the attackers and see where you stand.

How do you explain the value of red teaming to a reluctant or nontechnical client or organization?

Reinforce the fact that we are here to help, not break everything and walk away. This goes back to the natural adversarial stance between the two. We are here to emulate your worst-case scenarios in a controlled fashion, and afterward we will be here to help every step of the way. Too often people see red teamers as those who create more work or leave a bigger headache once the engagement is done, and are reluctant to perform red teaming.

> "Reinforce the fact that we are here to help, not break everything and walk away."

What is the *least* bang-for-your-buck security control that you see implemented?

Yeah. Definitely antivirus.

Have you ever recommended not doing a red team engagement?

Absolutely. I've gotten requests to have a red team engagement on X environment to demonstrate impact or "see how secure it is." There have been several times when doing an "offensive" architecture review or a review of the security controls in place may be more effective. This allows the customer to understand the theoretical attacks and how we would approach it, assume successful attacks, and approach implementing security controls accordingly.

What's the most important or easiest-to-implement control that can prevent you from compromising a system or network?

Implement the principle of least privilege wherever possible. This is cost effective and can prevent some major splash damage upon compromise. Also, keep everything up to date. Lack of patches will be your downfall.

Why do you feel it is critical to stay within the rules of engagement?

Not staying within the rules of the engagement is a breach of trust and also does not provide the exercise its due diligence. I think that breaking the rules results from a selfish desire to prove yourself as 133t or placing the priority of a breach over how it will affect the environment. If you breach the environment but topple over production systems, doesn't that make you the true bad guy? Your job is to provide business value to the organization, not obstruct it. Stick to the rules; they are there for a reason. If you disagree with the rules, kindly start a conversation as to why and promote a revision.

If you were ever busted on a penetration test or other engagement, how did you handle it?

I've always had pretty bad anxiety. I was on a physical penetration test, and after I got onto the floor, I selfishly sat at this lady's cubicle for two hours just casually performing the assessment. No big deal, just a new employee here. I even asked my "new co-worker" what the password to the Wi-Fi was. It wasn't long before people started to walk past me several times and whisper to each other before they asked for my badge and eventually called security on me. When they caught me, I shakily pulled out my "get-out-of-jail-free" paper and explained myself. They were pissed, and I just kept sweating and trying to laugh it off, hoping it would lighten the situation.

As I was getting escorted off the floor, employees were looking at me like I was a serious criminal, which didn't help my anxiety either. I shouldn't have stayed at the lady's desk. I had the LAN Turtle beaconing out as soon as I had gained access to the floor, so there literally was no need. To be fair, the mistake they made was escorting me to the elevator and not escorting me outside of the building, so I just went two floors down and sat at another cubicle. I was young and dumb, but looking back on it I still laugh.

What is the biggest ethical quandary you experienced while on an assigned objective?

I think sometimes the methods used to social-engineer people can get really dicey. I personally wasn't involved in this, but I heard about someone actually getting the client served a falsified court document instructing them to go to a website and schedule their court date. The website snatched their credentials, and they were successful. I don't have the gumption to do that. The emotional toil put on the client must have been pretty heavy.

How does the red team work together to get the job done?

Red teaming consists of a team of offensive consultants who bring a variety of specialties to the table working cohesively to accomplish the objective. You must rely on each other. For example, if you are a web guy and you pop shell on a web server, pass the shell off to the person with the most experience doing privilege escalation or lateral movement. Once again, you rely on your teammates and work selflessly. All the members of the team should keep good documentation and track everything they do, as it will be critical in the reporting phase. Each person should contribute to the report and, if possible, have a technical editor make sure everything is smoothed together and the language reads well. Delivery to the blue team should also be performed as a team. Either you can take turns walking through the break and explain which role applies to you, or you provide the attack narrative and have each member on standby to explain specifics if requested.

What is your approach to debriefing and supporting blue teams after an operation is completed?

I'm a big fan of helping blue teams, so I try to provide as much remediation support as possible. I take the time to understand their security controls and how things look from the blue team side. From there, I can try to truly explain what the failing control is. Lastly, I give them actionable remediation recommendations that are specific to their environment. You can just say "fix all input sanitization" and leave it to them to provide the solution. Help them out, understand their environment or predicament, and try to come up with the solutions together.

If you were to switch to the blue team, what would be your first step to better defend against attacks?

My first step is to provide education into offensive capabilities, attack scenarios, and true objectives and motivators of attackers. For example, I still do a ton of application development. Throughout my entire development lifecycle, I'm adjusting how I'm architecting solutions or how I'm developing stuff simply because I know how I would attack it. As you develop, or defend, you must keep the adversarial mind-set at the forefront.

What is some practical advice on writing a good report?

It sounds generic, but really know your audience. Your objective isn't to show off; understand that everything you provide should be actionable in some way. Also, your engagement isn't known for how sweet your hacks are, but for your deliverable. The report is the primary thing they are left with when you move on to your next gig, so make it count. It's like dropping off your résumé after you introduce yourself.

How do you recommend security improvements other than pointing out where it's insufficient?

Typically, I try to discuss security best practices as opposed to failed controls. Like, "Hey, client, it's standard to implement X because it prevents Y." It is the opposite of saying "Hey, client, you should implement X because your current X sucks." I realize that may have been overly casual, but you get the point.

What nontechnical skills or attitudes do you look for when recruiting and interviewing red team members?

The ability to communicate effectively and to understand the bigger picture. If you can't explain the l33t hacker hacks you performed, how can you expect the client to understand what their pain points are and effectively implement mitigating controls? Also, exercise sympathy. I get that you are excited about your l33t hacker hacks, but you're not here to brag. Sometimes you have to be able to step out of the terminal and understand the true objective.

What differentiates good red teamers from the pack as far as approaching a problem differently?

I think it all boils down to the ability to adapt. You see a lot of red teamers fold when the tricks they already know fail or the tutorials they read aren't giving them shell. I've seen several cases where the big break is right on the other side of banging your head against the wall because you are at the point of giving up. Being able to go that next step and leave the realm of comfort makes all the difference. Lastly, I think it goes without saying that a good teamer "thinks outside of the box." In this case, the box would be the comfort zone and the tricks you know so well. ■

> "There isn't just one type of red team job. There are quite a few subtle differences between different companies/groups that perform this type of work."

Twitter: @Zaeyx

Ben Donnelly

8

Benjamin Donnelly is an omni-domain engineer and the founder of Promethean Information Security LLC. Ben has worked as part of teams hacking such things as prisons, power plants, multinationals, and even entire states. He is most well known for his research projects, including his work on the DARPA-funded Active Defense Harbinger Distribution. Ben has produced a number of field-leading advancements, including the Ball and Chain cryptosystem. He has spoken at Derbycon and BSides Boise and has contributed content to multiple SANS courses. Outside of cybersecurity, he can often be found skydiving, producing underground electronic music, or starring in indie films.

How did you get your start on a red team?
I competed in a high school cyber-defense competition called Cyberpatriot. My team did quite well, and from there I managed to talk myself into getting invited to come out and compete in the first-ever NetWars tournament of champions. At this point, my entire skill set was still entirely from a blue team perspective—that was the only thing that Cyberpatriot had trained us in. Recently graduated from high school, where else was I supposed to learn the black arts ("red arts"?)?

But it turns out that my specialized blue team skill set quickly transitioned into red cell activity. I didn't win my first run at NetWars, but I did score in the top ~10 percent. Considering my age and that I was competing against professionals, I think that impressed some people. This got me a few job offers, and I took one working for a SANS instructor. I was supposed to just be an intern, but I kept throwing out knowledge and hard work. It wasn't long before I was getting called in to help with penetration tests, and my job title officially changed to penetration tester/security researcher.

What is the best way to get a red team job?

Define "best." If what you value is an interesting story, then perhaps your best way would be to do the old "black hat captured by FBI and forced to hack for good." Of course, assuming that your idea of best is to (as soon as possible) have a strong, well-paying, prestigious job "hacking things" legally, then there are a few things I can recommend.

You need to know your target audience, and then you need to impress them. There isn't just one type of red team job. There are quite a few subtle differences between different companies/groups that perform this type of work. From a high level, you'll find that there are two major types of hackers in this field. Both have places on different red teams, and both are really cool. The biggest practical difference between the two will be in their clientele.

The first type of red team is the computer network operator–type team. Their primary focus is going to be on access. They train to utilize hacking tools and frameworks, and they aim to impress. If you want to join one of these teams, you need to be focusing on training on breach simulation because that's what their world is all about. Their clients hire them to show exactly how an attacker might gain and leverage access to a network or system. This type of team is going to be dropped into a network, or onto a target system, with the goal of exploiting the system to its fullest extent and building a narrative they can present to the company's executive team detailing how they got it done. To join one of these teams, you almost certainly won't need a bunch of certs, and you probably don't need a college degree. What you do need are the skills to do the job and the guts to ask for it. To get there, find a team that you want to join, train until you're ready, and then prove yourself by competing or contributing to the community.

The second type of team is the security engineering–type team. This type of team is less likely to be dropped into networks with the goal of "simulating" a literal breach. Instead, they are likely to spend their time creating and building and auditing complex solutions to hard security-centric problems with the goal of improving the technical sophistication and security of a given software or hardware system. If you join one of these teams, you won't spend your time trying to create a narrative to describe how exactly you accessed a network via a simulated hack. Rather, you will spend your time analyzing systems from a multitude of perspectives and then applying your knowledge to answer tightly scoped questions such as "If an attacker had access to this network, could they bypass our host whitelist?"

For both team types you'll want some combination of computer science and information technology knowledge. You can gain these things in school or on your own time. The type of team that you want to join will influence whether you should be learning Metasploit and Active Directory or cryptology and software engineering. Once you know what it is exactly that you want to do, simply learn those skills and send in an application.

How can someone gain red team skills without getting in trouble with the law?

For me it was competitions. I kind of got dragged into them when I was quite young. I was in a cadet program in high school that gave me the opportunity to compete in Cyberpatriot back when it was just getting started. This competition opened my eyes to information security, though it didn't really give me red team skills. What it did do was to prepare me to be able to understand and parse red team contexts.

You can easily and legally learn the basal skills required to be ready to quickly transition into a red team role by working in computer network defense–type roles. You'll learn about what it is that attackers do as you learn to anticipate them. And far more importantly, you'll learn how to play with infrastructure.

Look, certainly part of red teaming is knowing how to actually exploit a system. You will need to know SQLi and XSS, and you will need to know how to pop a shell and pivot through it. Those specific things will not use up even half of your time. Even when you're actively "hacking," you will spend the vast majority of your time on building, manipulating, and traversing infrastructure.

If you want to be an amazing red cell member, here's what you need:

- Massive ability to manipulate infrastructure (gained from IT training)
- Massive ability to manipulate software systems (gained from CS training)
- Massive ability to manipulate social systems (gained from psychology training/high empathy/life)

I left out a few skills there, such as time management and report writing, but you get the idea. In the end, the crazy cool "hacker" things do not exist in a void. They are just the other sides of various coins you're already familiar with.

What is one thing the rest of information security doesn't understand about being on a red team? What is the most toxic falsehood you have heard related to red, blue, or purple teams?

Many people think what we do is magic. In the past, I've met incredibly intelligent and well-spoken people who treated us like gods. We absolutely do not deserve this praise. If we work hard, if we do a great job, then thank us. But our field isn't for immortals; it's just for lucky people who managed to find the opportunities and walk the esoteric path that led them here. You can be here if you so choose. Not to throw massive shade, but I absolutely can think of a few people who get tons of undeserved praise for simply existing in this field. And that's okay, until it makes other people feel like they don't measure up. There are absolutely wizards in the world; I defend this 100 percent. I've met some; I've worked with some. But the vast majority of the time, the gentleman professional running Metasploit and logging Nessus results is not one of the few rare and crazy-haired titans of computer science.

> "Many people think what we do is magic. In the past, I've met incredibly intelligent and well-spoken people who treated us like gods. We absolutely do not deserve this praise."

What is the *least* bang-for-your-buck security control that you see implemented?

Oh my goodness, firewall tech by far. All these expensive "security" devices that seem to keep selling like hotcakes are effectively capable of stopping 0 percent of technically sophisticated adversaries. It's quite unfortunate that these things sell so well, though it's certainly understandable. The people making these purchase decisions just don't know what's possible.

Take the example of deep packet inspection. I think a lot of even decently technical people making purchase decisions hear "This firewall will ensure only

HTTP traffic can exit your network by searching for HTTP header data sent via valid TCP routing" and they think to themselves, "That sounds awesome." This is one of the most sophisticated analysis methods we regularly see. I'm sure people are paying tons of money for it.

They're also paying me tons of money to walk into their network and wrap other protocols in unintelligible data globs sent as part of HTTP proxied traffic. This recently popped up on a test, where a client had exactly this technology in place. I just built a fake "update service" that polled a remote "update server" at random intervals, sending and receiving X-API-Key headers that contained arbitrary base64-encoded data. Normally such headers contain random strings encoded base64 or hex. In this case, we just piped any protocol/content of our choosing into that area.

For higher per-packet data throughput, we could have easily utilized a fake JWT/JWS-style header value containing multiple such random strings in the body tunneling data, with a fake signature section tunneling more data—or even better, a "JWT/JWE" wherein the encrypted body is entirely ours to play with.

Have you ever recommended not doing a red team engagement?
I've gotten right in the front door with a few companies. When that happens, often the rest of the test is a waste. Sometimes it's just an honest mistake—something like a default password left on an administrator account. That stuff happens even with high-level application developers (you wouldn't believe who). But more often than not, a test like this just becomes a slaughter because of the architectural failures of an application or system in general.

I've watched applications literally unravel from within by means of insecure direct object references (IDORs). The developers thought that it was fine to perform no authN/authZ prior to object access as long as the object IDs were long and random. Hint: that is almost never okay. In the specific case I'm thinking of, you could request a series of tokens if you knew only one starting tokenized value. They assumed you could get that token only if you were logged in as the user it belonged to. It turned out that you could find the token by requesting their password reset page with the user's email and then pull down a series of chained requests to compromise everything that belonged to the user.

In these architectural cases, the offer isn't to continue red teaming them. The offer is to help them rebuild their application from the ground up with a member of our team working with them to ensure they make valid security decisions.

What's the most important or easiest-to-implement control that can prevent you from compromising a system or network?
One hundred percent client (host) isolation. Unless the systems on your network absolutely must be talking to each other, you need to implement this, and you need to do it now. Especially in the modern world of AWS, GCP, and Azure, your business applications aren't living on-premises. They're living somewhere else, accessed via an external pipe that exits your LAN/WAN. Few organizations have any need for workstations to talk directly to each other. Not only is this functionality all but useless in most business use cases, implementing isolation stops a huge number of attacks that we would otherwise be able to leverage to gain access to and exploit your network resources. Without device-to-device access, how am I supposed to find and exploit unpatched servers or workstations on your network? How am I supposed to pivot laterally? How am I supposed to relay credentials or access a rogue SMB shared directory? You implement isolation, and I guarantee you will watch red teams fail.

Why do you feel it is critical to stay within the rules of engagement?

When it comes to causing harm, that's a huge no-brainer. You want to have a job? You want people to trust you? You want to not be in jail? However, I think people often get tripped up over some of the gentler rules surrounding things like scope and attack types. These are the gray areas where it's easier to just let things slide. You shouldn't do this. Don't let it slide, and don't purposely play in the gray areas. Here's what you need to do.

Have an open chain of communication with your client through which you can easily reach out at any time. When you bump into a gray area, don't just keep going. Reach out to your client and request clarification. If the rules of engagement or the project scope isn't matching the reality of the application/network/system, renegotiate it.

> "Have an open chain of communication with your client through which you can easily reach out at any time."

Literally everything is up for negotiation. Talk with people.

If you were ever busted on a penetration test or other engagement, how did you handle it?

I've never managed to get *hard* busted, yet though I've heard some great stories. I seem to be pretty good at living off the land to avoid detection in network pivots. As a result, I rarely get noticed by network security teams. When I'm blocked during external tests, I literally just round-robin out of their way and back into attacking.

I was stopped from entering a building once during a physical penetration test. I wouldn't say that they "caught us" as much as their security procedures didn't allow random people who showed up at the gate claiming to be "mold inspectors" to enter without a signed work order waiting for them. They asked us to head down to the security office, and they left me and my partner alone in their control room with just one guard checking out our credentials on his computer. When he didn't find our fake mold inspector badges listed for entry, he simply asked us to leave.

I know it's not a crazy cool story. But hey, maybe if you're nervous about how hard some of the heart-pumping, adrenaline-inducing portions of red teaming might be, even getting caught isn't always that bad. In the end, they just asked us to leave. We flew to another state and broke into a different facility for the same company.

What is the biggest ethical quandary you experienced while on an assigned objective?

"Should I report this to the vendor?" is a huge one, especially when it involves systems that you know are in production globally at a massive scale. The moral penalty for not reporting can be huge. But, there are certainly situations in which you'll find yourself locked into an NDA that limits your ability to share findings with a third party. In this case, it's often best to work with your client and have them report or permit a redacted report to be transmitted to the selected third party. This is yet another reason that it's good to have great clients. It's important to choose who you work with.

How does the red team work together to get the job done?

Personally, I find it a little bit harder or less efficient to work with others in many ways. The biggest issue is information flow. Interpersonal communication is hugely low bandwidth at best. Talking is a terribly inefficient way to transmit large amounts of information.

I think within red teams it's a huge hindrance that must necessarily be overcome. The work that we do is incredibly complex and terribly high in specificity. Especially when you bring in the issues that our perspective often adds to our tasks. We don't usually have a control console flashing lights and outputting debug information to tell us what a system is doing internally as we interrogate it. Instead, we have to work out what's happening inside by tracking huge numbers of variables indicated by external responses (such as error messages). Communicating exactly what is happening (and when) to each other can be a huge challenge.

When it comes to working with the defenders/blue team/product engineers, I'm a huge fan of the collaborative engagement model in which the "find a way in and tell us a cool story" method of black-box testing is replaced by the gray-box work with the engineering team testing discrete sections of the application/ network to understand the threats posed to exactly that portion of the system independent of any other protective layers. We don't want to find one "cool" way in. We want to find and patch all the many different ways in.

A lot of red teams are absolutely trying to prove something and come home with cool stories to impress their friends. They want to live the life of a hacker, and sure, it's cool to find XSS in a site and pivot that into full control over a site. You know what's even cooler? Actually helping the security team maximize the security of the application. You do this by forgetting about the glory and working directly with the security team to remove the "fog of war" around the application. Then you apply concrete adversarial-security engineering skills to building a model for a threat against any system/subsystem therein.

What is your approach to debriefing and supporting blue teams after an operation is completed?

Full transparency. My skill set isn't "running Metasploit," and my access doesn't rely on a bucket of zero days I pull from to impress people. We're kidding ourselves if we're not engineers first and foremost. Engineering is a skill that I hold inside my mind, and I don't lose anything by showing people what I've done. The next challenge will be different, the next project will be different, and I'll engineer my way through them as well.

You should be able to answer any and all questions asked of you by the product team. There isn't any special sauce here, and any red teamer who tells you there is is simply holding onto whatever weak power they might have for fear of losing it. If questioned, I consider it my job to tell the product team literally everything I know. If they can hold all that knowledge, then I as a red cell professional need to move on and discover more. There is no secret sauce.

We really do need to be the virtual explorers and cartographers of our field, helping everyone to follow in our footsteps as quickly as possible and then moving on to new horizons when they arrive.

If you were to switch to the blue team, what would be your first step to better defend against attacks?

Of course, the answer here depends on a lot of variables, such as the company or my delegated responsibility scope. But if I were to choose just one thing to push, it would absolutely be Active Defense. I've done a lot of work on Active Defense in a past life. It's something that I still think (even if some of the most common techniques are getting a little dated) is worth a huge amount (especially within the context of the average organization, wherein the cost of security engineers or custom software systems might be prohibitive).

With Active Defense, you're looking at interdicting attack methodologies as opposed to simply trying to "harden" everything. If your plan is to remove every last vulnerability from your network, you're going have a bad time. But if you implement systems that can anticipate adversarial actions and counter them to gain you something, you might just get positive play out of it.

I was the lead developer on Black Hills Info Security's Active Defense Harbinger Distribution (ADHD) for a few years. This tool was designed to tackle this exact problem space. We want to find ways to anticipate the types of actions that an adversary will take and then do things to hamper them—or sometimes, not even just hamper. If you look at tooling like Honeybadger (inside ADHD), you'll find that it's actually possible to track an adversary down to their physical location when they try to hack you.

There is a lot that can be done, and it's not even hard to do. Most teams just haven't thought to try. But you can, and you should.

This is a special question that's dear to my heart. If you're reading this and you're part of a blue team that wants to do this type of thing but have no idea where to go, please do reach out to me directly on Twitter, and I'll do what I can to point you to resources that can get you on the right track.

What is some practical advice on writing a good report?

Be detailed, correct, and honest. It sounds crazy simple, but in my experience, these are things people struggle with.

You need your reports to contain the necessary detail that any findings you produce should be easily understood and, in all possible situations, easily reproduced. You can check this by reading over it once or having someone outside of your project review it for you. If your writing makes any *leaps* from one idea to the next, you need to fill in exactly what you meant.

You should be correct in all your report writing. What this means is that you should ensure you tell the full honest and clear truth. Don't insinuate things that aren't there in order to make your team look better, and don't be overconfident. I like to write using words like *can*, *might*, and *may* unless I'm absolutely sure about something. So much of what we do is chaotic (highly complex) and filled with massive gray areas. It's unlikely that you will ever be able to say much with 100 percent certainty. Don't write like you know it all.

Finally, be honest in your report writing. Be brave even. Be willing to say that you found something truly damaging. Remember, your job is to play the part of an adversary. There aren't too many highly destructive adversaries in the world for one simple reason. People aren't often willing to risk it all. But rest assured, when a true villain strikes an organization, they won't pull any punches. You need to be brave, abnormally brave, when it comes to trying things that are hard. Be willing to run attacks that may fail, and be willing to be embarrassed if they do. Be willing to write about these attacks, and admit when you don't know things. Your clients aren't just paying you; they're relying on you. Act like it.

How do you recommend security improvements other than pointing out where it's insufficient?

You need to have at least a cursory understanding of what's actually happening in three areas if you want to be a good red team member.

You need to know what attacking is like: This is the first one that most aspiring red cell members rush to learn. They want to know "how to hack," so they rush out and start reading books and watching tutorials or talks looking to understand what the attack looks like/how it's carried out. This is great. You absolutely must know these things. But this isn't everything.

You need to know what your attack does: You need to understand what the attack is actually doing. Not just "Oh, the SQL injection string is injecting SQL." I've met people who knew ` or `1=1;` – who didn't know a drop of actual Structured Query Language. These are not serious people.

You need to know what your target system does when you're not around: Plain and simple, you need to actually understand what it is you're attacking. Perhaps not intensely or in depth, but you should have at least a cursory understanding of everything—every computer, every system, every person you interact with—outside of the context of your run.

If you know these three things, you can do your job, you can do it well, and you can provide the context modifications of your actions to the security team with professionalism and ease.

What nontechnical skills or attitudes do you look for when recruiting and interviewing red team members?

One hundred percent self-awareness. You look for the people who make fun of themselves. You look for the people who are willing to ask questions or admit when they don't know something. You look for the people who correct themselves.

In this field, your ego doesn't get to decide when you gain access to a computer system. Almost everything we do is reactive. We don't get to (often) write the vulnerability into the system beforehand. Therefore, you need to be 100 percent able to parse what's happening around you. That's what self-awareness is for. You need to be able to track the world without your ego attempting to force its own will on the world around it.

With self-awareness you can understand, control, and react to yourself. This means that you can put yourself aside and focus on the Herculean task of outsmarting armies of engineers and outperforming computers.

You'll be able to see what I'm talking about when you work on a team with both types. The difference is like night and day. Most people are stuck within themselves. I massively support and affirm those people who are (by right of birth or right of hard work) able to see themselves from a pseudo-objective perspective.

What differentiates good red teamers from the pack as far as approaching a problem differently?

I have met an inordinate number of exceptional red cell members who would almost certainly be considered to be somewhere on the autistic spectrum. If you've been in this field for even a brief period of time, you almost certainly have seen something similar. This doesn't mean you have to be autistic to be good. But it does imply that there is something going on.

It's probably true that the general autistic cognitive profile performs exceptionally in this field relative to the average or neurotypical cognitive profile: to be able to focus for extremely long periods of time, to be more apt to reason from first principles (axiomatically), to be highly sensitive to the specificity of your environment, and to be able to translate that into task-applied "detail orientation."

We welcome all types. If you know your stuff and if you can deliver, you belong here. But neurotypicals can in large part survive anywhere. As such, I do think that it's especially heartening to see neurodivergent people, who in many cases haven't ever before been able to clearly demonstrate their value to their peers/parents/community, absolutely kill it as part of a red cell. You take the "nerdy" kid who got made fun of for not following viral dance crazes in high school or whatever, you give him a laptop, and suddenly power plants start shutting off for seemingly no reason; it's beautiful. ∎

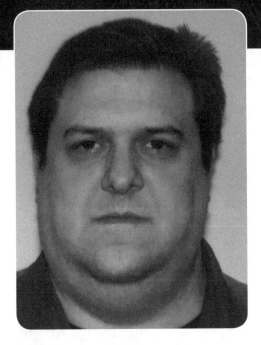

"Don't break the law! It's that easy."

Twitter: @passingthehash

Skip Duckwall

Alva "Skip" Duckwall started using Linux before there was a 1.0 kernel and has since moved into the information security arena, doing everything from computer/network auditing to vulnerability assessments and penetration testing. Skip spent three years on the U.S. Army red team, where he got to break into military bases and not get arrested for it. Skip's current work is as an independent security consultant.

9

How did you get your start on a red team?
I spent nearly a decade as a Unix system administrator before transitioning into the burgeoning full-time computer security arena. Unix sysadmin work routinely involves modifying an access control list (ACL) somewhere, be it a firewall, a file share, or whatever, so the transition to a security-minded role wasn't bad. I eventually transitioned into a position with the Defense Information Systems Agency (DISA), where I traveled to worldwide DoD sites and audited the sites versus the Security Technical Implementation Guides (STIGs). Having a deep background in day-to-day operations, along with a deep understanding of how various organizations attempted to keep their data secure in accordance with what are generally considered the top security standards, is what ultimately got me a job with the Army red team.

What is the best way to get a red team job?
A deep understanding of how the sausage gets made on a daily basis and how people involved with the process try to get their work done is key. Spending time

as a help desk/sys admin really helps to provide the foundational knowledge about how security operates. If you understand how the processes work, from the human level to the computer level, then you can find ways to subvert them. One of my favorite quotes I think highlights the point I'm trying to make: Ronnie Coleman said, "Everybody wants to be a bodybuilder, but nobody wants to lift no heavy-ass weights." In other words, you have to put in the time and effort to become proficient in the foundational levels before you can move on to the higher stuff.

How can someone gain red team skills without getting in trouble with the law?

Don't break the law! It's that easy. But seriously, who knows better how to subvert the functioning of the human body than a medical professional who has to stabilize or fix it daily? They understand that the wrong mix of chemicals/techniques could harm a human being. You have to understand how stuff is supposed to work and know how the whole Rube Goldberg contraption works front to back before you can routinely affect it in a desired manner. Vulnerability scanning, pentesting, red teaming, and so on all rely on target consent. If your target doesn't give you formal consent, then it's illegal, full stop. There are plenty of do-it-yourself labs and stuff online that you can use to break into stuff on your own network.

> "If your target doesn't give you formal consent, then it's illegal, full stop. There are plenty of do-it-yourself labs and stuff online that you can use to break into stuff on your own network."

Why can't we agree on what a red team is?

This link is from 1987:

https://www.washingtonpost.com/archive/politics/1987/08/24/navy-stages-commando-raids-to-expose-its-security-flaws/8b400370-92fd-4f6b-aa90-c1e1461ab63b/?utm_term=.d5797b93ae83

It talks about how a team of Navy personnel examined the security of various bases and some of the issues that came up. It also talked about people getting sued because of differing opinions of what the rules of engagement (ROE) were. I bring this up because this particular article is the first one I remember reading about what a red team cell is.

I was a member (as a contractor) of a service red team (Army). We were tasked with acting as a bad guy during military exercises and demonstrating in the most visible way possible how security lapses can affect the overall operations of the good guys. There were some rules in place, but generally we were tasked with a particular objective and not really given too much guidance about how to achieve it. If we were arrested for activities directly related to attaining these goals, we had letters that would (eventually) get us out of jail. As you can imagine, this offers a lot of flexibility about how to solve the problems on the way to completing the objectives. If we were really sponsored by a hostile nation-state, money, manpower, equipment, and time would not really be constrained.

Unfortunately, now the term *red team* has been somewhat diluted to mean something more than an average pentest. This could mean a normal pentest plus some sort of physical security assessment, for example.

There are generally two camps that argue about what a red team is: the folks who were on a service red team (or similar real-world teams) and everybody else. If you have had a job where you got to break into a military base several times a year and do stuff that, if caught, would get you thrown in jail, you have a different take on it than the rest of the world.

What is one thing the rest of information security doesn't understand about being on a red team? What is the most toxic falsehood you have heard related to red, blue, or purple teams?
A red team isn't a bunch of folks running rampant like a pack of hungry hyenas on the network causing maximum damage. A good red team is like a ninja—it sneaks in, maybe causes diversions or something, but eventually takes care of the task and disappears.

When should you introduce a formal red team into an organization's security program?
Ask the following multipart question: "Can you, within a 60-minute window, provide me with all of the following?"

- A count of all your computing assets, their locations, and any other relevant information within a 5 percent margin of error
- If provided a MAC address of a particular machine, its physical location
- A complete list of all internet access points as well as a diagram for each one of what your security stack looks like
- The last three days' worth of log data from (random machine)
- A written list of policies, procedures, runbooks, and so on for your SOC
- An overall network map, dated within the past three months
- Detailed policies, procedures, and results from the most recent security awareness testing

If the answer is no to any of these, then the organization's benefit from a red team would probably be minimal and they need some other sort of assessment. If they answer yes and can back it up, they might be ready for a red team.

What is the *least* bang-for-your-buck security control that you see implemented?
Threat intel. IMHO, pure snake oil.

Have you ever recommended not doing a red team engagement?
Frequently. I constantly recommend a full-scope pentest (on-site, remote, phishing, physical, wireless) before jumping to a red team. They have to survive and/or do well in a full-scope test before I'd give the go-ahead for an actual red team.

> "I constantly recommend a full-scope pentest (on-site, remote, phishing, physical, wireless) before jumping to a red team."

What's the most important or easiest-to-implement control that can prevent you from compromising a system or network?
Privilege separation. Understanding that the average office worker does not need admin access to their PC.

"The ROE are your boundary line between staying legal and opening up your liability for criminal and civil damages."

Why do you feel it is critical to stay within the rules of engagement?

The ROE are your boundary line between staying legal and opening up your liability for criminal and civil damages.

If you were ever busted on a penetration test or other engagement, how did you handle it?

Once on the Army red team, there was a group of us (5 to 10 people) in a conference room where we weren't supposed to be when a soldier appeared at the door asking if we had the room booked and what we were doing there. I responded with something like "We're here collecting metrics for the exercise. Ask Chief <deliberately messed up the name a couple of times, to which they corrected the name> about it. She said we're good."

The soldier seemed mollified and wandered off. Right after that, we packed up our stuff and walked out the door. While we were heading out to our cars in the parking lot, we were able to look in the window and see the soldier and some other folks wandering back to the conference room looking confused about where we had gone. In the after action, nobody asked us about it, so it must have been forgotten about.

The trick is to put on an air of confidence when challenged, have a story all ready to go, have names of people on staff, and so on, and then be willing to pull the plug if something doesn't seem right.

What is the biggest ethical quandary you experienced while on an assigned objective?

The toughest part of the gig is when the client decides as a result of your activities that somebody on their side has to be fired/relieved of their duties. I always try to ensure that everything we do is as nonattributional as possible, because often the problem is systemic and doesn't reflect the mistakes of one particular person. People can be retrained; at least the good ones can. If asked directly whose fault a particular situation is, I will always avoid using people's names. It might piss off the client, but ultimately I try to explain that it is usually not any particular person's fault and that it's a systematic failure that led to our successes. Generally the client is understanding, although sometimes they are not and have made wholesale staff changes as a result of our success.

How does the red team work together to get the job done?

From a teamwork perspective, everybody brings a different focus, different background, and so on. I've had many sessions where we spitball ideas about how to accomplish goals based on what we have in front of us, what we know, what we don't know, and so on. It's all about different perspectives. Keeping centralized notes in a wiki or something like that, making sure we had a central pile of screenshots, and then writing up individual summaries of actions taken, objectives achieved, and so on all helped with writing the final report.

What is your approach to debriefing and supporting blue teams after an operation is completed?

On the Army red team, we would hold a Q&A with the blue team. The big thing is that we would kick management out of the room. We wanted the techs and hands-on guys to ask us questions without fear of looking bad in front of management. We were honest and forthright with our answers too. We were there to make them better.

If you were to switch to the blue team, what would be your first step to better defend against attacks?
Take away local admin rights from the 95 percent of people who don't need them. The biggest reason it is in place is usually because there are not enough help-desk/support people to install software, and thus the populace gets to be local admins because they need to install software or do something that facilitates their work efforts.

What is some practical advice on writing a good report?
Understand that you aren't getting paid to break into the place; you're getting paid to write the report about how you broke in and what the client can do about it and what the implications are if an attacker did the same thing.

The report is *not* about how badass you are; it's all about the *client*. Does your report have actionable information that helps the client to remediate issues? Does your report effectively communicate issues to the C levels?

> "Understand that you aren't getting paid to break into the place; you're getting paid to write the report about how you broke in and what the client can do about it and what the implications are if an attacker did the same thing."

Also understand that in many organizations, the management won't take their employees' words at face value that something is wrong. They need an external third party to tell them it's wrong. Understanding the customer's motivations and then tweaking the report to help further their goals also leads to better report writing and ultimate client satisfaction.

How do you ensure your program results are valuable to people who need a full narrative and context?
Provide extensive documentation about how to fix the issue. Reporting is for the client and not for the tester. Imagine being on the other side and having this report landing on your desk. What information would you want in there to fix the issues?

What nontechnical skills or attitudes do you look for when recruiting and interviewing red team members?
The ability to effectively communicate your thoughts in a coherent manner, be it out loud or on paper.

What differentiates good red teamers from the pack as far as approaching a problem differently?
The degree of caution displayed. In some environments, one bad packet can kill your access. Good folks will test in a lab/VM environment first before trying it live on the wire. ∎

"From my perspective, the best way to get a red team job is to get involved in the red team community."

Twitter: @ronaldeddings

Ronald Eddings

10

Ronald Eddings is a Silicon Valley–based cybersecurity expert, blogger, and digital nomad whose ingenuity, dedication, and ambition have all earned him a reputation as a trusted industry leader. Over the course of his career, Ronald has garnered extensive experience working at various Fortune 500 companies and mentoring a multitude of fellow professionals. In addition to cybersecurity, he is well versed in software development, DevOps, and artificial intelligence. Currently, Ronald serves as a cyber fusion engineer at a cybersecurity startup and is an active contributor to several open source projects. He also holds a bachelor of science degree in information technology and an array of cybersecurity certifications.

How did you get your start on a red team?
My experience with red team, pentesting, and offensive operations came in phases. Before starting my career, I had a fortunate opportunity and became connected with hackers in the InfoSec community by being in the right places at the right times. When I first met Marcus J. Carey, I was still in high school and happened to be reading my first book on Linux.

Through Marcus, I met other hackers like Johnny Long, Marco Figueroa, Joe McCray, and many more. Through seeking and receiving mentorship, I learned that I could thrive in the field, and there was nothing in my way except for reading the material and understanding that mastery does not come all at once. At the time, there were not as many jobs for red teaming, pentesting, or anything attack related. Initially, I spent a great amount of time learning about how devices communicate and how to code in Python, JavaScript, and Ruby. Coincidentally, building a foundation of knowledge in those areas happened to be what the industry was looking for. Learning these topics did not come with ease but did make for a better time when interviewing and striving for my degree. While attending community college, I submerged myself in the newly organized InfoSec club and competed at events like Collegiate Cyber Defense Competition (CCDC). After mentioning my experiences to my college professor, I learned that he was a senior associate at Booz Allen Hamilton and recently opened a job requirement for a red team. Fortunately, I had stayed close with the idea that mastery does not come overnight and had been consistently making an attempt to become more versatile in the tools and programming languages available. When the time came to interview, I did everything to prepare—great meal, full night of rest, and showing up early to the interview. Since I was prepared and also had a reference, the opportunity was serendipitous and less stressful.

What is the best way to get a red team job?

From my perspective, the best way to get a red team job is to get involved in the red team community. There are many public events, conferences, and meetups that happen in various cities and online. It can also be a great start to participate and volunteer at conferences. This could be a significant start to diversify your peer group and ultimately strengthen your skills. Another strategy to get involved is to participate in CTFs and other public challenges. Practicing your craft for a set amount of time with a new set of challenges always goes a long way.

How can someone gain red team skills without getting in trouble with the law?

There has never been a better time to ethically obtain red team skills. Virtualization enables practitioners and enthusiasts to rapidly deploy infrastructure and applications. Today, my personal preference is Docker, which assists in creating a playground to attack devices and try new tools on various operating systems. To get started, there are many resources available such as books (e.g., *Tribe of Hackers*), online courses, conferences, and much more. My recommendation would be to become curious about what makes technology vulnerable and how to protect against attacks.

Why can't we agree on what a red team is?

It's probably a good thing that there are differences in red team definitions. Challenging current assumptions and searching for new solutions are what a red team is built on. I promote and encourage following a standard or setting out for a more optimal solution, since each organization has different requirements.

What is one thing the rest of information security doesn't understand about being on a red team? What is the most toxic falsehood you have heard related to red, blue, or purple teams?

A falsehood that I hear commonly is that a team has a single or few purposes. Red, blue, and purple teams have overlapping responsibilities with several teams. In fact, there are some red teamers who are doing more blue team work due to a lack of blue team resources. What can be toxic is attempting to stick to a single lane and not completely participating with the organization as a whole.

When should you introduce a formal red team into an organization's security program?

It can be difficult to determine when is a good time to introduce a red team into an organization. I'd measure a few key things: I'd assess if an organization had an incident response plan. If so, I'd ask, does the organization have a team to gather data and respond to such incidents? Lastly, I'd ask, does the organization have the capability and tools to eliminate and proactively protect against threats? If all of these are true, it may be time to introduce a red team. I've seen organizations invest in an existing team member to go to conferences and trainings to assist in building a new red team, which can go a long way if done with care.

How do you explain the value of red teaming to a reluctant or nontechnical client or organization?

With the growth and demand for InfoSec practitioners, red teams are appearing and growing to a larger size. Articulating the value of a red team is best done when threat research is done in concert. A red team that understands threats can perform more realistic tests based on previous attacks and events. Through documentation, it can be trivial to share details and metrics on what an organization is vulnerable to.

What is the *least* bang-for-your-buck security control that you see implemented?

To reverse the question, the most bang-for-your-buck control would be training. It's easy to buy a product and hope that it works. Vulnerabilities often exist because of a lack of training or hard-to-follow processes. Receiving training and optimizing processes go a tremendous way. As mundane as it may sound, regular security awareness training is effective—and serves as a precursor to red team tests.

Have you ever recommended not doing a red team engagement?

My background is working with larger organizations, which I've always found needing/requiring a red team engagement. The attack surface/landscape has grown by several orders of magnitude and is proof that security integration is continuous and ongoing. With the rise of applications, APIs, and IoT devices, there are always quite a few red flags identified. Red teams can help flag and assess these vulnerabilities to ensure other attackers are not taking advantage of such issues.

What's the most important or easiest-to-implement control that can prevent you from compromising a system or network?

A firewall. There's very little reason for many ports to be able to communicate outside of your organization. Most modern firewalls can also assist with creating rules that block malformed application requests.

Additionally, a firewall works great for blocking known bad addresses and other artifacts based on signatures and other techniques. As an organization matures, a firewall is a keystone resource to collect logs from.

Why do you feel it is critical to stay within the rules of engagement?

Red teams are being formed at organizations at an increasing rate because of the value that they can bring. Rules of engagement can help ensure a successful red team engagement in a production network. Existing outside the rules of engagement could lead to loss of profit and trust for an organization. More specifically, crashing an application or service that generates revenue for an organization is bad news for everyone. Rules of engagement are expectations that are set and agreed upon. If boundaries need to be adjusted, a professional red team will contact customers or stakeholders to adjust accordingly.

If you were ever busted on a penetration test or other engagement, how did you handle it?

Fortunately, I've never been completely busted. However, I have made several messy mistakes creating logs in sources I did not want to be seen in. More specifically, crashing an application can be an attacker's worst nightmare. When critical services crash, there are many logs created in several sources. It's the attacker's responsibility to clean up after themselves. I've had a few engagements where I've given an engineer a perfect opportunity to upgrade by crashing a service—which ultimately led to a patched vulnerability. If engineers have verbose logging enabled, there's a possibility that your payload will be revealed and give away the fact that an attack is underway. In situations like this, I make it my mission to find an alternative route for exploitation to ensure that I can clean up my logs and restart crashed services.

What is the biggest ethical quandary you experienced while on an assigned objective?

The biggest ethical quandary I face is teaching exploitation. With great exploits come great responsibilities. I spend part of my time teaching educational content on YouTube, with a portion of it being exploitation. While teaching this skill, I put in extra effort to narrow the focus on professionals in the InfoSec field and avoid viewers who are searching *How to Hack {Favorite Website Goes Here}*.

How does the red team work together to get the job done?

The red teams that show the most value are the teams that have great documentation practices. Detailed documentation leads to detailed reports and less stress at the end of an engagement. Taking the time to document your work is a team sport in itself. Just one individual not providing detailed documentation could mean missed learning opportunities for the entire team and less understanding of what was completed for the customer. Lastly, if the results are documented well enough, then debriefing blue teams will be a lot more straightforward.

What is your approach to debriefing and supporting blue teams after an operation is completed?

Before an engagement, I work with my customer or organization to set expectations and document each phase of my work. Assuming expectations are set beforehand, it's easier to collect data/create metrics on what is important. My approach to debriefing is typically sharing details on three pillars: evaluation, scoring/severity, and recommended fixes. My experience with organizations has been ongoing, and I've been frequently involved in applying the fix and assisting onboarding new application builds.

If you were to switch to the blue team, what would be your first step to better defend against attacks?

I find myself constantly working with teams focused on defense. There is an abundance of applications with open source packages and libraries. When I'm able to find vulnerabilities in source code, I work closely with engineers to patch and with blue teams to search for activity. After finding vulnerabilities, I enjoy hunting for evidence of similar discoveries. My recommendation for defense is to set up perimeters. It's vital to set up strong perimeters around your critical assets and entire organization.

Through this process, it's important to remember that security is ongoing and can't be solved in a single day. Sometimes turning on an alert will lead to an influx of events/incidents—it takes time to tune alerts and triggers. This should not be discouraging.

What is some practical advice on writing a good report?
Writing a report can seem like a daunting task if you've had negative experiences in the past. For a while, writing was something that I thought I couldn't get excited about. I learned that it's all about mind-set. By framing the work as valuable and exciting, I've made documentation and reporting the favorite aspects of my job. I've also learned it's the easiest way to show long-term value. I recommend shifting to a positive mind-set, making it fun, and being proud of the work. Documentation and reporting are the trophy case to your hard work.

How do you ensure your program results are valuable to people who need a full narrative and context?
Ensuring value can mean many things. It's important to first know what is the metric for your team's value. If your team is being measured on a number of engagements per year, then begin collecting that data on that metric and similar metrics. If a red team and blue team are working cohesively as a unit, then each engagement will introduce new results, and the data will reinforce this. If your red team is finding similar or identical findings each engagement, this is a cautionary sign that all teams are not working closely together or the importance is not being highlighted correctly. This is a great opportunity to get involved and provide more contextual information related to findings.

How do you recommend security improvements other than pointing out where it's insufficient?
Outside of basic security recommendations, it's vital to search for the root cause of what introduced a vulnerability. Introduce questions such as these: Is it a software issue? Is it an untrained engineer? Is there an organizational process that's delaying teams from patching? More insightful questions will establish more trust with the customer and make for more interesting red team engagements in the future.

What nontechnical skills or attitudes do you look for when recruiting and interviewing red team members?
I've spent most of my career working on larger teams, and I typically look for candidates with eagerness to work with a team. More specifically, I select candidates who can leverage other team members for help. I'm also an advocate of pair programming, hunting, and red teaming. The most beneficial nontechnical skill I find for the red team is the ability to ask questions. Thoughtful questions can satisfy and lead to more positive curiosity.

What differentiates good red teamers from the pack as far as approaching a problem differently?
What differentiates the best from the pack are habits. Acquiring the skills to become exceptional takes time and requires consistency. Often you see the greatest red teamers consistently attending the same meetings and conferences that help them continually succeed and avoiding bad agreements. It's most beneficial to prioritize what's most important and avoid distractions while learning and completing tasks. ■

> "The biggest asset of a valuable member of a red team is having a depth of knowledge in as many areas of computing as possible."

Twitter: @HackingLZ

Justin Elze

Justin Elze is the adversary emulation and threat research practice lead at TrustedSec. He has more than 13 years of experience in the information technology industry specializing in enterprise penetration testing, network security, social engineering, and red teaming. Prior to joining TrustedSec, Justin was a senior consultant for Accuvant Labs, Dell SecureWorks, and Redspin, where he led numerous red team engagements and penetration tests. Justin has worked in various industries including internet service providers, cloud services/hosting, DoD contracting, and services consulting companies.

11

How did you get your start on a red team?

For me, being on a red team was a natural transition from where I started in penetration testing and offensive testing. I always wanted to move offensive testing toward a more realistic model for clients, which was a real deciding factor in making that transition.

Looking back, I have been involved in IRC and computers since I was young, and I grew up with *Hackers* being one of my favorite movies. My actual start down a career pathway in computers was really fueled by two amazing high school teachers, Michelle Greenway and Meg McDonald, who supported my growth within the field and helped get me into a Cisco networking program, which really started my career and allowed me to grow into the person I am today. After that point, getting my OSCP and jumping from various IT-related jobs as a system engineer or network engineer enabled me to round out my experience until I got my first break into an InfoSec career.

What is the best way to get a red team job?

Most people get their feet wet with penetration testing, web application testing, or some other form of offensive testing as a first job in the field. Alternatively, coming from threat hunting or the blue team side gives you great insight into detections and how to circumvent them.

The biggest asset of a valuable member of a red team is having a depth of knowledge in as many areas of computing as possible. So, the best way to get a red team job may be gaining experience in as many other aspects of the job as possible, not just specifically offensive security.

"Today, there are tons of resources to help gain skills and tune the skills you have."

How can someone gain red team skills without getting in trouble with the law?

Today, there are tons of resources to help gain skills and tune the skills you have. Between CTFs and online offensive training courses, there are numerous bug bounty programs that will enable people to gain experience legally. Outside of that, Twitter has been a great resource where lots of people share tips and tricks.

Why can't we agree on what a red team is?

The major issue with defining a red team is the fact that people tend to bend standard rules of engagement to fit client requirements but still call it a red team job. Once you start taking large areas of testing away and implementing a ton of restrictions, you don't end up being able to replicate the behavior of attackers. This is where the lines begin to blur.

Red teams serve the purpose of adversary simulation for a client. It gives the client a chance to test their entire security stack against an attack meant to circumvent security controls and reach business goals.

What is one thing the rest of information security doesn't understand about being on a red team? What is the most toxic falsehood you have heard related to red, blue, or purple teams?

For a long time, there was a perception that red teams come in and destroy everything and always win. A lot of this was caused by companies performing red team engagements they were unprepared for.

If you look back, offensive security was "easy" for a long time—companies had huge gaps in visibility. Potentially, you could break in and avoid detection without a lot of forethought. Defense has made huge advances in the past few years. You can purchase EDR, SIEM, and other products giving you a huge technical advantage, whereas a few years back that would require a number of superstar employees.

Red teaming requires a lot of planning as well as a ton of development and research on the backend. You want to train the way you fight. I work with some very mature clients, and we constantly go back and forth. One quarter they might catch up and destroy every attack we make, while next quarter we come back with something completely new and make progress.

When should you introduce a formal red team into an organization's security program?

From a technical controls perspective, I would expect at minimum a security information and event management (SIEM) and collecting events from an endpoint. It would also help to have a formal IR process in place. Normally clients reach a point with penetration testing and their security program where they would like to see how the whole program does against a focused attacker with a business goal.

How do you explain the value of red teaming to a reluctant or nontechnical client or organization?

If a client is reluctant, then it's possible that they're just not ready for a red team. The value from red teaming comes in the form of seeing how an attack would play out. You end up being able to identify blind spots and areas of improvement—oftentimes to produce attack paths the client hasn't previously explored or built defenses around.

What is the *least* bang-for-your-buck security control that you see implemented?

The way this usually ends up is that the control itself isn't the issue. The control may be deployed wrong or isn't monitored—for example, an antivirus program that allows the end user to add exemptions and isn't responded to when it alerts.

A simple example of this is cloud-based email. Filtering solutions often come with a lengthy deployment guide. Often important steps get missed, like limiting IP space that can connect directly to your email server and circumvent the filtering service. This is common in companies of all sizes.

Have you ever recommended not doing a red team engagement?

It's fairly commonplace that I have phone calls with prospective clients who are looking for direction on future testing that may not involve doing a red team. The two most common scenarios are these: "We have done penetration testing for years but want to simulate real attacks over more time" or "We want to gauge the overall performance of the security program's ability to identify and defend from attackers." If the company isn't mature enough to support a red team engagement, I would recommend a purple team assessment, which would allow both offensive and defensive insights into understanding attacker behavior and techniques.

What's the most important or easiest-to-implement control that can prevent you from compromising a system or network?

Controls like two-factor are cheap for smaller companies, and while not perfect, if it is deployed across the board, it can slow attacks down effectively. I would also suggest separation of privileges and network segmentation along with password managers to companies in this situation. Creating an environment where attackers can trip up or have to switch standard tactics greatly increases the chances of catching them.

> "Controls like two-factor are cheap for smaller companies, and while not perfect, if it is deployed across the board, it can slow attacks down effectively."

Why do you feel it is critical to stay within the rules of engagement?
Staying within the rules of engagement is extremely important. However, when I work with clients to plan red teams, we try to remove as many restrictions as possible. It's rare we start an engagement with a long list of restrictions. The most common restriction is notifications prior to phishing a handful of key individuals. This usually includes contacting our point of contact and letting them know the pretext in case the high-profile target reports it and additional steps are taken. Clients are extremely receptive to limiting restrictions, as attackers don't work in strict rule sets.

What is the biggest ethical quandary you experienced while on an assigned objective?
The ethical quandaries usually present themselves in the form of things we are unable to do, for example, hacking a legit site and hosting malware, compromising employee cell phones, compromising employee social media, and other things that legitimate attackers would have no issues doing; we as ethical hackers wouldn't.

"No single individual will ever have experience in every part of technology you will encounter. You need a strong group to lean on and support operations."

How does the red team work together to get the job done?
It's called red *teaming*. I think many people forget that aspect. No single individual will ever have experience in every part of technology you will encounter. You need a strong group to lean on and support operations. Multiple people with different skill sets allow for a well-rounded team that learns and grows within itself. When attacking companies, you will always run up on technologies that you might have never seen before but chances are another team member has.

I was lucky enough to be able to build out the team at my current employer. I was also fortunate enough to build out the research team that backs offensive testing operations. Based on the increasing complexity of executing successful operations on clients, the research team allows us to have dedicated developers and researchers to provide new tools and techniques.

What is your approach to debriefing and supporting blue teams after an operation is completed?
Ideally, the approach to concluding an operation is having several debriefing calls or meetings. Normally, I would start with a large meeting involving team leaders of various teams. Breakout meetings for deep dives into technical issues and remediation steps would follow.

If you were to switch to the blue team, what would be your first step to better defend against attacks?
This is easier said than done, but ingesting endpoint logs into a SIEM or other searchable/alertable format would be my first suggestion. If you're not doing this, then you're operating blindly, and this is where the majority of threats start.

What is some practical advice on writing a good report?

Writing reports is par for the course in this job. It is most important to include relevant information the client might need for hunting after the report is delivered. Other pertinent information includes file hashes, dates, times, and accounts used. The more information delivered in an organized manner, the more useful and understandable it will be to the customer.

How do you ensure your program results are valuable to people who need a full narrative and context?

One of the areas a lot of people forget is showing what was tried and what failed, even if it went undetected. What attacks were tried gives significantly more context for the mind-set and approach that was taken. It also demonstrates client environment configurations that worked, deterring or preventing an attack path.

How do you recommend security improvements other than pointing out where it's insufficient?

I always include a section in the report that highlights positives. This may include anything the client is already doing that prevents or slows down the attack process. If you highlight things that the client is doing correctly, it helps to encourage them and show that they are making progress and headed in the right direction without losing hope or becoming agitated about their failures or where they are lacking.

What nontechnical skills or attitudes do you look for when recruiting and interviewing red team members?

The ability to work on a team and accept positive criticism is beneficial in this line of work. It's important to work as a team and support each other, giving each other new ideas or help when needed without dismissing their own ideas or thought processes. Communication is also key. It's necessary to convey sometimes very technical and wordy processes to a wide variety of audiences with varying technical capabilities.

> "It's important to work as a team and support each other, giving each other new ideas or help when needed without dismissing their own ideas or thought processes."

What differentiates good red teamers from the pack as far as approaching a problem differently?

First, creative technical problem-solving is an important attribute to have in a red teamer. It's fairly common that an attack or bypass that worked last week might not work this week. It's important to develop ideas and roll with the punches, but it is also a valuable quality to understand when you have exhausted what is possible and need to move on to another pathway. The ability to step back and have an adversarial mind-set is valuable. This includes achieving your goals with the smallest footprint and attack path possible. ■

"Challenge everything. Don't think more highly of yourself than you ought. Invest in people and relationships. Place first priority on growing in your character and learning technology second."

Twitter: @ustayready

Mike Felch

12

Mike Felch is a red team lead and security researcher at Black Hills Information Security. Prior to joining BHIS, he was vice president of Security Research for an InfoSec startup leading technical teams and exploiting hardware. Throughout his career, he's held roles as a software engineer, pentester, and system administrator. Mike is a divergent thinker who enjoys cognitive challenges and understands the power of collaboration. He's actively involved in the InfoSec community and regularly open sources red team tools. You will either find him with his wife, Angela, and daughters at InfoSec conferences or in prison, investing in the lives of incarcerated men.

How did you get your start on a red team?
I wish I had an easy answer, but my journey was not the typical path most people take. Most of my life I've been accused of being argumentative because of challenging the typical way of thinking by questioning everything, rarely giving up, and bending the rules. I grew up in a household where my dad reverse engineered my console games, Unix System V Release 4 was on floppy disks in my mom's Avon boxes, and I never had to worry about dial-up because we had 128k ISDN. Imagine being raised in a hacker's household during the boom of personal computers. Needless to say, the late '90s were filled with long nights of learning how to reverse engineer, coding, and crazy teleconferences (called c0nfs back then) with a fringe group of hackers exploiting the inner workings of technology without YouTube and wired on Jolt with ramen noodles. As you can imagine, an armed youth without direction resulted in global hell but, at the

same time, created the foundation of lifelong friendships where most of our journeys were cryptically documented and shared in ASCII ezines or dropped on full-disclosure mailing lists under numerous personas.

Over most of my career, I flipped back and forth between Linux administration, InfoSec, and software development until I finally decided to pentest full time. I was lucky enough to pentest for the corporate office of a large technology company that had dozens of subsidiaries, all running different technology stacks. This really helped grow my exposure to different technologies while also challenging me to grow my character because, little did I know, offensive security was actually less about breaking things and more about making other people better. I eventually left pentesting for a few years and took a role at an InfoSec startup as the VP of security research and development, where I managed a bunch of technical teams and security platforms and assisted with the corporate direction.

Even after working in the industry for a while, being on and off different teams and in different roles, I struggled to find a good cultural fit. Over the years, I uncomfortably forced myself to be part of the InfoSec community by volunteering to serve on the BSides Tampa and BSides Orlando teams. I eventually started attending local security meetups and building relationships, which led to me joining Black Hills Information Security (BHIS). While at BHIS, not only am I surrounded by super-talented friends who are more like family, but I have the privilege of red teaming within a culture that is so selfless.

What is the best way to get a red team job?

Challenge everything. Don't think more highly of yourself than you ought. Invest in people and relationships. Place first priority on growing in your character and learning technology second. Learn to contribute openly, even when you think what you're sharing is already known. Get involved in a local security meetup or conference. There are so many paths to offensive security that most people never consider. Red teaming is heavy on working together with others with the goal of making an organization better. Examine your heart; do you tend to glorify red over blue or only celebrate circumventing controls instead of defending them? Are you more concerned with looking good, or do you also celebrate the success of others?

Skill sets can be trained, but your character can make or break a team, create a service or disservice for a customer, and turn a company on or off to you as a candidate. Companies hiring pentesters require the candidate to be trustworthy and skilled in some area of technology, but even more important is the ability to get underneath others and push them to success. No one wants to work with someone who only brags about cracking a perimeter or bad-mouths a defender. Your character will speak louder in the circles you get involved in than the words you use to describe the latest cool hack you pulled off.

> "Skill sets can be trained, but your character can make or break a team, create a service or disservice for a customer, and turn a company on or off to you as a candidate."

How can someone gain red team skills without getting in trouble with the law?

Nowadays, there are so many challenging ways to grow technically. Capture-the-flag (CTF) competitions are a great way to train your mind to analyze a problem where a solution exists while exposing you to numerous technology stacks. Some people use CTF competitions to compete, while some leverage it for the learning experience. Additionally, while I am not a huge fan of bug bounty programs for organizations, they do create real-life experience opportunities for anyone wanting to bug hunt. Lastly, there are a number of online sites that offer pentesting labs like Hack The Box and Hack This Site. There are so many resources available today to build experience, connect with others, and learn how to operate as a team.

Why can't we agree on what a red team is?

This is a loaded question with answers that require all of us to address. A red team tends to reflect the experience of the one answering, which means, depending on their exposure, it could be accurate, tainted from marketing campaigns, or something much more made up based on their own misconceptions of the end goal. In my opinion, not all wrong answers are because of unintentional confusion.

I have witnessed a number of businesses navigating within the information security industry where they over-promise and under-deliver on quality within engagements with the intention of providing subpar services by capitalizing on customer ignorance. Another reason is most working InfoSec roles rarely have been responsible for defending or executing a red team assessment, which leads to a lot of false narratives, perpetuating the disagreement about what an actual red team is.

Personally speaking, it wasn't until I migrated from being a pentester into operating within a red team that I truly understood the difference between pentesting and red teaming. I casually used the terminology interchangeably throughout most of my career, not really understanding the difference and somewhat scared to ask for fear of being viewed as a fake. Little did I know at the time, most people seem to share the same confusion about a lot of different areas of our industry.

What is one thing the rest of information security doesn't understand about being on a red team? What is the most toxic falsehood you have heard related to red, blue, or purple teams?

One of the biggest problems facing InfoSec is this idea that red teamers have to know everything about all technologies. This crazy notion that it's the most technically difficult role in InfoSec and that only a select few can achieve success couldn't be further from the truth. Here are two realities: it's much more difficult to defend an attacker than to be one, and while red teamers know a little about a lot of technology because of experience, there's more we don't know than what we do. Red teaming is actually more about divergent thinking than knowing technology.

When should you introduce a formal red team into an organization's security program?

In most cases, businesses actually ready enough to benefit from a red team assessment tend to be those organizations that have matured in their security programs, leading to incident response plans in place, vulnerability management being fluid, and pentests occurring somewhat consistently. The common goal of red teaming is to make the blue team better, navigate security controls, quietly simulate an adversary, and assess the employees. This is much different than a standard penetration test, and while there is some overlap between a pentest and a red team assessment, an unprepared organization encountering a red team assessment can quickly become overwhelmed by the numerous findings that surface, potentially leading to a disservice to already burdened teams.

On the other hand, I've witnessed teams leveraging a red team assessment to surface necessary discussions and the need for funding to further their security program. Needless to say, it's not a one-size-fits-all scenario, and proper organizational context should be considered when determining whether a red team assessment is a blessing or a curse.

> "In most cases, businesses actually ready enough to benefit from a red team assessment tend to be those organizations that have matured in their security programs, leading to incident response plans in place, vulnerability management being fluid, and pentests occurring somewhat consistently."

How do you explain the value of red teaming to a reluctant or nontechnical client or organization?

Approaching an organization in a manner that communicates the end goal as one that helps, not just exposes problems, is critical to the success of a red team. I always try to challenge red teamers and pentesters to leave engagements with the customer feeling encouraged and valued, not exposed and vulnerable. Blue teams, developers, and other technical team members need to know you are on their side helping fight back. Your goal is not to give fodder to their leadership so they can hold employees responsible for vulnerabilities to the fire. How you communicate before, during, and after the engagement will determine whether they feel you are for them or against them.

What is the *least* bang-for-your-buck security control that you see implemented?

The existence of off-the-shelf antivirus products seems to be a common way enterprises are wasting their money. Malware and malicious payloads tend to modify their signatures with each iteration making signature-based detections a waste of resources. Microsoft has really stepped up its detection and mitigation strategies with Windows Defender. If the antivirus product isn't pivoting to a more anomalous behavior detection, then it's probably not detecting anything but old known malware that isn't a risk worth the extra cost and something that Windows Defender is already detecting.

To reverse the question, the most bang-for-your-buck security control is probably a strong and enforced password policy, which is one of the easiest way to drastically increase the security of an environment. This includes not re-using local admin passwords, having a 15-character password minimum, and making sure Global Policy Preferences don't contain passwords. All service accounts should have a distinctively different strong password generated that can't be memorized by employees. New account passwords should also be distinctively different, not predictable. This is a security control that can be deployed with minimum resources, has a low overhead, and is difficult to push back against and creates major problems for an attacker.

Have you ever recommended not doing a red team engagement?
I am just finishing up an engagement where the customer requested a red team when they really needed only a product within a specific environment tested. This led to more of an internal pivot assessment that put specific focus on the product and its configuration. By taking the time to discuss the needs of the customer and their expectations of the engagement, one can quickly determine a suitable engagement type that meets the needs and goals of the customer.

What's the most important or easiest-to-implement control that can prevent you from compromising a system or network?
The combination of a strong password policy and mandatory two-factor authentication on all critical services commonly results in major headaches on a red team. The larger an organization, the more difficult this can be to roll out, but for small and medium businesses this can be a quick win that grows with the organization while being enabled with a small budget.

Why do you feel it is critical to stay within the rules of engagement?
Aside from the legal issues that can arise, the goal of the engagement is to assess the security within the scope. If the rules of engagement outline specific details surrounding what's being tested, times of days, or other restrictions, then it's because that's what the customer deems the need to be in order to conduct the engagement. As a tester, we don't always know the impact an engagement can have on the environment or the employees who can quickly spin out of control. At the same time, a tester who listens well can make recommendations for the customer to consider, which may guide them into expanding the rules of engagement in a way that helps, not hinders.

If you were ever busted on a penetration test or other engagement, how did you handle it?
One of the beauties of red teaming is being able to face a well-equipped blue team that knows how to respond to an incident. On one red team occasion, we were leveraging social engineering attacks to phish credentials from a popular corporate social network that employees tend to use quite a bit. Now, I perform this type of technique a lot because it seems to be successful more than it fails, which means I have grown extremely comfortable executing the attack path to the point where I have targeted backend engineers, software developers, and even blue team members. It's a double-edged sword that, when performed successfully, can reap major access, but on the other hand, one misstep and the operation can be burned.

One day we were executing on an attack path and one of the targets, an internal recruiter, caught wind of our doppelganger profile on the social network. The informed employee reported it to the blue team, and immediately a junior analyst triaging the incident created canary credentials that were fed into our phishing portal. As soon as the credentials landed in our hands, our team concurrently worked on leveraging the credentials in an attempt to authenticate on multiple portals, simultaneously resulting in being fingerprinted and blocked and the creation of indicators of compromise, which forced us to step back and rebuild. The combination of a curious analyst, an unrelenting employee who reported the incident, and being over-confident led to us getting caught in the act. During the debrief with the blue team, we were able to praise the analyst in front of their peers, team lead, and executive staff.

When these types of wins occur, I add them to a special section in the executive summary of the final report so that everyone who reads them can celebrate in seeing the value of the team and the value of what worked.

What is the biggest ethical quandary you experienced while on an assigned objective?

I haven't really encountered too many ethical dilemmas while on an engagement. From time to time I receive one-off requests for a list of the accounts with passwords that I've cracked on an engagement, which can lead to awkward discussions. One time, I was instructed to test an exploit against a list of servers for an organization that never provided permission, which I refused to do, citing CFAA references. There was one interesting scenario where a company relied on Social Security numbers for their password reset form, and I leveraged the Social Security Death Index to hunt for accounts, but I suppose that's more of a moral dilemma.

Depending on what you are doing, what you might be researching, or how you might be going about something, offensive security can be ethically and morally risky. One guiding principle I've instituted in my life is to have a few close friends around who have earned my trust, whom I've given permission to check me at any time. We may not see eye to eye and I may flat out disagree, but if they speak up against an idea I have that might be risky, I submit out of reverence for them. I personally believe this principle can be applied in all areas of life where risk can sometimes be blurred due to tunnel vision, and most of the time the reward isn't worth the risk anyhow.

How does the red team work together to get the job done?

So many factors can alter how red teams operate, and I'm not sure there's a right or wrong way, maybe just ways that work and ways that don't. Sometimes team members have a technical specialty that can really assist the engagement, and other times it's a mixture of generalists who just work well together. In either case, it's common for a red team to have a lead who is responsible for a number of logistical and operational items like communicating with the customer and managing internal communications. A good team lead isn't a dictator, but a servant leader

> "A good team lead isn't a dictator, but a servant leader who equips, includes, coordinates, and oversees the engagement."

who equips, includes, coordinates, and oversees the engagement. They are also an active member from start to finish, since in some cases other members may join or leave mid-operation. This means the team lead is the primary voice during the rules of engagement meeting as well as the blue team debrief.

I've never been on a red team where each participant played an active role for only a specific area of the engagement. I suppose if it does occur, it's probably more with internal red teams than with consulting gigs. In most operations I've been on, there's a lot of communication among members, and while many attack paths might emerge, it's common for only one or two to be selected at a time. During the engagement, the teams I've been on found it best to work on the report collaboratively so that everyone pulls their own weight based on the work they contributed.

When I lead a red team, I spend time organizing engagement notes for the team in a way that outlines any questions they might have regarding the current operation. Need to know where the collaborative report is? Looking for the C2 infrastructure? Wondering where the VPN portal is and what realm doesn't require two-factor? Curious about the passwords we cracked from ntds.dit? Looking for the most current BloodHound data? Good communication is the key to moving swiftly and pleasantly with other team members.

If you were to switch to the blue team, what would be your first step to better defend against attacks?

Understanding the attack surface from an internal and external perspective would definitely be my first step. Think about how hard it would be to defend your home from a burglar if you didn't know all the entryways or rooms. Sure, you could strategically place a next-gen bear trap in the bathroom tub, but don't expect too much from it. It's much easier to defend when you know what you're defending.

I find this simple step to actually be true in most areas of my life. How can I attack an organization that I don't know? How can I be a better spouse if I don't know where I am failing? How can I be a better employee if I don't know my shortcomings? How can I find a vulnerability if I don't know the technology? This curiosity is what drives me and challenges me to keep digging.

What is some practical advice on writing a good report?

Report reading and writing can be such a necessary evil, and since it's the product of the engagement, special attention should be given so that it successfully communicates to the recipient. By splitting up the report writing into three sections, a tester can eliminate a lot of the common shortcomings that can occur with report writing and at the same time communicate directly to the correct audience. There are usually two groups of people reading reports: executive staff and technical staff.

The executive staff members typically care only about key deficiencies, what is working, what is broken, the overall risk associated with the engagement, and where they should go next. A good location for this information is at the beginning of the report; it should be short and to the point without any technical jargon. They don't care that the web server has multiple Apache Struts RCE vulnerabilities, but they do care that an external attacker can gain unauthorized access to customer data.

A report with a methodology outlining the attack path with screenshots is not only easy to write as you go but also provides a context to the recipient for how it all went down. It takes practice to write as you go, but it forces you to slow down in a healthy way. It's also useful for keeping a solid history of activity on longer engagements. There's nothing worse than skipping the methodology until after you chase a rabbit down a hole and have to remember everything that occurred.

Every report should have a findings section that you can glance at to see the overall vulnerabilities and their severity, but also read the findings details. The details should elaborate on what the tester observed, why it's a problem, recommendations for how to remediate, and resources that can help guide.

How do you ensure your program results are valuable to people who need a full narrative and context?

In the executive summary of each report, we not only discuss the key deficiencies but also highlight the key successes. This can range from technical security controls that performed well to employees who need to be highlighted for their vigilance.

In the debrief, I first try to honor the people who were involved by identifying their key contributions to the success of the engagement; this is especially true when the executive staff or leadership are on the call. Remember, we want to lift people up every chance we get because in a lot of cases they feel like we are about to call their baby ugly. It's much easier to deliver hard-to-swallow news when the recipient knows you are for them, that you care about their success, and that they aren't the sum total of their mistakes.

Uncovering weaknesses within an organization is just the start. A successful engagement is one where the results help the organization, not hurt. It's the responsibility of the tester to discover what the customer is hoping to reap from the engagement. It's obvious that a lapse in security controls can create risk for an organization, but a lot of times I learn they are actually hoping to leverage the results for funding or some other internal initiatives. Armed with this information, a red team can tailor the narrative in a way that encourages growth in a direction that aligns with existing initiatives and where weaknesses are well received instead of endured.

What nontechnical skills or attitudes do you look for when recruiting and interviewing red team members?

One of the most important areas I look for when hiring or interviewing a candidate is how they handle difficulty, because it flows into every facet of their work, team, and cultural contribution. How you leave your last gig is how you will arrive at your next one. Are they bad-mouthing their previous employer? That's a good indicator of what you can expect when they leave you. Do they complain about their last team or co-worker? You can probably expect their gossip to tear apart your team too. I'd encourage anyone interviewing a candidate for a red team role to spend more time discerning their character and understanding how they deal with confronting technology they don't already know. InfoSec tends to push certification paths and technical skills while neglecting the more important aspects of a person. This is one reason I tend to gravitate toward anti-certification; requiring specific certifications tends to create smoke-and-mirror scenarios. It's less about what they know and more about who they are and how they think. After all, we should be hiring for character and training on skill sets; instead, we hire on skill sets and end up firing for character.

What differentiates good red teamers from the pack as far as approaching a problem differently?

A quality red team lead is one who can successfully organize members, resources, and communication in a way that creates fluidity within the team. It's someone who can equip, encourage, and shine perspective without demanding their own way. A quality red team member works well at carrying their own weight when necessary, recommends solutions or techniques without running ahead of the pack first, and possesses a tenacious curiosity. Each team member has a direct impact on the success and failure of the team, so it's important that approaching a problem is carefully discussed before action occurs—otherwise, the entire engagement could be jeopardized. I really enjoy working within a team that moves together, communicates well, and uncovers small victories together.

> "A quality red team member works well at carrying their own weight when necessary, recommends solutions or techniques without running ahead of the pack first, and possesses a tenacious curiosity."

Red teamers who go into an engagement knowing it's broken somewhere tend to carefully turn over more leaves in comparison to the team member who gives up exploring because they encountered a roadblock. Resetting your mind-set before each engagement is a healthy habit to ingrain, which can help avoid developing bad habits that end up restricting a red team member from success. This is especially true when working as a consultant, who can go from engagement to engagement. ■

"Red teams are different because each organization has unique needs, which is why each job should be described in the scope of work."

Twitter: @KevinFigueroa

Kevin Figueroa

13

Kevin Figueroa is a passionate hacker and cybersecurity researcher. As a seasoned practitioner with 10+ years and vast, broad knowledge in cybersecurity, he has consulted in government, private, and public sectors. He focuses his discipline on network and web application penetration testing and vulnerability and risk assessments. Kevin's never-ending passion for learning different coding languages, threat research, lockpicking, and reverse engineering has led him to be a speaker at several conferences like DEF CON and InfoSec Connect; he is also a cofounder of the DCNYC Group, a monthly hacker meetup in New York City, and a cofounder of Unallocated Space, a hackerspace in Maryland.

How did you get your start on a red team?

I got started with red teaming several years ago, yet it feels so long ago. It took many years to acquire all the different skill set needed to be a great red teamer. Over the years, acquiring skills in networking, firewall, IDS, packet crafting, wireless, social engineering, lockpicking, mobile, and intricacies within different operating systems is fundamental to the red team. Of course, the major skill for red teaming is penetration testing, and I've conducted penetration testing for most of my cybersecurity career.

Being passionate about hacking and adopting more skills in addition to my three discipline strengths of networking, web application, and wireless penetration testing has given me the liberty to be a red teamer. Over many years and learning from different individuals and mentors, it has allowed me to grasp and learn other disciplines like lockpicking, mobile, and using neuro linguistic programming (NLP), which to me is the highest form of social engineering. Indeed, these aren't the only skills needed to be a red teamer, but they were the skills that got me started in red teaming engagements.

What is the best way to get a red team job?
Having a strong, diverse set of skills will make you a prime candidate to acquire a red teaming position. A major key skill set in red teaming is penetration testing, but penetration testing is not the only skill set that should be obtained. Two other skill sets that should be acquired and continually practiced are social engineering and lockpicking. These two skill sets sometimes are overlooked, but they could be extremely valuable when conducting a red team engagement. Lockpicking and social engineering must be practiced often. Attending lockpick villages at hacker conferences, using internet resources, gathering literature, and buying a lockpick set will get you started. Moreover, if you want to take your social engineering to the next level, continually practice NLP.

A couple of other useful skills are mobile, wireless, and radio frequency technologies. How useful could it be if you obtained an employee's phone and cloned the SIM? Or what about cloning someone's RFID badge to access a restricted area, maybe sniffing and finding a weakness in the Bluetooth protocol or in their wireless technology? These can all be entries into exploiting their security defense posture and also ways an organization could be compromised. So, as you can see, acquiring many different skill sets is essential to becoming a red teamer.

How can someone gain red team skills without getting in trouble with the law?
There are several ways red team skills can be acquired without getting in trouble with the law. Setting up a virtual lab environment with different vulnerable VM images is an extremely useful way to adopt the practice of penetration testing. One must continuously practice their penetration testing techniques due to the ever-changing technologies.

> "Setting up a virtual lab environment with different vulnerable VM images is an extremely useful way to adopt the practice of penetration testing."

For example, let's take network and web applications penetration testing. These are two completely different disciplines, yet web application testing relies on networking. Some may use a Linux/Unix environment, while others may use Microsoft Windows to host web applications. So, having a clear understanding of how networking works or how different web technologies integrate with one another will be highly necessary. Accurate knowledge is vital, whether networking or web application, and can consist of knowing several different web technologies and network appliances. The more exposure you have to what these types of vulnerabilities and weaknesses look like, the more you will be able to identify the weakness to exploit within an organization.

In the end, through many hours of practice, hard work, and continuous research, you acquire the tools to become a red teamer.

Why can't we agree on what a red team is?

I believe it's because there is no universal outline of what red teaming is. Red teams are different because each organization has unique needs, which is why each job should be described in the scope of work. Another reason is that organizations may have wanted a vulnerability assessment and called it a penetration test, or they may want a penetration test but are calling it a red team engagement. However, it is up to us, cybersecurity professionals, to understand a client's needs and explain the differences between engagement types. But one thing is for sure, exploiting vulnerabilities to compromise an organization is the main premise.

What is one thing the rest of information security doesn't understand about being on a red team? What is the most toxic falsehood you have heard related to red, blue, or purple teams?

Being disciplined in only one area of cybersecurity does not classify you as a red, blue, or purple team member. Being great at trolling doesn't make you a great social engineer, and conducting a vulnerability assessment doesn't make you a pentester. The fact that so many different buzzwords are being intertwined and used makes things within our industry so interchangeable, I believe it is causing all the toxic falsehoods.

> "Being disciplined in only one area of cybersecurity does not classify you as a red, blue, or purple team member."

When should you introduce a formal red team into an organization's security program?

Security maturity varies from organization to organization, but an organization should consider adopting a formal red team exercise into their security posture early on, and it should be performed at least twice per year. Another factor an organization should always consider is physical access to an authorized place. Sometimes small or midsize organizations overlook this aspect, and they should not.

How do you explain the value of red teaming to a reluctant or nontechnical client or organization?

Use relatable words with the client, use a relatable parallel story to explain why it's necessary, or even create a quantitative analysis to show the cost should a breach occur—all these should assist with understanding why red teaming is so important. In small to midsize companies, the security defense posture may be a second thought. However, showing the cost if the organization is compromised versus the cost of conducting a red team engagement may change how they approach security in their organization.

Have you ever recommended not doing a red team engagement?

Yes, however, that should be determined when engaging the client in the early stages. This will allow you to gauge the security defense posture of the organization. After explaining the reason why a red team engagement is not warranted, you should suggest an external penetration testing engagement instead.

What's the most important or easiest-to-implement control that can prevent you from compromising a system or network?

Access control and enforcing password policy. The small and midsize organizations I have come across lack in those two areas. These two tasks could be easily implemented by their system administrator. Another task that should be considered is a monthly vulnerability assessment. This will assist the organization's technology leaders in prioritizing the most critical vulnerabilities.

Why do you feel it is critical to stay within the rules of engagement?

This would be based on the scope of work and contractual agreement. It may be best to explain why one threat could lead to an exploit that compromises the organization and could possibly tarnish their brand. Also, let's say you're conducting a penetration test and run a SQL injection vulnerability program and the scanner drops a table and the company doesn't conduct regularly schedule backups of their database. The liability could fall on the red team for breaking the rules of engagement. Or what if the company has identified the vulnerability and has decided that the threat of the vulnerability is low enough for them to classify the threat as an acceptable risk and out of scope? This could make it appear as if the red team couldn't care less about the organization's rules of engagement, which may cause the organization to not award the contract to the red team for the next engagement.

If you were ever busted on a penetration test or other engagement, how did you handle it?

Yes, I was busted before on a red team engagement, and it was so bad, I almost was shot by an armed guard. This made me think twice about breaching a building with an armed guard again. Thank God, I printed an email by the POC of the organization as proof, but they still needed to call the POC for verification. Long story short, you should always keep some type of written proof of sanction by the organization when attempting to breach an organization's facility.

How does the red team work together to get the job done?

As I mentioned earlier, a red teamer should have a diverse set of skills. Working together shouldn't be an issue because you could play on each other's strengths. One thing is for sure, one teammate should always be selected to collect documentation from all other teammates and write the report along the way. This way, when the red team engagement has been completed, all team members sit together to discuss all the weaknesses in order for the organization to receive the best value from the results.

What is your approach to debriefing and supporting blue teams after an operation is completed?

The best approach in debriefing an organization or a supporting blue team is to be positive. The objective is to help improve the organization security defense posture, not explain how badly they are doing at implementing security defense. Identifying the weaknesses that could be exploited is one thing, but exploiting the weakness doesn't mean anything if you're not assisting them to understand why the weakness was there in the first place. That may cause the organization to rethink how they are prioritizing the vulnerabilities or to even set new policies within the organization.

> "The best approach in debriefing an organization or a supporting blue team is to be positive."

If you were to switch to the blue team, what would be your first step to better defend against attacks?

Personally, I would rather stay on the offense side of cybersecurity. However, if I were to switch to be on a blue team, I would engulf myself in continuous research on the new attack vectors that threat actors are employing. To better defenses, I would understand what type of log retention the organization has in place and become versed in the appliance or system that aggregates and correlates the organization's logs. Logs and monitoring are essential to begin tracking suspicious traffic and lateral movement within the infrastructure of the organization.

What is some practical advice on writing a good report?

First, do not over-write the report, meaning do not write a lengthy report, because business individuals in the organization will review about the first 10 pages, if that. Second, attempt to use the fewest words to explain the vulnerability without losing the meaning behind why this vulnerability exists. Finally, use screenshots or maybe even videos to show how you exploited the weakness, but make sure the words are simple and to the point. Don't just use buzzwords to put fear into the client.

How do you ensure your program results are valuable to people who need a full narrative and context?

To ensure the red team results are of value to the organization, a cost should be associated with each vulnerability discovered. Conduct a quantitative analysis that will support the vulnerability listed within your report while enhancing the client's report. Being able to discover a vulnerability in an organization's digital asset could be extremely important to the brand of the organization. Justifying the importance of the results and adding a dollar amount can drive the value as a necessary cause to the organization.

What nontechnical skills or attitudes do you look for when recruiting and interviewing red team members?

Looking for a candidate who is passionate about hacking and wanting to be on a red team is extremely important. Being able to identify a candidate with skills versus a candidate who can B.S. his/her way just to obtain a red team position is also essential. Having a small mock-up testing environment is a great way to find candidates with real skills. Also, a diverse background in different cybersecurity disciplines is a good attribute to hunt for (and is slowly dying out).

> "Writing great reports by giving great details of what, when, and how on an assessment could be the winning factor for the organization."

As for nontechnical skills used for red teaming, that would have to be writing. Writing great reports by giving great details of what, when, and how on an assessment could be the winning factor for the organization. Remember, using the fewest words to best describe what was found, when it was found, and how it was exploited will make a big difference.

What differentiates good red teamers from the pack as far as approaching a problem differently?

Because red teamers have diverse skill sets, they think differently about the approach to mission problems. Having people exposed to different technologies, in conjunction with having teammates with experience in different methodologies, is a major win. ∎

"From my perspective, skill trumps everything; over the years, I've aligned myself with way smarter people than me who have helped me grow into the security professional I am today."

Twitter: @MarcoFigueroa

Marco Figueroa

Marco Figueroa is a senior security researcher at a Fortune 50 company whose technical expertise includes reverse engineering, bug hunting, incident handling, and APT group tracking. He has a deep understanding of threat intelligence tradecraft across different market verticals and organizations to identify attack vectors, trends, and nation-state actors, and he utilizes the latest techniques from nation-state actor reports, enhancing his offensive security skills.

14

How did you get your start on a red team?

My first red team engagement was when I was a security analyst at a Fortune 50 company in 2006 and one of my co-workers cofounded a consulting company in India that had more than 100 employees. For about a week this co-worker, whom we will call Randy, was asking me security questions about specific network hacking techniques; at first, I thought he was interested in security because he was an Oracle DB developer, but then I finally asked him why he wanted to know all of these different techniques. He informed me that the company was being attacked every day and was playing whack-a-mole with the attackers. The questions he was asking me were to see if I was the right person for the job. He asked if I was interested in doing a pentest and wanted me to figure out how these intruders were gaining access. So, Randy gave me the scope of the engagement. The following Monday, we had a contract signed with the terms. To make a long story short, the perimeter was weak with default credentials on the router, and internally the switches had default credentials as well. The internal infrastructure needed to be hardened by the administrators. The lesson I learned from this back then was that it doesn't matter how big or small the company is, the red teamer should inform the stakeholder immediately about every critical impact vulnerability to the organization.

What is the best way to get a red team job?

From my perspective, skill trumps everything; over the years, I've aligned myself with way smarter people than me who have helped me grow into the security professional I am today. What happens when you begin to align yourself with like-minded individuals is it enables you to elevate your skills to a new level.

Here are my recommendations for how to do this and land the red teaming job that you want:

- Figure out who are the wicked smart red teamers in the industry, go to red team conferences, meet people, share ideas, get tips/tricks. People by nature love to help others, so if you have a well-thought-out question, then ask a person who you know will have the answers.

- Follow people on Twitter and use TweetDeck so you can create a group (named RedTeam). A few people I follow who provide me value through their tweets are @Tobyhush, @TTimzen, @0xDADE, @at1as, @invisig0th, @carnal0wnage, and @nnwakelam, but there are so many people delivering value that you can have many sleepless nights learning.

- Attend conferences like your life depends on it. I am where I am today because of the knowledge that I've gained by attending talks and hallway con conversations at conferences. Every single time I attend a conference I walk away with a bag of questions answered and a clear agenda of the things I need to implement and learn. I seek out people I know have more knowledge than I do to assist me on the roadblocks that I might be facing at that moment.

- This one simple thing is beneficial: follow up with people you meet. Make sure they remember you so the next time you see them, they will ask you about your progression on the question you may have asked them. Don't just friend a person on Twitter or LinkedIn; a two-minute email to a person you just met will go a long way. Some of the relationships that I've built over the years I now consider lifelong friends. Your persistence in seeking knowledge doesn't have boundaries, so why would you not be engaging with the community?

- Provide value to as many people as possible. When you do this one thing without expectation of anything in return, the doors will open for you. When I find something incredibly cool that I think a friend might like, I reach out to them and share the knowledge with them directly; this is how you build trust. I love helping people and sharing because this community has done so much for me.

How can someone gain red team skills without getting in trouble with the law?

This question is a no-brainer for me. Join the bug bounty programs and start hacking away. These companies are providing an incentive for bug hunters to find bugs, so they offer you training on their websites to get you started. HackerOne and BugCrowd are just two of the companies, but this space I believe will be crowded in the next few years. The company that wins this race will be the company that provides the most value to its community by going above and beyond for them. They can be providing you with every tool and training there is, but you must put the work in and type away on your keyboard to develop those skills to earn the bounties.

Some of the people and sites that have provided immense value to me these last few months are @jhaddix, @stokfredrik, @nnwakelam, @NahamSec, the

HackerOne website, Bugcrowd website, PentesterLab website, and Offensive Security Training.

What is one thing the rest of information security doesn't understand about being on a red team? What is the most toxic falsehood you have heard related to red, blue, or purple teams?

The value that the red team adds to an organization is invaluable. There was a team filled with top-notch skills, and they all left as a unit, one after the other, and went to another company. What does that say about the organization? I always inform upper management of the value of red teams. If you were on the front page of the WSJ in a negative way, what would be the price of that in dollars? If an adversary pops one of the company's servers and steals customers' data, then how does that company deal with the fallout if that data is sold on the black market or just dumped? Now, what if your organization had a red team continually working on looking for low-hanging fruit or reverse engineering binaries for bugs? People might say that's not red teaming, and my answer is the same thing every time: acting like the adversary is red teaming.

When should you introduce a formal red team into an organization's security program?

It varies tremendously between companies. I believe that a company should have a quarterly assessment regardless of its size. How I measure companies is that if your crown jewels are your IP or customer data, then you need to have a full-time staff red teaming. Companies think that being hacked won't happen to them, but if you look on HackerOne's Hactivity, you will be amazed at the innovative ways that companies can be compromised. From private keys leaked to RCE, it's an amazing time to be alive.

How do you explain the value of red teaming to a reluctant or nontechnical client or organization?

Luckily, all the companies that I've worked for have understood the value of having a red team, but one company that sells soft drinks found out the hard way about the importance of having a red team. This company had an incident that stopped the conveyor belt from pouring drinks. This incident cost them more than $100,000 an hour, and they learned a valuable lesson back then. The following month the company organized a security summit, and my manager at the time tasked me with bringing a "hacker" to talk about the importance of security back in the late 2000s (by the way, @at1as, you still owe me a drink for that one). This company eventually established a red team, and I want to believe it was that summit gathering that did it!

What is the *least* bang-for-your-buck security control that you see implemented?

To answer the reverse question of what gets you the *most* bang for your buck, an endpoint detection and response (EDR) product that allows you to deploy YARA rules.

Have you ever recommended not doing a red team engagement?

Yes. Instead I have recommended limiting access rights to users and training every employee on not being fooled by phishing emails.

What's the most important or easiest-to-implement control that can prevent you from compromising a system or network?

Make everyone in your organization part of the security awareness program. The adversary understands that employees will always fall victim to a well-crafted phishing email. For example, I ordered a package, and it was being shipped via UPS. That week I received an email that looked like a legitimate email from UPS, and it was perfectly crafted (kudos to that threat actor). It was 2010, and I remember it vividly because I spoke to my manager at the time, and the following week he received a similar email.

Why do you feel it is critical to stay within the rules of engagement?
One time I was on an engagement and a team member was out of scope and knocked over a critical server, and the server was down for a couple of hours. Besides the embarrassment of the call that we had with the manager, the engagement was immediately halted. What red teamers do not understand is that sometimes it's completely fine if you do not find anything; it's not the end of the world. You tip your hat and try harder on the next engagement. Not all engagements are made equal!

If you were ever busted on a penetration test or other engagement, how did you handle it?
I will give you the flipside version of this. I was contacted to investigate suspicious activity on a system. I received a binary and began to reverse engineer the binary. I said to myself that the binary I was analyzing was impressive. I reached out to the red team lead at the time and asked him if his team was performing any suspicious activities that I analyzed in the binary; the red team lead informed me that it wasn't the red team.

I immediately recognized that this was probably a sophisticated actor; I really admire cool binaries that I analyze. I give a lot of respect to the adversary for crafting sophisticated techniques. After investigating the binary further, I determined that it was a specific APT group and created some YARA rules to see how deeply they infected the network. It was the only box that was compromised, but I then had to investigate to see if they pivoted, and they didn't. We investigated the system, and we determined that the actor didn't compromise any other systems. Sometimes on operations the adversaries need to have operators on standby to pivot at a moment's notice. I know of adversaries who can run through networks within 30 minutes—those I consider supra actors. I love offense, but defense is where you learn bleeding-edge techniques from nation-states that you can use on the offensive side. I always read APT reports to learn the latest techniques that adversaries use. Playing both sides is crucial for your development as a red teamer!

What is the biggest ethical quandary you experienced while on an assigned objective?
When reverse engineering and hunting for bugs in software, you will always read a disclaimer informing you that you should not reverse engineer the software. When doing this, you have to know that if you find a bug, you should immediately report it.

How does the red team work together to get the job done?
If you're collaborating, then the communication between the team members is essential. I'd suggest having morning and evening stand-ups (10-minute meetings). Doing this will help the team figure out what the team is working on and their daily findings.

What is your approach to debriefing and supporting blue teams after an operation is completed?
I've always suggested to management that the red team members should write rules for the way they compromise systems. Many red teams do not want to do this because it hinders them in their next engagement. Many teams try to advise on specific ways to harden the system that was compromised during the engagement, but people usually do not want to write the detection rules. It's more work, but it will pay off in the long run.

If you were to switch to the blue team, what would be your first step to better defend against attacks?

I've played both sides over my career, and I find both sides fascinating. On the red team side, you're looking at things from a fresh perspective. My favorite is looking at new technology and trying to find ways to exploit it, and on the blue team side, it reminds me of the popular TV show *The First 48*. When something is detected, you must figure out what priority level the compromise is and then become a detective to figure out how to stop the bleeding. My reverse engineering skills allow me to work both sides as if I am ambidextrous; there have been times when I'm assisting the blue team side that I've had to pull in a red teamer to collaborate on an incident. I believe that red and blue teams are siblings, and they need to be aligned to work together for the common good.

What is some practical advice on writing a good report?

The thing that I will say about this is to figure out what are the most important things to the stakeholders in charge of the engagement. I do not believe a 500-page report is helpful. But they must be aware of all issues, that's for sure. Understanding what the stakeholders care about is so important, and providing value should be your number-one priority. Many pentesters in my experience hate writing reports, but if you learn how to embrace the task and provide an actionable report with clear steps on tackling the issues discovered during the engagement, then the organization and you win.

How do you recommend security improvements other than pointing out where it's insufficient?

I would point out the obvious things, but let's say the organization has an admin or engineer who doesn't know the why behind something that was compromised. I always believe in training the individual in depth on the techniques and mitigations, and I always recommend offensive training for defensive analysts. An example would be training on how Mimikatz is used. If an admin or analyst understands how it is used, then they will have the knowledge to write detections for it.

What nontechnical skills or attitudes do you look for when recruiting and interviewing red team members?

Positive attitudes, people who love to learn, and those who do not stay in their comfort zone. I had a friend who was an expert in skill Y. He knew the ins and outs of a specific skill set, and I asked him why he didn't learn another skill. He replied, "I'm the king of this sandbox, and I want to stay the king." That is an example of a teammate who would be hard to work with in different situations. A person with that mentality will not elevate team members. He won't let people get better than him in his sandbox. He will resent people on the team who can start playing better than him in that same sandbox. I think this would be a bad hire. You can sniff that out during the interview process; one question you could ask would be, "How would you learn new things that you've never learned before? Can you take me through that process?"

What differentiates good red teamers from the pack as far as approaching a problem differently?

I would say when a person loves the craft, that person will stand out immediately. I know a person who would absolutely be a first hire if I moved companies and built out a red team. I wouldn't take no for an answer when someone is creative and uses techniques to find ways to get the job done. I would consider them a person I can trust to do their best during an engagement. ∎

"Learn how to learn. Then teach yourself how to ship. And find or create a platform or community to share what you ship."

Twitter: @JFOLKINS

Jared Folkins

15

After surviving the dot-com crash of the late 90s, Jared Folkins went on to have a long career in systems and programming. In 2013 he turned a hobby into a career and has never looked back. Known for having technical chops and a high emotional IQ, he enjoys working with those who prioritize goals and people while placing egos last. He currently red teams for ThreatHound.com, blue teams for Bend La Pine Schools, and breaks down software while building up people at OpsecEdu.com. If you want his help or you just need a new InfoSec friend, contact him at JaredFolkins.com.

How did you get your start on a red team?

I had been a coder and a systems and database person for more than a decade. One day I started a project on the side where I was dismantling and reversing a Java application. The software's primary function was that it would back up your files and cryptographically seal them. It would then send this backup to the cloud, giving you an end-to-end encrypted archive. I wanted to see how it worked. While I was performing this work, I wrote my thoughts into four blog articles about what I was learning. I didn't detail the actual piece of software I was targeting but gave a general overview of the topics I was exploring. It was a great exercise, as I've found that teaching what I am learning really makes the lessons I learn in the problem domain stick.

A friend read my articles and asked if I wanted to present at a local hack night. Often afraid of ridicule and critique, I stepped outside of my comfort zone and took him up on his offer. The talk went over incredibly well, and someone I met that night asked if I'd like to moonlight by performing some security work. I jumped at the chance and have been consulting, adding tools to my red team toolbox and applying them ever since.

What is the best way to get a red team job?

There are so many inroads to getting a job in information security that I'd encourage you not to limit yourself to seeking "the best way." For me, I had a long career in systems and coding. When I implemented controls and systems to prevent my infrastructure from being hacked, I would test the actual proof of concepts I found online. I was discovering how to hack by trying to hack myself. I could put myself in the system admin's shoes or the developer's seat and think, "If I was under a deadline and needed to cut a corner, what corner would I cut?" Eventually I realized that I was pretty good at sniffing out vulnerable systems and code.

The one commonality that I've noticed in listening to many different individuals' stories is that everyone I admire can ship and produce with very little guidance. Learn how to learn. Then teach yourself how to ship. And find or create a platform or community to share what you ship.

How can someone gain red team skills without getting in trouble with the law?

Early in my life I built a home lab, and through many configurations I've had this home lab in place for more than 20 years. It has been the single greatest asset in my self-education. If I find a new piece of software that interests me, I install it in my lab and take a look. I get it configured, and I work to understand how all the pieces fit together. Then I start thinking about how to attack it and make the software perform and do things it isn't intended to do. I also appreciate when I've seen conference organizers release their CTFs, as many tend to be server based. I'll install those too and work through the problem. This ends up being a "safe" place for me to explore and learn without fear of having anyone else involved.

Bug bounties are also neat, but lately I wonder if the gig economy isn't taking advantage of some. It can be a safe place to learn, but that is and will always be my primary goal with bug bounties—learning. Not earning an income, but instead allowing me a safe place to educate myself and test some new ideas. Just remember to not deviate from the defined scope no matter how tempted you are.

Why can't we agree on what a red team is?

Computer science is a young industry. And although there are languages like Rust that are challenging the way we approach programming, we still can't even write a secure program that also meets the business requirements of the sales team. Buffer and integer overflows, SQL injection, XSS—attacks like these have existed and will continue to exist for some time. It is no surprise that information security, being an even younger discipline, is still struggling to define itself.

What is one thing the rest of information security doesn't understand about being on a red team? What is the most toxic falsehood you have heard related to red, blue, or purple teams?

The red team isn't sexy for long. Often you're whisked into an engagement and then whisked right back out. There often isn't time for modern or unique research. You are simply trying to help the organization find low-hanging fruit and move on to the next assignment.

The most toxic falsehood would be that the red team has more authority in the security narrative. Some people believe this and live in this belief, and it just drags people down. Don't do that, please. You exist to support the other teams equally. And you will truly succeed only when you seek to partner with them and not pwn them.

When should you introduce a formal red team into an organization's security program?

Folks think that getting a red team into the mix, especially an external auditing red team, will be *the* thing to push their organization's security story. Unfortunately, so many organizations haven't baked security into their culture yet. This is never more obvious than when I've been assigned to perform another pentest with the same organization and I find the same critical vulnerabilities that I reported on the previous engagement.

My advice is to figure out how to build a culture of security. How are you going to train and educate and build security people in your organization? If you don't know where to start concerning culture, hire a consultant—someone who can advocate and help you. From there you can dive into the NIST framework and make sure your team achieves 80 to 90 percent of what is on that list. Only then would I involve an external testing team.

Along with this I will say that you should give your staff and peers a small heads-up before a red team starts performing a test. "Within the next four quarters an external team will be accessing our staff and infrastructure." I've seen so much trust lost by leadership when they (a) haven't made security a priority in their culture and (b) performed a surprise pentest on their team. They've killed their team's motivation and sense of worth with a single misstep.

How do you explain the value of red teaming to a reluctant or nontechnical client or organization?

If you are a hacker or a nerd, I highly recommend taking a sales training course. This won't just level you up for red teaming; this will level you up in life. You can then apply these skills to understand that if you can't speak to the value your red team is offering, you won't be able to convince a single person on the leadership team to spend money on the initiative.

What is the *least* bang-for-your-buck security control that you see implemented?

A web application firewall (WAF) is probably the weakest control I've seen. If you are not familiar with a WAF, it acts as a proxy and sits in front of your web applications. It looks for malicious traffic, and if it detects it, the WAF blocks the traffic.

There are several problems with it in practice.

- The WAF can and often does tend to block legitimate traffic. Those old applications that people are trying to protect do in fact send traffic that is legitimate, but the WAF misinterprets it as malicious and blocks the legit traffic. You then spend a lot of time trying to tune the WAF to meet your organization's needs.
- Someone eventually finds a polymorphic attack and gets around the WAF's rulesets.

Instead, consider building a contractual relationship with your vendors where they agree in writing to also build a strong security story into their products, where they accept security reports from those in the information security community and where they perform routine and documented analysis to assess their product's security. This is not simply for liability, but the vendor should be signaling to you that they are actively trying to harden their products and truly want to harden their systems.

Have you ever recommended not doing a red team engagement?
Absolutely. If it becomes apparent that the organization seeking a pentest hasn't taken the time to really step through and build a solid foundation, I've offered to act as a for-hire CIO to help the organization build their security program, starting that culture of security that their organization desperately needs.

Mainly my recommendations rally the organization around the NIST Cybersecurity framework. At times I also get a sense of internal tensions for the organization, and I use the culture hacking skill set I've developed to try to disrupt things in a positive way. The goal is that I leave the organization in a much better position, in both security and skill set for the staff, than I found it.

What's the most important or easiest-to-implement control that can prevent you from compromising a system or network?
The biggest bang for your buck that I can think of is to make sure that the minimum password length for the users in your organization is 12 characters. From there, multifactor authentication and the use of a password manager that you can install on the desktop and browser will amplify this control.

Why do you feel it is critical to stay within the rules of engagement?
People who know me hear me talk about trust quite a bit. Not only can breaking the rules of an engagement get you into legal trouble, it will also lose you a ton of trust. And trust is the number-one currency in life. Without it, you will soon be severely limited in what you can accomplish, both personally and professionally. And so I advocate for people to always endeavor to build trust.

If you were ever busted on a penetration test or other engagement, how did you handle it?
I was testing a web application and was combing through the source JavaScript that was exposed on the client. I ran across a JavaScript comment where it appeared that a test username and password had been statically assigned for what I could only conclude was testing purposes. The comment had been committed out and shipped with the application. Bingo!

Following the rules of the engagement, I logged in with the credentials and had full administrative access and began harvesting screenshots of sensitive data. Unbeknown to me, those credentials were assigned to a developer who received emails when they were used. This developer wondered why she had received an email for those test credentials coming from a production host. To her credit, she followed through and about 60 minutes later there was an email in my inbox with the subject "BUSTED!" (To this day I have no idea why she was up so late, but good on her for acting on something that smelled fishy.)

At that point, the customer was awesome and used it as an opportunity to practice their remediation procedures for this type of event. They audited the host and the logs to evaluate what I (the attacker) had done. They then performed a full authentication audit trying to strengthen the story around test credential use. They educated all on their team about why it was brittle and asked their own team what should be done to harden their applications. They also liked the idea of credentials acting as a canary and kept some fake credentials in the source that would simply alert when used. It was a neat experience and not a bad way to get caught.

What is the biggest ethical quandary you experienced while on an assigned objective?

If you work in the security field long enough, you will eventually run into something that pushes your ethics. Instead of citing a particular incident, I'd encourage you to adopt a strategy of finding a small community of people whom you *trust* to bounce your ideas or problems off of.

These folks should care about you and your well-being. Also, they should have your permission to push back and disagree with you. This group should be rather small; I'd say fewer than six people. Work hard to vet them and also make sure their lifestyle and ideals signal things you value. I often ask myself the following questions:

- Does this person indicate they care about others?
- Does this person's personal relationships appear healthy?
- Does this person value the same things I value?
- Does this person differ in ways in which I feel I lack?

How does the red team work together to get the job done?

Communicate and collaborate! I don't care what the tools are (as long as they meet the operational requirements and threat models). Spend time understanding and planning how you will communicate and which person on the team is taking on what roles.

Having a team that collaborates to solve goals as a group is a true power-up. It amplifies your endeavors to new heights. When on an assignment, if I've sensed my group has a few egocentric contributors, I've also noticed that communications internally are generally lacking. With communication weak, when people get stuck, they appear unable to feel safe enough to ask for help, and we all need help. We all have strengths and weaknesses.

What is your approach to debriefing and supporting blue teams after an operation is completed?

I walk people through what I've found, but instead of always telling them how they should fix a problem, I instead often ask, "How would you fix this?" A lot of times there is that champion on the blue team who has been asking for the problem I've found to be fixed for years! By asking a lot of questions and encouraging a dialogue, you can discover this person and build an ally. Let me tell you, allies want to work with you again. This will lead to compounding interest in your career as people from your past, whose trust you have earned, seek you out again.

If you were to switch to the blue team, what would be your first step to better defend against attacks?

I still work on blue teams for my day job. Having good central logging is a must! Beyond this, filtering the alerts that are generated so that your team actually gets actionable results is laborious and requires planning and thought. I've seen many systems pwned despite an alert actually being sent out. Simply because of poor filtering, the blue team couldn't prioritize the value. They were drinking from a fire hose.

What is some practical advice on writing a good report?

Writing is a highly valuable skill. Instead of looking at it like a chore, hack yourself and learn how to write content and reports that leave people hungry to read more. Consider that reports will be read by many high-powered individuals in the organizations you test. Your name is on the report, so see it as an opportunity to market yourself.

Think about how often you try your hardest to get your résumé past the HR firewall. Here, you are going to have an audience with the very people HR often blocks you from speaking with. Use it! Learn how to write effectively and persuasively and remember that this work is another type where the interest compounds throughout your career.

I've also wondered often when red teams will start amplifying their results and reports by hiring a highly talented editor/marketer/writer/pentester type to help. If your reports come across looking bland and uninspiring, why not work hard to make them look awesome? It just is another way to set oneself apart.

How do you ensure your program results are valuable to people who need a full narrative and context?

Sometimes I'll segue into running a micro-tabletop exercise with some of the results that are severe if the people in the room need more context. This isn't traditional, but having been on the receiving end of the report and as someone who is technical, having someone else step your leadership through the potential issues by adding the weight of context is super valuable.

How do you recommend security improvements other than pointing out where it's insufficient?

During an assignment, as a team, keep a running list of things on your customer's infrastructure that caused you issues or prevented you from advancing. Then use this list to have meaningful conversations during your report by being honest and drawing upon this list to encourage them and build rapport. From there, if there is a system that gave you pause but you eventually were able to overcome, start a conversation about that. Ask them what they think could be done to turn that speed bump into a real roadblock.

What nontechnical skills or attitudes do you look for when recruiting and interviewing red team members?

"Tell me about a time when you messed up and hurt someone and have worked to restore that relationship." That is an interview question I'll ask often. Mistakes happen, and I find that good teams and the people in them often tend to have a solid characterization, evaluating their own actions and working to make themselves better. And there will be times that you are going to mess up and you will make a mistake, and you'll need to own it.

I'm not optimizing for people who, when faced with a mistake of their own making, simply move on. I want to work with people who will work to make it right and who will work to restore their team. It is a skill that I value highly both professionally and personally.

What differentiates good red teamers from the pack as far as approaching a problem differently?

Creativity and self-education are requirements in many facets of life, but this is no truer than with a solid pentester. Having the tenacity to explore and try to understand different problem domains is critical, but taking it a step further and applying it in a creative way to make an application or piece of infrastructure do something that it was not designed to do is paramount. I've seen some brilliant work in my career, and I've witnessed things I would have never personally considered trying.

So, take your creativity and combine it with the willingness to share. People like working alongside those who will graciously teach them. It will easily set you apart. ∎

"Everyone's path in this industry is different; it's all about obtaining the experience or expertise to do the job you want to do."

Twitter: @mubix

Rob Fuller

16

Rob has experience covering most facets of information security. He has helped design, build, and defend U.S. DoD networks as well as performed penetration tests and red team assessments against those same networks. More recently, Rob has performed numerous red team assessments against Fortune 50 companies. He is a frequent speaker, trainer, and volunteer at conferences and CTF events. He serves as a senior technical advisor for HBO's show *Silicon Valley* and hosts a show on Hak5. Rob has acquired a number of certifications, but the titles he holds above the rest are father, husband, and U.S. Marine.

How did you get your start on a red team?
Craig Balding (@craigbalding) gave me the opportunity to join my first red team, which turned out to be one of the most rewarding teams and jobs I've ever had the pleasure to be part of. I did this after being many other things, however. I had been a vulnerability scan engineer, a pentest consultant, a tier 1 and 2 incident responder, a forensic analyst, a firewall admin, an IT architect, an on-call help-desk tech, and an IT clerk. I believe that having this wide range of experience helped me obtain this opportunity and then nailing my interview successfully. Do you have to have the same path? Not at all. I have seen a mathematician make the leap directly over into pentesting and destroy networks because he understood steganography better than the network engineers did. I have seen stay-at-home moms become fantastic SOC analysts out of the blue. Everyone's path in this industry is different; it's all about obtaining the experience or expertise to do the job you want to do.

What is the best way to get a red team job?

Apply? This is like asking how to get a job, period. Red team jobs don't follow any particular set of rules. Apply for the jobs that are out there and be qualified to do so. Therein lies the tricky bit, though, right? First, you have to believe that you are qualified; then, you have to convince someone else (the recruiter/hiring manager) that you are qualified. Many hiring managers talk about the "hacker mind-set." This is the headspace where the intended use of something is ignored or expanded upon. The same process needs to be applied to getting a job. Hack it.

Think of qualifications as a list of intended uses, RTFM, and go from there.

How can someone gain red team skills without getting in trouble with the law?

Even in 2005, when I started learning about security, there were plenty of avenues to learn without committing felonies. Sure, in the BBS days and those of the "early" internet, resources were lacking, and many from that era still wear it as a badge of honor. This is fine; they learned the only way they could at the time. That time is long gone. If you think you have to break the law, then someone has misguided you. This does take one minor thing for granted—that you have a computer that you are authorized to use and have internet connectivity, which is not always the case, especially in third-world countries. If you have neither of these, then those situations may still be out there. I do not condone breaking the law, and no matter how I feel about the law in my own country, breaking laws isn't the way to fix them.

Let me put away my soapbox so we can talk about the ways you can actually do this in 2019. Red teaming can be made up of a ton of different skill sets including routing, switching, Active Directory, wireless (not just 802.11), physical security, Internet of Things (IoT), web, cloud, cryptography, databases, and so on. You can also come from a vast array of backgrounds and study an even wider variety of topics that wouldn't fit in this book without making a tomb of hackers. However, VulnHub is where I point most people. On VulnHub you download VMs and attempt to get "root" on them. The great thing about VulnHub is even if you are just beginning, you can download a VM, boot it up, have a go, realize you have no idea where to start, and read one of the myriad walk-throughs they have on the site for each VM.

There is zero harm in reading all of the walk-throughs many times over and practicing getting root the same way they do and eventually understanding why they are doing it.

Why can't we agree on what a red team is?

Because it means different things to everyone and that's okay. Why does it have to have a precise definition? Can you tell me what a security operations center (SOC) looks like in specific terms? Or what makes up a hospital even? We have a ton of collections of things that are defined by general ideas, and that is fine, such as the fact that hospitals include an emergency room but not all of them include long-term cancer wards or that a SOC must have screens on the wall for no reason whatsoever! Some are 24/7, and some are not.

These general ideas are accepted in society. Why isn't it okay for a red team to also be amorphous? The definition of a communicated word is one in which the parties involved understand it, and for the most part, when a customer and a consultant speak of red team engagements, there is an understanding of what that entails through mediums like the statement of work (SoW) and rules of engagement (ROE).

What is one thing the rest of information security doesn't understand about being on a red team? What is the most toxic falsehood you have heard related to red, blue, or purple teams?

I have no idea what the rest of the information security community/world/whatever understands or doesn't understand. One thing I wish was more prevalent is the core value that you are part of a team whose sole purpose is to make the company better and more secure. This doesn't happen by pointing and laughing like an outsider. The company has a vulnerability; that's your company (even if you are a consultant or contractor for them for the week). Get to work.

> "Run your own race to your personal goals. Don't worry about what the 'rest' of information security is doing or what toxic drama is next up on the internet."

Go to work, do good things, or build a company and do good things. Run your own race to your personal goals. Don't worry about what the "rest" of information security is doing or what toxic drama is next up on the internet. All of that is a waste of your time. You only get so much time on this earth, and you choose who you give that time to. Random security fads and drama are just not worth it.

When should you introduce a formal red team into an organization's security program?

As soon as they can afford it. Red teams are like human security unit tests. Everyone knows they need unit testing in their code, and they put them in as soon as it starts becoming needed or things start breaking. The same goes for the red teams. The moment you begin to need a blue team is about the same time you need a red team.

How do you explain the value of red teaming to a reluctant or nontechnical client or organization?

Listening. If you are there to help an organization genuinely, they will feel that and not be reluctant anymore. If they continue to be hesitant, then they don't want your services; you should let them make that decision and move on.

What is the least bang-for-your-buck security control that you see implemented?

Logs. But what is the most bang for your buck? Also logs. The problem with logs is that if you don't have a skilled team to look at said logs, they are useless, and moreover they cost more money the more you have just sitting around. So, even though AV or a SEIM or several other things can be considered unnecessary in different contexts, they usually don't cost you exponentially more money like logs do.

Have you ever recommended not doing a red team engagement?

Plenty of times. I did a talk called open source pentesting where I talked about the myriad of different offerings that I have offered and think other firms should offer because they fit better than a standard pentest or red team assessment or source code review. Ultimately, though, the customer is the one making a business decision to purchase your services. Counseling them to do something different may fall on deaf ears, or they may have a perfectly good reason for doing so that you have no insight into. You have to be okay with that.

What's the most important or easiest-to-implement control that can prevent you from compromising a system or network?

Good password management. Passwords are the bane of information security right now.

2FA/MFA is a solution, but it is still cumbersome or impossible to incorporate into the authentication platform a company uses. Most pentests and red team assessments that I perform these days start with some kind of initial toehold into the organization, and then the hunt for credentials begins—API keys, SSH keys, passwords, anything that can get me to a higher level or more access than that toehold. This is why I think a company should require the use of password managers for all work-based authentication; this includes API keys (vaulting products help make this a reality). A way to force this is to change your internal password minimum to something like 40 characters. Initial login (in order to get to the password manager) can be done via a smart card, FIDO, or another token-based product. Even mobile devices these days can act as FIDO devices, which would remove the need to deploy and manage a fleet of devices for authentication.

Why do you feel it is critical to stay within the rules of engagement?

Because it's a felony in the United States if you don't (breaking into a system without authorization), and liability insurance only goes so far. It's also an agreed upon document (rules of engagement).

If you were ever busted on a penetration test or other engagement, how did you handle it?

This happens a lot, and while I do get pissed (mostly at myself for being stupid in some way), it quickly becomes admiration for what the defense team put in place. I did a talk called Attacker Ghost Stories about several different occasions when I was caught. One of my favorite stories was the result of a honey pot (an intentionally vulnerable-looking software).

Once upon a time in a red team far, far away, my team had harvested a few sets of credentials from a phishing exercise, and I wanted to test them out on a web application page I found that showed a number of indicators that Active Directory authentication was in play on this page (such as a DOMAINjdoe). I proceeded to use each of the credentials the team had obtained, testing to see if the credentials were good and if they provided any higher-level access to the web application. Unbeknownst to our team, this was a page that did not actually have connectivity to any backend, much less Active Directory. It did, however, alert the administrators to every single user and password that we tried against that page so that they could disable them and have their passwords changed. This page was set up by a system administrator, not even the blue team (defense team), as a way to catch leaked credentials. Needless to say, our team was very displeased with me that I had burned all of their work.

What is the most significant ethical quandary you experienced while on an assigned objective?

There was a law firm I was testing. It was an internal test, and the responder was pretty new to the industry, so it was a pretty quick assessment. I was sitting there cracking passwords from the domain so I could access the target data for this assessment (dummy case records in their case data storage system) when I saw a credential crack for one of the top partners at this firm.

The password was poisonedher. This freaked me out. What should I do? Should I call the police? What would I tell the police if I called them? I had no proof of any wrongdoing. Did this person confess (as they secretly typed in their password every day) that they were poisoning or had poisoned some woman somewhere? Or did they just really like murder mystery books? I expressed my concerns to the engagement point of contact at the law firm, but I was agonizing over whether to tell anyone else throughout the whole week allotted for the test. A few months later the partner no longer worked at the firm, and that's the last information I got on the subject. The story still gives me the chills to this day.

How does the red team work together to get the job done?

It's a team, much like any other. Teams combine strengths and compensate for weaknesses, and every team is different. What works for my team might not work for yours. Good leadership and using a fast-fail approach when trying new things to find out what works best for your team have both been highly effective for me in the past. What platform works for most of the team when documenting findings? Is it Microsoft Word, OneNote, Google Docs, Etherpad? This is all about styles, personal preferences, and effectiveness. Communication about what works, what doesn't work, and what to try next is vital.

What is your approach to debriefing and supporting blue teams after an operation is completed?

That's easy. You give them as much as you can. Everyone has a schedule to keep, but if I had infinite time, I would go on-site with every single customer and fix every single one of the findings I found during an engagement. Every company is understaffed right now when it comes to security talent. Being that extra body, with intimate familiarity with the findings (since you found them), and showing the effort to find the right person and right fix would do leaps and bounds more help in this industry than shoveling reports over a table.

If you were to switch to the blue team, what would be your first step to better defend against attacks?

This really depends on what is considered the blue team. If that means incident response, then what I would do is forward Windows event logs, deploy Sysmon and OSQuery across my fleet of systems to talk to a central logging server, and set up alerts. I don't think this is done very much because it's a free solution and takes expertise (which is in high demand) to deploy.

Blinky boxes are still the highlight of InfoSec because they come with experts to implement and fix if things go wrong.

If by blue team we mean security teams in general, then I would focus on making security policies like minimum password lengths that force password managers and 2FA. I don't think this is done as much because it takes a lot of work to get approved and is usually a highly political process.

What is some practical advice on writing a good report?

Work with your customers to identify the most beneficial medium of reporting. While the industry standard is a 40-page report, it doesn't have to be this way. Many companies would rather reports be just imported into a ticketing system. Other companies prefer having their reports in the form of a slide deck with commentary on a conference bridge. If you never discuss the most efficient method, you'll never do anything different and probably just give them another PDF or DOCX to be ignored.

How do you ensure your program results are valuable to people who need a full narrative and context?

Objection! Leading the witness! In all seriousness, we in the industry are a lazy bunch. We spend a ton of time on things we find interesting and valuable, and the drudgery of writing reports, findings, and explaining our discoveries to others is tedious. We want to discover and be left alone. We have to overcome this. It's like working at McDonald's and sitting there making only the things we want to eat instead of the food being ordered. Part of maturity is learning that work is work because it involves things that are beneficial to people other than yourself. Put in the work to figure out the weaknesses, document how they were found, and then spend the time to research fixes, multiple if possible, and test those fixes. I've tested various "industry-accepted" fixes for common vulnerabilities that just don't work or work only partially. Do the work, and spend the time. You're getting paid to make the customer better, not show how cool you can be.

> "Part of maturity is learning that work is work because it involves things that are beneficial to people other than yourself."

How do you recommend security improvements other than pointing out where it's insufficient?

General Electric has one of the most well-known leadership tracks in the industry; companies worldwide send their managers to Crotonville. While I personally didn't attend any of the Crotonville training sessions, I had the fantastic opportunity to interact with a large number of peers and leaders who had. One of the main themes I heard most repeated from that training program centers around motivation—motivating others to do as you want them to. But, getting back to the question, "insufficient" is purely subjective, especially in the information security space. Chris Nickerson said it best in his TED talk where he said that security is a feeling, so you have to treat it that way. Identifying with how someone feels when you report a vulnerability to them and locating the right motivation to have them fix it can make a huge difference. If you go into a room huffing and puffing that you know better and that this change or that change will secure the company better, you are going to get ignored. We all have better things to do than listen to someone ranting and raving about the next "worst" thing.

What nontechnical skills or attitudes do you look for when recruiting and interviewing red team members?

I would say extreme curiosity is probably the primary nontechnical skill I look for in candidates. If you aren't curious, you aren't going to go digging through a pile of manuals to find the one URL that isn't protected by authentication or the one share out of 10,000 that happens to have a PASSWORDS.XLS in it. I use my insatiable curiosity regularly during red team assessments to poke at everything and anything (within the ROE).

What differentiates good red teamers from the pack as far as approaching a problem differently?

In my opinion, the most significant differentiator of people that I have seen as successful versus not is the ability to ask for help. The ability to ask for help is not as natural as it sounds. When you are knee-deep in a network or security vulnerability, it's hard to ask for help or let people into your "secret sauce." Letting go of that pride allows red teamers to go further, learn more, and be more successful overall. ∎

Twitter: @capt_red_beardz

Patrick Fussell

17

Patrick currently works as a red team operator and has more than 10 years of IT experience. After completing his time serving the U.S. Marine Corps, Patrick began working as an information security consultant, eventually moving on to a more focused role as a penetration tester. Patrick has been engaged to deliver a variety of services, such as the design and implementation of custom security assessments and penetration tests. Through his career, he has performed all phases of comprehensive testing including vulnerability, network-based security, and internet-based web application security assessments.

How did you get your start on a red team?

I would call it a fortuitous set of events. I had been pointing my career toward red teaming for a long time. I started out as a security analyst and then moved to full-time penetration testing. I knew at some point when I had developed my technical skill set in the right way that I might want to make the jump to red teaming. So I focused on learning the things that I thought might help me in that type of position. A few of my friends migrated to red team positions at the same time I started looking at the job market. After a few solid interviews, I had a stroke of almost dumb luck. I sat next to a hiring manager on an airplane who was looking for someone just like me to join a red team. We had a long talk that was a lot like an informal interview. About six months later I joined up.

What is the best way to get a red team job?

It seems like there needs to be some intersection of preparation and opportunity. The preparation comes from mastering the skills that make you a good candidate.

There seem to be many paths to get to that particular place. I say that because I think an ideal red team has some level of specialization within it. You have people who have different backgrounds and skill sets who work together because everyone can't know everything. Good red teamers can come from lots of different disciplines. There are probably some basic skill sets that make a stronger candidate. I do think everyone needs to be able to write code. Maybe not everyone needs to be an elite developer; however, code is the language of the computer, and you need to live in the land of the computer. Skill sets that mirror those of a good sys admin are useful.

This is the kind of list that could go on and on. Everything from networking to web apps come into play on a regular basis. In the end, the point is you can leverage your skills in interesting ways as part of an offensive security team. Showcasing your abilities by presenting at conferences, writing blog posts, publishing white papers, and contributing to open source security tools are all things that make it easy for a hiring manager to know if you are a good fit.

How can someone gain red team skills without getting in trouble with the law?

The cheap answer to this is to do what I did and work as a penetration tester for some years. This can be a great playground for developing the right skills. I was lucky to have a penetration testing job where the focus was always goal-based with a heavy emphasis on post-exploitation and lateral movement. I recognize not everyone will have this opportunity, though, so I think I would focus on the idea that a lot of skills you use for red teaming are not inherently illegal anyway. They probably look a lot like developing the same skills you might want as a system or network administrator.

Coding would be one of the easy ones. And this has an almost unlimited number of paths where you can spend time. You can write tools that do fun security-related things that will teach you things as you go. I think everyone should write a network port scanner at some point and make a real effort to understand how a socket really works. You can play with other people's code to learn how they conquer interesting challenges in the offensive security space. Learn enough code to understand how fantastic projects like BloodHound really work so that you can talk about what they are really doing in depth. Pluralsight has a ton of great content on Active Directory (AD). Set up AD in a lab and try to manage it for a few weeks.

This ties into what I think of as a classic answer to this kind of question, which is to build a lab. I would say this is almost a must. I have several labs I use on a regular basis. I recently purchased a laptop where I have a mini-Windows lab. I use Hyper-V to create a domain controller with one or two joined members. It just so happens this laptop is also great for gaming. The trick with the lab is to make it flexible and go use it. Install EDR or AV and try to get past it. Understand what works and what doesn't and why.

Why can't we agree on what a red team is?

This seems tied to the history of offensive security testing. At some point, the idea of offensive security was just hiring hackers to try to break into your stuff. Later, this got semiformalized and evolved. This resulted in a divergence of services offered and arbitrary labeling of what those services might be. Terms like *penetration testing* and *vulnerability scanning* got thrown around because organizations were willing to spend money on them and providers wanted to make money by providing them. This sort of Wild West of InfoSec industry spurred on by spending meant there was never really any formal basis for anything. In other industries, things like time or academia are allowed to help shape the landscape. So now we've gotten to the point where it's become apparent another type of service is needed (red teaming) to help organizations become more secure, but because of things like competition, there is no way for everyone to agree on terminology or standards.

What is one thing the rest of information security doesn't understand about being on a red team? What is the most toxic falsehood you have heard related to red, blue, or purple teams?

At some point in the past, there was a perspective that penetration testing was the sexiest type of InfoSec work. I would agree that maybe it was the most fun, but sadly that led to the idea that only the smartest, most experienced people could get into those roles. I can promise you that is not and never was the case. I think that type of thinking built this kind of elitism where people who did penetration testing were at the tip of this InfoSec pyramid. I really hate this perspective and do anything I can to disabuse people of the notion.

Red teamers are not the most elite of anything. Just like every other InfoSec job, it requires a specialized set of skills that you develop over time that make you good at that role. I learn so much from my InfoSec brothers and sisters in literally every kind of InfoSec job role almost every day. People who are passionate about their work no matter what their role can bring just as much (and maybe more) value to the industry as I can.

When should you introduce a formal red team into an organization's security program?

At some level, a good InfoSec program looks a lot like a really tight systems administration group. Because organizations develop their programs in so many varied ways, it's hard for me with my perspective to give a good groundwork for identifying a point in a cycle where you can say, "Yes, this is it, we have arrived." What I can say is that organizations that have InfoSec programs and are ready for red team engagements seem to have really good visibility into almost every aspect of the entire IT environment and its operations. They can reference assets counts and types. They understand how the various parts of operations conduct business and are plugged into the day-to-day of their operations counterparts. If I get on a scoping call and start asking questions about the network and get a lot of crickets because nobody knows who owns what part of a network, that is a red light.

How do you explain the value of red teaming to a reluctant or nontechnical client or organization?

A good place to start is to relate it to physical security. Start by trying to understand how the person thinks about security in general terms and find relationships with information security. Would you put locks on your doors? Why? Do you guard some parts of a building with more gusto than others? What is the reasoning behind that? Red teaming was born from the idea that you need to test things like physical security in an applied manner because vague exercises don't always expose the true reactions of people involved. Information security is no different in that regard. The critical difference is that an InfoSec attacker has almost zero risks and high reward.

What is the *least* bang-for-your-buck security control that you see implemented?

While I'm sure there are bad products out there, most types of security controls can provide value. You get less bang for your buck when you don't spend more of your investment on setup, configuration, and realistic testing. I've had lots of discussions over the years that went like, "Why didn't X control detect you?" to which I respond, "Well, that depends on exactly what you are logging from those systems," to which there are just shrugs and cricket responses. What good is an alerting system if it doesn't have the right logs?

What's the most important or easiest-to-implement control that can prevent you from compromising a system or network?
System-level firewall rules. Restricting the ability for systems to communicate with each other can make lateral movement around a network difficult or impossible. It can be difficult to execute from both planning and technical aspects, but I think it will provide immense value if done correctly. I often ask people, "Do your workstations need to be able to communicate on port X?" to which the answer is almost always no.

Why do you feel it is critical to stay within the rules of engagement?
Offensive security testing is tricky due to the complex nature of the organizations we do work for. There are a lot of places where it is easy to stray into behavior that can be destructive without intending to or even realizing you have done so. How can you be sure you are testing only assets that belong to the target organization? This can be something simple such as sending a phishing email that says a company will execute some action on a given date. The tester knows this is false, but not all recipients will. This may cause some significant confusion within a company. Setting ground rules that help avoid these situations benefits all parties and protects the interests of all stakeholders.

If you were ever busted on a penetration test or other engagement, how did you handle it?
I'd prefer not to relive that moment.

What is the biggest ethical quandary you experienced while on an assigned objective?
I once found evidence of an extramarital affair between two employees of a company I was doing work for while browsing chat logs. This same conversation had data relevant to the engagement. I tried to avoid including the conversation in the report, but the client was interested in the data source, and the logs kept coming up in conversation. This involved me getting a crash course in my legal and ethical obligations in terms of protecting data and privacy due to the high level of access I might have during an engagement. This was many years ago, and it still makes me uncomfortable to think about to this day.

How does the red team work together to get the job done?
I come from a military background, so I tend to think of a team as having a manager who acts as the enabler. The manager is responsible for ensuring the mission and assignments are understood by all and that progress toward the objectives is always happening. The manager makes sure the people are assigned to tasks to which they are best suited and that those people have exactly what they need to get the job done. As a member of a team, I've found my own focus tends to be on information sharing. Making sure everyone knows what I know often makes engagement more successful. Anyone who has worked on a team can tell you that can be harder than it sounds.

What is your approach to debriefing and supporting blue teams after an operation is completed?
This is often informed by understanding the needs of the client. Gaining insight into strengths, weaknesses, and capabilities means I can spend more time providing more specific data that will be of the greatest benefit to the client. In

line with this, building some rapport with the right people enables this type of behavior. For instance, understanding how a team is achieving a particular type of alerting lets me spend more time going over some activity we executed that maybe they missed. This might get highlighted in logs and reports but also might be overlooked if not communicated the right way.

If you were to switch to the blue team, what would be your first step to better defend against attacks, and if it isn't commonly done already, why do you suppose that's the case?

I think I'd investigate implementing strict host-based firewall restrictions. It seems like executing this in a way that still allows for easy system administration and monitoring is likely a complex and difficult undertaking. Messing it up would cause a lot of significant problems.

What is some practical advice on writing a good report?

The best practice I've developed over the years is to write as much of the report as possible as I go through the engagement. This will force you to slow down and think about what you want to record in your notes and ultimately write a much more accurate narrative. If you can focus on the quality of text, details, and formatting at the end because you wrote the broad strokes during, your client ends up with a better product.

How do you ensure your program results are valuable to people who need a full narrative and context?

This just requires keeping the objective of your writing in perspective. Yes, it's fun to talk about all the sweet shells you got, but each sentence you write needs to have a purpose. That purpose is to help your client. If you can't make a case for the point you are writing about being useful to your client, then you are just bragging.

How do you recommend security improvements other than pointing out where it's insufficient?

Thinking about the nitty-gritty details of how I would detect my own lateral movement techniques is a reasonable starting point. Understanding how people who are good at things—like alerting—do what they do means I can provide better feedback.

What nontechnical skills or attitudes do you look for when recruiting and interviewing red team members?

The ability to communicate complex technical ideas. The ability to speak about a complex technical issue, even with people with a similar technical background, is a skill like any other. Being good at it requires focus and effort. Being good at it means you are a much more valuable asset within a team. Imagine the phases of a red team engagement and how many opportunities there are for something to go wrong or right because team members are able to get across a difficult idea in a succinct way that everyone can grasp. I think this can be far more of a challenge than most people are willing to acknowledge.

What differentiates good red teamers from the pack as far as approaching a problem differently?

This seems to be tied to the ability to avoid assuming you know how something works. Good red teamers often enjoy the process of really digging down into something to understand how it works. ∎

"Challenge yourself to learn new technologies and find a way to share that knowledge in a broader sense through talks, blog posts, podcasts, white papers, mentoring, and so on."

Twitter: @carnal0wnage

Chris Gates

Chris Gates has been breaking things professionally for more than a decade via network and web application penetration testing, red teaming, and adversarial simulation. These days Chris splits his time being both a breaker and a fixer. Chris is the co-author of WeirdAAL, a tool for AWS reconnaissance, and contributes to other open source projects. Chris has spoken at the United States Military Academy, BlackHat, DEF CON, Wild West Hacking Fest, Toorcon, Brucon, Troopers, SOURCE Boston, Derbycon, LasCon, HashDays, HackCon, Bsides ATL, YSTS, IT Defense, OWASP AppSec DC, Ruxcon, Cactuscon, and Devops Days. Chris is also a co-founder of NoVAHackers.

18

How did you get your start on a red team?
In 2007 I transitioned from being an active duty Army officer to a government contractor position with the U.S. Army red team. Back then the various service red teams, along with other government agency red teams, were pretty much the only red team games in town. Most consultancies were doing pentest work, but commercial companies weren't facing the same threats that government/military were facing then from APT groups. My college degree (computer science), job in the Army (signal officer), and work with Joe McCray and LearnSecurityOnline gave me enough background and chops for the hiring manager to take a chance on me. In retrospect, it's laughable how much I didn't know, but I was willing to learn and put the time into learning everything I could and listened to my mentors about how to grow and mature in the field.

My real red team education started when I joined Lares. From there I was really exposed to how weakness in one of the three pillars—social, electronic, and physical—leads to weaknesses in the others and the numerous ways companies deploy protections for those three pillars.

The rest is history (and on LinkedIn).

What is the best way to get a red team job?

Put in the time and work to get experience. Demonstrate competence in one or more of the three pillars of red teaming—social, physical, electronic. Network with people, find mentors to help you fill in your knowledge gaps, and be willing to do the work they suggest you do to get to the next level. Challenge yourself to learn new technologies and find a way to share that knowledge in a broader sense through talks, blog posts, podcasts, white papers, mentoring, and so on.

These days, even with normal security consultancies you'll most likely be able to work on social engineering and even physical access attacks. All engagements and experiences are valuable, as you'll never know when something you did on some previous engagement becomes the thing that allows you to succeed on your current one.

How can someone gain red team skills without getting in trouble with the law?

Social engineering and physical access skills are a bit more challenging to acquire without on-the-job training. Social engineering CTFs exist along with organizations like TOOOL that can help guide people to be better at lockpicking or physical access attacks. In the end, you'll need to do the engagements with that get-out-of-jail-free letter.

On the electronic attack side of things, copious opportunities exist, including capture-the-flag (CTF) events, bug bounty programs, vulnerable hackable systems (Hack The Box, VulnHub, tryhackme, and so on), and vulnerable software repositories and local virtual machines/Docker containers. Coupled with thousands of hours of conference videos and online training, there is more material out there than someone could ever expect to consume. Pick a topic that interests you and go to work.

Why can't we agree on what a red team is?

Marketing, PR, and shady salespeople injecting their nonsense into what should be a straightforward definition. Rather than the quality of their work, research projects, conference talks, and so on, driving business, it's about making people believe via sales lingo that a less superior thing is the same as something else.

Chris Nickerson from Lares has been consistently on the leading edge of both the definition of red teaming and the art of red teaming itself.

What is one thing the rest of information security doesn't understand about being on a red team? What is the most toxic falsehood you have heard related to red, blue, or purple teams?

I had a battalion commander (think CEO) in the Army who said that on any given day it's better to be on active duty, a civilian, a contractor, or a local national (we were in Europe), and that always stuck with me.

Toxic falsehood #1: That any color is better than any other color. Maybe on Monday it's better to be red, but Tuesday it's probably better to not be. Without the success and work of one, there can be no success for another.

Toxic falsehood #2: That most people like/value red teams. Red teams are a toleration for most organizations. In general, all they do is identify broken things to add to the ever-growing pile of things to fix. The better I did my job on that engagement, the more critical and painful the things I threw on the pile. Want the opportunity to show value and shine? Be on the blue team. Helping a company prevent an incident or recover from one is when you can have a C level really be *happy* you work for the company that day. I've never had that feeling as a red teamer.

When should you introduce a formal red team into an organization's security program?

When the organization has moved from a reactionary security model to a proactive security model. Additionally, the organization should have had a few regular pentests under their belt. If your pentesters are regularly coming in and smashing everything, what good is it going to do to have someone social engineer their way in or pick a lock and get in and do the same electronic attack for two to three times the price?

> "If your pentesters are regularly coming in and smashing everything, what good is it going to do to have someone social engineer their way in or pick a lock and get in and do the same electronic attack for two to three times the price?"

How do you explain the value of red teaming to a reluctant or nontechnical client or organization?

It's most effective to not waste your time. In all honesty, if you have to really push, pull teeth, hand hold, and convince, then the organization isn't going to be in the right mind-set to receive or implement the things a red team engagement will find anyway.

What is the *least* bang-for-your-buck security control that you see implemented?

Vulnerability scanning when the organization doesn't scan for high-impact things, misunderstands what is a high-impact thing for them, or just doesn't do anything with the results.

Have you ever recommended not doing a red team engagement?

Quite frequently an organization would be *far* better off with an ISO 27001 risk assessment coupled with a penetration test to validate that the answers given to the risk assessment control's questions are accurate. A company with answers to the control questions, the accompanying policies/documentation, and the results of the penetration test validating each control will have a much better understanding of their security posture than someone breaking into their data center and rolling out with a server.

What's the most important or easiest-to-implement control that can prevent you from compromising a system or network?

Multifactor authentication. Ideally a username and password shouldn't get you access to anything in the external environment or, when possible, the internal environment either. The technology is sufficiently mature that 2FA SSH and SAML auth for web applications doesn't have a very high implementation bar.

Why do you feel it is critical to stay within the rules of engagement?

So you get your invoice paid by the client. A good/correct red team rules of engagement should have a pretty large swath of available options for attack. If your red team test doesn't allow physical attacks or social engineering, you have a pentest, and you should most definitely stay within the boundaries of the ROE.

If you were ever busted on a penetration test or other engagement, how did you handle it?

I've been caught many times. How did I handle it? Denial, anger, bargaining, depression, and acceptance. After acceptance, you pick yourself up, do some self-observation of where you messed up, update tradecraft (if applicable), buy drinks for getting busted, and move on. The beauty of doing this in an authorized fashion is you don't have strange people knocking on your door after you get caught.

> "I've been caught many times. How did I handle it? Denial, anger, bargaining, depression, and acceptance."

What is the biggest ethical quandary you experienced while on an assigned objective?

I did a job where the client was having credit cards stolen due to a multitude of misconfigurations and bad security practices. As far as I know, they didn't self-report this to any of the credit card companies or anyone else. I wanted to report them but ended up not doing it. I had to hope their auditor would take care of it.

On a more macro level, as a pentester or red teamer, you are going to see some *really* messed up stuff throughout your career. You are going to be under NDA, and you also have a responsibility to protect your client and their information despite what might be the utter ridiculousness and insanity of the situation you find yourself in.

How does the red team work together to get the job done?

The engagement lead manages the workload across the team members and has overall say for the engagement. Team members write up their respective sections for assigned work in the report. The engagement lead does the final edits. The implied task is creating a team that has the various skill sets and maturity to handle the various tasks for the engagement.

What is your approach to debriefing and supporting blue teams after an operation is completed?

"We are all on the same team." I start meetings with new teams with something like that. This is a bit easier when you are on an internal red team, but even as a consultant, you have the company's best interests as a priority. I explain it's not about getting someone fired or in trouble or "calling their baby ugly," but rather we are working to find things to improve on *before* a real bad guy does.

If you were to switch to the blue team, what would be your first step to better defend against attacks?
I did this at my previous job. I worked to add detection rules for the common things I do once I get on a host for host enumeration, post-exploitation, and then lateral movement. Those rules came in handy later.

What is some practical advice on writing a good report?
Tell the story of the engagement. Most likely the consumer of the report wasn't there, and you want them to understand how everything went down for the red team engagement. The report, where possible, should contain a sufficient level of detail for anyone in the organization to take that report and reproduce the electronic portions of the attack.

How do you recommend security improvements other than pointing out where it's insufficient?
If you are in a position and environment where you can give links to fixes, code snippets, or submitting (preferred) diffs for the issue, that goes really far. In my experience, the majority of people care about the work they do; it's really a time thing. Most IT people have a million competing requirements. When a pentest/red team drops a ton of findings, that's adding more things to the pile, more things they have to research to fix, and more time to allocate to fix. If you can provide the line in the config file to change, the specific patch to apply, or updated code, that helps tremendously.

What nontechnical skills or attitudes do you look for when recruiting and interviewing red team members?
A couple of nontechnical skills or attitudes I look for: the ability and willingness to admit when they were wrong, being willing to update their knowledge bank/skill set, and being humble. They must be able to accept criticism from the most junior member of the team up to the CEO. Most people don't have a problem with people above them, but on a "team" everyone should have the same amount of opinion, and it's up to the engagement or team lead to make a final decision. If you are the type of person to discount an opinion because of someone's years of experience, I have no time for you. I have similar feelings if you are "God's gift to red teaming."

> "If you are the type of person to discount an opinion because of someone's years of experience, I have no time for you."

What differentiates good red teamers from the pack as far as approaching a problem differently?
The same things I look for when I interview someone—the ability and willingness to admit when they were wrong, being willing to update their knowledge bank/skill set, and being humble—along with experience and the ability to call upon that experience when you are brainstorming approaches to any particular problem. ∎

"I think the most important three things you should do if you want to get a red team job are to decide you can, decide you belong, and decide you will chew through any and all gnarly obstacles encountered along the way and emerge, undaunted, as a member of a red team on the other side."

Twitter: @briangenz

Brian Genz

19

Brian Genz leads the red team at Splunk. He has information security experience spanning multiple sectors, including defense intelligence, manufacturing, finance, and insurance. Brian has worked in the areas of security assessments, vulnerability management, security architecture, and DFIR/threat hunting. He also serves as an intelligence officer in the U.S. Army Reserve with a focus on cybersecurity and is an instructor with GTK Cyber for the black-hat training called "Applied Data Science and Machine Learning for Cybersecurity." He holds two graduate degrees, an MBA and an MS in information technology, and multiple industry certifications.

How did you get your start on a red team?

I took a very nontraditional path to offensive security. I had just returned from a deployment to the Ninevah Province in Iraq in 2010, where I'd had the honor and privilege of serving as a long-range surveillance (LRS) company commander. Shortly after coming home, I went to work in the IT infrastructure group at a global manufacturing company.

I quickly realized that I had walked into a tough situation. The painful, hard-won knowledge and experience gained from navigating the persistent gaps, pervasive blind spots, and knowledge drain left in the wake of IT outsourcing seemed like an unending chain of insurmountable challenges. I frequently thought about how mentally and emotionally defeating that environment was, and I often compared it (in my head) to my low points during my time at the U.S. Army Ranger School a few years earlier.

Although I wouldn't have had the foresight to recognize what was happening at the time, it's clear now that I was following the mental playbook from Mountain Phase in Dahlonega, Georgia: "Just keep moving. Don't quit. Solve one problem at a time, and put one foot in front of the other. Just keep going."

I also followed my natural instincts to solve hard problems, to keep learning, and to continually look for ways to add a "particular set of unique skills" to my toolkit.

It takes a certain degree of measured, controlled insanity to follow the path of incident-driven problem-solving right up to the sketchy ledge of decision points like "Should I figure out how to get access to ACF2 and the mainframe environment to solve some sticky identity and access management (IAM) issues that no one seems willing or able to fix?" ("And should I mention in my request that I don't know anything about ACF2 or mainframes?") Sleeves up, heads down, solve the problem.... The forced fearlessness may have been irrational, but I always figured I could go back to hanging drywall if I accidentally deleted all the things and got fired. IBM Redbooks and Google were my friends for a while.

We don't always know where a path will lead or who we'll encounter along that journey. I began having more and more interactions with the global security team as a natural extension of the IAM troubleshooting I'd been doing across legacy mainframe systems and a new enterprise IAM system. That led to my first full-time role in information security, and it happened only because I'd been freakishly obsessed with solving sticky problems.

Because the global security team was relatively small, I had the opportunity to start from the ground up, focusing on vulnerability assessments and web application testing and even pitching in with forensics when the situation called for it. I suddenly had a new mission, a new set of professional development targets on the horizon, and a maniacal obsession with understanding how it all worked. Most important for me, though, was the natural alignment between my being hardwired to protect and the broader sense of being part of a community of professionals who, like me, are intrinsically motivated and driven to do whatever is necessary to protect the organizations we serve and the people who depend on our organizations.

What is the best way to get a red team job?

I think the most important three things you should do if you want to get a red team job are to decide you can, decide you belong, and decide you will chew through any and all gnarly obstacles encountered along the way and emerge, undaunted, as a member of a red team on the other side.

The first person you'll need to convince that you're capable, worthy, and willing to settle in for the long-haul, behind-the-scenes grind in your pursuit of a red team job is you.

Once you've negotiated those terms with your harshest critic, you're ready to go about the task of identifying one or more hops between where you are and where you're headed. I'm a fan of *What Color Is Your Parachute?* by Richard N. Bolles, and if you haven't had a chance to read it, I'd recommend taking a look. The mental models we often bring to bear on a new and scary challenge can be over-fit based on past experience, bias, and fear. This artificially constrains the set of options that appear to be available. It's as if our brains and biases conspire to perform a subconscious "zoom in 10x" operation without telling us and then present the reduced set of options as "Here's what we've got, deal with it." Refreshing our inventory of available mental models, as Richard does in his book, could help you identify paths from point A to point B that might not have been visible when viewed through the same old lenses of experience and unconscious bias. Even if you don't yet have a high-resolution, detailed image of the desired end state, the process of thinking deliberately about how to find potential paths to your objective may at least bring a rough outline or silhouette into view.

With that foundation in place, you'll be in an excellent position to start exploring the information security field and red team specialization, enumerating the list of skills and capabilities common among red team professionals, and evaluating options for acquiring those skills.

How can someone gain red team skills without getting in trouble with the law?

Andy Hunt wrote a book titled *Pragmatic Thinking & Learning: Refactor Your Wetware,* and the concepts from his book helped me develop a road map of professional development objectives.

While there is undoubtedly a wealth of other useful knowledge in *Pragmatic Thinking & Learning,* the aspect of the book that is most relevant to your quest to become a red team professional is the concept of the "journey from novice to expert." Hunt describes the Dreyfus model of skill acquisition, developed in the 1980s by Stuart and Hubert Dreyfus. The researchers were working to improve the state of artificial intelligence by building software capable of learning and acquiring skills in the same way that humans do. Hunt outlines the five stages of the Dreyfus model: Novice > Advanced Beginner > Competent > Proficient > Expert.

An important note about the model is the idea that you will likely land on different levels depending on the particular set of skills required for that knowledge domain. For example, you may be a Proficient Linux sysadmin, a Competent Python developer, and a Novice home chef. If you apply this model to your objective of securing a position on a red team, the foundational technology skills such as networking, system administration, and scripting proficiency can accelerate your progress.

Equipped with a structured approach to mapping out the skill acquisition you'll need, you're ready to identify a curated set of information and training resources related to offensive security. Here are a few helpful resources you might want to explore:

- SANS.org
- Cybrary.it
- PenTesterLabs.com
- github.com/enaqx/awesome-pentest

The key to moving from Novice toward Competent is consistent, deliberate, hands-on practice. The resources will provide a treasure trove of guidance that will enable you to chart a course based on your available resources.

A few guiding principles will assist in avoiding criminal and legal issues while developing your offensive security skills:

- "First do no harm."
- Don't break into places you don't own/have legitimate access to.
- When in doubt, refer to the first point.

Why can't we agree on what a red team is?

Different strokes for different folks. It will sort itself out. Information security is a relatively nascent field compared with many of the more established professional disciplines, and there continues to be a range of strongly held opinions about which bespoke approach is best.

What is one thing the rest of information security doesn't understand about being on a red team? What is the most toxic falsehood you have heard related to red, blue, or purple teams?

I try to avoid broad generalizations, in general. One thing I would want people to know about the red teams I'm familiar with is this: there are highly skilled, quiet professionals who are deeply committed to helping their organizations reduce their attack surface, improve their security posture, and increase the organization's ability to achieve their mission in a manner that protects the people whom they serve.

When should you introduce a formal red team into an organization's security program?

I can see where there would be multiple valid approaches to answering this question. Some people might recommend that an organization satisfy a series of progressive "gates" or milestones before adding a red team into the mix. For example, I would generally agree with the perspective that it's essential to focus on the fundamentals, the blocking and tackling components such as asset inventory, patching, IAM, backups, and the like. However, the question implies a sequential, upward progression from CMM Level 0, to CMM Level 1, and beyond. The logical consequence of that argument might be a conclusion resembling this: "And therefore, we can see (as the laser pointer dot jumps confidently to the top-right quadrant of slide 42) *here* that it would be imprudent to deploy a sophisticated red team capability until we reach *this* level of maturity."

If I were the Minister of Important Decisions for a day, I'd take an alternate approach. First, I would humbly submit for your consideration the idea that there is an inherent false dilemma built into the argument that we have to choose between option A, which is "Deploy the last few pennies of limited budget to finally solving asset inventory," and option B, "Unleash the red team, full scope." I think it's reasonable to suggest that this inaccurately reduces the spectrum of available options to these two extremes.

Second, I'm interested in Ground Truth. I want—no, I *need*—to know what the situation on the ground is, no matter how desperate. And, if the on-the-ground reality is bad, I especially want to know about that. We need to maintain a common operating picture of when and where there are weaknesses, exposures, misconfigurations, emerging flawed practices, and so on. If we don't deploy a red team capability that proactively seeks out gaps in our defenses by leveraging offensive security tradecraft, we are allowing preventable blind spots to exist, fester, and potentially get popped.

So, building or bringing in a red team capability should be done as early as possible so that leadership is informed about security exposures by trusted advisors rather than strangers. It's okay to use the red team to identify weaknesses before all of the basics are "solved" because those blocking and tackling aspects of managing infrastructure are unlikely to be "fix it and forget it" activities.

How do you explain the value of red teaming to a reluctant or nontechnical client or organization?

I've found that it's helpful to describe the portfolio of services that the team provides and to frame those services in the context of the organization's mission and objectives, as potentially impacted by a significant security incident.

If the services stop at the point of "Here's your 400-page PDF, good luck, and we'll see you next year (with the same stuff we just used)," a knowledgeable client or executive will not see the value regardless of how the narrative unfolds.

In this case, the team is essentially offering a service that keeps them employed rather than one that effects positive change for the client. That approach has a limited shelf life, given the options available to forward-thinking consumers of red team services.

What is the least bang-for-your-buck security control that you see implemented?
Commodity AV.

What's the most important or easiest-to-implement control that can prevent you from compromising a system or network?
I think one approach would be using a combination of the following:
• Implementing the principle of least privilege
• Establishing and actively maintaining effective processes for managing access during Add/Move/Leave events
• Using 2FA
• Actively improving detection and response effectiveness with adversary simulation and purple team exercises
• Limiting lateral movement with GPOs

Why do you feel it is critical to stay within the rules of engagement?
Adhering to the rules of engagement (ROE) is essential because this is the contract—the authorization and agreement that distinguishes the red team from the unauthorized adversary. It describes lines that trusted advisors cannot cross if we intend to achieve our objective of enabling leadership to make informed decisions based on identified risks.

To frame this in a kinetic context for emphasis, imagine a different scenario in which the red team is an infantry squad moving into a military operations in urban terrain (MOUT) site at Ft. Benning, Georgia. Let's suppose the ROE defining and governing the behavior by both offense and defense in the scenario includes a sentence, highlighted in bold, that says, "All participants in this evaluation will use blank ammunition. No participants will use live ammunition or other explosives. Live (and holy) hand grenades are right out."

If some inexperienced but eager soldier on the red team decides to go above and beyond the usual routine involving blank ammunition in the interest of providing even more value by simulating the actual behavior of adversaries attacking the MOUT site, that would be somewhat problematic for all involved. It violates the "first do no harm" principle, it may erode trust among the members of the offense and defense, and it will certainly fail to meet the established training objectives for the evaluation.

If you were ever busted on a penetration test or other engagement, how did you handle it?
I remember one situation a while back in which a member of the blue team contacted me to ask if a specific activity that triggered an alert was related to a red team engagement. Because I've been on both sides of this scenario, two things came to mind immediately.

First, I "fessed up" and confirmed that the activity was related to an ongoing operation we were running. For anyone who has scrambled a team and worked all night to investigate potentially malicious activity only to find out the next morning that it was the team 15 feet from your corner of the cube farm that was executing the attack, you can probably relate to this approach. As leaders, we need to know where the point of diminishing returns lies in a situation like this. We need to find the right balance between two competing perspectives: the desire to maximize the realism and training value versus the practical and humane considerations around taking care of people and not burning scarce cycles overnight (times the total number of analysts working instead of sleeping) in the name of "letting it play out."

Second, I notified several people who had likely been or would soon be looped in, via the grapevine, that there was a problem. The goal at this point was twofold: I wanted to make sure I spread the word at least as far as the probable blast radius of message traffic for the same reasons outlined earlier. (Think "snowball effect," but along the paths of an informal phone tree.) I also took the opportunity to give credit to the folks on the blue team for their excellent work in detecting the malicious activity, and I echoed that praise and kudos to multiple people in leadership. That was a genuine sentiment, and also, it's helpful from a relationship-building perspective to demonstrate our unwavering support for and solidarity with our brothers and sisters on the other side of the problem set.

How does the red team work together to get the job done?

One way I think about the required competencies and the division of labor for the red team is the concept of training an infantry unit. There are individual tasks and collective tasks. These are derived from the Mission Essential Task List (METL), and they are the building blocks of developing and maintaining the capability to perform the assigned missions. I think there's value in considering this approach as we build, sustain, and improve our red teams.

Here's an example: let's say we are members of an Infantry Rifle Company. One task we must be proficient in performing, as a group, is "Conduct an attack." There are collective tasks that the entire group must be able to perform together competently to complete the mission successfully. I'll list a few supporting collective tasks here to provide more context:

- Conduct a movement to contact
- Conduct an attack in an urban area
- Perform risk management
- Treat casualties
- Maintain operations security

Without drilling into all of the individual competencies or common tasks that each soldier must demonstrate, we'll consider just one example that is nested under "Conduct a movement to contact," and that is "Camouflage self and individual equipment."

Let's tie this back to the question of "How do you work together to get the job done?" on a red team. We'll call the mission Deliver Red Team Assessment to simplify. A random sampling of the supporting collective tasks might include some of the following (but with shorter names):

- Conduct red team assessment operational planning
- Perform OSINT reconnaissance
- Perform physical penetration testing
- Deliver bail money to appropriate jurisdiction and retrieve colleagues
- Maintain operational security
- Compose and deliver the red team assessment report

Now let's deconstruct the last collective task, "Compose and deliver the red team assessment report." There are specific competencies that individuals need to possess to be able to contribute to the collective task that the red team has to be able to perform.

I believe that the written and verbal communication skills required to compose and deliver a red team assessment report are essential for each professional in this role, especially senior-level professionals.

So, we can follow the example and call out one example of an individual competency that might be nested under "Compose and deliver the red team assessment report," and that is "Perform translation of technical security exposures into risk-based observations to executive stakeholders."

When thinking about how to divide the work and coordinate tasks across team members, it can be useful to consider the training and skill-building value of partnering individuals who are skilled in the competency of "Perform translation of technical security exposures into risk-based observations to executive stakeholders" with other team members with less proficiency in a particular set of skills.

Some engagements might warrant more crosstalk and pitching in across a wide range of tasks than others. It's important to find a balance that gets the job done while simultaneously enabling individuals to spend a decent amount of their time on the more traditionally exciting activities (breaking stuff).

What is your approach to debriefing and supporting blue teams after an operation is completed?

I build this into the requirements for the red team assessment. For example, in addition to the typical scope documents, I outline a specific approach for the red team to record and maintain records of all attack steps, with detailed host and network data that we use for a multi-session debrief with the blue team. Think of this in terms of having the red team maintain a detailed timeline of which hosts were compromised, when the activity occurred, and so on.

I've framed this as a way to build a tighter feedback loop between offense and defense. For example, in addition to providing the detailed list of impacted hosts, I'm interested in discussing the following with the blue team after the completion of the engagement:

- For each host that was involved in the intrusion, what evidence types exist (or previously existed but are no longer available): host/memory/network?
- For each host that was involved in the intrusion, what types of artifacts can the blue team currently view/acquire/retrieve?
- For each host that was involved in the intrusion, what types of artifacts can the blue team currently *not* view/acquire/retrieve?

These focus areas for the post-assessment review with the blue team can help to highlight visibility gaps. It can also add concrete examples to the business case the blue team needs to make when they're working to reduce visibility gaps in the environment.

If you were to switch to blue team, what would be your first step to better defend against attacks'?

I think this question will prompt some people to think about which defensive technique/config/"secret GPO sauce" will provide the maximum protection for the attack techniques (known today) for a reasonable level of effort and resources. Don't get me wrong—this is absolutely a valid approach in the sense that we should continually strive to identify structural, pervasive security weaknesses and remediate those to reduce our attack surface. I'll defer to my colleagues for those recommendations in this case and focus instead on answering the question I'm hearing:

How do we better defend against attacks, what would I do first, and why don't more organizations do this?

Prepare to be underwhelmed as I throw down a notional challenge coin with the longest and least sexy motto (that will never be on an actual challenge coin):

Know Your Terrain, Inventory, Patch, and Use the Intelligence Cycle to Create a Common Operating Picture for Practitioners and Leadership That Assumes Breach and Emphasizes Detection & Response.

I would do the following, in this order:

- Develop an initial plan to build the joint red/blue capability, calling phase 1 a 90-day iteration as an initial pass. I'd develop the rough outline of the approach, get feedback and buy-in from both teams, and then enlist the help of key players from each team to assist in preparing for the initial kickoff.

- Get the red and blue teams together for an off-site, or at least engineer a way to get as many of the senior folks from each time in a room with whiteboards. This series of planned discussions is a critical success factor for alignment on defining each team's scope, the services provided, and the set of capabilities each team brings to the fight now and a year from now.

I think each organization has its own unique challenges and maturity levels at a point in time, and my anecdotal sense is that it would be challenging for many organizations to allocate resources to "practitioner-defined strategy," given the volume and pace of tactical and operational workloads in play.

What is some practical advice on writing a good report?

I'm on a 10-hour flight back to the United States on a Boeing 787 as I consider this question, and I keep coming back to this thought about writing testing reports: why do aviation maintenance inspections occur, and how do the inspectors collect, evaluate, package, and deliver their results to the people who are responsible for making sure this aircraft is free of severe defects? (Also I'm wondering now whether aircraft maintenance inspectors complain about writing reports. If you currently work in that field and you do complain about that, please know that I, for one, really appreciate your time, expertise, and diligence, especially when there are people depending on you to protect them from preventable risks. Also a quick shout-out to the people out there who write testing reports for bridges, elevators, and airbags.)

Full disclosure up front: I believe that the era of rolling in, hacking all the things, getting domain admin by lunchtime, and then dropping a several-hundred-page PDF on someone's desk on your way out the door is over. Realistically, it's probably been over for a while, but old habits die hard (habits like "rinse and repeat" pentests year after year and also like watching *Die Hard* around the holidays because it is clearly a holiday movie).

It's essential to have a framework that guides the red team reporting activities that serve as the delivery mechanism that, if configured thoughtfully, will lead to establishing top-of-mind persistence in the leadership conversations and priorities.

One approach you might find useful is developing a customized "package" or bundle of work products related to a red team engagement. Here's how I think about that:

Who do we need to tell about what was identified as needing remediation, and what level of detail does each person need to take the required steps at their level to facilitate remediation? Every organization will be slightly different, but here are a couple of examples:

- *CISO*: We need to "inform the commander" or make the CISO aware of (1) the activities we performed, (2) the items we identified, (3) the impact of those findings based on a risk-based analysis, (4) the process we're following to ensure we are executing on our commitments to engage system owners to deliver risk intelligence and influence decisions in the direction of improving the security posture.

- *System owners*: We need to provide the right level of context alongside the technical components of the report. We need to keep track of "red team telemetry" and preserve key details about attack progression, systems compromised, and other operational notes for system owners so the report contents provide a way for them to perform further historical research and analysis as needed.

- *Blue team, as configured in your org*: Personally, I decided to schedule more debriefings with the blue team after a red team engagement because I knew the particular "report package" we were delivering to them would realistically warrant multiple sessions. Detection and response are crucial, and that drives my thought processes around developing a customized set of work products for the blue team in addition to the standard "Executive Summary, Scope, Methodology, Findings, Appendix."

- *Risk and compliance teams*: Depending on your organization's requirements, you may also need to consider specific report formats and content requirements based on frameworks like PCI and HIPAA.

These are just a few examples of how you might take the "recipe" found in any of the available penetration testing frameworks and then customize the final product or report template based on your organization's requirements. I'd recommend considering the approach of designing the baseline report and then augmenting that with additional sections or appendixes as needed, based on the particular stakeholder group.

One quick tip I'd recommend: begin with the end in mind when collecting and presenting system details in the report. Think about the "last mile" of delivery when it is handed off from, for example, a member of the red team to the system owners. Keep in mind that "system owners" probably means something a bit different, in a practical sense, than it did before virtualization, and I'd argue the same dynamic is in play in terms of "cloud."

The system owners you're working with may need to track down and divvy up some of the remediation goodness with other system owners. So, please consider providing a separate spreadsheet or CSV file that lends itself to being analyzed, parsed, and chunked into smaller data sets in addition to dropping IP addresses and host names into a Word doc and then exporting to PDF.

How do you ensure your program results are valuable to people who need a full narrative and context?

One way to identify and close any gaps in perceived value in reports related to red team operations is to solicit feedback. One caveat—we are leveraging the collective experience and expertise of the members of our red team to provide intelligence to leadership about the organization's security posture. Therefore, we are not in a position to do any less than that, regardless of what consumers of our reports might prefer. Said a different way, the consumers of our reports should not be allowed to "downvote" items identified under the guise of "the customer is always right."

There is a practical, proven model of soliciting feedback for research or other types of assessments that you can adapt to whatever scale makes sense for your situation. You could have a verbal discussion with the stakeholders and ask questions like, "What about this report, and this process as a whole, is working well in your opinion?" "What isn't working as well, and why?" It would also be useful to ask them questions about how the information flows downstream from the report review meetings. Do some recon, understand their operational processes and workflows, and take time to view the most recent report review process through their lens just long enough to understand some of the challenges and context that might be contributing to any criticism they share about the reporting process or related work products.

How do you recommend security improvements other than pointing out where it's insufficient?

It's always challenging to find the right balance between delivering the insights about identified risks and calling someone's baby ugly.

One approach that can be a reasonable middle ground is to build relationships with the key teams and individuals who will be the consumers of the recommendations you make. If possible, it's helpful to develop those relationships early and often to avoid having a first conversation that necessarily revolves around a significant finding and the corresponding unsolicited recommendations.

As we build relationships with people (notice the distinct absence of the sterile term *stakeholders* here) who have different roles, accountabilities, and priorities than we do, I think it's helpful to try to walk a kilometer in their shoes. Consider this to be a mental exercise in seeking first to understand and then making a genuine effort to move from knowledge to empathy.

If you can actively look for opportunities to recognize and give kudos to the people you're advising as a steady-state, ongoing approach, you effectively accomplish two things: you establish a pattern of providing advisory feedback, and you end up providing both positive feedback and recommendations for improvement over time.

What nontechnical skills or attitudes do you look for when recruiting and interviewing red team members?

We need people who are humble, driven, resilient, teachable, and fearless, but in a first-do-no-harm manner. We need people who understand what servant leadership means in the context of information security. We need people who are hardwired to protect. We need people who are willing to do the less glamorous, behind-the-scenes work required to keep the lights on and answer the mail. We need quiet professionals who stand shoulder to shoulder with colleagues in our common cause of applying technical and tradecraft expertise to the mission of protecting the organizations we serve. We need people who can translate technical details into a narrative that frames security weaknesses in a risk-based context.

What differentiates good red teamers from the pack as far as approaching a problem differently?

I think one characteristic that differentiates good red teamers from the pack is a combination of resilience, tenacity, and tradecraft expertise that is laser-focused on the objective of delivering risk intelligence surfaced via the red team assessment. ∎

"I honestly don't know that there's any one best way to get a red team job. Penetration testing and red teaming are more about your ability to think creatively than a certain sort of education or background."

Twitter: @jaredhaight

Jared Haight

20

Jared has been in information security for five years now and is currently a consultant specializing in adversary simulation-style engagements. Before entering InfoSec he spent time in the operations side of IT, working in help-desk and desktop support before spending a decade as a systems administrator. Over the years he's released a couple of open source tools that have been well received, including PS>Attack, and he is a core developer behind the Faction C2 Framework. He's given talks and training at cons like Troopers, DerbyCon, CarolinaCon, and numerous BSides events.

How did you get your start on a red team?

I had what I feel is a pretty traditional path into red teaming. I've been in IT for about 14 years now; I started as help desk, then desktop support, and eventually systems administration. One day the company I was working for told me they were starting a security team in IT, and they wanted me on it. I'd always been a generalist, and I enjoyed that. It was cool to work on networking one day and virtualization the next, bouncing around various aspects of IT operations. I'd always been security-minded in my IT roles, probably more so than most people, but I wasn't sure how I felt about specializing in security.

I quickly realized that focusing on security would give me an excuse to learn the offensive side of things, though, and I was sold. Pretending to be a bad guy and getting into things you're not supposed to is so much fun! I quickly started studying for my OSCP and made some friends in Charlotte, North Carolina (where I was at the time), in the InfoSec scene, which all led to my first job as a penetration tester.

After some time in the industry and a lot more friends later, the opportunity for my current role came up; now I'm dedicated to adversary simulation and red team exercises.

What is the best way to get a red team job?

I honestly don't know that there's any one best way to get a red team job. Penetration testing and red teaming are more about your ability to think creatively than a certain sort of education or background. My advice to anyone trying to get into the offensive side of security is always the following:

- Learn the basics of programming language. It doesn't matter which one, but you should know how logic works (`if` statements and stuff like that) and how to read and write files.
- Understand basic networking. Know the difference between TCP and UDP, how DHCP and DNS work, and how HTTP/HTTPS works.
- If you have a local InfoSec community, get involved. You don't have to give talks or anything (though that's awesome if you want to), but talk to people, learn what the local InfoSec industry is like and what skills are in demand. In addition to helping you learn new stuff and understand where you need to focus your studying, the people in your InfoSec community can help a lot when you're on the job hunt by recommending you for positions or getting you in touch with other members of the community.

These will help a lot if you're new to the industry and trying to get a penetration testing position. If you're looking to get a red team position where you're performing adversary simulation, I'd first recommend some background as a penetration tester or another InfoSec role. Most of these engagements rely heavily on stealth, so to be successful, you have to know what actions you can take without being detected. This sort of knowledge typically comes from some experience in the field either as a defender or as a penetration tester.

In addition, it's important to remember that red team engagements are about adversary simulation, so pay attention to what's going on in the world. A lot of great companies like FireEye, Cyberreason, Cisco's Talos group, and Microsoft publish white papers on how threat actors operate. This provides great insight into what's happening in the wild and can help to align your actions to actual threats.

How can someone gain red team skills without getting in trouble with the law?

Several companies offer red team labs that you can play in, such as Pentester Lab and Hack The Box. Chris Long (@centurion on Twitter) has also released a phenomenal project on GitHub called DetectionLab. It's a set of scripts that handle building out a heavily monitored Active Directory environment. It provides a wonderful opportunity to try attacks and see what sort of noise they make.

I also think there's a lot of value in building your own lab. A red teamer's job is to make recommendations on how to mitigate threats, and having the experience of building and implementing the solutions you've recommended better enables you to make realistic, practical recommendations.

Why can't we agree on what a red team is?

I think the big issue is that there are two competing definitions for *red team*. The first is an offensive security team, or the opposite of a blue team (the defensive side of InfoSec). By this definition, if you hack into stuff professionally, you're a red teamer. I believe this was actually the most common interpretation of the phrase up until a couple years ago.

The other definition is more about the process, using *red team* as a term specifically for adversary simulation. Whereas a traditional penetration testing engagement is focused on finding as many vulnerabilities in a given network as possible, a red team engagement assesses the company's detection and response capabilities. These engagements are usually goal-based, have a wide scope, and focus on stealth and evasion.

What is one thing the rest of information security doesn't understand about being on a red team? What is the most toxic falsehood you have heard related to red, blue, or purple teams?
I *hate* the statement "Red has to be right once; blue has to be right all the time" because it sets an unrealistic expectation that the defensive side of the house has to be perfect. Instead, the reality is that as a red teamer, I'm on blue's turf, and everything I do could potentially be monitored and alerted on.

Instead of worrying about being right all the time, blue teams should focus on hardening what they can and funneling me toward heavily monitored choke points. This helps to turn those tables where red must be right all the time, else they're going to be detected.

When should you introduce a formal red team into an organization's security program?
This is a hard question because I don't know that there's a universally correct answer. In general, I think it's important to have a blue team in place before introducing a red team, or else you won't have anyone to fix the findings. I'd also recommend that some basic security hygiene be in place, such as managed patching, some sort of logging and monitoring, and limited administrative access. This way your red team can work on harder issues and provide some real value instead of making obvious recommendations.

How do you explain the value of red teaming to a reluctant or nontechnical client or organization?
Empathy. The biggest pushback I get is from technical people who are worried we're just going to trash their work or try to ruin whatever they have going on. They see security as the people who just say no to everything. Most every department within a company is operating with less time and a lower head count than they would like, and they're just trying to do their job as best they can. I worked in operational IT for a long time; I know I've cut corners and done things that weren't the most secure option because I had to move on to the next task. In all but the most extreme cases, I can't fault people for doing the same.

One of the things I try to make sure that customers (internal or external) understand is that we're here to help. In a lot of cases, we can be an advocate for the customer and their pain points, for example suggesting more staff or a change in process to make security easier. I also make sure that the narrative of my report focuses on the systemic issues that led to a particular vulnerability. In most cases, there's no single person to blame for a security issue in a company—it comes down to a process failure.

What is the *least* bang-for-your-buck security control that you see implemented?
A lot of companies will spend massive amounts of money on AV, EDR, SIEMs, etc., and then never provide enough people to monitor those things. You can't expect someone to chase down (or even notice) an anomaly in the logs if they're also working on a dozen other things in the environment.

Have you ever recommended not doing a red team engagement?
Usually by the time I get involved with an engagement, all these details have been worked out. I think for a red team engagement to really be valuable, a company should already have a pretty mature security posture, though. In casual conversations, I've recommended that people instead perform a penetration test or purple team, as these tend to focus more on working with the customer to immediately address issues that arise.

With a red team engagement, most people don't know it happened until they get the report. This can be a real surprise to a blue team that is still in the process of getting established or up to speed, and can feel pretty unfair.

What's the most important or easiest-to-implement control that can prevent you from compromising a system or network?
Have your email gateway add an "EXTERNAL EMAIL" message to outside emails. It's a super-simple, low-impact solution that has been really effective at lowering phishing success. The other two things I would recommend are implementing Microsoft's LAPS, which is a free solution to randomize local admin passwords and leverage Windows Event Forwarding to centrally collect logs from your Windows environment. Windows Event Forwarding is built into Windows and makes for a pretty good log aggregator.

Why do you feel it is critical to stay within the rules of engagement?
Trust is the most important part of being in offensive security. We are handling incredibly sensitive data and operate in production systems. Our clients, company, and co-workers need to know that we can be trusted with this responsibility. Rules of engagement are put into place to protect the company, protect the red team operator, and focus the engagement on areas of interest. If you step outside of the ROE, you risk lowering the effectiveness of the engagement and raising concerns that you may cause harm to the environment with your actions.

If you were ever busted on a penetration test or other engagement, how did you handle it?
Once I get past the initial disappointment of being busted, it really is a positive thing that should be celebrated. I always make sure to congratulate the person who caught me, especially if they aren't in a security role, because it's not their "job" to be on the defense. Most findings are always going to be suggestions for improvement, so it's really nice to be able to say, "You did really well here!"

One scenario that comes to mind is a physical I was doing against a company. Usually for a physical I'll do some recon and figure out what the company's badges look like. I'll then Photoshop up a badge, print it out, and paste it onto a HID card. In a badge case, it looks pretty convincing, and most badge readers make the same "beep" noise whether the badge is valid or not. So, if someone asks you to badge in after you've tried piggybacking off of them, I can just hold the door, make the badge reader beep, and go about my day. I've had a couple of my badges inspected by security officers who never noticed that they were fakes.

This one engagement, I'd already hit a couple of their buildings and was feeling fairly good about myself. I came to my next target around lunchtime and approached the back patio where everyone was eating. I caught the door as someone was entering and went to step into the building. A security guard was seated nearby and asked me to badge in. No problem, I hit the badge reader with my fake badge and stepped inside. The security guard stopped me; he actually noticed that the LED on the badge reader blinked red instead of green. Who notices that!?

Alright, no biggie. I handed my badge to him—the same badge that two other people had already closely looked at and let me on my way. This security guard noticed that the badge looked off, pulled it out of the badge holder, and then peeled my Photoshopped badge off the card. I'd done this trick a dozen times across a bunch of companies and never had anyone notice it. I was floored. I made sure to congratulate them and let the point of contact I had for the company know that they did an excellent job.

What is the biggest ethical quandary you experienced while on an assigned objective?

I don't know that I've ever had any real ethical quandaries about an objective. If there's ever anything I'm not sure about, we work with the client to make sure that everyone is on the same page. For example, in a recent engagement there was some concern that our malware may have ended up on users' personal computers. We worked with the company to identify ways we could key our malware to their corporate assets to make sure that things didn't get out of hand.

I do always feel a little weird going through people's emails, but it's also one of the best sources of information you can have. I make sure it's an in-and-out sort of thing, though; I don't want to spend more time reading people's emails than I have to.

How does the red team work together to get the job done?

We have different people (or sometimes entire teams) with their own specialties, and we will tap them in as needed. For example, we have a social engineering team that is incredible at intelligence gathering, phishing, vishing, and so on. We have a hardware team that handles things like dropboxes and some of the infrastructure we need. Among the operators, we all have our personal strengths and can tag in and out of an engagement as needed or just bounce ideas off each other.

We have a loose standard for how we store information, so it's easier to share and store artifacts that are created throughout the engagement, but most of it comes down to communication. We're all remote, so each engagement has a dedicated chat channel, and we spend all day in there sharing things as we find them and keeping each other in the loop. For each engagement, someone acts as the lead, and they're responsible for the overall strategy of the engagement. They also handle working with the team to assign work and responsibilities.

When it comes time to generate a report, we usually split it up into sections and assign them to members of the team. The lead then handles putting everything together and doing initial QA. During our reporting we also work with the blue team so we can make sure we accurately present their perspective with regard to what was detected and how they responded.

We present the final report to both management and the blue team, typically in separate meetings. This is where we can really dig in with the blue team and work through recommendations to make sure that we're offering advice that works for their needs.

If you were to switch to the blue team, what would be your first step to better defend against attacks?

My first step would be monitoring. You can't protect yourself if you don't know what's happening. It's not an easy problem, though; it's incredibly easy to completely overwhelm yourself with log volume. I think the best approach here would be to start small. Log a handful of important, ideally high-fidelity alerts, like when a service is created in Windows and when the membership of a high-value group changes. Get that under control and then expand what you're logging.

What is some practical advice on writing a good report?
Write for your audience. There are typically three groups that are going to read your report:

- *High-level management*: These are generally people who aren't as technical and are very busy. You want to focus on the important details here. Their concerns are going to be more focused on the big picture of "How is my company doing; how bad is the risk?" This is typically where a "High-Level Recommendations" section helps. Summarize what's wrong and how to fix it in an easy-to-parse list.
- *Technical management*: These are going to be more technical people who are concerned with how they're going to task out the work your report is going to create. They need to know what's wrong, why they need to fix it, and what the impact of the fix is going to be. This is where an overview of findings, their impact, and suggested fixes come into play. This shouldn't be a technical deep-dive, but it should be enough information that they can have a good understanding of what's involved. I also like to include a narrative in the report that walks through how the engagement played out. This helps technical managers to better prioritize fixes and understand the context of why a given fix is important.
- *Technical staff*: These are the people who have to actually implement fixes. Make sure they have all the information they need to understand the problem, how to fix it, and any considerations they should be aware of. In a lot of cases, this staff won't have the full report available to them, so your descriptions and information here should be able to stand alone.

I try to write my reports with the understanding that no one is going to sit down and read it from cover to cover, so I write each section as if it's going to be its own stand-alone document. This sometimes involves a lot of repeating information, but I think it's the right approach.

How do you recommend security improvements other than pointing out where it's insufficient?
I think it's always important to try to provide systemic recommendations when possible. Instead of focusing on "Patch X wasn't applied," try to figure out why it wasn't applied. Do they have patch management? Was this server omitted from it? Was this patch omitted? Why?

This is where it's really useful to talk to the blue team before finalizing your report. They can help to offer perspective around the problems you're seeing, which can help to make better, more thorough recommendations.

What nontechnical skills or attitudes do you look for when recruiting and interviewing red team members?
The number one for me is ego. On the team, we need to be comfortable asking for help if we get stuck on something. It's not going to help the team if there's a member who's too full of themselves to ask for help or if they're going to be condescending when they offer feedback and advice.

What differentiates good red teamers from the pack as far as approaching a problem differently?
Situational awareness and a constant focus on the objective. For any given situation, there's going to be dozens of different options for how you can proceed. Being constantly aware of the environment, how your actions in the environment will affect it, and what the end goal is allows a red teamer to quickly assess what they feel is the best next step. ■

"Critical thinking in the moment is a big skill that really can't be taught; it's something that is learned over time, and some have the knack for it right away."

Twitter: @tothehilt

Stephen Hilt

21

Stephen Hilt is a senior threat researcher at Trend Micro. He focuses on general security research, threat actors, malware behind attacks, and industrial control system security. He enjoys breaking things and putting them back together with a few extra parts to spare. Stephen is a world-renowned researcher, having spoken at Blackhat US, RSA, HITB, and many more. His research has gained him Dark Reading top hacks of the year twice. Stephen is a Nmap contributor and has written some Nmap scripts for ICS and other mainstream protocols. This work took him into becoming an expert on ICS protocols, and he co-authored the book *Hacking Exposed Industrial Control Systems: ICS and SCADA Security Secrets & Solutions*.

How did you get your start on a red team?
I started working on network operations mostly with routing and switching. I slowly started taking on responsibilities of the security-based systems from a networking stance. Shortly after this, new compliance regulations came down from the regulators who oversaw my company at the time, and I became a subject-matter expert in networking and started doing compliance-based assessment prior to auditors coming in. I built a reputation of doing good work in this field, and the security operations group offered me a job to move over and I accepted. There I started by doing more incident response and forensics at an enterprise level. Eventually I wanted to do more than just being on the blue side would provide, so I looked for a consulting job and took the time to

learn more and more offensive skills and was hired to do several black-box assessments for vendors and customers.

What is the best way to get a red team job?

Focus on the fundamentals of the area you want to be in. If that means you want to be a web app exploit dev, then sometimes the best way into that area is by getting a web app dev job to understand the fundamentals of how the systems are designed, built, and deployed. Then build strong security skills along the way and you'll be red teaming before you know it.

How can someone gain red team skills without getting in trouble with the law?

There are multiple ways of doing this. Set up your own lab and attack your own infrastructure. If you find exploits, bugs, or insecurities in deployments, responsibly disclose these items through many different avenues, such as bug bounty programs. Participate in bug bounty programs; these will build up your ability to legally try finding bugs and exploiting them in systems. However, remember to follow the rules of the bug bounty; otherwise, your efforts won't be paid. Third, capture the flags (CTF) are a great way to legally go after systems, break into them, and exfiltrate data. With capture the flags, this is not only expected but is rewarded by some CTFs with monetary prizes.

> "Participate in bug bounty programs; these will build up your ability to legally try finding bugs and exploiting them in systems."

Why can't we agree on what a red team is?

Why can't we agree on many things in InfoSec? I think the reason why we can't define roles, and specifically what a red team is, is that the scope that defines a pentest, red team, and black-box assessment blur together in many avenues. But the real difference is who is aware of the test before the test starts.

What is one thing the rest of information security doesn't understand about being on a red team? What is the most toxic falsehood you have heard related to red, blue, or purple teams?

Red teams are often seen as hostile toward blue/purple teams and as distracting from the real work that blue teams have to do. This is because in most cases you are doing your job when you show that someone else is not doing their job, which for me was a difficult part of the job to deal with and eventually a reason why I went back to the blue and purple sides of security. It was hard to stay on the side that just points out the holes versus the side that does lots of work to also help remediate the issues.

When should you introduce a formal red team into an organization's security program?

This one is dependent on the company. But the overall security mentality of the company, executives, and board of directors should be very mature.

How do you explain the value of red teaming to a reluctant or nontechnical client or organization?

Honestly, the most effective perspective is that if you keep doing things announced and well planned, you'll never know what the attackers will see or how they may come at your company.

What is the *least* bang-for-your-buck security control that you see implemented?

The default "click, click, done" kind of security awareness training. Conversely, I've been to places where the whole workforce has a security-first mentality. When you make everyone responsible for security, then that's the most effective control.

Have you ever recommended not doing a red team engagement?

Yes. If you feel that their maturity is not able to handle a red team, then you have to do what's right for them even if that means to tell them that. Some companies will benefit more from just having someone talk to them about their processes and to make sure that they will be effective for day-to-day operations. Introducing a targeted attacker may not be the best idea for their security posture.

> "Work with every user to make sure they understand the importance of security to the company and what information and processes may be the most critical to the business."

What's the most important or easiest-to-implement control that can prevent you from compromising a system or network?

Monitoring your systems, learning normal states, and alerting on things outside of normal, even if that's monitoring how much bandwidth is being used at the ISP. Work with every user to make sure they understand the importance of security to the company and what information and processes may be the most critical to the business.

Why do you feel it is critical to stay within the rules of engagement?

The ROE identifies what the company wants to be tested. It's not your own personal task to find anything else. If the company is hiring you to look at the new system that is being deployed but you find issues with another system, one they already knew about, then you took time out of the overall scope of the project and did not focus on the items the company wanted you to focus on.

If you were ever busted on a penetration test or other engagement, how did you handle it?

I was sitting in a conference room using one of their ports that a phone was plugged into; I switched my MAC to the one of the phones to avoid NAC and was trying to find a system that I was supposed to target. I had managed to compromise the AD infrastructure and started making accounts for myself for later use. At this point someone stormed into the conference room demanding that I explain myself. They managed to track me adding accounts to the room I was in. Luckily, I had the scope of work and rules of engagement with me, so I presented them to them and asked them to call the person who had authorized me to perform the assessment. I also complimented them on their ability to track down so quickly where the attack was coming from, and told them I was going to make sure I would note that in the report.

What is the biggest ethical quandary you experienced while on an assigned objective?

When someone is trying and doing the right thing and you have to convince them they are wrong. Say you are doing a physical security assessment and someone stops you, but you have to convince them that you are authorized, and sometimes this will go on for a while. Sometimes I just want to stop there and say, "Good job, you saw something and you acted on it."

How does the red team work together to get the job done?

Teams are always the best method; no one person has the skills to do everything. I have found it helpful when in the middle of breaking a system to ask another person on the team to take some notes so I don't have to piece it all together from memory later. This then helps when writing a great report, and then when debriefing it to the customer, you can tell personal stories from when you found the system and how the "team" reacted. It adds more human elements to the story for real impact.

What is your approach to debriefing and supporting blue teams after an operation is completed?

If blue and red teams don't work together, the issues won't ever be fixed.

If you were to switch to the blue team, what would be your first step to better defend against attacks?

I have already. I now use a lot of the skills I learned on the red side to learn how to defend, stop, and even track down the attackers.

What is some practical advice on writing a good report?

Having a standard template to start from helps a lot. Also, it's easier to write if you are passionate about what you did. Write up as many positives as possible; that way, you feel like you are discussing not only negatives but the positives that the company was able to show. I have never written a report for any client that wasn't doing *something* right you could compliment them on.

How do you ensure your program results are valuable to people who need a full narrative and context?

Be humble in your own skills. Compliment them more than you do yourself.

How do you recommend security improvements other than pointing out where it's insufficient?

Rank the findings based on the company's priorities, which means you need to understand the business of the company. This shows them where their top-dollar spend should be to fix the findings that you have discovered in a way that makes sense to their company.

What differentiates good red teamers from the pack as far as approaching a problem differently?

Critical thinking in the moment is a big skill that really can't be taught; it's something that is learned over time, and some have the knack for it right away. It's the ability to realize you are against a wall and to look at the problem a different way that then sometimes will solve the issue that you are running into. ∎

"The laws surrounding hacking are gray at best, but they will most likely not be in your favor."

Twitter: @bk_up

Brent Kennedy

22

Brent Kennedy is the red team director at Capital One Financial Corporation, where his team is responsible for conducting advanced, objective-based offensive operations that emulate threats faced by the organization and the financial industry as a whole. Formerly, Brent led the penetration testing team at the CERT Division of the Software Engineering Institute (SEI), where his team supported and assisted in the development of the Department of Homeland Security's Risk and Vulnerability Assessment (RVA) and Red Team programs.

Brent is a graduate of Carnegie Mellon University ('10), where he received an MS in information security policy and management, and of Washington & Jefferson College ('08), where he received a BA in information technology and economics; he holds OSCP and GXPN certificates. Brent is also an adjunct professor at Carnegie Mellon University's Heinz College and at Norwich University, teaching courses in ethical penetration testing and information security.

How did you get your start on a red team?
In a previous job, I worked for a Federally Funded Research and Development Center (FFRDC) that partnered with a federal agency to conduct penetration tests for other government organizations. Over time, some customers' security posture greatly improved, which increased the need for stealthier tradecraft and the demand to test their monitoring and response capabilities. A red team capability was spun up with the more experienced testers on the team. This was an extremely valuable time in my career: I got to explore and improve my tradecraft and really see what did and did not work. Many lessons were learned!

What is the best way to get a red team job?

First, make sure red teaming is what you really want to do. It is different (not better or worse) than penetration testing, requiring a different set of skills and mind-set. Then, focus on learning about tactics, techniques, and procedures (TTP) and operations security (OpSec) at a deep level. Those core fundamentals will be essential in learning how to best execute because you may get only one shot. Finally, spend some time with the blue team. Having an understanding of how blue teams work to monitor, detect, and respond will go a long way to being a good red team operator as well as making your output relevant, whether you are successful or not.

How can someone gain red team skills without getting in trouble with the law?

As a professor who teaches an ethical penetration testing course, I always sternly caution my students to act within the law and always be cognizant of where they are operating. The laws surrounding hacking are gray at best, but they will most likely not be in your favor. That being said, there are a few platforms out there now that provide sandboxed testing environments that are an invaluable tool for testing skills and tools in a real networked environment.

Red teaming is also about having the right mind-set. You can gain great red team skills by spending time with defenders and reading about strategy. Many of the strategic techniques that are used in warfare are applicable to red team operations.

> "Red teaming is also about having the right mind-set. You can gain great red team skills by spending time with defenders and reading about strategy."

Why can't we agree on what a red team is?

Often, the term *red team* is used to describe anything in the offensive security realm, especially as it's become a buzzword in the tech industry. If you ask someone what the differences between application testing, penetration testing, and red teaming are, you start to get more consistent answers. I think the biggest disagreement on the term comes when red teaming is being defined as "advanced" pentesting. Red teaming has the connotation of being the next level up from penetration testing, when in reality the objectives of the two services have significant differences, and both are valuable.

In discussing red teaming with leads from other organizations, I'm always interested to see the different ways their red teams are organized and how they operate. On the surface, these can look like differences, but it's really just each team applying the same core red teaming principles to best fit their organization and customers. Doing so is an important part of internal red teams.

What is one thing the rest of information security doesn't understand about being on a red team? What is the most toxic falsehood you have heard related to red, blue, or purple teams?

Not many people understand the level of planning that goes into a red team operation from both a management and technical perspective. It is not as simple as getting an idea, opening up the computer, and starting to hack. A great deal of preparation goes into getting the necessary approvals, making sure the right people are "in the know," and planning the actual execution. Also, setting up the proper infrastructure can take a large amount of time and resources.

A toxic falsehood is that red and blue cannot work together and naturally work against each other. Sure, blue is trying to detect and prevent red from being successful, but that is only one facet of the job. Behind the scenes and after the fact, the two teams can and should work closely together to fully understand what each party did and close any identified gaps. The success of a red team ultimately relies on having a great relationship with blue. At the end of the day, I believe that the red team is an extension of the blue team, not a completely separate entity.

> "The success of a red team ultimately relies on having a great relationship with blue. At the end of the day, I believe that the red team is an extension of the blue team, not a completely separate entity."

When should you introduce a formal red team into an organization's security program?

An internal red team should be one of the final pieces of a security program. An organization wants to make sure they have mature processes in place to monitor, detect, and respond to intrusions before they have a red team potentially create events. A red team is valuable in helping to fine-tune an existing security program, not find holes that are already known.

How do you explain the value of red teaming to a reluctant or nontechnical client or organization?

When explaining what a red team does to a nontechnical audience, I always highlight the world *real*. I explain that a red team is emulating a real bad actor and using only the resources that a real bad actor has at their disposal. It is always important to be humble in these discussions to make your customer know you are not there just to make them look bad. It helps to explain that when a red team goes into an operation, they do not know if they are going to be successful, and that is the point. This helps create a partnership, as if it's a puzzle that both of you are trying to find the answer to.

Have you ever recommended not doing a red team engagement?

Yes! Many times customers want a red team exercise because they assume that is the most advanced offensive service, and why not go with the best? In reality, though, the customer is looking for a more targeted assessment of their product or application that better fits in the application security or penetration testing realm. It is critical to figure out what the customer is really looking for in terms of output and what they really want evaluated. This will help drive selecting the right assessment type. Not one of these services is better than the other; they are simply oriented to different demands, and it's important to help your customers identify which is the best fit.

What's the most important or easiest-to-implement control that can prevent you from compromising a system or network?

Proper account configuration, namely, applying the principle of least privilege. Smaller businesses have the advantage of being just that—small. Before their environment grows too big, they can work to keep access tightened up and allow access only where needed on an individual basis. To a red teamer, an over-privileged account is gold because it can be used "as intended," and this often does not get caught.

Why do you feel it is critical to stay within the rules of engagement?
It's important because the rules of engagement (ROE) are, above everything else, an agreement of trust. No matter how much the customer welcomes and believes in red teaming, they want you to behave in a manner that is best for the organization. Going rogue and breaking that trust will lead to a bad relationship that could spread throughout the organization.

If you were ever busted on a penetration test or other engagement, how did you handle it?
Getting caught is not a bad thing! Being on a red team means being kept (somewhat) in the dark as to what new defensive measures are being rolled out. Getting caught can mean that those defenses are working, and every red teamer should expect and want to get caught...sometimes.

> "Getting caught is not a bad thing!"

On one such occasion, I was working toward the objective of spreading malware when my mule host, which was hosting the malware payload, got discovered. This became a race against time with blue now being able to better track where I was. Ultimately, I was still partially successful but also burned. This created a great opportunity for red and blue to work closely together. We both did some things well and some things poorly, but it created a discussion on how to better stop an attack of that nature at the root level.

What is the biggest ethical quandary you experienced while on an assigned objective?
There have been some social engineering pretexts that made my stomach churn, such as leveraging a natural disaster or national tragedy. You just know you are pulling on people's heartstrings and exploiting the good in human beings, so that makes it hard to pull the trigger. However, I have to remind myself that the real bad actors are using these techniques, so it is all for the greater good (I hope!).

How does the red team work together to get the job done?
The duration of an internal red team operation will differ from organization to organization, but there's a good chance they are all shorter than the length of a real adversary's campaign, so working as a team is the only way to accomplish everything on time.

During an operation, it is best to have well-documented processes and procedures that ensure that all team members are properly documenting their work and communicating it with the larger team. It is also good to ensure that the customer POCs are kept in the know based on our ROE with them. This is all managed by an operation lead who is responsible for ensuring that our procedures are followed and that any outstanding issues or impediments are properly communicated up the chain.

Afterward, I recommend a service that is centered around burning any TTP that was successful during the operation. This is accomplished by the red team and blue team working closely together to replay the TTP, determine what evidence is present, gain full awareness of all associated IOCs, and then put a plan in action to prevent and/or detect the activity. This teamwork between the groups has been amazing in gaining increased defensive measures in a short time.

What is your approach to debriefing and supporting blue teams after an operation is completed?

My belief is that the blue team should have full knowledge of an operation and the tactics that were used after an operation is complete. Simply put, if the red team can be successful, then so can the bad guy. Being able to burn TTPs and increase defenses as a result of a red team operation is why they are conducted in the first place.

It is sometimes not enough just to hand over a report. Ideally, red and blue should sit down and work through the attack path again so that everyone can see it working in real time. I have found that this allows for "light bulbs" to go off and for defenders to come up with innovative solutions.

If you were to switch to the blue team, what would be your first step to better defend against attacks?

I would focus on getting offensive training for all blue team members. Through teaching in the classroom and mentoring in the workplace, I have had the privilege to train many blue team folks on offensive techniques. These people are extremely skilled at their jobs but have never had the opportunity to experience an attack from the other side. Being able to understand how an attacker operates and thinks is extremely useful and creates "light bulb" moments that result in full situational awareness of the problem and creative solutions. I believe this allows defenders to triage events more quickly and come up with root-cause analysis rather than just fixing problems on the surface.

"Technical writing is an art, and doing it well comes with experience."

What is some practical advice on writing a good report?

Technical writing is an art, and doing it well comes with experience. A common misbelief is that a good report is long, but that is certainly not the case, and you're just making more work for yourself. I encourage my team to focus on the facts and tell a good (and accurate) story. Be concise in your writing so that your reader doesn't get lost in technical jargon but instead can follow along and understand what you, the attacker, did and why you did it.

How do you ensure your program results are valuable to people who need a full narrative and context?

This speaks to the art of writing a good narrative. An operation's story should include the weaknesses that were exploited, but it shouldn't call them out in a way that makes the audience feel dumb. The report should speak in terms of what an "attacker did to our network" instead what "I did to you." Results should be presented in a manner where you are back on their side of the fence and discussing what improvements can be done together, for the better of the organization. State the facts of what happened and how the collective "we" are going to fix them.

How do you recommend security improvements other than pointing out where it's insufficient?

It's best to come prepared with real, plausible recommendations to the problems you are pointing out. It's also imperative to be humble and admit what you do not know. As a red team, you exploited a weakness, and that's a fact. Now present what you know in terms of how you could be stopped in the future, while welcoming additional input to the solution. It's also important to recognize that the ideal fix may not be a reality. There are many forces at play (politics, prioritization, money, and more) that can prevent a defender from implementing a solution. In some cases, the problem may already be known, but a red team exploiting it may serve as the leverage needed for leadership to prioritize remediation.

What nontechnical skills or attitudes do you look for when recruiting and interviewing red team members?

Check your ego at the door. Internal red teams need to be able to work with each other and defenders to achieve the same common goal. Any bad attitude can kill the team dynamic, and an ego can ruin internal relationships. On the other side, someone who has a passion for tradecraft is a dream candidate. I want the person who is always willing to learn from others and spends time honing their skills because they know that job is never complete. They will become an excellent red teamer in no time and will never stop growing.

One of the best nontechnical skills is the ability to convey technical information at a high level. It's not just about the words that you choose but also being able to read and understand your audience. You must have patience with a nontechnical audience, and explaining complex concepts in relatable terms can go a long way to connecting with all the other important teams within the organization. It's imperative to remember that your organization is full of really smart people, but not everyone is specialized in every area. Teach others and let them teach you.

> "It's imperative to remember that your organization is full of really smart people, but not everyone is specialized in every area. Teach others and let them teach you."

What differentiates good red teamers from the pack as far as approaching a problem differently?

Patience and creativity. On red team operations you sometimes get only one shot at exploiting a weakness, so you cannot be too eager to jump in. The red teamer who can take a step back, spend time assessing the situation, and come up with a cunning solution will not only be successful but also set a great example for the rest of the team. ■

"Even though the term *red team* has been around, there is still much debate on what a true definition is and what constitutes a red team with regard to cybersecurity."

Twitter: @HackingDave

David Kennedy

23

David Kennedy is the founder of two organizations: TrustedSec and Binary Defense Systems (BD). David is an avid gamer, a father of three, and passionate about coding, hacking, and red teaming. David previously was a chief security officer (CSO) for a Fortune 1000 company with offices in more than 77 countries. Considered a forward thinker in the security field, he is a keynote speaker at some of the nation's largest conferences and a guest on several national news organizations. He also worked on cyber warfare for the U.S. Marine Corps (USMC) and on forensics for the intelligence community, including two tours in Iraq.

How did you get your start on a red team?

Even though the term *red team* has been around, there is still much debate on what a true definition is and what constitutes a red team with regard to cybersecurity. Red teams outside of the industry would be defined more as a way to challenge current rationale and thought and to provide alternative contexts and forward-thinking ideas. I remember the term *red teaming* in the intelligence community when I was working for the U.S. Marine Corps; it was used as an early form of challenging current mission strategies and providing additional outcomes as alternatives to mission-critical objectives.

I for one believe that red teaming is the ability of more of an advanced organization to conduct real-world simulations in a way that emulates adversary attackers who are within the capabilities of an organization's threat model. While that might be a mouthful, red teaming's intent is to understand the capabilities of adversaries and to emulate them in a way that bolsters an organization's defenses through the way an adversary would.

Why this is important in today's world is that most organizations are at a "basic" form of cybersecurity. What I mean by that is organizations rely primarily on technology to fix non-technology-related problems. For the few that have risen above the purchase-to-protect model and for organizations that understand their business objectives and how to protect them, red teaming can be a way to test the effectiveness of the program and to advance it.

I would say my first true red team was when I got out of the Corps in 2005. I was working for a small boutique consulting shop where we were performing full-scope engagements against companies. One of my favorite and first ones was for an energy company. They wanted to assess their ability to withstand a hostile entity attempting to take control of the organization. I remember doing early stages of open source intelligence gathering (OSINT) and profiling the company and finding the best entry point into the organization. I also looked at what their major threats would be, and with a low internet-facing presence, we decided to focus on the physical entry path and place a device that would call back from their network.

We started off first during the day by going through and understanding the traffic flow (ingress/egress) of the building. The place was staffed 24/7 with armed guards, and we decided night entry might be the best route. We first climbed over a barbed-wire fence through a helicopter pad and to the facility's back entrance right by the parking garage. We had previously done reconnaissance and decided that it would be the best entry point into the building because of the camera placements through the day. We got to the door and realized...no door handles. Oops. We noticed a small gap on the top of the door and started applying a substantial amount of pressure to the door frame—boom, door opens up. No alarm. Golden.

We then proceeded to the objectives; our first target was the CEO (based on the customer request). This part is pretty funny—to get to the CEO desk, we had to go through the main lobby second-story foyer. This is where the security guards sat. On the first floor, there was a command center in the lobby area with monitors plastered everywhere showing all of the cameras. You could literally see us on the monitors as we tiptoed behind the back of the security guard on the second floor as we walked into the executive area. The guard wasn't paying attention, luckily for us. We placed a keystroke logger on the executive's desk and then proceeded to the data center. We were able to use lockpicks to get access to the back exit into the data center. Conveniently enough, there was a bathroom in the data center; we had been going at it for a few hours, and I really needed to use the restroom (sorry, TMI). It was the first time I had ever seen a bathroom in a data center. I was really fascinated about this.

We had completed all of our objectives; we verified that our device was establishing a connection back to home base and that we had visibility into their full network. It was time to call it quits, grab a beer at the bar after, and high-five each other. As we were leaving the building to go back to the same entrance we had initially breached in the first place, there were saloon-type doors (double-sided doors that swung back and forth). There was a large crack in the middle of them, and I peered through the door to check the hallway to ensure we were clear. Immediately I panicked—there was a security guard right on the other side walking to the doors. I looked at my partner and said, "We are f'ed."

As soon as I said that, the guard walked through the door, and the total shock and fear on both his part and ours is something that I will never forget. My heart sank into my feet, and I began to freeze up. I noticed the guard moving his hands toward his holster as if to draw his gun. At this point, I didn't know what to do; I couldn't even say a word. He looked at both of us dressed in all black, lockpicks in hand, throat mics for communication—classic burglars.

Officer: "Whoa, whoa. What the heck. What are you two doing here, and who are you?" At this point I didn't know what to do; I literally just said the first thing that came to mind.

Me: "Uh, whoa, dude, sir, we are here in IT; we had a server crash and have been working all night. This thing was a mighty big pain in the rear. We got it up, though. I didn't mean to startle you."

I probably should have told him who we were, that we were authorized to conduct physical activities on this company, and come clean—especially with someone who is armed, but I didn't.

Officer: "Phew. Okay, wow, you guys almost gave me a heart attack. Glad everything worked out, and have a great night."

That was my first red team. After that, I never looked back.

What is the best way to get a red team job?

A red team is a culmination of multiple skill sets, usually compiled into both technical and nontechnical. Having experience in different areas can land you a red team gig and allow you to dedicate yourself full-time to red team engagements. For example, usually during a red team exercise, all avenues of going after an organization are on the table including physical, wireless, external, internal, social, and more. Honing your skills in these areas can help you get a red team job. Some of the best red teamers I've met were former developers, systems administrators, network engineers, and law enforcement.

> "Having experience in different areas can land you a red team gig and allow you to dedicate yourself full-time to red team engagements."

For most red teams in general, at least most of the ones we focus on, being able to perform large-scale open source intelligence gathering on an organization, building threat models against adversaries, and being able to create customized infrastructure and tooling can help land a red team job. This comes with experience and practice. Red teaming is not an entry-level position but one that spawns from having skill sets in multiple areas around cybersecurity. Penetration testing is a great start and you can expand yourself from there.

I remember a number of years ago working as a CSO for a Fortune 1000 company and we hired Lares Consulting, which is run by Chris Nickerson and Eric Smith, to come and do our red team for that year. I felt pretty good about our security program and where we were headed, but I needed validation on where we were. I knew it was far from perfect and never would be, but I wanted to understand where I needed to focus my efforts. Chris and Eric did a physical assessment, and I piggybacked with them on it. I remember going to the front of the building and Chris had some copper wiring in his bag. We had a small gap in the front of our building, and there was a crash bar, but it was activated by touch (energy). Chris wedged the door open and placed a wire from one side of the door onto the crash bar and used his hands to generic static electricity. The door opened. We all started laughing hysterically about how cool that was; then we moved through the building, which was monitored 24/7 by armed guards. Walking through the building waving at the cameras and then getting to each of the objectives, I realized I had a lot more work to do both physically and soon on the network as well. Once they were inside, they plugged some hidden devices in and were able to gain access to key objectives on the network. I learned a lot of great new tricks that day.

For me specifically, my job started off doing everything—risk assessments, penetration tests, physical assessments, forensics, wireless, and more. I started learning each of the areas around cybersecurity and expanding my skills. I started writing my first tool, called Fast-Track (exploitation framework), and crafting my skills. The ability to create your own custom stuff, including crafting exploits, command-and-control frameworks, and evasion when it comes to red teaming, is important when emulating more advanced adversaries. I looked up to a number of inspirational people in the security industry, including Mati Aharoni, Chris Nickerson, HD Moore, FX, Bruce Potter, Mudge, and a number of other just amazing, brilliant people and learned from them. I also learned the soft skills from a longtime mentor of mine, Scott Angelo, who I really credit for my ability to talk to executives and higher-level individuals but also stay grounded.

When I was working at the boutique security company, Scott left and went to a Fortune 1000 company and brought me over to run their security program as their CSO. I credit a lot of my success and my career today to him, but most importantly, he guided me in a fashion that allowed me to stay technical but also focus on strategy and program-building. Chris Nickerson and Scott Angelo are key role models and the reason why I started TrustedSec, and I leaned on them heavily when I was looking to leave a perfectly great job to start my own companies. Long story short, surround yourself with amazing people and friends who are willing to help you make decisions and guide you when making huge ones to validate that you aren't crazy. Thanks to Chris and Scott, my companies have more than 170 employees worldwide and are trusted by some of the largest companies in the world. Now I get to work with friends every single day and make the world a better place!

How can someone gain red team skills without getting in trouble with the law?

There are a number of organizations out there that you can join, especially in consulting, where you learn as you go and learn from others. For me, learning from others was imperative and important early on in my career. My biggest advice for anyone looking to get into red teaming is to drop the ego and recognize that you have a ton to learn and will always have a ton to learn. Learn from anyone who is willing to teach you and build on your own experiences. Learn from others—that is the best skill you can learn.

When it comes to honing your skills, pick up easy ones such as lockpicking, understand wireless technologies, and take jobs that build on your skills, such as penetration testing. Those will help you start to gain knowledge on red teaming. Remember, you don't need to be the best at everything; focus your skills on the areas in which you learn the best and that you enjoy the most and be average at the rest. For me, after getting out of the military, I joined a small boutique consulting shop that allowed me to dabble in pretty much everything and grow my skills over time.

More on the technical side, learn as much as you can with cyber ranges, capture the flags, and offensive security courses. They are applied learning where you have to go and actually attack systems in a controlled environment to learn some of the finer arts around penetration testing and exploitation. Their course curriculum scales as well, from pentesting with Kali all the way to advanced Windows exploitation. I remember sitting at BlackHat a number of years ago with the instructor Matteo Memelli, who absolutely blew my mind on kernel exploitation. I remember sitting there with Dave from Dual Core, and we were literally competing back and forth trying to see who could finish the exercises first for fun. Learning this way and keeping it fun and exciting is critical to learning and it's also critical to learn in a way that's ethical and legal. I can't emphasize this enough—stick with your ethics. Don't do things illegally, and learn the right way!

Why can't we agree on what a red team is?

I think most of the security industry agrees on the term *red teaming*; the deviations or questions center on what the purpose and intent of a red team is. A red team is not a penetration test; a penetration test is not a red team. Let's just be clear there. A red team is a group either internal to the organization or external (consulting as an example) that understands the capabilities of the organization that is being attacked, understands the threat models the organization faces, and can develop ways to emulate and circumvent to achieve certain objectives. This includes going after an organization with any means possible (within the rules of engagement). Where the confusion comes into play is how organizations interpret red team results, or the purpose or intent of a red team. It isn't to demonstrate that your company's security sucks; it's to demonstrate that there are ways to improve.

There's a lot of debate right now on disclosure of new research techniques and whether red team research should also contribute to large conglomerate companies that are using the research industry as a way to secure their own products. At TrustedSec, we have an entire group dedicated to researching new capabilities for more of our advanced customers to simulate more precise and targeted attacks from high-end nation-states. In stating that, we don't hoard zero days and responsibly disclose them; however, we do keep close to our chest specific techniques, customized infrastructure and agents, and capabilities or bypasses for products in order to effectively do our jobs. In stating that, we always work with our customers to build detection capabilities in them. Justin Elze runs our practice on the red team side and Carlos Perez is on the research division, and we are always super cautious and balance the need to release attack vectors that could do substantial harm versus keeping real-world simulation tools at our disposal to do our jobs effectively.

Real-world simulations keep you sharp and test pretty much everything an information security program is designed to do, including your incident response, detection capabilities, vulnerability management, and more. It literally stress tests your entire security program that you strive to make better. The after-action items are where you need to improve and raise the bar to make the organization more resilient to attack.

What is one thing the rest of information security doesn't understand about being on a red team? What is the most toxic falsehood you have heard related to red, blue, or purple teams?

We get a number of organizations that want a "red team" because it sounds cool and they want something different than a penetration test. Most organizations are not designed to handle red team engagements because it requires a certain level of maturity in the security program. For example, if you don't already have visibility into your organization through monitoring and detection capabilities, a red team probably isn't the right fit for you. It's true that a red team can be used to show how ineffective the current program is and use that as leverage, but most of the time it's overkill and more expensive than other methods.

Another falsehood is that the red team's mission is to destroy the organization without remorse. The purpose of a red team isn't to be this amazing force that is so elite that the organization can't build defenses. Our whole purpose as a red team is to work and strive for the organization to get better at defenses and to be an expert on attack patterns and how a compromise is uncovered within an organization. That's why more of the purple team approach fits most companies.

A purple team is the blue team (defense) and the red team (offense) coming together to work and build defenses together. This is often more of a simulation, where the red team comes up with scenarios and objectives and works through each of the phases of an attack in conjunction with the blue team being in lockstep with every move. When an attack is launched, the blue team is there looking to identify if it can be seen. The objectives are for red to understand the defense but most importantly for blue to see whether they can either prevent or detect the specific phase of an attack. This goes from initial exploitation all the way to post-exploitation and exfiltration and every step in between.

When should you introduce a formal red team into an organization's security program?

When a company has reached a level where they have the visibility needed (which can and should change frequently) and they have a team that is actively looking for indicators of compromise within their organization, then it's probably a good time to introduce the red team. Prevention in general takes a substantial amount of time to implement within an organization; however, detection usually doesn't. Red teams can help prioritize and prepare both the long-term prevention strategies as well as gaps in visibility that you may have in your organization. If your monitoring capabilities are still immature, a red team probably isn't in your best interest or your best use of time. At this point in the game, endpoint logs are a must for visibility.

This also gets into the conversation around third-party managed security providers (MSPs). If you are leveraging a third party, ensuring that the organization is comfortable with red team engagements or collaborative purple teams to get better is important. I highly recommend making sure your current vendor is supportive of these types of simulations for the MSP to get better at detection as well.

How do you explain the value of red teaming to a reluctant or nontechnical client or organization?

Understanding the objectives of a red team and ensuring that the reasons for conducting them are fully explained is important. The purpose is to simulate what an adversary that is similar to those that would target your organization would do if they spent time going after you. This is about as real as it gets without having an actual adversary compromise you. If you've built a security program and you want to test its effectiveness, a red team is a must. Communicating the value and ensuring that the program is heading in the right direction can help reassure the reluctant folks and push the objectives forward.

> "If you've built a security program and you want to test its effectiveness, a red team is a must."

What is the *least* bang-for-your-buck security control that you see implemented?

Data loss prevention. It's usually more static in nature over specific business processes looking for Social Security numbers and credit card data. It almost never detects attackers as exfiltrating data occurs. In fact, I can't think of one time I've ever seen a company detect exfiltration of data with data loss prevention in my 18 years in the cybersecurity industry. Information classification within an organization is an extremely daunting task that requires an entire culture shift in order to tag data appropriately within an organization. I really haven't seen many companies fully implement this; as a whole company it's just difficult to scale and to enforce.

Have you ever recommended not doing a red team engagement?

All the time. It's important for organizations to understand the level of maturity needed to conduct a red team and the objectives of it. Most organizations need a penetration test in order to identify what gaps they have. Most organizations don't have a long-term strategy around capabilities and focus more on the tactics and procedures of attackers versus the techniques. Most organizations aren't ready for a red team.

In the industry, people need advisors and people to help them build their security programs. If they aren't designed to handle or ingest what a red team produces, it shouldn't be something you start off with.

What's the most important or easiest-to-implement control that can prevent you from compromising a system or network?

Enabling the Windows Firewall on workstations. Seriously, do this. One of the main ways we move laterally is by compromising one system and then moving onto the next. While this isn't a perfect solution, it does prevent me as an attacker from moving from one workstation to the next by harvesting either local admin credentials, cached credentials, Kerberos tokens, or other areas for data. While this doesn't protect your server infrastructure, it removes a substantial attack surface and forces me into the servers.

Application control/application whitelisting. While it might not be the "easiest" to do, there are a number of solutions that you probably already have that can stop several attacks out there. For example, Microsoft has Software Restriction Policies, AppLocker, and Device Guard. Just by doing simple things like blocking PowerShell from regular users and blocking non-code-signed binaries in user profile directories can have a *huge* impact on your infections and thwart a number of attacks.

Why do you feel it is critical to stay within the rules of engagement?

Rules of engagement shouldn't be so restrictive that they tie up the entire engagement in a way that doesn't allow a real-world simulation. However, there should be some limits to what is acceptable and the level of engagement you are willing to do. We've had engagements in which we crowbarred a door open and caused physical damage. That might not be for you, and rules of engagement help define what the objectives of the engagement are and ultimately what the outcomes are.

If you were ever busted on a penetration test or other engagement, how did you handle it?

There was one that comes to mind where we were doing an engagement for a retail customer. We decided that the daytime would be the best time to get into the building physically. We piggybacked and got into a side entrance to the corporate headquarters of this retail company. That was the easy part; the next phase was to get access to the data center, and there were specific objectives to do once in the data center. We found an open conference room inside the corporate headquarters and behind the security checkpoints and called 0 for the company directory and found the extension to the data center. We called the data center and had a pretext that we were auditors coming to do a survey of the data center and to let us in.

<Ring, ring, ring>

Bob: "Hello, this is Bob from the data center. How can I help you?"

Me: "Hey, Bob! It's Joe from security. We have some auditors here in the conference room going through our PCI audit, and they need to review the logs of everyone coming in and out of the data center as well as access to walk freely to look at the camera placements and the physical controls for our data center. I'll be sending them down; can you let them in?"

<Long pause>

Bob: "I'm sorry, who did you say this was?"

Me: "It's Joe Smith from security; my extension is 1111."

Bob: "Um, I'm best friends with Joe, and you definitely are not Joe. What is going on here?"

<Phone click>

Frantic running to a different location. We ended up cloning a badge from someone leaving the data center and then getting access to the data center, but we got so busted initially.

What is the biggest ethical quandary you experienced while on an assigned objective?

Social engineering is a tough one for me, especially morally. I pride myself on being an honest person, but in social engineering it's the exact opposite of that. You have to remember that you are doing this for the greater good and an attempt to identify how education can be more effective or how controls may fail. You are doing this to help others. I always attempt to do social engineering from the perspective of positivity and do not try to use negative persuasion as a method to achieve my objectives.

How does the red team work together to get the job done?

It really is a team effort. For red team engagements that I've been on, we each play a critical role in attaining the objectives. For example, if I'm breaking in physically, someone assigned to the physical reconnaissance and best entry points is paramount. Once inside, someone handles the implant or technology that will be used to establish access to the organization or meet the objectives. If we are talking more externally, having expertise in applications, perimeter defenses, and more becomes really important. Oftentimes for a red team, when we gain initial code execution on a system, understanding the capabilities of the organization and what will get us flagged is important. Having team members who can communicate and help evade detection is important.

Lastly, remember that the red team uses mutual respect and collaboration between red and blue to help bolster an organization's defenses and to understand where the security program can improve through real-world simulations.

What is your approach to debriefing and supporting blue teams after an operation is completed?

There are a few different approaches. One of the more collaborative approaches is purple teaming, where the exercise is conducted in real time with both red and blue working together at the same time. With red teaming, the ability to reproduce your steps with examples, timing, and artifacts is important in order to respond after the fact. Out of a red team should come two objectives—strategic and technical remediation efforts. Technical means a specific fix, detection, or preventative measure that could stop the techniques used. Strategic means figuring out how we prevent the tactics and procedures (or detect them) in the future so these types of attacks aren't successful or are stopped earlier.

If you were to switch to the blue team, what would be your first step to better defend against attacks?

When looking at not just today but tomorrow, there is no longer a castle mentality to protecting an organization. We don't have archers, moats, heavily fortified walls—we have a tent city with patrols occurring through the streets and distributed across a vast expanse of land. In this type of model, our traditional security principles don't fit, and we (in security) have to adjust appropriately. The priority is not on how much we can protect a company with shifting technology, but how we can minimize the damage in the event we have a lapse in security. Do we really care if Bob in sales is compromised? Well, maybe. However, in the grand scheme of things, Bob isn't going to cause a substantial breach that will cause the company a significant amount of damage. Can we detect Bob's computer as it's compromised or shortly after? Possibly. If we do, can we stop the spreading (lateral movement) to other systems? Yes.

> "The priority is not on how much we can protect a company with shifting technology, but how we can minimize the damage in the event we have a lapse in security."

We now live in an era where protection takes a substantial amount of time to implement, and detection has to become our number-one priority to move as fast as new attacks are coming out.

What is some practical advice on writing a good report?

Communication on findings and how a company can ingest what occurred during a red team is *the* most important element to any test. I, for one, enjoy writing reports because it is a representation of the work and time that went into trying to effectively test the company's security controls. Focus both on the positives that they do well and on where they can get better. It's about telling a story and how you got to the point you are at now. Instead of thinking about how much reporting sucks, think about the value you are providing them and, if they implement everything you say, how much harder and how much more of a challenge it will be in the next go-around.

When writing a report, know your audience. Executive summaries are your time to shine and tell your story about what happened and why. At a high level, summarize what you accomplished—the good and the areas for improvement. Focus the narrative on how the organization is doing when confronted with targeted attacks and how they can improve (from a high level). Then, from there, focus on telling the story more technically, focusing on the same thing you just explained in the executive summary, and move into the meat of the report—the findings. Make sure they are reproducible and provide as much information as possible in order for the reader to clearly understand what they are looking for. Recommendations shouldn't be to visit a site; it should be a clear road map and strategy around fixing the problems identified.

I remember when I coauthored the book *Metasploit: The Penetration Tester's Guide* with some of my good friends. Our publisher was No Starch Press, and Bill Pollock (an amazing individual) was peer reviewing the book. I remember I wrote this one chapter; I think it was on post-exploitation, and I thought it was the greatest chapter ever. Bill literally emailed me saying, "Dave, while this is cool from your perspective, a reader going through this would be completely lost. You need to rewrite this entire chapter." At the time, I was frustrated and upset. How could he say that? How could he make me rewrite the entire chapter? I then decided, you know what, let me have someone who isn't in cybersecurity read this and tell me what they think. After page 2, they stopped reading and said, "Listen, this sounds cool, but I don't know what any of this means." Bingo. From there on out, I always tried to write anything from the perspective of the individual reading what I wrote.

How do you ensure your program results are valuable to people who need a full narrative and context?

A red team approach isn't about showcasing weaknesses or your team's individual skill sets. It's to showcase how well a company does (both strengths and weaknesses) and where the bar can be raised. When you look at a security program, there are multiple pieces that consist of what we call security today. Ranging from governance to vulnerability management and everything in between, a security program is complex, and oftentimes an organization feels they are in a good spot, but are they really? Or they aren't sure where to prioritize next. That's where red teams can help—both strategy and validation.

How do you recommend security improvements other than pointing out where it's insufficient?

A good example of this is pointing out the positives of a security program and where it does well. Then focus on where it can continue to move forward and which direction it can improve on. It's not saying it's insufficient; it's stating that anything can be improved upon. When you look at an organization's threat model and the sophistication of different adversaries, being able to model your attacks on relevant attack vectors that are a high likelihood can help map what level of attacker is needed and the types of controls you have in place. Maybe your program is adequate to a certain level but deficient in others based on the capabilities of other attackers.

What nontechnical skills or attitudes do you look for when recruiting and interviewing red team members?

Red teaming is not just about technical skills—although in certain circumstances they are still very important. For me, the number-one skill is the ability to communicate what they performed in a way that everyone can understand. Sometimes how we attack can be complex, and the story or message we tell back can be equally confusing or complex. Being able to break down and communicate complex messages in a way that all audiences can understand is a desirable skill and one that a lot of us lack in the cybersecurity space. A good example of this is someone I hired who is memorable for me, Jason Lang.

"Being able to break down and communicate complex messages in a way that all audiences can understand is a desirable skill and one that a lot of us lack in the cybersecurity space."

In the early DerbyCon days, I remember someone whom I had never met came up to me and at the time was a developer and interested in security. He pulled me aside at the Hyatt, right outside of the capture-the-flag room in the back, and said, "Hey, Dave! I'm looking to getting into security; I'm an application developer—what thoughts do you have for me?" I remember just listening to his experiences and where he wanted to go, and I was already blown away at his ability to explain his vision and grasp what we were looking for. I gave him some words of advice and how I would approach cybersecurity and spent about 10 minutes with him.

Flash-forward several years; Jason starts to publish his own tools and is on a red team and doing what he enjoys. He now is one of our top senior security consultants on the red team running in our adversary emulation team. Most importantly, Jason's soft skills and his ability to communicate what he does to others has landed him as a regular favorite with customers. We just had a customer today ask for Jason specifically by name because of his thoroughness and the way he communicated to the customer. The customer's reaction was this: "We took everything Jason did for us last year and incorporated it. It's going to be super challenging for you folks this year." We love that!

"Red teaming is a culmination of skill sets. Not one person alone knows all that there is to know about a specific subject."

What differentiates good red teamers from the pack as far as approaching a problem differently?

Red teaming is a culmination of skill sets. Not one person alone knows all that there is to know about a specific subject. Being able to pool one another's strengths and weaknesses to create a cohesive team is important. Having time for research and development (R&D) or a completely dedicated R&D team for capabilities and infrastructure is equally important. There's no question that defense is getting better within many companies, and that is an awesome thing to see. It's increasingly harder for us as hackers to break into organizations. To continue forward and to stay current, you need a team that has time to develop their tactics, techniques, and procedures and to incorporate them into the team. You need to be able to understand defenses, how they apply, and most importantly how you can evade them. At the end of the day, we are only as good as the team we are on. We work as a team, and we fail as a team.

I remember one engagement we were on where we ran against a blue team that literally shut us down on everything we did. It was bad (for us), and we honestly took that to heart. As a red team, we felt defeated—we were both impressed with the capabilities of this organization and vowed that we would do better next time and not let that happen again. This striving for greatness and mutual respect to get better can make a world of difference. ∎

> "Build on your existing strengths and add some computer hacking skills to help you get your foot in the door."

Twitter: @doratexplorer17

Maggie Ligon

Maggie Ligon exercises her passion for security as a pentester at a fast-paced consulting firm, performing assessments of wireless, network, web, and physical environments. She specializes in web app tests and architecting reporting tools and techniques for her team to maximize writing efficiency while also producing high-quality, useful reports. After hours she can be found drawing, looking for dogs to befriend, and enjoying time with her friends and family.

24

How did you get your start on a red team?
After pentesting on internal teams for a few years, I decided it was time to take on a new challenge and started applying. I got a few callbacks from online applications, but what actually worked the best was going to InfoSec meetings and meeting people, which introduced me to teams I didn't even know existed.

What is the best way to get a red team job?
If you're starting from an InfoSec position, I'd recommend looking into consulting companies that offer red teaming as a service and really huge companies that can afford their own internal red teams. Additionally, I highly recommend visiting your local InfoSec groups; someone is always hiring or has their ear to the ground and can point you in the right direction.

One of the great things about InfoSec is all the wildly different backgrounds people have. I've known people who started as suburban stay-at-home parents, juvenile delinquents, journalists, veterans, software developers, accountants, retail workers, you name it! If you're coming from a background that doesn't

"One of the great things about InfoSec is all the wildly different backgrounds people have. I've known people who started as suburban stay-at-home parents, juvenile delinquents, journalists, veterans, software developers, accountants, retail workers, you name it!"

seem related, I'd first try a little thought exercise: write down five skills you have that could be applied to breaking into a company. Example: "Retail workers and parents: you're able to negotiate with highly irrational people." This is *great* for social engineering.

Build on your existing strengths and add some computer hacking skills to help you get your foot in the door. To actually find and secure a job, take the same steps as the InfoSec folks: apply with confidence to either consulting companies or huge firms, and go to local InfoSec meetings.

How can someone gain red team skills without getting in trouble with the law?

Software and hardware hacking:

- Join a bug bounty program.
- Do capture-the-flag (CTF) exercises.
- Learn how to build whatever you're interested in tearing down, such as code or locks.
- Work on vulnerable practice environments (the "Damn Vulnerable" series, for example).
- Attend local InfoSec group meetings and conferences.

Search engine skills: these are hugely important for red teaming; try to figure it out on your own as much as possible. The ability to learn is far more important than being an expert in one niche thing, especially on a red team.

People hacking and physical security: there are many resources for technological study and growth. For the more human side of social engineering and physical assessments, legality can be more difficult to achieve. One way to practice is to put yourself in uncomfortable (but still legal and safe!) situations. What people group/situation brings out your inner "nope"? Do you hate crowds? Hit up a busy mall on a Saturday and go into every open shop and identify one security flaw or feature, such as distracted staff or a camera. Don't feel like you belong? Good! Embrace that and *act* like you belong. Are you that one person in InfoSec who loves crowds? Go somewhere where you're expected to be alone and silent, like a peace garden or a museum. Sit in it. The goal is to be able to read a space and adjust to the atmosphere without thinking about it, with no reference to your comfort level.

Active listening and empathy will open all sorts of doors. People love to be heard, and the more relaxed they are, the more they'll share. Two-for-one exercise: practice actively listening to a friend or family member. You get practice and an opportunity to deepen your relationship!

Why can't we agree on what a red team is?

Computer science and InfoSec are pretty young fields, language is fluid, and *red team* sounds cooler than *security scanning* or *pentesting*. People naturally want to play up the awesome sides of InfoSec to sell services and look cool.

When should you introduce a formal red team into an organization's security program?

Minimum level: you've had several pentests from independent parties, your information is that valuable, and your existing security teams are more or less able to do their jobs. This means you have offensive and defensive people working full time and their input is taken seriously at all levels of the company.

"What are you doing *not* having a red team?" level: the data you want to protect is highly valuable, your company has a big attack surface, and your security program includes offense, defense, and a secure SDLC.

What is the *least* bang-for-your-buck security control that you see implemented?

For the love of all that is blue, red, or purple, if you don't understand basics like input validation, you're not going to configure that tool correctly. It doesn't matter whether it's the world's best monitoring system, an expensive WAF, or a bike padlock. Basically anything on which you spend money before you've hired at least one knowledgeable person is only going to go so far.

Annual security slideshows with little quizzes also do nothing. The people who care *already* care and the people who don't are just going to click through and learn nothing.

What's the most important or easiest-to-implement control that can prevent you from compromising a system or network?

Knowledge and buy-in. Management and employees with a healthy amount of paranoia and the ability to secure their work are formidable opponents. Great Aunt Matilda operating the building entrance mantrap is much less effective than Paranoia Patrick guarding the open-plan office from a folding table. Aunty M. will of course let the nice young pregnant lady in! How sweet, she's bringing cookies for her husband, Frank! Patrick will ask why she's not on the visitor list, call Frank and find out he's not married, and ask her to leave. It's not the easiest to implement, but it's definitely the most important.

Easiest? Look up *secure configuration <myTechnology>* and go wild.

Why do you feel it is critical to stay within the rules of engagement?

Because I'm not a big fan of being incarcerated (or destroying my client's business).

If you were ever busted on a penetration test or other engagement, how did you handle it?

On one of my earlier formal (internal network) tests, the defense team noticed when we connected to the network and ran a scan. They quickly paraded over to our area and let us know, and my senpai's response was to get as excited as they were. You caught us? It's 8:35 a.m. on Monday! Guess I'll have to up my game; thanks for letting me know.

If you're sincere and truly appreciative of others' skill, saying so can build alliances. Share information. Ask what they caught you on and tell them what you've been doing; both teams can improve together.

I also got caught cold-calling people, but in my defense they were all security people, so they knew better. I just got off the phone and didn't let on. Then died inside.

Here's a more fun story: I was looking very, very sketchy roaming around an office looking through desks, and Greg (correctly) asked if I needed help, who I was with, and so on. So I told him I was working with the InfoSec people and... he let me wander off. I can't be sure he didn't report me, but I wasn't told that he had. Mwahaha.

What is the biggest ethical quandary you experienced while on an assigned objective?

Maybe not the biggest but the most omnipresent: drawing the line regarding scope. I know that a server has SQLi, but it's out of scope or I'm out of time. Stepping away at that point is always rough, but other clients need tests, and jail isn't fun.

How does the red team work together to get the job done?

Soft skills: Have humility, stand up for what's right, communicate, and be able to disagree and commit.

Hard skills: Writing wordz gud, being able to answer technical questions at a deep level, and being able to reproduce issues.

What is some practical advice on writing a good report?

Having been on both the receiving and sending ends of pentest reports, I highly value clear instructions on how to re-create issues. This is a little self-serving; when I do retests, I want to get through them without having to re-learn the whole environment! From developers I hear more concern about clarifying risk. After all, it's usually the developers who have to get upper management to sign off on risk acceptance.

Also, everybody likes charts and pictures; not so many like reading.

How do you recommend security improvements other than pointing out where it's insufficient?

Point out security strengths and show how they can be bolstered even further by related controls. If there's a chance to grab lunch with the blue team or have a similarly casual conversation, you can also talk about previous tests (obviously, don't breach confidentiality) or stories you've heard from other testers. Red teaming is very cool, and lots of people love to hear about interesting technical finds, narrow escapes, and epic failures, and they might absorb some useful info along the way.

What nontechnical skills or attitudes do you look for when recruiting and interviewing red team members?

A hunger for learning that massively overtakes any earned or unearned ego and the desire and ability to listen. People who refuse to learn or communicate can't adapt.

> "No single type of person is the ideal red teamer. Everyone brings something unique."

What differentiates good red teamers from the pack as far as approaching a problem differently?

No single type of person is the ideal red teamer. Everyone brings something unique. If you're on the team, you have something to offer, so offer it with confidence. What seems obvious or natural to one person can be a totally novel approach from another person's point of view. ∎

i hack

> "My idea of a perfect red team exercise is total and utter failure coupled with early detection."

Twitter: @MrJeffMan

Jeffrey Man

Jeffrey Man is a respected information security expert, advisor, evangelist, and co-host of the security podcast *Security Weekly*. He has more than 35 years of experience in all aspects of computer, network, and information security. Jeffrey has held various information security roles within the DoD as well as private-sector enterprises, is a former PCI QSA, and was part of the first penetration testing red team at the NSA.

25

How did you get your start on a red team?

I first became involved with ethical hacking in the early 90s while working for an organization entitled the Fielded Systems Evaluation Branch within the Information Systems Security Directorate (INFOSEC) at the National Security Agency (NSA). The mission of this branch was to perform security assessments against all cryptographic and communications systems developed by the NSA and currently in use by such entities as the U.S. Armed Forces, the Department of Defense, and the Department of State. One area of focus in the branch was networked systems, and my interests gravitated toward that group because they were talking about things that I had learned about by seeing such movies as *WarGames* and *Sneakers*. We basically started learning how to hack computers and networks by targeting each other's workstations and by trying to gain "root" access to our own local area network.

Shortly after I began working in the Fielded Systems Evaluations branch, the world as we knew it changed forever with the initial release of Mosaic, published by the National Center for Supercomputing Applications (NCSA) on January 23, 1993. Although we were already working with workstations, networks, and even the internet, the release of Mosaic greatly popularized the internet (or World Wide Web as it was called back then) for the general public, and this got the attention of executive leadership at the NSA. Months of extensive analysis and planning resulted in the formation of the first Center of Excellence for Network Security at the NSA, which was named the Systems & Network Attack Center (SNAC).

The formation of the SNAC involved the relocation of numerous branches and divisions from all over the INFOSEC Directorate to a single location, which ended up being a building that was part of NSA's Friendship Annex (FANX) complex near what is now Baltimore/Washington International Thurgood Marshall Airport. Our branch was included in the move, and the small group of us that was focused on learning hacking skills ended up getting our own office from which to hone our skills and practice our craft.

We were focused on learning everything we could about hacking skills, and as part of that wanted to embrace as much of hacking culture as we were able to and live the lifestyle. We built our own network within our office, bought a refrigerator and stocked it with Mountain Dew, and dubbed the name of our hacker space The Pit.

We had few tools back then to help us and very little in the way of automation. Hacker conferences weren't really a thing yet as conferences like DEF CON were just getting started (and weren't exactly friendly to "feds" anyway). There were few or no training courses available, and automated tools were almost nonexistent. What tools did exist were mostly "designed" to help network and Unix administrators secure their systems.

What we did have was eagerness to learn and access to as much information as was publicly available at the time (you just had to know where to look for it), and a few "sacred texts" such as *Practical UNIX and Internet Security* by Simson Garfinkel and Gene Spafford, *Firewalls and Internet Security: Repelling the Wily Hacker* by William R. Cheswick and Steven M. Bellovin, and of course *The Cuckoo's Egg* by Clifford Stoll.

We learned hacking skills and how to exploit "features" of many operating systems. We developed a methodology for performing what we called a vulnerability and threat assessment (VTAM); the DoD loves acronyms, after all. We performed VTAMs for many internal customers and for other DoD customers using classified networks. We were also in demand for other non-DoD and unclassified networks, so we also learned how to navigate the bureaucracy and the NSA Charter and ultimately developed a strategy for engaging with our "customers" in a reasonable time period.

We didn't call ourselves a red team at the time—that term did not exist. We were hackers.

I will put forth my definitions of the various activities in question, not with the intent of changing anyone's mind about the meanings, but simply for understanding and perspective:

Vulnerability scanning: An automated tool that reports on vulnerabilities and/or misconfigurations of targeted systems generally without any context of overall business operations

Vulnerability assessment: A process of researching, interviewing, observing how an entity's business is conducted, computing and networking operations, application development, etc., to provide recommendations on how to improve the overall security of the entity

Penetration testing: A manual exercise, performed by skilled hackers to test the defenses and/or detection capability of a target entity. Targets may vary as well as the scope of the engagement, but the overarching objective is to see how well an entity holds up to attempts at breach or compromise. In simple terms, a penetration test provides threat emulation and focuses its findings on the weaknesses in processes and operations that led to any negative result.

Red team: Still kind of a new concept for me, but I've heard most people describe a red team exercise in a similar manner to how I describe a penetration test. They go on to describe a penetration test as largely an automated process (using vulnerability scanners) to report on as many vulnerabilities as can be discovered given the targets, scope, and time frame of the engagement.

What is the best way to get a red team job?

This often seems to be the most coveted job in cybersecurity. I personally think that the majority of penetration test/red team exercises are pointless—particularly when they rely on scan results and only report on vulnerabilities. But then, I might be blurring the definitions—but that's okay since we can't universally agree on what red team means.

I'm not saying there isn't a need for skilled red teams, I'm saying that even today most companies that engage a red team aren't really ready for the exercise, so they are more often than not wasting their money.

A better engagement for the majority of companies out there would be to perform a vulnerability assessment. Some might call this a tabletop exercise, but ask any decent red teamer and they will tell you they have a pretty good idea of how they are going to break into a company just from their initial interview/kick-off session with the target.

So, the best way to get a red team job is to have demonstrated skills. But I would ask this question: Why is there so much enthusiasm/focus/training for breaking things, and is there the same emphasis on making things that are resistant to attack compromise right from the start?

> "Why is there so much enthusiasm/focus/training for breaking things, and is there the same emphasis on making things that are resistant to attack compromise right from the start?"

How can someone gain red team skills without getting in trouble with the law?

Don't do anything illegal. There are plenty of ways to practice in safe places such as CTFs or hacker spaces or build your own network/system (which is a great learning exercise anyway) and then break it.

Why can't we agree on what a red team is?

Probably for much the same reasons that nobody can agree on other terms in our industry like *security*, *risk*, *vulnerability*, or *threat*. The primary reason for lack of agreement on terminology is largely that there is no authoritative source for creating such definitions or rather, the private sector is not aware of/does not acknowledge what used to be considered the authoritative source, which was the National Information Systems Security (INFOSEC) Glossary published by the NSA in 1992.

Beyond that, I'd say the biggest problem with our terminology largely stems from lack of agreement or standardization on what are the activities, goals, or objectives of whatever-you-want-to-call-it but might be a vulnerability assessment, a penetration test, or a red team exercise.

I think it is extremely important to set expectations with the customer/target and determine the goals and objectives first, followed by rules of engagement, timing, reporting, and so forth. I began working in the private sector in 1997, delivering vulnerability assessments and penetration tests. Well, we usually performed vulnerability assessments even though the customer always asked for a penetration testing exercise. Whenever I would start talking to the customer about what they wanted in terms of services, I would ask several key questions:

- Do you want us to find all the holes that would enable an attacker to break into your environment (vulnerability assessment), or do you just want us to find one way in and see how far we can get (penetration test)?
- What do you want to get out of the engagement (goals)?
- What do you plan on doing with the results of our testing (objectives)?

Most of the time the customers had read or heard about the need for a penetration test but when pressed, they really wanted a vulnerability assessment. I usually had to coach them through the rest of the process to develop reasonable goals and objectives for the engagement but ultimately to produce a successful result.

We measured success not by being successful in gaining "root" access to the network, but in either a) being caught/detected or b) the customer learning from the experience and making real changes to their systems and their processes.

We failed more often than not.

What is one thing the rest of information security doesn't understand about being on a red team? What is the most toxic falsehood you have heard related to red, blue, or purple teams?

That red teaming should not be the ultimate goal of anyone interested in this field. There are numerous ways to make a contribution, so why do we regard red teaming as being the apex? I think building something that resists compromise is way cooler than breaking stuff (and harder too).

As for toxic falsehood, I'd pick the belief that an organization's cybersecurity program or posture begins, ends, and revolves around the hackers. Also, the vast majority of companies simply don't have the infrastructure or resources to have such things as red, blue, purple, or even IT teams. This means that the vast amount of focus on this type of craft is on a relatively small number of organizations, leaving all the rest to fend for themselves. Enter the product vendors.

When should you introduce a formal red team into an organization's security program?

When the organization has effectively built a security program starting with a basic but comprehensive understanding of what the organization has or does that has some value that is worth protecting. This could be proprietary research data, customer PII, continued operations, brand recognition, and any number of other things. Once an organization knows what it needs to protect, it needs to describe how it will accomplish this task through a series of documented policies, standards, and procedures. Then, it needs to train its employees in what they individually and collectively need to do to follow the rules put forth in said security program. They need to have put as many detection, logging, and monitoring processes in place as they can afford and to have tweaked and tuned it and trained on them. They need to have practiced through various exercises, fire drills, and tabletop exercises; reviewed the results; put in place lessons learned; and developed a certain level of appropriate paranoia for what's at stake. Then they can go ahead and hire a red team to pretend to be a bad guy and see how well the organization holds up to attack (and if it even sees the attempts).

> "Once an organization knows what it needs to protect, it needs to describe how it will accomplish this task through a series of documented policies, standards, and procedures."

How do you explain the value of red teaming to a reluctant or nontechnical client or organization?

I'm usually explaining why it's mostly unnecessary given the lack of maturity of the organization (customer) whom I am advising.

What is the least bang-for-your-buck security control that you see implemented?

Any pentest/red team exercise when the organization is not ready for it, which is most of them.

Have you ever recommended not doing a red team engagement?

All the time, especially back when I was selling/managing/performing penetration tests/vulnerability assessments. I learned to do this early in my private-sector career because one of my first engagements was to perform a pentest (red team exercise) for an organization that had recently connected to the internet but had gone out and purchased the leading firewall solution at that time and had put several folks through the firewall training. They were set, and they knew it—and I think their motivation was really to justify the investment to their skeptical management, who might have thought they were spending a little too much time and effort on something as trivial as direct internet access.

I began the reconnaissance phase of the engagement, which included attempting a port scan of the targeted IP address space. I was perplexed because I immediately started seeing results as if there wasn't a firewall in place at all. Our methodology at the time involved starting remotely and trying to gain access to the customer's network, but then we would also go on site and perform additional testing from "behind" the firewall to see where we could get throughout the network. We pretty much had a field day from the outside, so we quickly moved on site to perform additional testing. We had been testing for only a short time before we were approached by the admins accusing us of "bringing down their network." We hadn't really been doing much of anything, so I called a timeout, and we asked to see the firewall rules. You may have already guessed that the last rule was "IP ANY ANY ALLOW."

That was the point when I called off the penetration test and convinced the customer that they needed us to perform an architectural review and basically really help them set up a secure network and get the most out of their firewall.

The life lesson I learned came when we presented our report on the engagement to the CFO of the company. He commented that he was extremely impressed that we had done right by them and helped them get better instead of needlessly sticking to the letter of the contract and doing only what we had been hired to do (and then billing them for additional time for the work we ended up doing). My takeaway was that we should always do right by the client—they ended up being our customer for years after that engagement, and we ended up being not only their pentesters but their trusted advisors as well.

"We're in the security business, and when you're trusting a company/individuals to potentially gain access to everything of value in your organization, you need to know you can trust them."

What's the most important or easiest-to-implement control that can prevent you from compromising a system or network?

I don't think the answer is technical. I think the answer is to teach them what they don't know. Then they can make better informed decisions on how to invest their scarce resources. That, and outsource—with the caution that passing on responsibility for security to a third party does not automatically mean that you have passed on your potential liability. Big difference.

Why do you feel it is critical to stay within the rules of engagement?

Integrity and trust. We're in the security business, and when you're trusting a company/individuals to potentially gain access to everything of value in your organization, you need to know you can trust them. So, be trustworthy.

I learned another early lesson when I was working for a client that hired us to do a penetration test of a single IP address (which was their perimeter firewall). We were explicitly asked not to scan or attempt to gain access to any other IPs surrounding that single IP address. We did notice from a simple port scan that there were other systems responding in their registered address spaces, and just by connecting with a browser, we deduced that they were likely out-of-the-box web servers. When we reported to the big boss at this company, I presented our findings (which weren't much against the actual target) but also provided a footnote that during our reconnaissance we noticed what appeared to be default web servers that would have more than likely given us complete access to their internal network and bypassed their very tightly configured firewall. I think this time it was the CIO. His response was priceless and provided me another early life lesson. He turned to his staff and asked, "What's wrong with our processes that we are letting people get away with doing something like this?" Process. The real vulnerability wasn't the default web server—it was that someone was able to put it out there in the first place and that nobody saw it or said anything about it.

If you were ever busted on a penetration test or other engagement, how did you handle it?

In my early days in the private sector, I would sometimes port scan a "prospect" as part of the reconnaissance to help determine what kind of help they needed. I remember one time I scanned a bank that was somewhere in Europe. They had some detection mechanism in place, traced the scan back to our registered domain, and ended up sending a rather nasty "cease and desist" email to my company's CEO. When I found out about it, I contacted the originators and commended them for their detection capabilities. They were not amused.

What is the biggest ethical quandary you experienced while on an assigned objective?
The biggest quandary I can think of was in my days as a qualified security assessor (QSA) for the Payment Card Industry (PCI). One of the PCI requirements is to perform annually both an internal and external network penetration test. As a QSA, I had to first find out if the required penetration testing had been performed and then I had to obtain a copy of the report and review the findings. Too often, I had to grimace and accept a "pentest" report that was merely a Nessus report with a cover page. The big ethical quandary was when the pentest/red team was hired by my own company.

How does the red team work together to get the job done?
It's been quite a while since I was part of an active engagement, but back in the day the "team" aspect was generally a) divide and conquer, especially when coming from outside and inside; b) collaboration when necessary to try to solve a problem; c) letting each member of the team do what they did best, which meant I did most of the talking and writing and left others on the team to do the technical aspects. We would all participate in reporting and presentation of findings, as we were all eager to teach how to prevent the things that we were able to accomplish.

If you were to switch to blue team, what would be your first step to better defend against attacks?
I wouldn't, as I am not active anymore. But, I think the first step to better defend against attacks is to figure out two things—what you are protecting and what/who you are protecting against.

What is some practical advice on writing a good report?
Most, if not all, of the reports that I have had the pleasure to review over the past 15 years are heavy on automated findings output and extremely light on what I would call custom or tailored content. My idea of a good red team report is that you describe at some level the methods/techniques you tried and describe not only success but failures as well. Remember, my idea of a perfect red team exercise is total and utter failure coupled with early detection. When there is a finding, the focus should not be on "we found a vulnerability and exploited it," but rather it should be "the presence of such and such vulnerability indicates that a particular process or set of processes is failing." This should be followed up by detailed recommendations for how to address the process issues and not simply "we need to install a missing patch" or "we need to change that shared admin password to something other than Secret123."

> "My idea of a good red team report is that you describe at some level the methods/techniques you tried and describe not only success but failures as well."

How do you ensure your program results are valuable to people who need a full narrative and context?
First, insist on a presentation of findings so you can talk things through. This is always better than just delivering a poorly written, light on the right kind of details report. I always found it best to start with something positive (no matter

how hard that might be) and work your way into the details—what I call the good, bad, and ugly format for presenting bad news.

How do you recommend security improvements other than pointing out where it's insufficient?

I try to start with the basics and work my way into the more detailed/nuanced recommendations from there. The real audience is not always the group that hired you but some level of executive management, and they (no offense) usually have no clue what any of us are talking about. This is where it becomes persuasive speech, in that you are trying to make someone understand why they need to change behavior or attitudes and, most often, spend money. Context is everything, and the challenge is to explain the complexities of what needs to be done in a way that the recipient can understand it. I call it the "Art of the Jedi Mind Trick," and it involves things like listening, knowing your audience, learning to speak their language, telling stories/making analogies that fit within their frame of reference but get the point across, simplifying things, framing the discussion in the context of the business and its business processes, and not assuming they get it on the first try. Engage a feedback loop, ask them what they heard, and above all try not to overwhelm them with how bad things are. The old African proverb says, "How do you eat an elephant? One bite at a time."

What nontechnical skills or attitudes do you look for when recruiting and interviewing red team members?

I certainly would mention having good communication skills here, but I usually hear that from folks who proceed to demonstrate it poorly. Beyond that, I can only suggest what has worked for me, which is having a certain skepticism about everything, a tenacity to keep digging, not taking no for an answer, and always looking for another way—I think we can call that the hacker mentality, which is not in and of itself a technical skill but certainly goes a long way to helping one be successful in this field.

"To me the best red teamers are the ones who will walk away from or redirect a customer away from a red team exercise if they are not ready for it but will work with them to get them ready."

What differentiates good red teamers from the pack as far as approaching a problem differently?

To me the best red teamers are the ones who will walk away from or redirect a customer away from a red team exercise if they are not ready for it but will work with them to get them ready. I think what is also important is to understand what motivates a customer to request a third-party red team exercise in the first place. Is it a regulatory or compliance requirement? Have they previously been breached or compromised and now have the right attitude?

In other words, accurately defining not only what is the "problem" but putting it in context with goals, scope, objective, and expected outcomes. The best red teamers are also teachers, and teaching starts from the beginning of and lasts through the entire engagement, ideally until the customer becomes adept at catching the wily hacker. ■

> "Some really smart penetration testers I know would probably get bored if they realized how much tedious recon and planning goes into a red team campaign."

Twitter: @malcomvetter

Tim MalcomVetter

Hi! My name is Tim MalcomVetter. I started using, building, and breaking computers in the 1980s as a kid and started getting paid for it in 2000. Along the way, I've:

- Consulted with Fortune 500s
- Hacked mainframe sockets to web APIs, fuel pumps to mobile apps
- Led e-commerce dev teams
- Deployed enterprise security solutions
- Made plenty of mistakes

26

Currently, I'm quite fortunate to run a great red team program at the world's largest company, simulating adversaries across five continents with fantastic teammates I've been able to recruit/retain (hobby and career aligned)!

How did you get your start on a red team?

Right place, right time, right skills, right attitude. I like to think that red teaming really pulls in all the skills I've learned from every job I've ever had—in security or otherwise. I don't think I can downplay any past experiences as not playing a role in my ability to get my career where it is—including part-time retail jobs in high school and college. I'm the sum of those experiences.

I also have to acknowledge how being a trusted advisor to an important client was a major contributing factor in my career. I was in the right position to help an organization grow to the point where they were ready to branch out into red teaming, though I didn't know it at the time. I didn't realize how important it was to take technical concepts and break them down simply, without any condescension, so that any level of audience could understand the material and make the best-informed decisions, from nontechnical business stakeholders to executives to engineers. Because my attitude was—fortunately for me—in the right place (let's chalk that up to maturity—I would *not* have been ready when I was younger), the opportunity not only to do red team work but to build a red team program from scratch fell right into my lap.

What is the best way to get a red team job?

So many people say they want to do red team work. I'm not convinced all really do. Some really smart penetration testers I know would probably get bored if they realized how much tedious recon and planning goes into a red team campaign. To them, red teaming is just the next level progression of penetration testing, which could not be further from the truth. Red teaming isn't necessarily better than penetration testing; they're different disciplines. Other people definitely want to do red team work for the wrong reasons. In their minds, it's the ability to play out a Hollywood script in exchange for a paycheck.

You may need to get some experience in other roles first. I'm not a hard and fast believer that you have to follow a certain recipe of steps in order to get a job doing red team work or to be good at it, but certain experiences certainly won't hurt you. If you have spent time outside of InfoSec in IT, your experience shipping features to support a business's mission will make you better at red teaming. Programming skills aren't required, but it certainly helps. The best red teamers I know are at least proficient with what I've heard others call *combat coding* (writing quick tools on the fly). Experience defending networks and systems most certainly is a *huge plus*. You will hit a glass ceiling in your performance if you don't understand how to defend against your attacks. You can't know offense without knowing defense and vice versa. The more experiences you have had, the more intuition you'll be able to draw upon in this work.

Let's say you really want to do this kind of work, for the right reasons, but you're newer to the field. My advice would be to connect with people already doing the work. Ask questions. Stay humble. Basically, take on a mentor without that person realizing they're mentoring you. Figure out where your skill gaps are and address them on your own because there are more people wanting these jobs than there are available jobs. There may be a talent shortage for InfoSec jobs, but every time I have an opening to hire a red teamer, résumés come in from all angles—which is *not* the case for other types of roles, unfortunately. You will likely have competition for the role. It's a good idea to connect with somebody and do some personal development on the side while you have a different IT or InfoSec role.

Whatever your path is, congratulations when you arrive. This is a fun and important field. The personal development work is not done just because you landed the job. In fact, the pressure will likely ramp up. There is a never-ending stream of new things to learn and new areas where you will recognize yourself as deficient. That's all part of the fun.

How can someone gain red team skills without getting in trouble with the law?

It's really simple: don't break the law. Regardless of where you live, that probably means you shouldn't mess with somebody else's computer. It's so easy today to spin up a virtual lab at home for practically no expense (compared to back when I walked to school both ways, uphill, and in the snow—back in the day when we had to build our labs on physical hardware boxes because virtualization wasn't a thing).

Why can't we agree on what a red team is?

Because it's a simple label for a hot commodity that everyone wants to have and do, that drives marketing hype, and that inspires shallow sales pitches by people who aren't technical, don't understand the nuances, and won't put in the time to learn.

To borrow from Winston Churchill, *red team* might be the worst label for what it is we do, except for all the other labels. Like it or not, it's an industry standard, and the great thing about standards is there are so many from which you can choose!

InfoSec didn't originate the term, of course. We borrowed it from WWII era military doctrine, when the United States was blue and the USSR was red. I heard a little rumor that in China, they call this work *blue teaming* because their flag is red; therefore, the red team is the good guys. Maybe someday we'll have a better name.

What is one thing the rest of information security doesn't understand about being on a red team? What is the most toxic falsehood you have heard related to red, blue, or purple teams?

I frequently hear "red has it easy" or "blue has to be wrong only once for red to win." In the past year, I'm starting to see people understand the other side to this, but not everyone gets it yet. If you do red team work and it's easy, either you're not helping your clients grow their security programs or you're taking money from clients who aren't ready for red teaming. Against a tough, well-defended target, it's a give-and-take at best—and quite honestly it could be a landslide for blue. Yes, blue has to make mistakes (or more realistically, have a finite security budget that results in gaps), but red also has plenty of opportunity to create mistakes and result in detection and containment before objectives are met. It's complicated and nuanced.

I also see a pattern of putting red teamers on a pedestal over blue teamers. I think there are a couple reasons for this: a) some amazing defense work happens behind closed doors and nondisclosure agreements, where it will never be discussed publicly, but most of the offense work happens in consulting, where publication of work is often the best marketing strategy, or by internal teams trying to recruit security talent, so we all hear about it; and b) we like to glitz up the work like Hollywood, forgetting the real purpose behind the work: a red team's job is to be the personal trainer, strength/conditioning coach, and nutritionist for the prize fighter, which is the blue team. Few people can remember the trainers for top athletes. We need to keep that mind-set.

When should you introduce a formal red team into an organization's security program?

There is little benefit for red teaming an immature organization—little, not zero. At the minimum, an immature organization can have a severe "wake-up" experience that can jump-start their security program immediately, but they don't need recurring red team exercises until they get fundamentals going. I've done my share of those—they can be effective if presented correctly.

If the organization is growing its security program and has invested solely in prevention (versus detection and response), then a red team exercise will be like hiring a team of professional sudoku puzzle-solvers. They will eventually figure out the correct sequence of events to traverse all the networks, clouds, and people to achieve their objective. Since nobody is watching (detection), nobody will notice all the failed attempts to run the gauntlet of prevention controls. The only benefit for such an exercise is to figure out how long red took—and that's not really that valuable because it could be because red wasn't familiar with a given prevention control (but a real adversary might be), so it slowed them down, or it could just be that red took their time. After red figures out the attack path, it's a lot like watching professional video gamers make their two-minute runs through Super Mario Brothers, beating the entire game. It's entertaining to watch, but that's where the value stops.

Ideally, the security program has its fundamentals: it has a basic asset inventory of what's important to them to actually protect (always start with inventory!), it has a basic set of access controls around that inventory (prevention), and it has logs going to a centralized process where there is a combination of technology and humans alerting on the logs. Even with that, it would be advisable to start "unit testing" basic detections based on behaviors from MITRE ATT&CK first. Finally, the organization needs to know what is valuable to the adversary so it can be modeled.

How do you explain the value of red teaming to a reluctant or nontechnical client or organization?

I always like telling my stakeholders how we focus on realism. We don't talk about theoretical vulnerabilities that can be exploited only when you stand on one foot the night the stars are all aligned on every third blue moon. It's binary: either we achieved our objective or we did not. Our job is to prepare the business for the reality that an attacker may play unfairly without their knowledge or consent.

What is the *least* bang-for-your-buck security control that you see implemented?

I don't think I can pinpoint a single security control that has the lowest ROI, but I frequently see and hear about organizations whose security spending priorities are out of touch with reality. For example, if the organization spends the majority of its budget on state-of-the-art hardware security modules (HSMs) to encrypt its crown jewel assets but leaves the front door open with single-factor authentication and hasn't figured out how to block simple month-plus-year passwords, that's obviously going to be a really poor choice once red teaming begins. I'm not sure why, psychologically speaking, we see so many security practitioners do things like this, but it's super common for defenders to worry about zero days and nation-states when the fundamentals that are much more likely to be exploited are neglected.

Have you ever recommended not doing a red team engagement?

My default response to someone requesting a red team exercise is to point them in a different direction, but that's because I'm not a consultant trying to sell red team exercises as a revenue stream. As an internal team, we try to choose our targets and scenarios based on a wide variety of inputs and risk concerns, and we basically never inform the stakeholder we're coming before we begin, as a general rule.

Typically, if a project owner/stakeholder comes to me and asks for me to "red team" the project, I decline and politely redirect to different teams that perform risk reviews, threat modeling, source code reviews, and application penetration testing. That's usually what they really want anyway. *Red team* to the person asking to be red teamed typically means "Come throw your ninja pirate monkey laser sharks at my assets, please; I want it to be secure." To us, *red team* means simulating an adversary moving toward an objective—typically to acquire data they can monetize and never with advanced knowledge they're coming. The adversary's objective isn't to claim king-of-the-hill in your fancy new application or environment; they may traipse in and out of it, but only if it takes them closer to their actual objective. As a result, the request from the stakeholder becomes more of an input into our process for queuing up future work, which we then validate against other concerns, FAIR risk calculations, and other general business needs.

What's the most important or easiest-to-implement control that can prevent you from compromising a system or network?

I don't have just one simple control to recommend, but you can get a ton of mileage out of doing these three things: multifactor authentication on all external services, use least privilege (nonadmin) accounts on all user endpoints, and send as many logs as you can to qualified and competent security monitoring personnel. You'll never eliminate all of the vulnerabilities in any environment, but you can make them meaningless if you have a good detection and response program.

Why do you feel it is critical to stay within the rules of engagement?

Besides the legal aspects, rules of engagement are the contract for how red and blue interact and execute the exercise. If nothing else, violation of the rules of engagement results in broken trust. Broken trust results in a lack of growth (on both sides). Lack of growth results in zero progression toward better security. And zero progression really makes you wonder why the organization is paying you to do red team work. Red teams are an expensive cost center (unless you're a consultant, then you're a profit center for your firm, but you're still an overhead cost to your client). If the organization isn't directly benefitting, the work will stop. So, following the ROE, as well as jointly reviewing it with blue to make sure it's as effective as it can be, is required—no ifs, ands, or buts.

If you were ever busted on a penetration test or other engagement, how did you handle it?

Contrary to what the internet will have you believe, a good defensible organization will catch you, and if you perform numerous red team cycles with them, they will catch you frequently.

The first time this happened, it came as a surprise. We did not see it coming. We were disappointed in ourselves, surprised we were contained and cut off, and as a team literally started slow golf-clapping our blue team over a red team video chat session in all-out admiration of their work. As much as our egos would love for that to have been the only time, it's far from it. Each time, we embrace the mixture of personal disappointment with pride in our blue team. We try to immediately determine what indicators and other operational mistakes we may have made so that we have a couple hypotheses before we postbrief with the blue side. "It was X, wasn't it?" Our goal is to constantly improve. That means we will make mistakes. As they say in Jiu Jitsu, "Either you win or you learn." And we learn a lot.

If you have a healthy program, you will be caught as often as you succeed. If either side starts to "win" (I hate this word in this context, but it's the easiest way to convey the intent) more often than the other, then that is a direct indication the program isn't working, and it probably means the winning side isn't sharing enough data in postmortem analysis. We had red team challenge coins minted, and right there prominently on the coin is a phrase we borrowed from the NSA's team: "If we win, we lose." That dichotomy drives us. We want to "win" (hit our objectives). We allow our ego to help push us to achieve that goal, and in the process we're the iron sharpening the iron of the blue team. But if we achieve that goal, we approach it with the humility and gravity of what that means—it means that we as a security organization failed. We want that not to happen just as much. So, we make sure—as soon as the exercise is over—that we realign our egos toward making our sparring partner, the blue team, better than they were before we began. I promise that if this attitude is genuine, it is only a matter of time before the blue team will return the favor.

To us, red teaming is fun. It's a game. We get paid to play a game we love that just so happens to also be super valuable for our stakeholders, if done correctly. Just like your favorite video game, we don't want to keep replaying the same level over and over again on novice. We want to level up. Beat a level, push it up a notch, run it again. Getting caught is just part of that process. We align that "caught" experience to our team's understanding that it means everyone is getting better, and it isn't a problem.

Also, sometimes we execute a sequence of events and *expect* to get caught. Why? To ensure that detection controls still work and response processes are still effective.

What is the biggest ethical quandary you experienced while on an assigned objective?

The biggest quandary is probably the legal restrictions that keep us from fully simulating a real adversary. Real adversaries can compromise third parties, use them as infrastructure, and maintain simultaneous attacks on numerous organizations at once. You probably can't do that legally, and simulating it is very difficult unless you are very creative, bending your environment to make things appear certain ways, but you still have to tread carefully to ensure you stay on the high road.

How does the red team work together to get the job done?

Some people will tell you they do red teaming, but when you ask them about it, you'll find out they operate solo. A "red team of one" as we call it. Sorry, but that's not a red team. It's probably just a penetration test with a large scope. We find that a "team" of fewer than a couple operators severely limits success, for a number of reasons.

First, you'll be doing this work for a real paycheck. You probably get paid every other week, regardless of whether you hit your objectives on a red team campaign. A criminal adversary doesn't get paid until they can reach the objective and monetize the data. That changes their motivation—they'll be laser focused on achieving that goal and possibly work around the clock with fierce dedication until they achieve it. You, however, probably need to take time off for a dentist appointment, want to meet that friend for dinner, or maybe have a vacation planned. Maybe you just want to take a break away from a screen for a bit. You, as a red teamer, can do that without fear you won't get paid. That changes things. To keep up the intensity, having a team of three or more operators allows you to cover the calendar and time off and ensure someone is there to catch that shell when it phones home, putting it to good use before it times out and dies.

Second, contrary to what the internet will tell you, red teamers do not know everything there is to know about all things related to all types of systems and all security technologies. Having a team with a diverse skill set allows you to bring in subject-matter experts as issues arise. The deeper the bench and team roster, the more likely someone on your team will have seen X before and have a creative idea what to do with it.

Third, it helps to have multiple people so the work can be divided up for time. You may realize some access you currently have will be short-lived, it will likely generate indicators of compromise, and in a few short minutes or hours, you will probably lose that access as the blue team catches up on your timeline. If you have multiple sets of eyes and hands to review the access you have, you can divide and conquer the territory faster. A "red team of one" will never be able to do that.

Fourth, having a team allows you to simultaneously chase the access you have *and* capture data for debriefing. A phrase I've heard other teams use is "sniper, spotter" where one person has hands on the keyboard "chasing the access" and the other is collecting screenshots, log output, and other artifacts for debriefing without slowing down the action. That's a process we follow a lot—sometimes with as many as five or six operators watching the same terminal if we're brainstorming how to navigate a tough situation. In those situations, one or two operators may be testing a technique on lab systems outside of the operational environment to support the team's decision about which step to take next. A "red team of one" can do this, but at a three to ten times slower execution rate than a group, and in well-defended organizations, that will typically mean getting detected, contained, and eradicated.

What is your approach to debriefing and supporting blue teams after an operation is completed?

First, we collect a near-real-time log of events in sequence in a space where an invited member of the blue team called a *trusted agent* can observe. The trusted agent's role is to be a nonactive member of the detection and response effort, primarily ensuring that the exercise doesn't impact the business (e.g., by taking a production system offline as a containment step) and collecting logs of any missed detections so that the blue team can review why the detection was missed during debrief, which may occur weeks or even months later. The trusted agent does not take any active defender role or inform the red team about the presence or status of events.

Second, we try to map all events (in near real time if we can do it) back to MITRE ATT&CK so the technique IDs can be reviewed during postbrief to ensure better detection coverage.

Third, we find nobody reads or enjoys massive written reports—neither the red teamer who was forced to create it nor the blue team nor the stakeholder of the operating environment. So, we don't create long reports. We do frequently create a simple one-page executive summary, and we are constantly honing our craft, telling our breach stories with slide decks for audiences that want to dive deeper than the one-page overview.

Fourth, we do log findings that are actionable. We don't bother with hypothetical or theoretical—only findings that we definitely exploited and are related directly to our recommendations.

Fifth, we *never* create "red team debrief decks." We always create "purple team debrief decks." The red team operators involved in the exercise meet with blue team trusted agents and engaged responders to draft the final deck together, without managers present. This is important. We want to focus on the technical content first and reiterate to both sides during the reporting phase that everyone is on the same team. After the draft is done, then it is reviewed by red/blue management and begins its circulation with executive, technical, and stakeholder audiences.

All of this is an art form that gets better with practice.

If you were to switch to the blue team, what would be your first step to better defend against attacks?
My answer to this today will be different than my answer months from now since this is a moving target (your environments should always be improving and becoming harder targets). But, today, I am most certainly fascinated by threat intel teams that track attacker infrastructure before it is used against an environment. Friends of mine in several different organizations are beginning to identify common indicators of command-and-control (C2) servers from large internet scans, identify the type of C2 server applications, and sometimes even extract their implants' configurations—*before* those ever hit the stakeholder's environment. Many of these C2 servers are discovered through lazy or sloppy adversaries—both real (financial or nation-state groups) and pretend (red team) threat actors. I find it fascinating that when threat intel results in the discovery of a C2 endpoint before it is used, the endpoint IP/domain are tagged and blocked in the environment before malware ever lands in a phish, and the threat actor is basically lost before they ever began.

So, if I were defending an organization with all of the fundamentals in place and a strong detection/response program, I would most certainly chase some tactical threat intel, blocking common C2 endpoints, and keep a close count every time an endpoint got blocked trying to connect.

What is some practical advice on writing a good report?
My friend and fellow hacker Alex Lauerman once said, "We hack for free but get paid to write reports." So true.

Practical advice for writing reports? Don't do it if you can avoid it, especially long ones. Nobody reads 100-page reports. Few will read beyond three pages. Drive an interactive discussion of the exercise (use slide decks for this as necessary). Keep the storyline simple—putting yourself in your audience's seat to make sure they will understand everything you're presenting without any confusion. Keep a good flow and avoid going too far down in the weeds, or at least be very judicious about where you do get into the nitty-gritty. Then boil the whole narrative and recommendations down into an easy-to-consume single-page document (or less). If you can't do an elevator pitch version of the exercise, then you probably don't really comprehend the real value and impact of the exercise yourself. Practice until you can and do.

I have seen red teamers really proud of all the subtle aspects of their work. Those nuances matter but not to all audiences. Don't go into the report thinking you're writing the red team version of *War and Peace* and that your reader needs the first-person omniscient view of your perspective of the last several weeks of work. Remember, less is more.

If you're a consultant, definitely don't meet with your client and read a 100-page Word document to them over a video conference screen share. I've seen it done. It's painful. Nobody wants that. Everyone says they hate PowerPoint decks, but they hate Microsoft Word as a replacement for PowerPoint way more.

There's an art to PowerPoint. This isn't a security conference, so leave the memes at home. Sanitize everything in the deck. All customer, contractor, or employee names, user IDs, and every last byte of trophy data you exfiltrated—show enough to imply you got what you said you did. If they don't believe you, you can show them unsanitized data later. But the reason why it's important to sanitize the deck first is because of the ping-pong after-effect the deck will have internally for your customers. They will pass the deck around, and people will see it. They will figure out who fell for the social engineering, who broke policy, or who made the security mistakes. It can demoralize the organization's culture, so sanitize everything by default.

How do you ensure your program results are valuable to people who need a full narrative and context?

Empathy drives everything. If you can empathize with the system admins, employees, contractors, customers, executives—if you can empathize with *all* of them—you will naturally gravitate toward making your final deliverable something that will naturally benefit them, and you will care less about whether your skill set is highlighted.

The fact is, a year after the debrief, the executives, engineers, and other stakeholders won't remember 99 percent of what you tell them. They will, however, remember how you made them feel. Did you make them feel stupid? Did you make them feel like you have far superior knowledge and intellect? Did you telegraph to them just how arrogant you are? Or did you make them feel like you were their partner, helping them through a tough situation so they would never have to repeat the experience again? That's what will matter.

How do you recommend security improvements other than pointing out where it's insufficient?

Since we always debrief a "purple team" slide deck, the improvements are always "ours." One team. One set of recommendations. One voice. The nerds sort the technical conflicts long before they go to the executives. This way we can focus on the opportunity (where the insufficiencies are) without it being a pejorative or negative experience. We will highlight strengths and wins, but since we do so many of these iterations, our core team doesn't have to spend copious amounts of unnecessary time crafting consolation trophies for showing up to the exercise. We can just focus on the gaps and constantly drive the program forward. One vision: make it a harder target each time.

What nontechnical skills or attitudes do you look for when recruiting and interviewing red team members?

I focus on team fit over technical skills. There are many people interested in this work. Unlike most InfoSec jobs where recruiters often toil to drum up more interest in their role than similar roles at other organizations, there is usually a line around the block of qualified candidates for red team jobs. So, we focus on attitude and aptitude first and then skill set diversity second. We don't usually need three or more people with the same core skill sets because that's an opportunity cost to the team—we could have hired somebody who is skilled in an area where we have zero coverage. Skill diversity has paid itself back many times over.

When it comes to attitude, I focus on internal locus of control versus external locus of control. This is a social-psychology concept (Google it for a better explanation) that can basically be summed up as "Does the candidate feel in control of their successes and failures?" You can tease this out by questions like these: "Tell me about a time when a project you were working on failed. What happened?" If the candidate says, "My teammate dropped the ball," "The boss made the wrong call and the project failed," or something similar, it implies external locus of control, whereas a candidate with internal locus of control might say, "We missed a detail, and I learned to make sure X didn't happen again." This might seem silly—like some sort of general self-help guidance for managers—but when your red team gets contained and blue wins, a person with an external locus of control will ruin morale for both sides. If you want to keep the right attitude and a healthy relationship with red and blue, prioritize this character attribute. Learn to ask questions that tease it out. Start by trying it on yourself, and when you hear the external locus of control come out of your own mouth, arrest the thought midsentence, and start correcting your own mind-set.

What differentiates good red teamers from the pack as far as approaching a problem differently?

A good red teamer will question everything, every time, making hypotheses from the beginning to the end, testing them, eliminating variables, and approaching everything systematically. This includes thinking about the team as a single organism and realizing that the only way for the team to succeed is if all of its resources are used at full capacity.

A good red teamer will realize that a force multiplier is to mentor the junior members of the team—the more they learn and know, the faster the team can operate together in the future. The investment of time necessary for the mentorship generally pays off within a single exercise.

A good red teamer is never satisfied with the results, even if the objective was met. A good red teamer will ruminate on the sequence of events, focusing on how to be more efficient and realizing the opportunities for detection and containment that were missed by the blue team. They will red team themselves, like a chess grand master turning the board around and playing against herself.

A good red teamer will build up tons of intuition over time. Each iteration, whether a practice in a lab or memory of someone else's work from a report or blog, will deepen a neural path in their brain and increase their confidence. A good red teamer can typically spend as little as an hour in reconnaissance of a target and have a rough idea of not only how mature the security program is but also the most likely and successful avenue of attack. Don't read that to mean you need to spend only an hour in recon! It just means they have a good hunch, and as a good red teamer, they will spend more time on recon and planning than any other phase because they realize the more time spent on recon, the easier the exploitation and actions on target will be.

The best red teamers are really indistinguishable from the best blue teamers. This is probably the most astonishing detail for somebody new to this field. The best red teamers (and vice versa, the best blue teamers) see both sides of the same coin so well at once that the only question is what their objective is. They can tell you where the security controls should be. They can tell you how the attack can be detected and contained. They can tell you how defense should triage and process any single action of their attack, if it was identified by blue, because they themselves are world-class incident responders. They can tell you when the attacker's motivations are important to the sequence of events and when they are not. They can swap tactics with minimal planning. They can emulate multiple types of attackers. They can think in strategy—not just tactics and techniques. They are driven by realism; while they respect what some of the best penetration testers and exploit developers do (and maybe they themselves could do that work), they are motivated to make the red team exercise as realistic as possible. They will not be satisfied until they realize the only way they can make it more realistic is if they actually commit a crime. Their drive for hyper-realism will make them fascinated by reports of real breaches, and they will armchair quarterback both the attacker's and defender's mistakes in each story.

The best red teamers will also make great threat hunters. Why? Because they want to red team the real adversaries. Their drive to win, to be the best, and to make the exercise as authentic as possible will make them want to crush any real adversary in the operational environment—that is, after all, the red team's playground, and we don't like to share our playground with the real adversaries. ■

> "Develop your skills from multiple angles. Blue, purple, and red experience makes you better in InfoSec in general. Cross-pollinate."

Twitter: @13M4C

Brandon McCrillis

27

Brandon McCrillis is a cybersecurity professional, a veteran of the U.S. Navy, and a former U.S Air Force government civilian. He is a former network exploitation operator with the DoD, senior technical lead for computer network exploitation (CNE), and team lead, while standing up U.S. Cyber Command's Cyber Mission Forces. Brandon has led a team of more than 150 multidisciplined cyber operators to conduct more than 10,000 operations globally and now assists organizations of all sizes and verticals to better understand business risks and build industry-leading information security programs. Brandon joined Rendition Infosec in 2015 and serves as CEO.

How did you get your start on a red team?
I started in pentesting and offensive cyber operations and made the move to red teaming when we started up Rendition Infosec.

What is the best way to get a red team job?
Work hard at what you do. Continue learning. Demonstrate creativity, aptitude, and perseverance.

How can someone gain red team skills without getting in trouble with the law?
Social engineer your life and break things when legally able.

Why can't we agree on what a red team is?
Gartner.

What is one thing the rest of information security doesn't understand about being on a red team? What is the most toxic falsehood you have heard related to red, blue, or purple teams?

"Red teaming isn't simply pentesting. The red team needs to operate as an offensive actor but have the ability to tie their results back to something meaningful for the business and stakeholders."

Red teaming isn't simply pentesting. The red team needs to operate as an offensive actor but have the ability to tie their results back to something meaningful for the business and stakeholders. The most toxic falsehood I've heard is that you need to pick a team and stay there.

Develop your skills from multiple angles. Blue, purple, and red experience makes you better in InfoSec in general. Cross-pollinate.

When should you introduce a formal red team into an organization's security program?

Get the basics out of the way first and then gradually reshape some of your pentesting engagements into red team assessments through creative discussion and planning. Tabletop red teaming is an easy way to increase maturity without making massive changes to your current testing cycles and requirements.

How do you explain the value of red teaming to a reluctant or nontechnical client or organization?

The value in red teaming is understanding and exploiting the business's worst fears. A pentest goes only so far, and the objectives are different. Red teaming requires the ability to combine many aspects of traditional security audits into an engagement that crosses the bounds of simply "checking the compliance box."

What is the *least* bang-for-your-buck security control that you see implemented?

Buying an expensive tool before understanding your risk appetite, procedural maturity, and the skills of your people.

Have you ever recommended not doing a red team engagement?

Yes. Some organizations are just not ready for a red team assessment. In these cases, I usually recommend a more collaborative technical evaluation or capabilities gap assessment first.

What's the most important or easiest-to-implement control that can prevent you from compromising a system or network?

Multifactor authentication (to include verification of visitors), incident response policy, and password length.

Why do you feel it is critical to stay within the rules of engagement?

Know your scope, especially in an environment with less maturity. The politics and culture of the organization have a lot to do with how successful the red team engagement will be and the value of it to the business.

If you were ever busted on a penetration test or other engagement, how did you handle it?

Whip out that "get-out-of-jail-free" letter, and if that doesn't work, run like hell.

What is the biggest ethical quandary you experienced while on an assigned objective?

Social engineering can be difficult for some. When you have to lie to someone about your sick infant you're taking to the ER, it can feel awkward, especially if you have a child at home.

How does the red team work together to get the job done?

Many different testing aspects have to come together in a ballet of sorts; reporting can also be difficult due to differing testing perspectives and methodologies.

What is your approach to debriefing and supporting blue teams after an operation is completed?

The red team exists to make the blue team better. You need to appreciate the fact that you're there to increase defenses through calculated exploitation opportunities and detailed attack reporting/narratives.

If you were to switch to the blue team, what would be your first step to better defend against attacks?

Increase network visibility and monitoring surrounding IoT devices and "support devices" such as printers and multifunction devices. Ensure my organization has clear incident reporting procedures available to all levels of employees.

What is some practical advice on writing a good report?

Spend extra time writing the attack narrative, keep the executive summary short and geared to a third-grade reading level, and put all of your technical data in an appendix.

How do you ensure your program results are valuable to people who need a full narrative and context?

Break out the attack narrative and background of the engagement. The executive summary should be clean and to the point. Also, consider adding a technical summary for executives who have some tech background but won't get value from technical findings alone.

How do you recommend security improvements other than pointing out where it's insufficient?

Tie it back to the business. Make your findings relatable to the industry and audience you are trying to reach.

What nontechnical skills or attitudes do you look for when recruiting and interviewing red team members?

Charisma and stage acting ability. I also look for members who demonstrate creativity and out-of-the-box thinking.

What differentiates good red teamers from the pack as far as approaching a problem differently?

An ability to solve problems in unconventional ways. Also, an ability to tackle technical limitations without a linear path of thinking. ■

"Trust is a big thing in this industry."

Twitter: @Oddvarmoe

Oddvar Moe

28

Oddvar is a red teamer working at TrustedSec. He has more than 18 years of experience in the IT industry and is passionate about Windows security—so passionate that Microsoft has awarded him the Most Valuable Professional Award three years in row. As a speaker he has delivered top-notch sessions at conferences such as DerbyCon, IT Dev Connections, Paranoia, HackCon, and Nordic Infrastructure Conference. He also actively contributes to the security community, and he is most known for his contributions around the LOLBins/LOLBAS and the Ultimate AppLocker Bypasslist. He has also discovered several weaknesses in the Windows operating system and found new persistence techniques.

How did you get your start on a red team?

Prior to working with red teaming at TrustedSec, I was a penetration tester working in Norway. When I was working as a penetration tester, I always felt that the adversary part was missing in my engagements. Running a lot of noisy tools was something I felt would not be a natural thing to do if I was working as a real adversary attacking my customers. I could always try to simulate a red team, but even the noisy tools I ran were often not detected, so my customer base was not mature enough for red teaming.

I was lucky enough to get noticed on Twitter by Dave Kennedy, and it ended up in him hiring me as a red teamer on his Adversarial Emulation and Threat Research (AETR) team. I got noticed by him since I shared a lot of blog posts, tweets, and research projects to the community on various topics around red teaming, security research, and penetration testing. I especially got a lot of recognition from the community from my work on the Living Off The Land Binaries and Scripts (LOLBAS) and getting the term LOLBin out there.

I always dreamed of getting the opportunity to work as close as possible to a real adversary, and that is what red teaming is all about.

What is the best way to get a red team job?

I don't think this is something that can be answered easily. The most practical approach would be to look for job openings and apply to them. When applying, it is important that your résumé reflects skills that are fit for a red team and of course that it is true. If you can provide links to projects that you are active on, that's really clever to get better noticed. It is also important to understand that it is not necessary for every pentester to strive to become a red teamer. When performing red teaming, you are reliant on not being detected, so it is a more strategic approach where you work in a slow pace rather than a "fire-all-the-tools-at-once" approach. Often, this is compared to the ninja versus the pirate, where the sneaky ninja is the red teamer and the noisy pirate is the pentester. It also requires you to be able to change existing tools so that they are not detected; therefore, some coding skills are required in my opinion. If you are a person who is not patient and rather like that things happen fast, then red teaming is probably not the best fit for you.

If you, however, feel that this is something that is perfect for you and you want to get a job as a red teamer, then I think the best way is to make sure you share interesting information and become an asset to the InfoSec community. One way you can do that is by providing relevant content, doing talks, writing code, helping others, and simply sharing your passion for InfoSec. (Also, be nice. Nobody wants to hire a douche bag.) Doing these things will often end up with you networking with others who become your friends. And if someone asks your new friends if they know someone they should hire, chances are that they will point in your direction. To be honest, I would rather hire someone who was recommended to me by someone I know than a person who did an okay interview. Trust is a big thing in this industry.

How can someone gain red team skills without getting in trouble with the law?

I think the best approach is to build your own environment where you set up a good detection using free products (ELK stack, Windows event forwarding, Splunk free, etc.) and try to sneak an attack in without triggering detections. There are a lot of interesting projects out there that can help you to build a good detection lab—that way you will learn what defenders are doing to detect you, and you become better at evading detection. Also try to customize existing tools and techniques to avoid detection; this is also a good way of getting more skills. There are also several red team labs you can buy access to so that you can get hands-on experience, and you can also download vulnerable VMs that you can try to attack. If you currently are doing penetration testing, you can always start the test by trying to get access without being detected to practice red teaming, assuming that is okay with your customer, of course. Another good source for learning more about red teaming is to read reports on advanced persistent threat groups and study their TTP to learn from them and try to evolve them into something new.

Why can't we agree on what a red team is?

I think part of the problem is that there are so many different opinions on what a red team should be. Many companies sell this as the best pentest they can offer and do not understand the aspect of adversarial simulation; others say it is an advanced penetration test. I have even talked to customers who thought the red team was something you hired when you had a breach to get help. Ideally, this book will help to make everyone better understand what a red team is.

When should you introduce a formal red team into an organization's security program?

In my opinion, the organization is mature enough when it can respond to security alerts and actually has good detection in place that can be put up to the test from a red team.

Furthermore, the organization needs to be able to improve in areas where there was a discovered gap in detection or even routine failures as a result of a red team. If the customer cannot act on the results of the red team, then they are not mature enough.

How do you explain the value of red teaming to a reluctant or nontechnical client or organization?

When we invest in backup solutions, we make sure to verify the backups afterward to make sure the solution works as intended. If the backup does not work, we can make changes so it works as it should. It would be incredibly boring to not have a working backup in the event of a disaster, and the reason why would be that we did not test it. The same goes for red teaming; we want to test that our security detections and routines work as they should so we know that our organization can handle a real attack. It would not be a lot of fun to find out that an attacker can easily hack into our environment undetected and isn't stopped just because we did not test the security of our organization properly.

What is the *least* bang-for-your-buck security control that you see implemented?

I would say everything that companies buy that they don't follow up on. I often see a "set-and-forget" mentality when I am around.

This is a typical dialogue with customers:

> Me: "What sort of security products do you have?"
> Customer: "We have products X, Z, and Y."
> Me: "Do you monitor them? Or respond to their alerts?"
> Customer: "No, we don't have time for that."

You want to invest a lot of money in people to get the most bang for your buck. One person can make the entire difference in the security level of your organization, in my opinion.

In terms of specific product types that give the least bang for your buck, I would say an expensive IDS/IPS that cannot inspect SSL.

Have you ever recommended not doing a red team engagement?

Many times. For example, a customer asked me about getting a red team, but the customer did not fully understand what that meant. The customer assumed he was getting the best security test. I asked if he had a blue team or any good monitoring in place. The customer responded that they did not have either of them. After that I explained that there are different levels of maturity in terms of what sort of security test you should get. It turned out the customer had never gotten any testing done in the past, and I recommended starting with a vulnerability scan, both external and internal, and then taking it from there.

What's the most important or easiest-to-implement control that can prevent you from compromising a system or network?

I feel the "free" security controls that you already have license for (assuming you have a Microsoft environment) can be used to really make it hard for someone to compromise you. If I were working in a small company and had little money, I would focus on application whitelisting using Microsoft AppLocker, remove admin rights, enable BitLocker disk encryption, configure Windows client firewalls to prevent client-to-client communication, establish Microsoft Deployment Solution to easily re-deploy machines that get infected, deploy Microsoft Security baselines using Group Policies, and also invest a lot of time into training employees so that they are aware of what attackers attempt and to raise awareness.

Why do you feel it is critical to stay within the rules of engagement?

This comes down to trust. The customer trusts that you follow the rules of engagement and so does your employer. There are often several reasons for having rules of engagement in place; one could be that the customer wants to focus on certain areas that they want to improve. Also, not following the rules of engagement could mean in some scenarios that you are doing something illegal, and we should never do something that is illegal.

If you were ever busted on a penetration test or other engagement, how did you handle it?

I was caught on my first red team. I did not have a lot of experience doing red teams, and we were done with the OSINT and figured a good start would be to do a password spray against OWA. I started the password spray and was immediately caught by the customer. The customer sent an email in a way that triggered me in the wording they used (in a good way). I felt kind of bummed out since this was my first red team and I was already caught by something as simple as that. I learned a lot by getting caught, and I changed my tactics completely when it came to password spraying. I started to leverage things like proxy canon to use a new random public IP on each attempt and also changed my username list to no longer be in alphabetical order. On my next engagement where I did password spraying, I was not detected at all. I think the best way to handle failure is to learn from it and evolve.

How does the red team work together to get the job done?

To be a successful red team, you need to have different skills. We cannot all be experts at everything. It is important to be able to leverage each other's skills to benefit the engagement. During our red teams we share notes and have a dedicated chat room for the specific engagement where we can share our information so that everyone can see what is happening and it is also easy to ask the other team members for advice. Documentation is something that is done during the entire engagement from beginning to end. Normally during our engagements, we do quick status meetings with our point of contact at intervals and have a report walk-through with the blue team afterward. During these meetings and the walk-through, all the red team members are normally present. We make sure that the blue team understands the gaps that we found so that they can better enhance their detection and response capabilities.

If you were to switch to the blue team, what would be your first step to better defend against attacks?

There are many things I would do for sure, but the most effective technical and easy things would be to disable macros and associated script files (HTA,

WSF, VBS, JS) so that they open in Notepad instead of executing the code. Even if this is really easy to implement, there could be many reasons why it is not implemented, such as the organization relies on macros for their day-to-day business or they need to be able to run script files. Many times, when I have engaged with customers who claim they need macros or need to be able to run script files, just 10 percent of clients actually need this capability. This means you can disable them for 90 percent of clients, which makes it so much harder for the attackers to get in and it does not impact the customer. The exceptions should never be the deciding factor on the level of security you should enable.

Furthermore, I would make sure the following things were implemented:

• Application whitelisting on all clients
• Removing all admin rights for the end users
• Deploying endpoint detection and response clients
• Deploying hardening baselines
• Installing a client firewall
• Streamlined OS patching and OS upgrades
• Collecting client event logs centrally

Of course, I would also do a lot of awareness training with all the employees so that the entire organization matures.

What is some practical advice on writing a good report?

The report is the product of all you do on a test, and you should take great pride in creating it. This is the result that the customer gets from a test. When I write reports, I always try to think as if I am the customer who reads the report. That way, I should be able to understand what we did and be able to improve based on that. If that is not the case, then I need to rewrite it. Correct screenshots are also important, and you should never assume that everyone knows exactly what you know. Remember, you are the expert, and you are (or should be) trying to explain it to someone who is not an expert.

How do you recommend security improvements other than pointing out where it's insufficient?

It is important to always have concrete things that can be done by the blue team to improve the security in the gap that was identified. For instance, if you discover during a red team that you can log in to the VPN solution with a username and password, you need to make sure that you recommend multifactor authentication. If you also did most of the internal compromise through the VPN and it was not detected, then you need to recommend improvements to the logging and what sort of activities they should be looking for.

What nontechnical skills or attitudes do you look for when recruiting and interviewing red team members?

I am not responsible for hiring, but if I were to recommend someone to come work for us, that person would have to be passionate about security. Also, they would need to be someone who wants to change the security industry into something better and not just do a job. Other skills that are beneficial for a red teamer are the ability to be social and talk to people, having a sense of humor, learning new things quickly, having patience, being curious, and being humble. ■

> "The precursor to getting better at any craft is to understand it from as many viewpoints as possible."

Twitter: @indi303

Chris Nickerson

29

Chris Nickerson, CEO of Lares, has spent the last 20 years of his career leading, inspiring, and sometimes irritating the security industry. With Lares cofounder Eric M. Smith, he created the unique methodology used at Lares to assess, implement, and manage information security realistically and effectively. Collaborating with a group of other InfoSec researchers, he founded the Penetration Testing Execution Standard (PTES) and is working with the Red Team Alliance Training Collective to create a certification for red team testing. Chris is one of the founders of the Security BSides conferences, and he's been a keynote, speaker, and/or trainer at more than 50 InfoSec conferences worldwide, including DEF CON, CyberWeek, and BlackHat. He's a member and certification holder with ISACA, is on the board of CREST, and holds CISSP, CISA, BS7799, and NSA IAM certifications. His book *Red Team Testing* is upcoming from Elsevier/Syngress. Despite all that, he is perhaps best known for his appearance on the TV show *Tiger Team* on TruTV and his TED Talk *Hackers are all about curiosity, and security is just a feeling*.

How did you get your start on a red team?
In my early days at Sprint we had a task force put together to show the actual impact of vulnerabilities identified. Over time, the scope grew and began to include attacks from the physical, social, and electronic realms. Although this team was called a "tiger team," it was really my first professional exposure to mixed-discipline attacking over multiple execution surfaces.

What is the best way to get a red team job?

Earn it. The main reason to have a red team is to be able to simulate a wide range of adversarial tactics over the entire attack surface. The operator needs to have a broad background in problem-solving and quick thinking. Knowledge of one discipline can be tactical but is not sufficient when tasked with simulating many different adversarial models. The operator must be able to mimic not only tactics but thought patterns. With that in mind, the best way to get a red team job is to practice everything *besides* red teaming.

How can someone gain red team skills without getting in trouble with the law?

Practice in a controlled environment. This may come in many forms, from picking your own padlocks to creating pentesting labs. The precursor to getting better at any craft is to understand it from as many viewpoints as possible. There are boatloads of classes at conferences and standalone. My advice would be to take a solid mix of classes in pentesting, social engineering, and physical security. Oh, and don't forget to have mastery of your audience's language. We can be the best red teamers in the world and will not get a single stitch of credit unless we can effectively and appropriately communicate our actions.

> "Practice in a controlled environment. This may come in many forms, from picking your own padlocks to creating pentesting labs."

Why can't we agree on what a red team is?

It *is* a fairly standard term in the military. Since the invention of the German 19th-century kriegspiel (wargame), it has had a few names, but the sentiment has remained the same. The Army said it well in TR71-20 TRADOC:

> "A structured, iterative process executed by trained, educated and practiced team members that provides commanders an independent capability to continuously challenge plans, operations, concepts, organizations and capabilities in the context of the operational environment and from our partners' and adversaries' perspectives."

So, from that standpoint, the world has had a great definition of it. Why can't "we" agree? Well, we will have to ask who "we" is. If you mean "people in cybersecurity," I would quickly point to the sales and marketing departments. Since such a small talent pool existed when the terms started to gain popularity, they wanted to cash in on the interest. Just like *penetration testing*, the term was watered down and manipulated to mean "whatever engineering talent I have to sell you." Bruce Schneier (https://www.schneier.com/essays/archives/2007/04/how_security_compani.html) captured this so elegantly while comparing the information security market to American economist George Akerlof's paper "The Market for 'Lemons,'" which is a body of work that looks at markets where the seller knows a lot more about the product than the buyer. That's partly the same issue we have in *red team* definitions. The customer doesn't know what to expect, and the sales team makes up a slick sales sheet that says the words they are looking for and the buzzwords that make them "feel" like they are doing it right.

What is one thing the rest of information security doesn't understand about being on a red team? What is the most toxic falsehood you have heard related to red, blue, or purple teams?

Red teamers, or the offense, thinks they are better than any other teams. Look, I am all for having confidence in yourself and even more so confidence in your team. But, there is no place or need for some pseudo-hierarchy. Members of this team should be the *most* similar. They should all be committed, passionate, and mission-driven. They should be using their talents to drive progress. They should be the instrument of change no matter how hard it is or how long it takes. This isn't a field for people who don't want to make a difference. We're all part of the same crayon box and, when used in concert, can create something much bigger than our individual contributions.

> "This isn't a field for people who don't want to make a difference."

When should you introduce a formal red team into an organization's security program?

Coach Bear Bryant said, "Offense wins games. Defense wins championships." The key lesson here is that you *need* to have a defense to win. Having an active state red team requires an active state blue team. That's not to say that one cannot get some value from "sparring" with the red side, but to realize the full potential of the organization's ability to progress and improve through the challenge of red teaming, they must have a team dedicated to that constant improvement. This may be a "hunt team," or it may be a group of dedicated defenders charged with the proactive improvement of the environment. Either way, the commitment to challenging the status quo is being able to act on it. The teams that are ready for a red team are the ones who are ready to put in the work to own the findings, measure the results, and drive the organization forward.

How do you explain the value of red teaming to a reluctant or nontechnical client or organization?

The sparring analogy is one that I usually find most people understand. Whether it's the Mike Tyson–style "Everyone has a plan until they get punched in the face" or the idea that you join a fight club to see what it really feels like to be in a fight or something even deeper. The entire sentiment of red teaming is to challenge the status quo—not through some type of theoretical or mathematical model but to learn and evolve through experience. It makes me think of those silly T-shirts that say, "There's no patch for human stupidity." They are totally wrong! The patches that we get are called *experience*, and the more experience we get, the more prepared we are. This applies to the sparring partner analogy. If you are a beginner, you need to always be punching up above your skill level—not too far, because you need to build your confidence. Let's face it, if you jumped in the ring day one with Iron Mike, you'd likely hang up the gloves forever. As you progress, you need to move from sparring in your class to the next level above it. Each time you turn the dial to make the sparring partner a bigger challenge, you will build confidence, experience, and skill. Eventually, when you get to the pro level, it's no longer about fighting someone better; it's about someone who has a different style than you. You may be the baddest thing to ever hit the ring, but the variables you experience in the challenger or adversary are the things that can catch you off guard. At this point in the game, you need a sparring partner who can act "just like your opponent." It will prepare you for the inevitable fight ahead and give you trust in your skills. It will also point out opportunities in your game plan that may have never been tested. Not everyone is ready for a title fight, but the ones who are trained for it with every breath.

What is the *least* bang-for-your-buck security control that you see implemented?

To answer the reverse question, training. Investing in your people will always beat your tools. It is a common misconception that you can buy your way to being secure. As you can see from common statistics, that idea isn't working so well. There is nothing on this planet that can beat a dedicated and educated member of the team. The thing that most people don't consider is that security tools constantly have vulnerabilities just like everything else. So, at the end of the day, every time you buy a new tool, your attack surface *increases*, not decreases. There are more things to attack, more openings, more everything. Now, with a highly trained team, you would be able to know that and engineer around the blind spots created. Without that training and investment in your team, you are increasing the likelihood that the very thing you bought to protect you will be the thing that gets you owned.

Have you ever recommended not doing a red team engagement?

Most people are not ready for a red team engagement. It is an extremely deep look into an environment's real-world effectiveness to defend itself in multiple different modalities. Oftentimes, the companies asking for exercises like this do not have the technology/staffing in place to even make progress on the findings. Back to the sparring analogy, they are amateurs trying to spar with Tyson in his prime. It's counterproductive to the program, and we regularly guide companies to testing types that they are more prepared for. This may be pentesting or even a broader defensive controls analysis to determine what they are actually equipped to handle. It often doesn't end well, and they go with another vendor willing to sell them the "term" they are requesting. I still feel firm in the decision to do what's right for the client even if they don't see it at the time. Now, have we ever done a red team job on someone who was woefully underprepared? Absolutely! How did it end? Just like we told them: a string of attacks that you aren't staffed or engineered to deal with. Surprisingly enough, about 10 percent of them recover from the shock and awe and actually make a massive change. The others just don't call back.

What's the most important or easiest-to-implement control that can prevent you from compromising a system or network?

Two-factor everything. Passwords are the Achilles heel of modern access. It's the most common way I see access and lateral movement happen. There are plenty of 2FA solutions out there that are free to low cost and provide a massive leap in security above the single-password solution.

Why do you feel it is critical to stay within the rules of engagement?

The rules of engagement aren't just a contract, they are your word. The bond of trust that is required to allow a stranger to see the darkest secrets of your business is one that requires a far more emotional connection than words on paper. It requires honor, purpose, intent, and overall trust. The foundations of that trust are memorialized in the rules of engagement. It's a catalog of your mission and your commitment to the progress of the organization.

If you were ever busted on a penetration test or other engagement, how did you handle it?

Oh boy, I have had some weird ones. One time I was working at this large healthcare facility. It was about 2 a.m., and we had made our way into the IT operations building through a chat with the cleaning staff. As time went on, the cleaning staff left, and we stayed on the network. After collecting the artifacts of access the client requested, we went exploring. We were looking for some final flags of raw patient information, data, persistent physical access, and additional bypasses. I found myself in the basement looking at a few boxes that looked just like a key box, I swear. Anyway, I picked the box open, and the alarm went raging. I knew right away that this was the alarm central unit and the tamper switch had been triggered. I heard a faint yell from my teammate upstairs, "Are you kidding me? Nickerson, what are you doing down there?" I ran up the stairs, beet red and totally embarrassed. We both convened at the alarm keypad to see if we could find a way to disarm it. We checked everything close to the panel and found nothing. As a last-ditch effort, we popped the external housing, and on the inside of the casing was the number 4757. Coincidentally that was also the number of the building we were in. We punched in the code, and the cacophony of sirens immediately stopped. "Whew! We're good," I laughed. I was met with the "I'm not impressed" look, and we started to collect our things.

Not more than three minutes later, the road up to the facility was drowning in blue and red. "Well, here we go," I said, as I started to reluctantly unfold my engagement letter. We immediately went outside and waited for the police to show up. Like any pride-stung red teamer, I thought to myself, maybe if I go first, they will think I am supposed to be here. So, as soon as they were in the parking lot, I waved them to our side of the building. "Officer! I'm so sorry. I have been here all night working on this server being down, and the cleaning lady locked me in. I just came out here for a smoke, and the dang alarm started going off. I tried to turn it off, but the call already went out." He let out a faint giggle and grabbed a flashlight to shine in my face. After a few minutes of questions, he actually bought the story. I helped him do a sweep of the area, looking for anything suspicious, and he reassured me that "this kind of thing happens all the time" since I was worried about having to pay a fine for the emergency response call. They eventually left, and we packed up and alarmed the building in good conscience that if anyone else broke in that night, they were surely going to jail.

What is the biggest ethical quandary you experienced while on an assigned objective?

Red teaming is a really strange duality. On one hand, you are being paid to conduct a test to find potential weaknesses and measure the success of a program. On the other hand, you are doing all the things your mom told you to never do, and you are doing it for money! It's a really strange place to be in. Also, there is a palpable intensity to it. You are breaking into a building. You are doing this highly criminal thing, and no matter how you justify it, you feel those butterflies. But unlike with a criminal, the intensity doesn't stop there. You see, when a criminal gets caught, they know that's a potential result of the game they signed up for. When you, a red teamer, get caught, you no longer have the feeling of the criminal act or the intensity of going from hidden to exposed. You immediately switch to an entirely different fear. You go from "OMG, I don't want to get caught" to "OMG, I'm getting caught. I'm a phony. I'm terrible at my job. Everyone is going to know. My career is over. My peers are going to ridicule me. The client is going to think I suck. And on and on...." It's vicious. There are other ethical aspects of the job that we come in contact with that have some effect or give me pause, but there is nothing like listening to my mother's voice in my head, telling me that the thing that I am in the process of doing is just wrong.

How does the red team work together to get the job done?
The team is everything. No one can do it on their own. Even if it is a one-person job, the entirety of my team is there to support the operator every step of the way. You need a pump-up? We got you. Need someone on the cameras at 4 a.m.? We will get on. Need someone in your ear to walk you through the office you should break into to try to get part of the safe codes? We will be there, digging through mailboxes and shared folders trying to help you narrow the 1,000 offices down to the ones that likely have the code. This doesn't stop at the operation. Afterward, the same rules apply to our blue team counterparts. You need something? We are there. We are an extension of your team—there to make sure that when you tackle the next big issue, you know that we have your back. Findings, remediations, brainstorming sessions, or just a late-night call to vent. We are just as invested in the program growing as they are. Together we make it happen.

What is your approach to debriefing and supporting blue teams after an operation is completed?
We start the process as early as possible. If we are allowed, we let members of the blue team "ride along" with us to gain both sides of the experience. I can remember some pretty famous faces in the InfoSec industry coming on a gig with us as blue teamers. Some of them used it as inspiration to create revolutionary defense programs, and some of them used it as a launchpad to move the offensive industry further than we could have ever expected. The one thing that was the same in every engagement was that the more we engaged, the more we all learned.

If you were to switch to the blue team, what would be your first step to better defend against attacks?
Basic defensive inventory. Most companies have been bullied by compliance to buy tools and technologies they don't even use. They have had Gartner in their ears for decades, telling them what to buy but not why. Situational awareness and home field advantage are the biggest assets of the defensive team. The best teams in the world use those two things to move mountains and respond to attacks in real time effectively.

What is some practical advice on writing a good report?
Collaboration. Work with your peers, work with your clients, and work with your team. Try a few different styles of reporting and see what resonates with the customer. Not everyone learns and communicates the same way. The more versatility you get in your reporting, the more likely the customer is to understand the intent of the attack path as well as the remediation. If our goal is to grow, let's push it from every possible direction.

How do you ensure your program results are valuable to people who need a full narrative and context?
This is something that is crucial to the pre-engagement phase. Both sides need a road map. Both sides need to set clear expectations for what the exercise will cover and how it will be delivered. Don't just spend time selling; spend

time listening. Spend time learning about the business and the members of each team that is part of the test. Learn their differences and how they need communication to unfold. Define pathways to success and a picture of what success looks like. Throw out the work language for a little bit and just speak like humans—ones who are about to embark on a deeply emotional and distinct journey together—and make sure everyone is comfortable. That comfort and trust will be the foundation of the exercise and ultimately the thing that separates your success from your failure.

How do you recommend security improvements other than pointing out where it's insufficient?
Metrics. This is no longer a binary game. There is a way to distribute the information in a testing engagement without the fear, uncertainty, and doubt. We must first understand that the discipline of security is a capability. It is something that can be measured on a standard capability maturity model integration (CMMI) scale. As testers, we rarely know the actual impact to the organization beyond our theoretical impact. "OMG, I got domain admin! You are hosed." Well...maybe, but is that a fact? Not always. It does, however, drive fear. Fear is the last thing wanted as an outcome. Remember the Tyson scenario. We can't break the will and confidence of the team; our job is to show the opportunity for improvement and track its progress. That said, we need to use metrics to enrich the data over time. We can't just say "red team wins." We need to measure the varying level of success of the program to protect and detect the threats we simulated. We then need to work together to improve our capability maturity tactic by tactic. You know what I think is insufficient? The graphs you see from every security tool tell you that it stopped "X number of threats or attacks." You know what it doesn't tell you? "Out of how many." How many did it miss? How well is it really doing? The red team is there to fill out the rest of those metrics for the defense team. The red team is not there to decide for them or even suggest what products they need to stop the attack. The red team is there to provide the metadata needed to empower the blue team to make the best possible decisions.

What nontechnical skills or attitudes do you look for when recruiting and interviewing red team members?
Drive. Pride. Honor. Respect. The technical skills can be taught to just about anyone. The aforementioned traits are something that are inside someone. The willingness to be behind the scenes, grinding, is the thing I see as the most valuable trait of a red teamer. Everyone is going to get pushed to give up, red or blue. The ones who can carry on in the face of adversity because of their dedication to the cause have the selfless nature that moves the needle. One breath at a time, one hack at a time, one collaboration at a time—they know that the mission is everything and will stop at nothing to get there.

What differentiates good red teamers from the pack as far as approaching a problem differently?
Being able to switch modalities. Removing the route to the issue allows you to see it from a different perspective. It may not be a shot you can take from the outside. It may not be a phish that lands. It may not be a cred you can find or a pivot you can make from the outside. It may not even be the guard you try to trick your way past. A good red teamer is ready to execute on any and every part of the battlefield. A great red teamer is one who knows how to spot the weakness and knows how to leverage the collective power of their team to get the job done. ■

"Red teaming isn't a smash-and-grab. The red team is there to support, train, and collaborate and to strengthen the organization."

Twitter: @redteamwrangler

Ryan O'Horo

30

Ryan is a red team lead engineer and has spent many years in security consulting. He has a particular interest in process analysis, continuous improvement, and building better teams.

How did you get your start on a red team?

I was working as a consultant doing penetration tests, putting an enormous amount of work into finding and exploiting vulnerabilities, but there was no end in sight. Some clients would fix a bunch of stuff, but I'd come back and find my way back to compromising Active Directory or an entire fleet of workstations. Worse, almost none of my clients could see what was going on during penetration tests. I was noisy and pervasive and didn't raise any red flags.

So, I sought to give my clients a way to detect attacks, as it seemed quite impossible to prevent them all. That's when I found red team as a concept, started attending blue team conferences, and proposed we start a red team practice.

Why can't we agree on what a red team is?

Red teams really need to be in tune with their organizations. What they do is highly dependent on what's needed, so what that is differs for every organization.

If you're consulting as a red team, the approach is usually quite different from an internal team. You have to be all things to a variety of organizations.

What is one thing the rest of information security doesn't understand about being on a red team? What is the most toxic falsehood you have heard related to red, blue, or purple teams?
Red teaming isn't a smash-and-grab. The red team is there to support, train, and collaborate and to strengthen the organization.

A verifiably false narrative is that a red team should remain siloed, with no organizational visibility, as if there's an attempt at preserving objectivity or the flawed assertion that threat actors work from zero knowledge. You're wasting valuable resources going from zero to full compromise in a silo. You're holding back on your organization's ability to learn from what the red team knows.

When should you introduce a formal red team into an organization's security program?
If you have an incident response program with analysts who work cases all day, it's about time.

How do you explain the value of red teaming to a reluctant or nontechnical client or organization?
You have detection, prevention, and response capability. How do you measure the quality of those capabilities? How do you know you're getting what you're paying for? The red team brings assurance that a wide range of threats would be made visible and manageable in your environment.

Have you ever recommended not doing a red team engagement?
As a consultant, I constantly told clients they weren't ready for a red team. I had several maturity-related screening questions to make sure I wasn't wasting everyone's time and money. Since it was in my wheelhouse, I normally recommended a vanilla internal penetration test. These will usually illuminate where prevention is greatly lacking and give you an opportunity to ask, "If this happened to us, how would we know?" If I felt the organization needed additional detection and response capability, I'd recommend companies that offered consulting on building a blue team practice.

What's the most important or easiest-to-implement control that can prevent you from compromising a system or network?
If your business is making widgets, your expertise is primarily in making widgets. It shouldn't fall entirely on your organization to onboard expertise in information security. Leveraging cloud services where security controls are managed by a much more capable and well-funded organization than your own is by far the best way to protect SMBs.

Why do you feel it is critical to stay within the rules of engagement?

> "The business depends on trust, and not just within security."

The business depends on trust, and not just within security. Where the red team is given the most latitude, it requires that much more trust to maintain. The rules are designed to protect the business, and if they aren't to your liking, you've either not done the legwork required to change them or don't understand the reason they employ you.

Many simply can't afford an acceptable level of assurance and put themselves or others at risk. I'm interested in ways to democratize access to information security.

What is the biggest ethical quandary you experienced while on an assigned objective?

I'll be honest, the day-to-day work doesn't bring *Law & Order*–quality drama. The biggest ethical challenge in my professional life is the unequal distribution of information security. Both people and organizations buy and sell a certain level of assurance for the safety and privacy of others. Many simply can't afford an acceptable level of assurance and put themselves or others at risk. I'm interested in ways to democratize access to information security.

If you were to switch to the blue team, what would be your first step to better defend against attacks?

Operationalizing intelligence is the core skill of a red team. Blue teams can and should have the same core skill. There's a world of difference between looking for a hash in an environment and determining whether a particular cross-process access event is benign or malicious based on numerous factors, like memory-protection flags.

Analysts may have a hard time contextualizing certain behaviors during an incident response unless they've seen that particular activity through the eyes of an attacker and their objectives. Studying intelligence and understanding how it can be used to defend an organization requires an attacker perspective, and it shouldn't just be the red team that applies that knowledge. Your engineers and analysts should be trained in offensive techniques.

What is some practical advice on writing a good report?

People learn best through storytelling. Reports should lead with a compelling narrative that communicates the story of your findings—what they mean in terms of real, honest risk to the business, not highly dramatized what-if scenarios.

Every finding should come with a proof of concept that an average engineer can execute and validate. Remediation advice should take into account that what often seems like an easy thing to do is nearly impossible or impractical at enterprise scale. Suggestions on how to prevent and detect should be included. You should also explain, at a high level, how to prevent similar findings from surfacing in the future to avoid whack-a-mole remediation.

How do you ensure your program results are valuable to people who need a full narrative and context?

The one true goal is to improve the organization and its people. That should be done through more than operations—where the lessons learned are primarily through data points. Group training, shadowing, and other one-on-one time is crucial for delivering on the one true goal.

What differentiates good red teamers from the pack as far as approaching a problem differently?

A good red teamer is never afraid of new detection and prevention technology. There's always a way to solve the problem of getting the job done, even if it doesn't solve the problem as presented. The confidence that there is a way creates a way. ■

"We all have a bias in several areas, and it is constant work to identify where we need improvement."

Carlos Perez

31

Carlos Perez has been active in the security community since 1999, working for the government of Puerto Rico, helping secure networks and performing internal pentests. He later joined Compaq/HP, where he worked as a senior solution architect for the security and networking consulting practices covering 33 countries in Central America, South America, and the Caribbean, helping customers to design and implement security solutions that helped meet their business needs in a secure way.

Carlos also worked as the director of reverse engineering at Tenable, Inc., where he was in charge of all remote code execution checks and finding zero-day vulnerabilities on products tested. He is currently the practice lead for research at TrustedSec, where he researches and develops both offensive and incident response tools for the consulting teams. Carlos is best known for his contributions to open source security tools like Metasploit, DNSRecon, and others. He has presented and provided training at conferences like Derbycon, DEF CON, Troopers, PSConfEU, HackCon, and BSidesPR.

How did you get your start on a red team?
It depends on the definition of red teaming. In the context of critical thinking and providing alternative thinking to technological projects with a business/operation impact, it started while I worked in consulting at Compaq. I was part of a team that would consult with customers to identify risk areas of new projects after gaining a deep understanding of the needs, goals, and perceived risks of the company. In terms of long-term simulation engagements, it was while I

worked at the beginning of the Compaq/HP merger, where I was outsourced to Microsoft to help in a large government contract where I was part of a team responsible for the security of the project.

What is the best way to get a red team job?
Let's start with the type of role you would like to have in a team. Most consulting organizations, as well as internal red teams, are at the technical emulation of the quadrant; it is also the one most practitioners promote and push, since most of their background is technical. For adversarial emulation, you will need

- A solid base in programming logic. By having this you will be able to adapt to most scripting languages in a short time. This will allow you to automate workflow, create new tools, and modify existing ones as needed.
- Good networking knowledge. Most actions will traverse an IP network, and an understanding of this environment is critical.
- System administration skills in the desired areas of expertise. You will need to understand how systems are configured, maintained, and secured so as to better understand areas where critical thinking can be applied.
- A self-didactic workflow. This is a field of constant learning, and having a defined method honed by constant practice for learning new skills is one of the most valuable tools you can have.
- The ability to identify and work against technical bias. We all have a bias in several areas, and it is constant work to identify where we need improvement.

On the nontechnical side:

- Learning about how teams work, are structured, and communicate. You will be part of multiple teams and eventually lead them. One thing to remember is that in red teaming the biases and political structure of an organization will be reflected in the technical reality, so understanding what composes the systems is of great value.
- Constant monitoring and learning new trends and best practices in the technology industry, not only the security field but the industry in general. Cloud and DevOps are great examples of technologies that many practitioners ignored for a long time and that are critical nowadays.
- Media skills. I know it is an area many feel uncomfortable with since many in the field are introverts. The idea of working to better communicate ideas and concepts is a scary one for many. At the end of the day, if you are not able to convey the risks, mitigation, and supporting information in a manner that decision-makers can use and comprehend, then you have failed.

How can someone gain red team skills without getting in trouble with the law?
There should be no reason whatsoever to engage in questionable or illegal actions to gain skills for this type of career. Information, training, and reference material to learn all aspects of it are available publicly, and all can be simulated in a lab environment to test and validate concepts.

Why can't we agree on what a red team is?
This is a very good question. The term and practice come from the military on the general side, and on the technical side, it was pioneered by Sandia National Labs IDART teams, yet we find that many practitioners keep redefining the terms

and actions. I do believe that one of the most common definitions boils down to a longer pentest with fewer restrictions and specific goals. This sets the playing field and causes customers to have the idea that red teaming is just that, since it is what is being pushed by the consultants offering the services. If we go further back and look at how it is taught at the University of Foreign Military and Cultural Studies (UFMCS), how multiple branches and agencies define it, we can see the emulation aspect is still there. However, emulation is not the main role of red teams (as we see many InfoSec consultancies push it as part of its definition). Red teaming is more providing an adversarial perspective to planning and operations, where personnel with critical thinking skills and an understanding of the technology, business, cultural, and political areas of the organization provide a noninstitutionalized way of thinking to help address areas of possible risk and also of improvements. It will take a paradigm shift on the InfoSec side to go beyond the comfort and self-gratification and include the other areas outside of pure emulation, but I believe several in the industry are seeing it and moving to expand their skill set and processes so as to expand the service portfolio they offer.

What is one thing the rest of information security doesn't understand about being on a red team? What is the most toxic falsehood you have heard related to red, blue, or purple teams?
That one needs to keep new exploits and techniques secret, even from customers, because otherwise one would lose the advantage in other engagements. It means that the only red team action you can provide is an emulation and that you have failed in cultivating a relationship with the customer—if you do not succeed over them then you have failed. In other words, expectations and metrics are not what they should be.

When should you introduce a formal red team into an organization's security program?
This is a hard one, since an organization's maturity level is not only technical but also political and operational. There has to be a culture of involving security at the start of a process, when it makes sense to have it, and a willingness to hear alternate critical ideas of plans when presented. Not many are willing to have their projects, in-place operations, and systems tested and be told of flaws. Also, there has to be a buy-in to put in the effort to eliminate or mitigate presented risks; in some rare cases it may mean completely abandoning a project once risks are identified that were not thought of.

> "There has to be a culture of involving security at the start of a process, when it makes sense to have it, and a willingness to hear alternate critical ideas of plans when presented."

How do you explain the value of red teaming to a reluctant or nontechnical client or organization?
After an initial meeting to understand what they did, how they operated, and what their worries were, I had to go and do research on the risks and security events that companies in their industry and their competitors had. I also

looked at who their customers were and their overall numbers. Once I had the information on their industry, how they operated, and their worries, I was able to justify a tabletop exercise. This was an organization that had multiple pentests done for compliance, and the security team made sure they were not the ones where we just run a scan and call it a pentest. I noticed little was being done between teams in terms of information sharing and process review and refinement, so a short tabletop exercise that would not be too expensive (with a focus on their industry and events of concern) was an easier sell. The engagement showed huge gaps in response time, access to information, and monitoring. Once value was shown from adversarial thinking, this opened the door to more services, from routine tests many times a year to being brought in for advice on new initiatives.

What is the least bang-for-your-buck security control that you see implemented?

The purchase of a tool or suite of tools with no training and metrics developed around its users and value. Many solutions without the properly trained personnel or a proper set of goals with metrics (and the results it hopes to achieve) are just blinking boxes in a rack providing a placebo effect for those who signed the check.

Have you ever recommended not doing a red team engagement?

Yes, many times. Especially when I see that the organization is not technically or operationally ready for it. For example, on the technical side, asset inventory, centralized logging, and patch management might not even be in place. On the operational side, if the security team is not part of the overall decision process and the political environment is one of competition and conflict between the security team and other teams, any value from the exercise would be watered down or completely lost. In many cases, helping develop proper IT infrastructure after a gap analysis or helping develop a proper vulnerability management program is of greater value.

"By following best practices from the vendors, you would be surprised how many avenues of entry would be blocked, allowing small teams to focus on automating detection of abnormal behavior."

What's the most important or easiest-to-implement control that can prevent you from compromising a system or network?

Address the most common avenues of entry first. Phishing and the use of malicious files are still very effective. Most companies do not block or control the execution of HTA, Windows Scripting Host, or Office macros. By following best practices from the vendors, you would be surprised how many avenues of entry would be blocked, allowing small teams to focus on automating detection of abnormal behavior. Profiling what is normal in an environment takes time to develop because it requires information by systematically addressing the most common techniques and putting monitoring in place; with time, the payoff is high.

Why do you feel it is critical to stay within the rules of engagement?

You are providing a service to a customer, either internal or external, for which one of the core foundations is trust. By breaking the ROE you are breaking the foundation, hampering the effectiveness of any recommendations provided.

If you were ever busted on a penetration test or other engagement, how did you handle it?

During one engagement, my established remote access sessions to the implants/agents started dropping, even the backup ones to alternate infrastructure and different beaconing intervals were seen. In the call, the customer mentioned they found them and started listing them one by one. My initial inner reaction was dread, but it quickly turned into excitement when I changed the way I was thinking. From "I'm busted, I lost" to "Man, they have their act together; they rock! This is awesome!" I reminded myself that my task is to help them test their security, and my main goal is to help them be more secure. Getting caught meant they had learned from previous engagements and were putting stuff into action. It meant I had made a difference, and I congratulated them on it. Then I went over every action and helped close any other small gaps to help them do even faster detection.

How does the red team work together to get the job done?

First, you need to have a clear understanding of what type of event it is and what is to be tested. Everyone should know the details of meetings and understand the client. Planning is done as a team; each member has an opinion that is considered for the initial plan. Depending on the size of the team, leads are selected based on their skills for parts of the plan, and one lead may have one or more areas to lead. An initial plan is discussed and agreed on; this includes the project manager, who will interface with the customer. As the engagement progresses, regular meetings are held to discuss actions and plan others, always taking input from the other team members. After an engagement, a debrief should be done where egos are left outside and people are honest about what needs improvement. Areas of improvement and action items are discussed and worked on as needed. New techniques or tools are documented and shared with the rest of the team so as to improve the collective knowledge base of the teams.

What is your approach to debriefing and supporting blue teams after an operation is completed?

Check your ego at the door. I try my best to make sure that they know I'm there to help them make their environment more secure and do not plan to be adversarial with them. I would start by complimenting them on all I found they are doing well, telling them which of their controls had the biggest impact in terms of tools, and explaining the tempo of operation in the engagement. Once we have shown what was good, we move on to how to improve their controls and processes. Asking questions also ensures it is a team effort and not just one side saying what they should do.

If you were to switch to the blue team, what would be your first step to better defend against attacks?

Look at the chain of attacks that would have the most impact on the environment so as to identify common links among them. Once those links are identified, I would look at how those links can be severed or monitored better, not only from a technical side but also from an overall operational side.

What is some practical advice on writing a good report?
I would say we have to adjust the way we view report writing. It is our final deliverable—the thing we will be measured on. It is in many ways a representation of our professional abilities. We must not see it as a painful activity but as one that can really have a valuable impact on the customer. When we change our view of the report, I believe it changes how we feel when we do it. A customer can tell by the quality and wording how much work went into the final deliverable they paid for. By not putting in the effort, we simply devalue the work that was done and how we are professionally seen.

How do you ensure your program results are valuable to people who need a full narrative and context?
You have people on your team with business and soft-skills knowledge who are able to work with members of the customer team to set the narrative. If such a relationship is not present, then clearly defining and understanding why you were hired will help you figure out how to tailor the recommendations and wording in the report. This means putting the proper amount of work into the pre-sales stage and in the definition stage of the SOW before the engagement and building proper relations during the engagement, when possible, with the parties of interest.

How do you recommend security improvements other than pointing out where it's insufficient?
When possible, I try to learn why something is the way it is before making a recommendation. Sadly, it is not possible every time, due to time constraints or being unable to learn details from the client for some reason. When I know the why of multiple areas, it is easier to provide solutions that may have bigger impact than just a log to monitor or a setting to change. This is where it is important to have that trusted advisor relationship that makes it easier to gather these extra pieces of information. Even so, I do try my best to understand how the recommendations may have impacts on the business processes supported by the affected systems. This makes it more likely that the team's recommendations will be adopted.

What nontechnical skills or attitudes do you look for when recruiting and interviewing red team members?
It is important to be teachable and to always be open and in search of learning new things, even if they are outside the person's comfort zone. One critical skill is to be able to put one's ego aside and be humble enough to say, "I do not know, but I will learn it."

What differentiates good red teamers from the pack as far as approaching a problem differently?
The breadth of knowledge a team has. This is more than the mastery of certain techniques. A red team must be able to cultivate a relationship based on trust with its customer, be it via consulting or internal to the organization. The strategic goal is always to help a customer see and mitigate all possible risks and to provide advice. At a tactical level, the team should develop the skills in the technological and business operational areas that will allow the team to succeed in achieving its strategic goals. ■

> "The main thing required to get hired as a red teamer is to have passion and determination as I showed; everything else is easy and falls into place."

Twitter: @0katz

Francesc Rodriguez

My name is Francesc Rodriguez. I am a 21-year-old Toronto-based Cuban-Canadian penetration tester and security researcher who likes to drink all the booze and hack all the things. During the day you can find me hacking for the government. By night you can find me doing research on binary analysis, endpoint security, web security, and network security research. I am the creator of the Temple of DOOM CTF series. This CTF series was made for beginning to intermediate skill levels looking to grind and get some new challenges thrown their way.

32

How did you get your start on a red team?
I was addicted to video games in middle school and was not producing satisfactory grades, mainly because I skipped classes to come home and play games on my PlayStation 3. My father would always get calls from school that I skipped school, and he would break my game discs. I had to figure out a way to make him think that I was no longer playing on my PlayStation, so I learned how to jailbreak my PlayStation and installed all the games internally. Back then, it was really easy. All you needed was a USB and custom firmware that George Hotz had released to jailbreak your console.

This sparked my interest in programming mods and cheats for games in C++. After I got bored with game hacking, I started reading books about security, as it gained my interest and sort of tied it together. From the first book, my interests and desires grew more and more. I started reading a book in two weeks and then some in a week. I found myself reading almost all day in my senior year of high school. This is around the time I began thinking I needed more challenges. After talking to some peers in the community, they pointed me to information security. Already being well versed in several programming languages and having good scripting skills, I decided I could give this a go. I installed Kali Linux and began learning some of the tools. This felt very "script kiddie" to me, but I was assured by many people in the InfoSec community that this was how it was.

Before I knew it, I was running scans and getting shells on systems. Again, my eagerness to learn and move forward pushed me to learn and to be quieter. Scans were making too much noise on the event loggers, and I wanted to find out how to be silent. This is around the time I enrolled in college for computer networking and really started seeking peers in the InfoSec community. I met a guy who went by Dead Rabbit. He was mysterious, he knew a lot, and he was willing to share it, but he was a ghost. He would come and go, but anytime I needed him, he was there.

Before I knew it, I was ranked #71 on Hack The Box, a virtual lab for hackers all over the world to sharpen their penetration testing skills. This really added to my CV and skills. From there I began seeking work in the field. My first job was as an SOC analyst, nothing lavish. I watched SIEM logs and reported findings to management and escalated issues as needed. It paid the bills, but it did not fill my desire to learn more and achieve. I left that job after a few months and found myself in a penetration testing/red team role for the government.

"Certifications and experience are something hiring managers look for in a red team candidate, such as the Offensive Security Certified Professional or Offensive Security Certified Expert certification, but that is not always the case."

What is the best way to get a red team job?

The main thing required to get hired as a red teamer is to have passion and determination as I showed; everything else is easy and falls into place. Certifications and experience are something hiring managers look for in a red team candidate, such as the Offensive Security Certified Professional or Offensive Security Certified Expert certification, but that is not always the case.

Fruits come in all shapes and sizes, and red teamers come from all different backgrounds. At one point computer engineers were programmer heavy, then they shifted into system administrators, and now there is a huge influx of cloud operators. All of these roles have relatively the same duties, but each is a different art. Red teaming is the same. The best way to get into the field is to have the will and desire, put in the work to get the knowledge, and keep learning. If you have the skills to do the job, look past those job requirements and apply for the positions. A lot of people look at the job requirements and get discouraged because most of them require five or more years of experience in the field, but I applied for a senior penetration tester position that required five-plus years of experience when I only had five months of experience on my résumé working in a SOC, but my technical skills helped me get past those requirements. This was because of my confidence and my ability to show my knowledge to the interview board.

How can someone gain red team skills without getting in trouble with the law?

The best way to gain red team skills without getting in trouble with the law is through free resources built by the InfoSec community. Hack The Box is a prime example of a free resource for hackers by hackers. This platform, in my opinion, is the best way to practice and improve your skills. I have gained most of my skills through their platform, and they even have a dedicated red team lab called RastaLabs where you can hack a very realistic Active Directory environment, which requires skills such as OSINT, phishing, local privilege escalation, persistence techniques, enumeration and exploitation, lateral movement techniques, and exploit development, as well as creative thinking, patience, and perseverance. Home labs also help a lot; this is where people use commercial-grade hardware in their homes. This creates a sandbox of a virtual world where all kinds of operating system distributions can be spun up and configured differently. There are also vulnerable instances of operating systems that can be used to help people learn.

Why can't we agree on what a red team is?

I think this is because there are so many dynamics at play; penetration testing is a loose end off of red teaming, but red teaming engages it more in a theoretical real-world scenario. Where penetration testers might send an attack here and there and see what is broken, red teamers will attempt to break in as many ways as they can. They also attempt to break the security overall, including firewalls, IDS, IPS, host-based security, physical security, and so on. Penetration testers can focus on just sending XSS attacks or attempt to utilize publicly disclosed exploits to gain access to a system and when it works, move on. Red teamers will run a realistic attack as if Russian or Chinese hackers were trying to break into the NSA's data center. There are no limitations on the engagement, and the red teamers can attack everything. Due to red teaming being a larger form of penetration testing, many people disagree about where it fits. The truth is, red teaming is penetration testing but with a goal of running through the logical space and getting as much access as possible, whereas penetration testing might focus on a single application to make sure there is input validation, error handling, and other security functions.

> "One thing I don't think the other groups realize is the level of effort put in by red teamers."

What is one thing the rest of information security doesn't understand about being on a red team? What is the most toxic falsehood you have heard related to red, blue, or purple teams?

There are many different aspects of information security, such as cybersecurity, threat management, risk management, compliance, penetration testing, and so forth. One thing I don't think the other groups realize is the level of effort put in by red teamers. I don't want to say that as red teamers we are the cream of the crop, because the other groups also pitch in, but we simulate realistic attacks on the enterprise and identify vulnerabilities and gaps. The most toxic falsehood I've ever heard is that one element is more important than another; without a red, purple, or blue team, your organization would be incomplete. They each play a part and, while not equally important, are all required to play their parts.

When should you introduce a formal red team into an organization's security program?

Honestly and bluntly, the second your product hits production, you should have had thoughts about a red team having at it. If you are putting an application or service out there without a red team, you are opening a can of worms. For example, if you put your product into production and get a customer who begins processing data on your system, and then a hacker breaches that system and obtains that data, that would be a very bad time because of negligence in terms of the security program. Security needs to be in place from the beginning, not added on at the end; while the red team might not need to be there, there would need to be other security tests, but before going live, the red team should have a go at the whole platform.

> "If you are putting an application or service out there without a red team, you are opening a can of worms."

How do you explain the value of red teaming to a reluctant or nontechnical client or organization?

I think this is the same as any security language. Adding the red team element adds no difference. Speak to those people at a high level in terms they understand, and make sure they understand why it is important. For example, you could explain to the client to think of it like this—a Ferrari will get normal wear and tear, and without the proper tune-ups it can break. This would include shocks, suspension, oil change, and so forth. Red teaming could be one of those elements. It is something that is needed; the language just needs to be at a level the person will understand.

What is the *least* bang-for-your-buck security control that you see implemented?

The worst security control I have seen implemented in an enterprise is McAfee VirusScan+ AntiSpyware Enterprise. This is an all-purpose security solution that doesn't include endpoint monitoring. A small percentage of compromises are caught by endpoint antivirus. The game has changed and gotten more complex, and a second line of defense is now needed to fully protect from the unknown adversary. Traditional endpoint protection is no longer up to par for this task.

What's the most important or easiest-to-implement control that can prevent you from compromising a system or network? For example, how can we help small and medium businesses who have a smaller budget and staff?

The simplest way to achieve this is to outsource. Depending on the scope, if a small organization cannot afford to maintain these people, they should outsource the task to a third party.

Why do you feel it is critical to stay within the rules of engagement?

There are legal reprimands if you do not stay within the rules of engagement, and these are very costly fines. More than that, it would ruin your firm's reputation as a red teamer if you don't follow the rules of engagement on your contract. If this is an internal red team, it would create a null result. If things were found outside of the scope, it would waste man-hours as well as possibly compromise those systems.

If you were ever busted on a penetration test or other engagement, how did you handle it?
I have never been busted thanks to @dollarvpnclub.

What is the biggest ethical quandary you experienced while on an assigned objective?
I have found time and time again "juicy" exploits. I don't want to go into the specifics of the exploits, but it was client data on these systems that would be considered confidential. However, because of my morals and ethics, I report my findings immediately to management and relieve the burden from my shoulders.

What is some practical advice on writing a good report?
Reports should include the relevant information in a clear and concise way. This isn't a time to play dress-up and make it look all pretty. It is effective when it delivers the information in a manner that flows and allows the customer to understand what the findings were and the recommendations made.

How do you ensure your program results are valuable to people who need a full narrative and context?
A mixture of screenshots and context in text will alleviate this issue. The customer or intended recipient of the report needs to understand what is going on and be able to get a full picture rather than what the red teamer thought was important. A standard operation process from the red teamer's organization could help immensely here.

How do you recommend security improvements other than pointing out where it's insufficient?
Over the years I have learned that the best method is to provide proof detailing what the issue is and why it happens, rather than just saying it exists. For example, I've discovered backdoors and zero days before even any exploiting; this was done by thinking out a potential issue and seeing it through. I was able to identify a vulnerability in a self-password reset that is used in a lot of enterprises to avoid having to go through the help-desk team for support. I pointed it out to my team, and they just kind of shrugged it off at first, but the next day I came back with a SYSTEM shell without authenticating to our work computers, and they began to take the issue seriously. The way to recommend anything is to show the issue and bring forth solutions as recommendations. Additionally, analyze the inherent risk and put in controls to reduce it to just residual risk.

What nontechnical skills or attitudes do you look for when recruiting and interviewing red team members?
They need to have good communication, and if they don't but have very good technical skills, we just need to add someone who can put their thoughts on paper. Recruits should be confident but not have too big of an ego or signs of toxicity. People like that bring down the overall productivity of the team, which would be counterproductive. The most useful nontechnical skills by far are writing reports and communicating issues and findings. ■

> "I often joke that I have one of the only jobs in the world where it's my duty to make my job harder tomorrow than it was yesterday, but I wouldn't have it any other way."

Twitter: @_r00k_

Derek Rook

33

Derek is an industry veteran with more than 15 years of experience spanning systems administration and engineering, web development, security engineering, and offensive security. In the office, he devotes his time to building and running an internal offensive security practice. Out of the office, he splits time between family, martial arts, teaching for SANS, and building his own consulting practice, Corvid Security. A NetWars Tournament of Champions winner and NolaCon black badge holder, he can often be found participating in whatever CTF competitions he can find. Derek holds several security certifications, including GCIA, GNFA, GCIH, GWAPT, GXPN, and OSCP.

How did you get your start on a red team?

I kind of fell into it. By that, I mean offensive security was a career goal of mine since 15-year-old me saw *Sneakers* for the first time and found out I could do criminal stuff legally (with permission) and get paid for it. After that, I took every tech job I could get ahold of. I bounced from web development back in the heyday of Allaire Cold Fusion to help desk to Linux admin to systems engineering and finally into a security role. I had been doing security engineering for a while and pursuing offensive security as a hobby. I was kind of working three jobs at the time, with my day job, my YouTube channel, and doing as much research and lab building as possible to teach myself the various skills I'd need to transition.

I think my work in the community got me noticed because I got a call from someone in my extended professional network. They were putting together a new product security team and asked if I wanted to build the internal offensive security practice. I not only got to pivot into full-time offensive security, but I got to build my own team and define my own program.

What is the best way to get a red team job?

Professional networking. Keeping up to date on the latest trends, comparing notes on new techniques, and even just getting a heads-up about new positions opening up can be a huge leg up. Offensive security and red teams are still relatively rare, so there's a lot of competition for positions.

How can someone gain red team skills without getting in trouble with the law?

The dirty secret is that most red team skills are just system administration and development skills. Utilize virtualization and free/cheap cloud accounts to practice setting up infrastructure. Learn how things fit together, why different services are required, what purpose they serve, and so on. Not only will that help you understand how to abuse misconfigurations and move through an environment like a normal user would, it'll also teach you how to set up a resilient command-and-control infrastructure. Blue and red are the same skill set with different intentions, and you can learn a lot without ever simulating malicious activity.

Why can't we agree on what a red team is?

I think we get too caught up in titles sometimes. Everyone's job at a company is to participate in making the company money. Our job in security is to de-risk business decisions as much as possible, while doing our best to balance priority #1 (making money) with protecting our employees and customers. If we could all agree on that, I think things would move more efficiently for red and blue alike.

What is one thing the rest of information security doesn't understand about being on a red team? What is the most toxic falsehood you have heard related to red, blue, or purple teams?

One thing I think a lot of people don't internalize very well is that our job is to help the company attract and retain profitable customers—not to "hack the crap" out of the company or roadblock potentially risky progress. I've heard this in a few places before, and my current CISO is fond of saying, "We put brakes on cars so we can go faster."

When should you introduce a formal red team into an organization's security program?

Well, I was hire #1 in a new product security group, so I'd say whenever. I will say there have definitely been challenges associated with that decision, though. Frequently teams are just unsure how to handle working with my team and start trying to slot our service catalog into more traditional security roles like source code analysis or asset discovery. That being said, I'm willing to bet every offensive security or red team ran into similar hurdles in their inception, regardless of the maturity of the surrounding organizations. Honestly, the forward thinking of the company to want an offensive team so early is one of the things that drove me to my current employer.

How do you explain the value of red teaming to a reluctant or nontechnical client or organization?

An organization spends money systematically securing their company and/or product. They develop best practice and hardening guidelines. They implement vulnerability discovery and management programs. All of this is an attempt to anticipate how an adversary would approach attacking their company and to try to preempt that attack with proactive defenses. They do all of that guessing but stop short of having adversarial-minded professionals simulate an attack. These simulations are ways to benchmark the defensive programs put in place and put vulnerability findings into context and priority.

What is the *least* bang-for-your-buck security control that you see implemented?

Security information and event management (SIEM). It's not that SIEMs aren't useful, but I often see organizations implement them to "solve security" but give zero consideration to what is feeding them. They're often either grossly over- or under-fed. Having too many alerts is just as bad as having no alerts because people tend to ignore everything and useful data gets lost in the noise. A deliberately fed and monitored SIEM can be extremely useful; I just wish it were more common.

Have you ever recommended not doing a red team engagement?

I kind of get to cheat on this one since I run an internal team. We're constantly tuning what we recommend based on what needs to be done. We don't have to worry as much about billable hours and whether the red team has a higher rate than pentesting. We still do a formalized SOW process, but it gets to be more fluid. Sometimes we get in the middle of an engagement and realize that a different type of engagement is warranted, and luckily we have the flexibility to do that.

What's the most important or easiest-to-implement control that can prevent you from compromising a system or network?

Educate your users. We need to get rid of the concept of yearly security awareness. We also need to stop dunking on the concept of idiot users. Sure, they're our biggest attack surface, but they're also our biggest defensive perimeter. They are the biggest and most sophisticated IDS in the world. When "something is weird with my computer," no IDS could pick that up. Sure, they're not super specific sometimes, but with education they could be. Eight hours a month (total, not per security person) can develop an awesome ongoing education program and have better results than hundreds of thousands in "blinkenboxen."

Why do you feel it is critical to stay within the rules of engagement?

Rules of engagement are what separates explicit consent from unauthorized. It's the explicit consent that separates offensive security from crime. I've seen the community sometimes start blurring the lines in the name of "But adversaries wouldn't obey the rules." It's important to remember that we are *not* adversaries; we only simulate them in engagements. It goes back to the whole "We're there to make the company money, not hack the planet" thing.

What is the biggest ethical quandary you experienced while on an assigned objective?

In our line of work, we often gain access to data we shouldn't have, such as HR data, PII, or PHI. In general, I'm pretty good about recognizing things based on location and filename, but sometimes a keylogger grabs more than we intended, or a file with potential credentials in it has more info. Thankfully, nothing I've gained access to has had legal implications so far, so I try to act as I would if I didn't have that info as much as possible.

How does the red team work together to get the job done?

None of that can happen in a vacuum. There's this perception that all hackers are wizards, capable of bending computing infrastructure to their will with only their mind bullets. Nothing could be further from the truth. Humans are just more effective overall when they specialize. Teams become truly awesome when you blend people with complementary, but different, specializations together.

I'm fortunate that the team I've built so far is a diverse group with different perspectives, backgrounds, and skills. We work insanely well together, and we prove our value to our company constantly.

All of that, though, is useless if all we do is hack stuff, drop mic, repeat. Working with the blue team, product teams, and even (and especially) nontechnical staff to shore up our defenses and make our company more resilient is vital to performing our duties. It's not even just about security in the traditional sense. Complexity often introduces many security concerns. We've worked with development teams to simplify their solutions. Sure, it made them more secure, but it also made them more performant and reduced development overhead for that team moving forward. We're all a cohesive team, working toward the same goal.

What is your approach to debriefing and supporting blue teams after an operation is completed?

If we're not working a covert engagement, we're usually in constant communication with operations, development, and security staff. We provide nightly progress reports and oftentimes are in Slack with them discussing current findings and potential paths forward.

In covert engagements, we often try to bring a nonoffensive person onto the team to be part of the team for the engagement. At the end of the engagement, we divulge everything and work with the various teams involved to help them understand what we did and how we did it, and try to identify remediations, process updates, and whatever would help in stopping us from doing that again.

My goal is to never be able to do the same thing twice. I'm in offensive security because I love learning new things and diving deeper into my understanding of old things. I often joke that I have one of the only jobs in the world where it's my duty to make my job harder tomorrow than it was yesterday, but I wouldn't have it any other way.

If you were to switch to the blue team, what would be your first step to better defend against attacks?

That's probably too environment-dependent for me to answer specifically. I will say that I think it's good for everyone to hop the aisle every once and a while. The 15 years I spent in nonoffensive tech gave me fantastic insight in how companies run and how defenders defend. I apply that intuitive understanding in my job every day. When I eventually hop back to blue, or into a more hybrid role, I'll be applying the lessons I've learned as an attacker to my defenses. One thing that I think isn't done enough in companies is training people to think like an attacker. They don't have to be trained to be full-on hackers, but getting people to break out of their shells a little and understand how software and systems can be abused will make them much more effective developers, operators, and support staff.

What is some practical advice on writing a good report?

Write the report like it's your job. Here's the secret...it is your job. All the 1337 h4x0ring in the world is no good to anyone if you can't articulate what you did and what the impact is and offer good, actionable recommendations on how to effectively mitigate or respond to your report.

Writing the report while you test is important. Taking excellent and comprehensive notes as you move not only improves your ability to internalize the information you're discovering but makes report writing a lot more fluid. Most people who are researching their next attack or payload are already reading about the defenses they'll need to circumvent or what misstep in the defenses allowed them to breach them in the first place, so make notes of those and learn more about them as you go. This will make your attacks more effective and assist in making excellent remediation recommendations. Most hackers love learning. Report writing is just another opportunity to learn about attacking and defending.

How do you ensure your program results are valuable to people who need a full narrative and context?

Our reports have a few different sections to illustrate our findings from different perspectives. We have an "Attack Scenarios" section that contains our attack maps and descriptions of the different paths we took through an environment. They link back to specific findings, but in general it provides a wider view of the engagement, as well as context for why specific findings matter. We have a detailed findings section, where security deficiencies are listed with remediation recommendations. It's not just vulnerabilities, but process and policy deficiencies, and so on. Lastly, or firstly, we have additional sections in our executive summary that talk about things that went well during the engagement and areas for improvement. This gives us a place to highlight things that were done well by all of the nonoffensive teams involved in the engagement. It keeps the report from being an overall negative message and crafts an overall more complete message.

How do you recommend security improvements other than pointing out where it's insufficient?

Get people invested and involved in their own security—not just their work security but personal and home security. I gave an internal talk a couple companies ago that included a 15-minute hacking demo. It was a "From phish to watching your webcam and stealing your tax documents" flashy-magic-show-hacking-demo. The chief council asked if he could talk to me about their personal life security for 15 minutes. Fifteen minutes turned into an hour and a half, and I think it was the most productive hour and a half I could have spent in that company. They became an advocate for security there, and a lot of things changed as more people bought into that.

What nontechnical skills or attitudes do you look for when recruiting and interviewing red team members?

Curiosity, hands down. If someone has the drive to understand the what, how, and why of something, they can be taught rote technical syntax. I spent eight hours over the last two days reading help documentation to understand how some arcane utilities operated, resulting in pivoting opportunity I wouldn't have found otherwise. It's hard to maintain that sort of focus unless you're intellectually invested in the answer. I think the word *passion* is a bit of a cliché in our industry, and it's often used as an excuse to provide awful work-life balance to one's employees. I'm passionate about making sure my employees have good balance and don't work too much. I think curiosity is what provides that drive and focus while still being able to have nontechnical hobbies.

What differentiates good red teamers from the pack as far as approaching a problem differently?

Their ability to not take things at face value. Red teaming is about challenging assumptions and testing other potential avenues of reasoning, even if it runs against common convention. Red teamers are the type of people who look at a situation and instead of thinking "This is what this means," they think "This is what I can make of this." I think people can be taught that skill, like teaching developers to think in terms of abuse cases or attacker stories in addition to user stories, but some people consider alternatives naturally. ∎

Twitter: @isaiahsarju
Image: Gregory Rothstein

"If you don't showcase what you did in a report, you never did it."

Isaiah Sarju

Isaiah is a curious hacker with a love for people. He's been hacking things since elementary school when he started tinkering with computers. His first formal information security position was at the Microsoft Malware Protection Center in 2008. Since then, he's conducted numerous offensive security engagements and helped others become top-tier security practitioners. He relishes a good hack, and his favorite part of any engagement is performing postexploitation activity. When he's not hacking, teaching, or fighting for a more equitable future, he plays tabletop games, swims, and trains in Brazilian Jiu-Jitsu.

34

How did you get your start on a red team?
To answer this simply, I started doing network penetration testing consulting and eventually transitioned into red team work because I desired more technical challenges. The skills that have served me well come from a life of asking "What happens if I do this?" all while I built technical experience through IT help desk, systems administration, and the like.

What is the best way to get a red team job?
Develop your skills and then play to your strengths. Build a well-rounded portfolio of offensive security knowledge and then specialize in one or more areas that interest you. Red teams need a diversity of skill sets to take on a wide range of projects, but they also need folks who can go deep in specific areas. For example, if you've specialized in attacking infrastructure hosted in AWS, look to join a red team at an organization that has moved, or is moving, to the cloud.

"Consulting is one of the fastest ways to hone the skill sets that you will use in red teaming. You will get a diversity of experience and build the communication skills necessary to provide the consultative services that red teams often need to provide."

Don't make an organization that's never heard of infrastructure as code your first choice.

How can someone gain red team skills without getting in trouble with the law?

Consulting is one of the fastest ways to hone the skill sets that you will use in red teaming. You will get a diversity of experience and build the communication skills necessary to provide the consultative services that red teams often need to provide.

If consulting isn't an option, ask for authorization to do offensive work during your day-to-day work. Penetration testing, and subsequently red teaming, is often malicious systems administration. Do not discount the skills that you already use, and learn how you can use those same skills for a little fun and profit.

Why can't we agree on what a red team is?

There's a conflict between what's sexy and what's needed. I argue that most companies do not need a red team. Sure, they need folks with offensive attack knowledge, but they have to cover the basics first. If they are consistently getting wrecked on penetration tests, they need to invest in basic security. Red teams exist to help the security organization level up, not to be their patch management program.

Even though it's a resource drain to invest in a red team, many organizations want to build one. Perhaps someone learned at a conference or from a blog post that they "need" to have one. Or maybe they want the technical talent that's attracted to a position like "red teamer." So we end up with folks who are capable of legitimate red teaming working at companies that aren't even ready for a stock penetration test. This makes it hard to accurately describe the team: they're called a red team, made up of red teamers, but they're tasked with running a vulnerability scanner.

What is one thing the rest of information security doesn't understand about being on a red team? What is the most toxic falsehood you have heard related to red, blue, or purple teams?

It's not cool spy stuff all of the time. By being specialized, you're often the go-to for guidance. Your job is not just to wreck networks with mic drop attacks. It's a lot of education and finding ways to convince folks to stop doing what they've been doing for many, many years.

Red teams don't need to be antagonistic all of the time. Yes, they need to test the organization, and they need to relish in cool hax; that's their job. But when they position themselves as the enemy of the blue team, they stop seeing themselves as being on the same larger team with the same goal: to make the organization better.

When should you introduce a formal red team into an organization's security program?

After building, maintaining, and fully utilizing an internal penetration testing team, some organizations try to jump from third-party penetration testing to red teaming. They often don't have the infrastructure ready to support an internal team. Many times the organization doesn't uniformly understand what the red team is going to do. And most critically, the other functions that the red team is meant to help level up (SOC, IR team, etc.) are frequently too immature for ongoing red team testing. There is learning, growth, and practical infrastructure that emerges from deploying an internal penetration testing team. These same steps help an organization grow into red teaming.

When the defenders are no longer challenged by the internal penetration testing team's work and the testing team naturally starts to do more complex adversary-style engagements, then the organization is ready for a red team.

How do you explain the value of red teaming to a reluctant or nontechnical client or organization?

An effective step for me is to ask them to enumerate the types of threats that their organization faces. I then ask if standard penetration testing is emulating those threats.

As a side note, even if there are advanced adversaries in an organization's threat model, it doesn't mean they're ready for red teaming. It likely means they need to level up quickly because they're in over their heads.

What is the *least* bang-for-your-buck security control that you see implemented?

Whatever the last vendor tried to convince you would solve all of your security woes or a problem you don't have. We don't need to invent problems; we're surrounded by them. Many problems are solved by improving processes and fine-tuning the technology we already have. Whenever someone would rather sell you a new product than help you get to the root of why you're broken in the first place, run the other way.

Have you ever recommended not doing a red team engagement?

Absolutely! I'm probably not a very good "company man" when I am consulting. I rarely upsell clients. Sometimes I have an eager client who will ask me if they are ready for a red team, and I kindly remind them of the test I just conducted.

I have recommended and continue to recommend investing in organizational changes that build security into day-to-day processes. You get more bang for your buck buying U2F tokens for everyone than paying to have a one-week engagement where they pick locks (you know are bad), install backdoors on unlocked laptops (you know aren't monitored), and elevate to domain admin (in an environment you know is full of weaknesses). Similarly, you get more bang for your buck if you hire two SOC analysts and have them build robust SEIM correlation logic than if you hire a wizard hacker who costs four times as much.

What's the most important or easiest-to-implement control that can prevent you from compromising a system or network?

System: All users use nonadministrative credentials for day-to-day work.
Network: Pervasive 2FA.

Why do you feel it is critical to stay within the rules of engagement?

It is the document that makes everything we do "legal." Without it we could be "accessing a computer without authorization, or in excess of authorization." (See 18 U.S.C. ¬ß 1030.)

If you were ever busted on a penetration test or other engagement, how did you handle it?

No one specific occasion comes to mind. One of my biggest pet peeves on penetration testing engagements is when the client asks me to "simulate an APT" with a two-week scope! What aggravates me even more is when someone actively works to disrupt my test but would not detect my activity without prior knowledge. Something that happens occasionally is someone, privy to the test, sees that I am using a service account and then they rotate a password that hasn't been changed in over three years. When they do this, they are basically raising their hand and saying "I'm arrogant, I don't want to look bad, and I have limited judgment." They make themselves my number-one target and will inevitably find their credentials in the report (masked out, usually). I especially appreciate when they use their domain admin account to come kick me off a system and end up handing me their juicy credentials.

What is the biggest ethical quandary you experienced while on an assigned objective?

I've been lucky; my work has been free of these.

How does the red team work together to get the job done?

The first "team" that the red team is on is the organization's. This means they're on the same team as the blue team. It is important to remove the "us versus them" political mentality or the desire to point fingers and laugh. Hacking stuff is sexy, but building a resilient security program is magical. Red teams need to see blue team wins as their own, not distinct.

When it comes to the team aspect of getting the job done, it's in the diverse skill sets it takes to reach and then perform actions on objectives. You need folks who can establish footholds through phishing, zero days, or physical compromise. You need other folks who know how to stealthily move around a network. You need other folks to perform everything in between. No one person can do all of that (in a reasonable amount of time).

> "I am on the same team as my client, so my work isn't done until their work is done."

What is your approach to debriefing and supporting blue teams after an operation is completed?

I am on the same team as my client, so my work isn't done until their work is done. This can be different for internal versus third-party red teams, but the mentality can be the same. Internally, I am there to provide as much information as possible to help them identify what I did (pcaps, commands, timestamps, etc.). As a third party, my goal is to provide as much information as possible to avoid my client needing further assistance. Third-party red team engagements should always be scoped to include support during remediation and retesting.

If you were to switch to the blue team, what would be your first step to better defend against attacks?

Teach blue teamers to test their own monitoring, alerting, and response solutions using offensive techniques. Just as we preach test code as it's built, we should test our monitoring, alerting, and response solutions as we deploy them.

Defense and offense are taught as separate disciplines, but they should not be. We can specialize in one or the other, but we need more shared knowledge.

What is some practical advice on writing a good report?

The first step is reframing how we look at it. Instead of seeing it as a burden to be done as the last step, at the last minute, see it as a showcase of your 1337'ness. No one will ever know how much of a badass you are unless you show them. Often the report is the one thing that a customer is paying for, so treat it as such. If you don't showcase what you did in a report, you never did it.

On a practical note, some techniques that work well for me are report as I go, screenshot everything, and have my first draft done well in advance. This way I have evidence for everything I have done, especially if I find something that is not reproducible later. Additionally, I like to write a report, sleep on it, edit it once, give it some time, edit it a second time, give it some more time, and do a final read-through. Having strong reporting skills not only makes me look good but helps me with my main objective: to make folks better.

How do you ensure your program results are valuable to people who need a full narrative and context?

Stick to the facts. Avoid talking about problems as isolated issues. Discuss their larger impact and articulate how improved processes will impede a future attack. Narratives are powerful tools to provide context, especially with multistage attacks. Due to their compelling nature, it's also a great place to highlight what could have stopped that attack. Saying something like, "Credential reuse and single-factor authentication allowed the consultant to take credentials found in the general user environment and use them to compromise the super-secret environment" is powerful. It doesn't point fingers, but it still drives home the impact.

How do you recommend security improvements other than pointing out where it's insufficient?

The first step is in how we talk about insufficiencies. It should never be "Well, some idiot did this." It should be "If your goal is to achieve A, then you need to be doing B, and here's why." It depersonalizes blame and shifts the focus to solutioning.

What nontechnical skills or attitudes do you look for when recruiting and interviewing red team members?

Communication and the ability to teach. You can be the best hacker in the world, but I don't want you on my team if you can't teach others, whether that's a fellow team member or a project manager whose product you just hacked.

What differentiates good red teamers from the pack as far as approaching a problem differently?

The belief that they're never done learning and that there's always a new way to attack a problem. ∎

> "In my opinion, some of the most fulfilling work on the red team is being able to work with your blue team to fix your areas of weakness."

Twitter: @0x_90

Mary Sawyer

35

Mary Sawyer is currently a member of the red team at Palo Alto Networks. In addition to her work on the red team to stay ahead of the attackers by embracing their mentality, strategies, and tactics to test the organization's security posture, Mary is also innovating on the purple team program.

Mary has a bachelor's degree in computer science, with a certificate in information security, from the University of Texas at Austin. She is a strong advocate for inspiring and empowering girls through technology.

How did you get your start on a red team?
I really got my start in offensive security by joining the security club at my college. I had a lot of fun learning and teaching other students about security concepts and cool script-kiddie stuff I had read about online. A sponsor of that club heard about my work and generously invited me to come hack their stuff for a living.

What is the best way to get a red team job?
I'm a little partial to my own approach, which was to join a security club. It allowed me to explore a wide range of topics and gain access to a larger audience. I think there are other, less college-focused ways I could recommend like Twitter or security conferences. Even if you don't work in security, I think you can easily make a name for yourself if you find a cool research topic.

How can someone gain red team skills without getting in trouble with the law?

Antihacking laws can get complicated, but a general rule of thumb is that you must have permission from the owner. So, my advice would be to hack your own stuff! A good starting point could be hacking into your own Wi-Fi with Aircrack, testing an exploit on cheap phones you can buy online, or hacking your own computer with Kon-Boot or any other lab equipment that is owned by you.

Why can't we agree on what a red team is?

I think it's a maturity issue. The needs of a young security organization aren't remotely the same as those of an older organization. Even if the young organization is well funded, they are still putting out fires that an older organization contained a while back. Every company is also structured a little differently, even if we have similar names for things. The field of information security itself is still young compared to others, so I think these things will work out with time.

> "The needs of a young security organization aren't remotely the same as those of an older organization."

What is one thing the rest of information security doesn't understand about being on a red team? What is the most toxic falsehood you have heard related to red, blue, or purple teams?

I've observed a lot of people interested in joining the red team. A lot of people think that if they join the red team, they won't be worried about getting hacked anymore because they are the ones who are going to be doing all the hacking. If anything, being on the red team makes a person even more paranoid! After learning how simple a lot of the APT hacks are and how cheap it would be for a random developer or IT person to replicate the same attack, I can at least speak for myself and say that I have a lot harder time believing that everyone is as calm as they look. This leads me to my next point: most kids I've talked to who want to get a job on the red team believe it will be shells all day, every day. You really don't want that. In my opinion, some of the most fulfilling work on the red team is being able to work with your blue team to fix your areas of weakness.

When should you introduce a formal red team into an organization's security program?

I think security programs can start building a red team as soon as they have the power in an IT organization to ask stakeholders to fix holes in their security. If you don't have the power to actually fix *any* of the findings from a red team assessment, then there's little value in building one besides having a handy list of assets that a threat actor can exploit.

How do you explain the value of red teaming to a reluctant or nontechnical client or organization?

Some people are only ever going to be concerned about security when they face the consequences of doing something insecurely. Red teams can be extremely useful in this respect. We air out the dirty laundry for our organizations before it gets into the hands of nation-states, organized crime, script kiddies, and so on. This usually means big money is at stake, which gets tickets closed and issues fixed a lot faster than a polite vulnerability scanner.

Have you ever recommended not doing a red team engagement?

Not everyone is ready for a red team assessment! If you know that there are deficiencies in an environment and still request someone to exploit them, there are two outcomes: you end up with no new insight into your environments or with a tremendous backlog of tickets that no one is actively fixing anyway. My recommendation was to enable the people in charge of working on the backlog of tickets and to have a red team assessment afterward to assess what should ideally be a secure environment. That's where the true value of a red team lies.

What's the most important or easiest-to-implement control that can prevent you from compromising a system or network? For example, how can we help small and medium businesses who have a smaller budget and staff?

From my experiences, the most important control is going to be some type of password management solution. If you do it right, it makes lots of attacks useless (i.e., password spraying, default passwords, password reuse, etc.). It's easy to get wrong and hard to fix after you messed it up the first time. That's why I think small and medium businesses especially can benefit from focusing on this first.

How does the red team work together to get the job done?

Being part of a team means constant and robust communications. Because our work is sensitive, it's also important that our chat programs are end-to-end encrypted. Some of the best work is done in a pair programming style, though. It's inevitable that we will hit a wall sometime during the day. This makes it so that everyone contributes and learns from one another. When we move on to reporting, we sit down and write out the story, add details, and then edit in a circle until we're satisfied. Working with the blue team is like a consultation. They ring, we answer (depending on who broke what).

What is your approach to debriefing and supporting blue teams after an operation is completed?

This depends on whether they catch us. If they catch us, the jig is up. We drop everything and start the cleanup phase together, sharing our timeline and what commands we ran and where. If they don't, we usually wait until we officially call off the exercise and present our findings formally with an overview of affected systems and compromised data. Later, we'll then have a postmortem meeting where we share the timeline with details and work through where they could have caught us. After that, we'll work with them in creating alerts as consultants on the technical details.

If you were to switch to the blue team, what would be your first step to better defend against attacks?

I'm lucky to work in an InfoSec organization that encourages a lot of open collaboration and sharing of information between the red and blue teams. It leads to a lot of awesome innovation on both sides. If I were to switch to the blue team, the first thing I would do is to ask the red team: What do you want me to fix? What are the biggest problems facing the blue team? A lot of people have the knee-jerk reaction of "Oh, we're on opposite sides. I can never, ever talk to them, especially not about how insecure our stuff is!" I think it should be the opposite.

What is some practical advice on writing a good report?

I think you should start out by writing a story. You know that your job is cool; now write about how cool it was in the report! Then, add the details and screenshots. If you have a template, start copying your story over, and you will naturally begin the editing process. Take a coffee break, and then go in again and edit one more time before handing it over to a colleague for editing again. If at all possible, try to get some creative writing classes! It doesn't have to be a painful process. The more you get used to the writing process, the better the reporting cycle will be for both you and the consumer.

How do you ensure your program results are valuable to people who need a full narrative and context?

We provide a few different sources of information from red team exercises that go out to different people. To our managers, of course, we showcase our skill sets. In reporting that goes outside of our InfoSec organization, we highlight areas where other teams have improved to give credit where credit is due. Most of what affected parties actually see as a product from us are tickets that are added to regular development sprints by their product managers, so it's a relatively painless process.

How do you recommend security improvements other than pointing out where it's insufficient?

I draw on my experiences as a developer to put things into terms that other developers want to hear: issues or tickets with detailed instructions (bullet points telling them where to click is optimal) or code samples that they should use to replace the bad code. Sometimes the fixes are more complicated, which means that your reporting process needs to be more complicated. If possible, it's best to sit with developers or IT or whoever you need to in order to ask them what they think is wrong and ideally provide guidance so that they'll do it the right way in the future.

What nontechnical skills or attitudes do you look for when recruiting and interviewing red team members?

The skills that have been most useful for me include writing skills, presentation skills, empathy, and a good sense of humor. Writing skills are probably my number-one skill. You need them for report writing, explaining vulnerabilities (ones that you find and other people's depending on the quality of their original write-up), and a million other random tasks. Good presentation skills are especially important, as you will inevitably have to talk to senior directors, VPs, project managers, and other stakeholders. If you are bad at explaining what you did during a red team exercise or elsewhere, it will essentially erase some of the critical work you did in discovering vulnerabilities in the first place. The last two skills, empathy and a good sense of humor, become important when talking to someone impacted by your work. While everyone wants their own work to be properly respected and praised, you won't get that by making fun of the developer whose account you took over or rubbing it in to the blue team.

What differentiates good red teamers from the pack as far as approaching a problem differently?

I think the best red teamers are good communicators. Everyone seems to think that the way to be the best red teamer is to find a zero day in everything or get a shell on the CEO's laptop. Yeah, that's also an important part of the job, but if you want to elevate the craft, you need to be able to tell other people what went wrong and how to fix it. If you can do both of those things really well, you're sitting pretty. ■

"I am a self-taught penetration tester and ethical hacker. I learned the craft by setting up my own lab at home and practicing there."

Website: https://www.linkedin.com/in/bradleyschaufenbuel/

Bradley Schaufenbuel

36

Bradley Schaufenbuel is VP and CISO at Paylocity and a principal consultant at Schaufenbuel Advisory Services, Inc., which has been performing red teaming engagements commercially since 2010. He has held security leadership positions at numerous companies in the financial services and technology industries over his 22-year career. Bradley has MBA, JD, and LLM degrees; is a licensed attorney; and holds 23 professional certifications. He is a prolific author and speaker and serves on the advisory boards of multiple venture funds and startups.

How did you get your start on a red team?

I am a self-taught penetration tester and ethical hacker. I learned the craft by setting up my own lab at home and practicing there. When I felt I had mastered the basics, I sat for and passed the Certified Ethical Hacker exam from EC-Council. Nine years ago I started a cybersecurity consulting firm and began offering traditional network perimeter penetration testing. Although I was good at finding and exploiting network and infrastructure vulnerabilities, I was less skilled at finding and exploiting application vulnerabilities and performing social engineering. So I began to contract with others to supplement for my weaknesses. I also began to work more closely with my clients' blue teams. It was at this point that I truly graduated from penetration testing to red teaming.

What is the best way to get a red team job?

The best way to get a red team job is to master the skills of a red teamer and then obtain objective third-party validation of those skills through education and/or certification. I would suggest building your own lab of vulnerable hosts and then practicing vulnerability elicitation, vulnerability exploitation, lateral movement, and so on. I would suggest learning everything you can about the threat landscape, vulnerabilities, exploits, social engineering techniques, and so on. If you are able to obtain a formal education in cybersecurity, that helps. If formal education is not in the cards, then at least obtain industry certifications such as the Offensive Security Certified Professional, Certified Ethical Hacker, and Certified Red Teaming Expert. The good news is that there is an acute shortage of red teamers, so if you have a passion for this work, you can find a way onto a red team.

How can someone gain red team skills without getting in trouble with the law?

I personally learned my red team skills by setting up my own lab and practicing there. Many educational institutions and red teaming boot camps have been giving their cybersecurity students more realistic red team exposure by offering willing organizations free red team engagements. Aspiring red teamers can also obtain access to third-party labs from red teaming training organizations. There is absolutely no reason that a red teamer should practice their skills on a network they are not authorized to test, and there is no good excuse for doing so.

Why can't we agree on what a red team is?

In my opinion, the biggest obstacle to obtaining agreement on the definition of a red team is widespread abuse of the term—commercially and internally. Red teaming is more comprehensive than penetration testing, which is more comprehensive than a vulnerability assessment. Pricing naturally tracks to the comprehensiveness of the testing and the skill required for delivery. Some service providers use the confusion between these terms to overcharge clients or undercut competitors. I cannot tell you how many times a prospective client has selected a competing proposal for a "red team engagement" based on price alone and then been delivered the raw output from an automated vulnerability scan of the perimeter as their "red team report." I have also seen the term abused by security professionals, who refer to their app sec team or their vulnerability management team as their "red team," even though they are not actually doing red teaming. Until the consumers of these services are more discerning about what they are actually paying for and security professionals stop using the term so loosely, there will be differing definitions of what it truly means to be a red team.

> "Red teaming is more comprehensive than penetration testing, which is more comprehensive than a vulnerability assessment."

What is one thing the rest of information security doesn't understand about being on a red team? What is the most toxic falsehood you have heard related to red, blue, or purple teams?

The one thing the rest of the information security profession does not understand about being on a red team is just how hard this work is and how difficult it is to keep up with developments in the space. I believe that a lot of people have an image of red teamers as Mountain Dew–chugging punks happily pounding away at their keyboards as they break through one layer of security after another, high-fiving one another along the way. In reality, a good red teamer must be organized and methodical. They spend more time documenting their activities than they do executing them. And they spend countless hours studying new threats and new vulnerabilities and improving upon their techniques. Although exhilarating, it can be grueling work.

> "I don't think an organization will obtain the true value of having a red team until it has a relatively mature security program and a fully functional blue team."

When should you introduce a formal red team into an organization's security program?

I don't think an organization will obtain the true value of having a red team until it has a relatively mature security program and a fully functional blue team. You don't get much value from testing something that is not yet complete. The whole point of a red team engagement is to learn and improve. If you don't have the basics in place and you don't have a team of defenders to apply the lessons learned, there really is no point.

How do you explain the value of red teaming to a reluctant or nontechnical client or organization?

I explain the value of red teaming as a relatively inexpensive way of determining whether your past investments in people, process, and technology are providing the results you expected and what areas of future investment will provide the organization with the biggest bang for its buck. A red team leverages the same techniques that a determined adversary would, so there is no better way to measure the quality of your defenses without incurring the impact of an actual attack.

What is the *least* bang-for-your-buck security control that you see implemented?

The least bang-for-the-buck security control I see implemented is an un-tuned security information and event management (SIEM) platform. If an organization does not take the time to ensure that only the highest risk events bubble up as alerts, then security analysts on the blue team quickly get bogged down reviewing tons of low-value alerts. The more crap a security analyst has to sift through, the easier it is for a good red team to hide its activities.

Have you ever recommended not doing a red team engagement?

I had a prospective client approach me about a red team exercise. As we began to scope out the exercise, the client admitted that the organization had not invested anything in security and had no security program or organization whatsoever. If fact, he assumed that we would own his environment in a matter of minutes. He wanted to do the red team exercise to scare his executive management team into investing in security. I told him that an important objective of a red team exercise is to not only test an organization's technical controls but also to test the timeliness and effectiveness of its incident response capabilities. Without any investments in security controls and no blue team to speak of, I suggested he consider having a basic vulnerability assessment conducted instead. It would be far less expensive than a red team engagement and would likely achieve the same result, i.e., a report containing a sea of red to spark management action.

What's the most important or easiest-to-implement control that can prevent you from compromising a system or network?

The easiest and cheapest control that a small- or medium-sized client can implement to prevent me from compromising its network or systems is basic patch management. The fewer vulnerabilities I have to exploit, the harder it is to achieve the objectives of the engagement. It's maybe not the easiest to implement, but the second most important control is multifactor authentication on all public-facing interfaces. Many systems include an MFA option, and, if not, there are many affordable third-party MFA add-ons. Without MFA, it is child's play to compromise user credentials through password spraying or via phishing attacks. Public-facing interfaces are the first place that a red team will go to compromise credentials and get in. They need to be protected accordingly!

> "Public-facing interfaces are the first place that a red team will go to compromise credentials and get in. They need to be protected accordingly!"

Why do you feel it is critical to stay within the rules of engagement?

The rules of engagement are a contract between you and your client. If you disregard them, then you have breached that contract. If you have breached that contract, then your activities are no longer authorized. If your activities are no longer authorized, then you are no longer an ethical hacker. If you are no longer an ethical hacker, then you are a criminal.

If you were ever busted on a penetration test or other engagement, how did you handle it?

I was conducting a physical penetration test at a large community bank. The bank's disaster recovery site was a server room located in the back of a large branch. I posed as an AT&T technician and walked into the branch. I approached the branch manager, showed her a fake work order and ID card, and said that I needed access to the server room because that is where the circuit I was working on terminated. She seemed to buy the story hook, line, and sinker and took me back to the server room. Better yet, she left me unattended in the server room. Score! I took some photos with my cell phone and then plugged my laptop into the network switch and started to do my thing. A few minutes later, I heard voices and footsteps approaching. I turned around and saw the branch manager with a police officer, who promptly ordered me not to make a move and to identify myself. It turns out that the branch manager was suspicious of me but played it cool and called the IT manager, who stated that he had not ordered any work to be done. A police office just happened to be doing his rounds outside, so the branch manager flagged him down. Fortunately, I had a "get-out-of-jail-free" letter on me. A quick call to the CISO that authorized the testing resulted in me being sent on my way without being incarcerated. But it was pretty embarrassing.

What is the biggest ethical quandary you experienced while on an assigned objective?

The biggest ethical quandary I have experienced occurred when I found child pornography on the personal drive of an executive while moving laterally in a client's network during a red team exercise. Under the laws of the state in which the client was located, I had an affirmative obligation to report my findings directly to authorities. I informed the client of what I had found and my obligation under state law. The client wanted to handle the matter internally and asked me not to report my findings to law enforcement. The client threatened to sue me for breach of contract, claiming that I had an obligation not to disclose my finding to a third party under our mutual nondisclosure agreement. I refused to break the law and reported the finding to the local police department. I lost the client, and they refused to pay me for the work, but I feel that I did what was both right and legal. Child pornography is no joke.

How does the red team work together to get the job done?

The most effective red teams are composed of people with a very diverse set of skills and perspectives. One person may be a social engineering guru, another may be a scripting junkie, another may be app sec focused, and so on. Rarely is one person a guru at everything. When folks with diverse but complementary skill sets and a common objective come together, magic happens. Given that each member of the team has his or own area of focus, it is relatively straightforward to divide up tasks like report writing and debriefing, with each red team member contributing where their area of focus is highlighted.

What is your approach to debriefing and supporting blue teams after an operation is completed?

In the best-case scenario, my red team is working directly with the blue team during the engagement; in other words, we are conducting a "purple team" operation together. For a more traditional red team exercise, where our activities go undetected or client reactions were not appropriate or timely, my debrief includes recommendations for ways in which the blue team can enhance its monitoring and incident response capabilities to find and react to anomalous events more expeditiously.

If you were to switch to the blue team, what would be your first step to better defend against attacks?

I freelance as a red teamer on weekends and oversee a blue team during the week, so this is not actually a theoretical question for me. Assuming common perimeter security controls are already in place (including a robust patch management program), my first step as a blue teamer would be to leverage multifactor authentication for any public-facing interface. As a red teamer, executing successful password spraying attacks on public-facing interfaces with single-factor authentication (or collecting credentials via phishing campaigns) is like taking candy from a baby. It is cheap and easy to do. The biggest obstacle to the deployment of MFA is the use of older public-facing interfaces that don't support an integrated MFA option or SAML, e.g., Outlook Web Access.

> "Let's face it—writing a red team testing report sucks."

What is some practical advice on writing a good report?

Let's face it—writing a red team testing report sucks. It is time-consuming and boring compared to conducting the engagement itself. That being said, it is an essential component of the job. The customer is paying you to learn about his or her vulnerability to attackers. Your report is how they will learn. Your report is also a reflection on the quality and comprehensiveness of the red team exercise you conducted. Your audience for that report is often not only your customer but also its customers and/or its regulators. If your report is of poor quality, these stakeholders will question the quality of the red team testing as well. A good report walks the reader through all of the actions that were taken by the red team, all the weaknesses that were found, and what the client can do to remediate those vulnerabilities.

How do you ensure your program results are valuable to people who need a full narrative and context?

My red team report reads a little bit like a Grisham novel. It guides the reader through all of the plot twists and turns. I describe the techniques of the red team that failed as well as those that succeeded. I also point out the strengths of the customer's controls as well as their weaknesses. I describe the times in which our efforts were thwarted by the blue team as well as the times in which our efforts succeeded. The red team is not infallible. It is important to give credit where credit is due and not just trash the client.

How do you recommend security improvements other than pointing out where it's insufficient?

In my final report, I include step-by-step instructions for remediating any vulnerability that I exploited in the red team exercise. Where my activities were not detected by the blue team, I include recommendations for implementing methods of detecting that activity going forward. Where social engineering techniques were used with success, I recommend enhancing security awareness training. I also like to include a road map for achieving the next level of maturity for my client's security program. In other words, I advise the client on where they should focus their efforts after they fix the vulnerabilities we exploited in this engagement.

What nontechnical skills or attitudes do you look for when recruiting and interviewing red team members?

I look for an inexhaustible supply of intellectual curiosity (necessary since there is always more to learn). I look for extraordinary persistence (necessary to achieve the red team's objective in the face of a determined blue team). I look for unflinching personal integrity (necessary in a profession where crossing over to the dark side can be very lucrative). And I look for a passion for this field (necessary to sustain the first three over time).

What differentiates good red teamers from the pack as far as approaching a problem differently?

Ordinary red teamers immediately jump in and start testing. Extraordinary red teams spend time planning and strategizing before testing. Ordinary red teamers leverage prewritten exploits. Extraordinary red teamers write their own exploits. Ordinary red teamers try techniques one at a time and move on when one alone fails. Extraordinary red teams creatively combine techniques to obtain results. Ordinary red teamers look for opportunities to stand out from the crowd. Extraordinary red teamers look for opportunities to work together to exploit collective synergies. Ordinary red teamers give up when they have exhausted all common techniques and have not achieved the objective. Extraordinary red teamers persist day and night until they achieve their objective. ∎

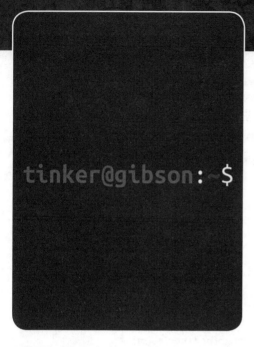

`tinker@gibson:~$`

"Spend most of your time hunting for a job by going to local meetups and conferences. Join some reputable online groups as well."

Twitter: @TinkerSec

Tinker Secor

37

Tinker is a full-scope penetration tester with experience in testing and bypassing the security of logical, physical, and social environments. He has conducted social engineering operations as part of red team engagements in the United States, Canada, and Europe. Tinker has built up, managed, and trained red team and penetration testing teams. Prior to this, Tinker served in the SOC trenches as an intrusion detection analyst. Prior to that, he served in the United States Marine Corps.

How did you get your start on a red team?

A burly man named Bubbles approached me after a meeting of the Dallas Hackers Association. I had given some talks in the local community concerning how I had approached kinetic attacks and defenses in the U.S. Marine Corps and technical talks on how I had trapped Chinese malware for analysis. He said I had the right mind-set for being on a red team and wanted to know if I wanted to be on his team. He promised me training and guidance. I told him no. I was working on a blue team and had just started a project that I wanted to see through. Six months later, I finished that project, and he reapproached me. This time I said yes.

I went through the interview process and was offered the job. They assured me that in the beginning, they would ease me into the job gently. They'd train me and let me shadow other team members. After half a year, they would let me start doing my own gigs.

Right after I started, my new company got bought out, and most of the team left. I, one other newbie, and our technical lead were what was left of the team. My title was changed to senior penetration tester, and I was flown to Los Angeles to hack into two different targets. After several long days, sleepless nights, drawing on what was left of my team, reaching out to local friends for technique advice, and a shit ton of adaptation, I managed to take complete control of both target networks and got my start on red teaming.

What is the best way to get a red team job?

Just like getting any job, you split your time between building up the skill sets required and networking.

Build up skill sets: Study the following: systems, networks, virtual environments and cloud, thick applications, web applications, mobile applications, scripting, physical environments, social exchanges, basic attacks, basic defenses.

You will not become an expert at any one of these until you actually start doing it. Just get a feel for everything. It seems daunting, but don't do deep dives on anything just yet. Study high level and see how it all connects. Later, you'll start to do deep dives.

Also practice the following: participate in scripting challenges, build a virtual lab inside your cheap laptop and install systems and connect them together through networking, and do capture-the-flag exercises online or at conferences.

Professionally network: With a foundational skill set, you get the job through networking. By all means apply for jobs online, but don't spend too much time doing that. Spend most of your time hunting for a job by going to local meetups and conferences. Join some reputable online groups as well. If you don't have local meetups or conferences, create and organize one. Beyond just going to conferences, volunteer for them. In-person networking is the best, but this is limited by money and means and being away from large cities. Do the best you can and take advantage of any resources that are presented, such as scholarships and volunteer reimbursements (some places cover airfare and room accommodations for volunteers, etc.).

It's who you know (networking) that gets you the job. It's what you know (building up skill sets) that will help you in meeting and knowing other people. It's an upward positive cycle. Breaking in is the hardest part. After that, as you continue to build experience, skill sets, and professional reputation, it gets easier.

How can someone gain red team skills without getting in trouble with the law?

It's an old trope that you need to break the law in order to learn hacking. That was built out of a time when there weren't many resources and the only way folks learned was by messing with other folks' stuff.

Nowadays, if you can get your hands on an old laptop (cheap on eBay or freely given out by community organizations—hunt around!), you can build a virtual environment using free tools and practice all the skills you need. Use a free Linux operating system, install VirtualBox for free, download free vulnerable virtual machines from vulnhub, and attack those machines.

If you can get to a CTF in person or online, participate in those. Get books for free online or at the local library. Take free online courses at Cybrary, EdX, and Coursera. Everything you need to learn and train is free and legal.

"The whole point of 'offensive security tests' is quality assurance of established security apparatus or demonstrating gaps in established security apparatus."

Why can't we agree on what a red team is?
We've tried to take a wide variety of security assessments and boil them down into a couple of catchphrases. It's as simple as that. The whole point of "offensive security tests" is quality assurance of established security apparatus or demonstrating gaps in established security apparatus.

If you want to test a specific implementation, you conduct a "targeted penetration test." If you want to test a specific environment, you conduct an "open scope penetration test in a target environment." If you want to test all environments against a specific threat scenario, you conduct an "open scope penetration test of all environments based on threat scenarios of the following threat actors."

The term *red team* is just easier to say when speaking about these more open-ended assessments. The problem lies in where that line is drawn. When does a targeted penetration test become a full-blown red team engagement? To add to the complexity, we've established defenders as the blue team, so all offensive testers are the red team, so any action they do (even white-box security audits) can be considered red team actions.

Finally, we have folks in marketing who love the concept of a red team because it sounds sexy and cool, and we can use it to sell all the things! So *red team* is further muddied. Don't worry, all concept terms lead toward meaninglessness through denotation creep.

When should you introduce a formal red team into an organization's security program?
Security quality assurance assessments and penetration tests can and should be conducted at all stages of a security maturity model. Initially it can help demonstrate the very need for security, prioritize initial steps, and help establish a baseline benchmark. Throughout the maturity model it can establish continual benchmarking that can assist in trend analysis and further security prioritization.

When does a company move from outsourcing this need from third-party consultants to in-house? It's the same as any other job: when the cost-benefit analysis outweighs outsourcing to bringing in a resource internally. Generally, when a company is large enough to support the overhead and the need for a vibrant security model requires continual testing, it is a good time to have a dedicated person or team conduct offensive security assessments.

How do you explain the value of red teaming to a reluctant or nontechnical client or organization?
I boil red teaming down to quality assurance. That's all it is. If a reluctant or nontechnical client sees a need for security in the first place, they see a need to test that security to make sure it works. If that same person does not see a need for security, I show them how a red team or penetration assessment might prove that need.

Ultimately it depends on that person's threat model. What are their priorities, what are they worried about if those priorities are attacked, what sort of apparatus do they want to build to protect those priorities, and how do they want to test and ensure that the security apparatus works?

What is the *least* bang-for-your-buck security control that you see implemented?

This is an interesting question. What do I see that folks put in as security but does little to stop attacks as compared to other security controls? Truth be told, I don't see much security in general, so something is generally better than nothing.

But that said, I'd say the least bang-for-your-buck security control that I see is a vulnerability scanner. It's not that I don't like vulnerability scanners; they're great if they're actually fully used. But they never are. I'm also not saying this because I think penetration tests are better than vulnerability scanners. They both are security QA that cover different areas and have different strengths and applications, and companies should employ both.

Here's a typical scenario that I see: ACME Company implements a vulnerability scanner from a top provider. It's a solid scanner. It can detect a decent percentage of known vulnerabilities, simple misconfigurations, and lack of patches.

ACME runs this scanner once, and it puts out a massive report of everything that is vulnerable! Great! Now what? Well, you've gotta fix the issues. After multiple meetings, the findings are paired down to Critical findings and some High, and, after several months, a very small number of those have been fixed. The remaining Medium and Low findings are ignored (even though fixing many of them is easy, with good, quick returns).

But that was an ad hoc, point-in-time scan. No vulnerability management program was built during that time. No patch management policy. So, ACME scans again, and an even greater list (as new vulnerabilities and new detections for old vulnerabilities have been added) is generated.

The metrics say that the initiative is falling behind.

So, ACME uses the vulnerability scanner to do continuous scanning, but the scan results are never (or so infrequently as to be never) acted upon. Add to this that most scans don't cover full CIDR ranges; rather, they use known IP and host information and therefore miss rogue or orphaned systems. Also, some systems are so out of date and vulnerable that the vulnerability scanner knocks them over, so instead of making the system robust, they're removed from scanning outright and then forgotten.

Have you ever recommended not doing a red team engagement?

Many folks don't need a full-blown red team. Of those, if the client believed and trusted me, they would often get a lot more out of white-box security audits.

Often, though, either folks don't have the experiential background to understand what could happen or they don't know me personally or through trusted reputation to determine whether what I say can be trusted. This is fine. Often the proofs of impact that come out of red teams are crucial, or the prioritization and benchmarking that come out of full-blown penetration tests are highly valuable parts of their security approach.

For those customers who do know me, have a culture of security, and don't need a black-box test, I often recommend a more white-box approach. For example, I'll do an open security audit where I look at everything—network schematics, firewall rules, group policy preference, physical walk-throughs, etc.—and then conduct analysis on what I could do based on what I see from the top down. Or, I'll conduct a more limited and targeted penetration test that assumes a certain level of access from a malicious actor and focuses on a key area of their security apparatus.

White-box assessments often take less time and less cost to conduct. I recommend them where appropriate.

Why do you feel it is critical to stay within the rules of engagement?
Rules of engagement (ROE) are crucial for a couple of reasons. The first is that there may not be a need to test everything. If a client, for example, knows that they are susceptible to phishing attacks and has already begun a process of mitigating that vulnerability, they would not get much from a test that breached them via phishing. What would it prove that they didn't already know; what would it suggest other than what they were already in the process of mitigating? So we might add to the ROE "no phishing attempts" in order to direct our assessment to other things that could allow a breach and assist in minimizing the attack surface further.

The second is that ROE helps prevent actual damage. I might demonstrate that I gained enough access and privilege to delete all data, but I would never actually delete all of the data. I can take a picture of a laptop that was left in an employee's car, but I'm not going to break their car window to steal the laptop. Aside from the legal issues (I'm not going to break local laws to conduct a test, even if a malicious actor might), we want our tests to help stop actual harm, not cause the actual harm ourselves. So our ROE will specifically have language that shows that we might demonstrate access or privilege but not conduct proofs of impact that would have a high likelihood of causing actual damage.

If you were ever busted on a penetration test or other engagement, how did you handle it?
It's rare that I'm "busted" in the traditional sense. Often after I've gotten access and shown proofs of impact, I'll get louder and louder until I'm (intentionally) caught. I then set a benchmark of detection that helps the client know what they could see and what they missed. That said, I have been outright stopped several times. I like to highlight these times by telling stories, giving presentations, and going on podcasts. Some of those have included my "Singing the Blues: When Blue Team Kicks the Red Team's Arse" series.

So let me think of one I haven't spoken about quite as much.... I was hacking into a website from the internet. I found a vulnerability that let me conduct blind SQL injection attacks and access the backend database. After some tentative probing, I opened up with sqlmap and let it do its thing. On three separate days, I conducted attacks and dumped pieces of the database.

Getting full authentication hashes was tough, though. The web app was not the most robust, and the blind SQLi attacks required a lot of tuning to get reliable output. Before I could get key account information, I was stopped cold.

My IP address was blocked, and, more importantly, the vulnerability was patched. I and another colleague bounced IPs and found a new attack vector, but that was patched, and the new IP addresses were blocked. When we had exhausted several IP addresses and could not find any more attack vectors, I sent a final note to our target through their login portal:

    (test' UNION SELECT "Hello SOC and Dev Team! Good Job!"--)

I meant it sincerely, but apparently we spooked them. They thought they had antagonized an actual threat actor and were worried that actor would come back in force. This caused their team to work over the weekend fixing every vulnerability they could find in their own web app. After the debrief, I offered my apologies by taking them out for drinks. It was the least I could do.

What is the biggest ethical quandary you experienced while on an assigned objective?
I specifically do not put myself in ethical quandaries, even if they are allowed within the scope of the assessment. I don't target people for social

engineering using their personal lives. I don't conduct attacks that could have consequences outside the scope of the test. I might point out that information gained during open source intelligence gathering could be used in that manner, but I won't do it myself. There is always another way. There are plenty of attack vectors to exploit.

Part of this mentality comes from an early experience while pentesting. I had gained access to a person's workstation and needed to show proof of access. Nowadays, I generally take a screenshot of their desktop. At the time, I thought that I should take a screenshot of their Documents and Pictures folders, as this would show tangible proof of access. I opened their Pictures folder and found many images of that person in a bikini on the beach. There was nothing wrong with those images being in that folder. There was nothing unethical or against policy for that user. But I didn't feel comfortable looking at them. It was part of their personal life and was not needed for the test. I deleted them from my Loot folder and found another way to prove access.

In conversations with other testers since then, I found that I was lucky that that was the only thing I ever found in a Pictures folder.

How does the red team work together to get the job done?

Most folks on a red team come from a generalist background. They can do a little bit of everything. This happens because most penetration tests involve only one or two people, so the current state of the industry requires that they be generalists across a wide spectrum of technologies focusing on the specialty of attack methodology and skills.

During a full red team engagement, we have the ability to bring in a more diverse group of folks with more skills and specialties. Either we can use generalists who have developed specialties in various things (e.g., antivirus evasion, infrastructure and command-and-control buildout) or we can hire specialists (e.g., software developers, nontechnical social engineers).

As with any other team, tasks are delegated based on the particular team member's skill set and the needs of the operation as a whole. A person who is good at breaching or phishing might get an initial foothold and pass shells on to other members who might be particularly good at privilege escalation or persistence. Every member takes notes, screenshots, and pictures of their actions and writes part of the report. One person, often the lead, will collate all of the reporting and put it into one single report. During debriefing and mitigation planning, that lead will guide the debrief process and bring in the various team members to speak about their parts of the red team assessment.

What is your approach to debriefing and supporting blue teams after an operation is completed?

This depends on the client and their needs. Sometimes a client just needs a report of our actions and initial guidance on what to prioritize during mitigation. We ensure that our reports are thorough and include detailed steps on how to re-create the situation and resources on how to mitigate the vulnerabilities.

For clients that want us to help mitigate the issues afterward, we often pass our work to other teams that are tasked with building out the mitigations and building up security. We assist them throughout that process.

For clients that want a more purple team approach, we'll include blue team members in our operations or sit side-by-side with them. We'll work out whether they see our actions and help them tune their tools until we reach a desired end state.

All of this is sorted out during the scoping process of the project.

What is some practical advice on writing a good report?
Use templates and report generation tools.

- Set up template reports around common assessments. The template reports should include detailed information on how the assessment was approached, a list of most probable actions taken, and a list of the most probable tools that were used. These should be generalized. For instance, the tool list should include multiple toolsets that are often used. If a tool wasn't used or was used and wasn't listed, it's easier to add or remove that from a robust list later.
- Set up templated findings that hold generalized summaries, generalized recommendations for mitigations, and detailed lists of resource information. Often the red team finds common issues across multiple clients and targets. If they can pull those issues from a template and tweak the template to meet the specific finding of that assessment, a lot of effort is saved in generating the report.
- Tweak all templates to describe the specific issues found during that assessment. With the bulk of the reporting already taken care of with the template, the focus is then on the issues that were unique to that client or target. This prevents the tester from glossing over issues that the tester understands but the client may not. This allows the client to have an in-depth amount of information at hand that the tester doesn't have to write out each time an assessment is finished.

How do you ensure your program results are valuable to people who need a full narrative and context?
The biggest thing is to go through the attack methodology and show what worked in the attack and what did not work in the attack. A documented methodology will show the client what was attempted and how the test was approached. An attack narrative will give the details as to the context of where the tester began, where they ended up, and how they got there.

In addition to showing negative findings or vulnerabilities, it's important to highlight positive findings. Positive findings will include the security apparatus that prevented specific attacks as well as times where the blue team detected, responded to, and contained the attacks.

How do you recommend security improvements other than pointing out where it's insufficient?
Pointing out vulnerabilities is the first step toward security quality assurance. Building mitigations or remediating vulnerabilities is the second step. It's important to offer multiple ways to mitigate or remediate issues, as each client or business unit is in a different situation. Often, we'll offer both triage recommendations (things to do immediately for a quick win) and long-term solutions (things that will address the underlying issue and prevent further issues over time).

If the client or business unit allows the red team to assist more actively in the remediation process, discussions around threat modeling, budgetary constraints, and prioritization allow for the best security given specific constraints.

What nontechnical skills or attitudes do you look for when recruiting and interviewing red team members?
The mind-set and approach of looking at everything and saying "How can this be used against me?" and "How can I use this against someone else?" A lot of military folks, hackers, and criminals have this mind-set. The hard part is finding someone who has that mind-set and also has a professional bearing and good communication skills. ■

"If you want to get a really good red team job and be effective as a red teamer, understand all the details of how the blue team functions, and that will make you a way better adversary."

Twitter: @jaysonstreet

Jayson E. Street

Jayson E. Street is a co-author of the Dissecting the Hack series. He is also the DEF CON Groups Global Ambassador and the VP of InfoSec for SphereNY. Jayson has spoken on a variety of information security subjects, including events at DEF CON, DerbyCon, GrrCon, and several other cons and colleges.

38

How did you get your start on a red team?
I believe I've always had that red team mentality, even when I was in physical security, patrolling a new building or starting at a new site. I would always look at the defenses and check to see whether the camera placements were correct to make sure that the perimeter was secured. I made sure that the doors were locked and there was no way to circumvent the door, so I was always thinking with that mentality—how I would break in and be the bad guy. I didn't actually start doing the official red team role until probably midway through my career. When I started looking at the physical aspects, partly being inspired by watching some other red teamers give talks at conferences, I realized, "Wow, that's a whole other avenue I could start looking at," so I started doing red teaming in my organization. They were very supportive and let me do these kinds of things, which helped perfect my skill and got me more confidence to actually start going after it—it was a great fit. Their support benefited them, and then it benefited me in the long run.

What is the best way to get a red team job?
I think the best way to get a red team job is to start off with the blue team. I always recommend to people that red team jobs are fun, and for some reason we make them all seem like they're sexy people like, "Oh, look at these

guys breaking in and stealing stuff. They're breaking into the network and downloading all the crown jewels." That's cool and everything, but I don't think you can be a really good red teamer unless you understand what the defenses are, how the defender thinks, and how the defenses are made, built, and monitored. I'm sure everyone has been talking about different ways to go about getting the job and places to interview, but forget about that part if you want to be a good red teamer. If you want to be someone who is really good at their job, start off at the blue team doing the defender's job. Learn their processes, learn how they escalate issues, and learn what they're monitoring for so you can circumvent them. If you want to get a really good red team job and be effective as a red teamer, understand all the details of how the blue team functions, and that will make you a way better adversary. At the same time, you being a better adversary will bring value to your clients because the role of the red team is to actually assess and help the blue team.

How can someone gain red team skills without getting in trouble with the law?

I've always said the main difference between a hacker and a criminal is permission. The key way to do that is if you're in a blue team position right now, contact your upper management, get involved with them, tell them that you would like to do a red team exercise and that you would like to approach it from the adversarial position. See if you can get upper management to buy in to that process and explain to them this is a free assessment. Give them some good arguments that makes them take that chance and actually grants you permission to go in and do it.

Why can't we agree on what a red team is?

I have no earthly idea. I think because everybody has an ideal of what the red team is supposed to be. I've already described red team, and I'll say it again—I think that the red team is not just a physical aspect of the job of penetration; I think it is also network based. I believe that red teaming is different from penetration testing or vulnerability assessments or things like an audit. It's an adversarial way of thinking. You still have to stay within the scope of the defined agreements that you've made with your client, but it is a more adversarial role in which you are trying to think outside the box by channeling what an actual attacker would do and breaking into the network. It's not just firing up Nmap and scanning to see whether they've exposed ports or running a Nessus scan. It's literally going in and looking for a way to create a payload to send in an infected PDF or to leave a USB drive in the parking lot. You have to think like an adversary, and when you give them that report, the blue team will benefit from that information.

What is one thing the rest of information security doesn't understand about being on a red team? What is the most toxic falsehood you have heard related to red, blue, or purple teams?

I think one of the main things the red team forgets about is that they exist only to benefit, help, and improve the blue team, period. There is no other part of it. The only function a red team has is to make the blue team better. I'm going to say that just one more time for the people in the back—red teamers are only there for the blue team; they're not separate, and they don't exist in a separate field to audit or just to show where everything is broken. Their job is to facilitate making the whole company more secure, instructing the blue team by giving them information on where their flaws and gaps are, and showing them how to shore those up and fix those.

I think the most toxic falsehood is that there's much of a difference when it comes to red, blue, or purple teams. At the end of the day, we should all be on the same team—the team of trying to make things better and more secure. We're doing different functions, but we are all on the same team. We all win at the end of the day when the company is more secure than before we started.

When should you introduce a formal red team into an organization's security program?

One of your biggest indicators that you're ready to do a red team assessment is that you know where all your computers are. Have a full asset management program. Know when a new machine pops up on your network, especially one that's not supposed to be there, and report on it and investigate it. How is an organization going to detect when someone else gets in, puts a new machine on the network, and starts doing callbacks if they don't even have that part managed? They have bigger issues to address first.

Second, if you don't have proper patch management systems implemented to make sure that machines are patched and you want red teamers coming in and doing damage to their network, that's not right. You need to have a totally incorporated working network department IT support line and information security department. You have to be communicating together, be well organized together, know how to work together, and share information and alerts from different devices you own. You need to be able to detect all those things and be able to report on it in a way that makes it more effective for defense. Because if you can't get that part down, which is mostly policy, procedures, understanding, and discovery, then you're not ready for a red team.

How do you explain the value of red teaming to a reluctant or nontechnical client or organization?

I think the best way to explain the value of a red teaming engagement to a reluctant or nontechnical client is simple. We need to stop building defenses as if we are expecting to be attacked by honest criminals and then inspect them as if we would expect it to be done. A lot of defenders build and a lot of programmers program things for honest people. Locks keep honest people out; they don't keep criminals out. I've seen a lot of networks that were really great until someone who was "thinking bad" was able to find a vulnerability because they were thinking like a criminal—they were thinking like an adversary.

What is the least bang-for-your-buck security control that you see implemented?

Any device that you have on your network. Be it an IDS, IPS, firewall, WAF, or whatever it is, if you have that device on your network and you haven't taken the time to understand what the signature baseline is for your environment or how to configure it specifically tailored to your network, then that is one of the worst things to have, and that's a waste of money. That is throwing money out the door. I've seen so many people put in an IDS system, but they don't properly tune; therefore, everybody is ignoring any kind of legitimate signature because they consider it just another false positive. You have to configure these devices so that when someone sees an alert, they take it seriously.

Have you ever recommended not doing a red team engagement?

I actually have a story where on the first day of my red team engagement, I went to the CEO of the company by the middle of the day to tell him that I couldn't continue. I started by doing a preliminary look at what was going on, and this was before the engagement actually even started. I told him that I could not in good conscience actually do a red team on him and that he needed to take the money that he was going to pay me and hire a network consultant or a new network administrator. Their current network administrator had put everything on a 10.0.0.X network, and there was no DMZ. It was a totally flat network. The mail server and the web server were reachable by anyone on the network! Everybody was on the same network, including the guest Wi-Fi.

What's the most important or easiest-to-implement control that can prevent you from compromising a system or network?
I know this is a broken record, and I know there's also some people who like to debate about it, but if you have a small or medium business and you have a small budget and a small staff, then the least you can do is to patch.

Why do you feel it is critical to stay within the rules of engagement?
Because I don't like going to jail! If you do an engagement and go off script, you could actually be responsible for damages and for information that you weren't supposed to gather. You may have compromised something that you weren't supposed to. You could be scanning or going into another network. I've had friends who have said that they've been on jobs where they actually broke in and they found themselves on a network. Then after further recon, it turns out it wasn't the network they were supposed to be on; they got the IP address wrong, and they actually compromised another company. You have to make sure that you stay within the rules of engagement. Understand what your scope is, and even if it's a narrow scope, you have to stay within the confines that your client has set because that gives you a shield from any kind of liability. If you stay within the parameters of the engagement, you're going to be okay.

If you were ever busted on a penetration test or other engagement, how did you handle it?
Actually, on all my engagements I try to get caught at least once if not more times. I always handle it as a learning experience. It is a great thing to happen, and it's even better when you weren't expecting it to happen. That's a cause for celebration. You should be happy for them because they're doing what they're supposed to be doing. They did everything right, and that's what you want. You're not supposed to just be trying to find their flaws; you're supposed to see what they're excelling at, what they're doing right, and making sure you document that as well. Celebrate those victories because they did a good job. So, you have to make sure that attitude is transferred when you do get caught. You shouldn't be resentful like, "Oh, crap, you got me on this one, but I got you over here." No, it should be, "Good job. Well done. Can I have your name so I can give you the recognition?" In a lot of these reports, there are so many people and so many instances where they have to look down upon what people did wrong. Make sure you give them something to look up to, and make sure you give them someone to look up to. That helps the medicine go down, so to speak.

What is the biggest ethical quandary you experienced while on an assigned objective?
I think the biggest ethical quandary I have is hurting people's feelings. It's difficult for me, and it gets me because I'm lying. I'm lying to people, telling them I'm here to help their network run faster, or I'm there to give them new equipment. I mean, I literally told one manager at this bank that I was going to re-outfit his whole entire branch and give them all new equipment, and when I had to tell him at the end of the engagement that I was lying, I felt like I'd kicked a puppy.

I mean, this guy thought it was Christmas, and I'm telling them there's no Santa Claus because I shot him, which was horrible. I still feel really bad about that.

How does the red team work together to get the job done?

Usually the people doing networking (or several people all doing network-based or physical-based attacks) are the red team. For me, red teaming is working with the blue team. It's the collaboration. A company does not hire a red team to break in and cause damage or show where all the damage can be caused, not even to show where all the holes are. That's not really what the client is paying you for—they are paying you for the report and the collaboration that you have with them after the incident is over. You're showing them where they need to do better, where they are doing well, and how to fix it and make it better. That's what they're paying you for. You're not being paid to break it; you earn your paycheck by showing them how to fix it.

What is your approach to debriefing and supporting blue teams after an operation is completed?

The best way that I approach debriefing and supporting blue teams is quite simple. I let them know at the beginning, before I start, that I am not an adversary. I'm an advocate, there to help them be more secure. I'm giving them assurances that when I'm done, they are going to be better for it. They're going to get the ear of management to find out where they need more support and more funding to get things fixed, to get things done the way they should be done. And they probably have been saying this for years, and no one has listened to them. I'm their advocate in that regard, and I make sure they understand that before I even start. So when we're debriefing and supporting the blue team or the operation, they understand already that there are no hard feelings. There are some instances where people still get a little upset when they find out how easy it was to get in. But at the end of the day, they still understand you're there to help them, and you always approach it that way.

If you were to switch to blue team, what would be your first step to better defend against attacks?

In my case it would be, "What would I do if switched back to the blue team? Because I started out on the blue team." And I think the first thing I would do, again to reiterate an important point, is make an assessment of all the devices on our network. I'd check our current patch status. I would do a complete inventory and create an open dialogue between all the major groups that are, in some way or another, partly responsible for information security. Then I would get the users on board to let them understand that they're part of information security too! I would also create a comprehensive security awareness team, because I also think that is very important.

What is some practical advice on writing a good report?

I do believe I am an expert on how not to write reports! I'm not very good at them, but I think it's the most important part of a red team engagement. The only difference between the people you hire and all the other people currently attacking your network is you're getting a report from the ones you hired. You're paying for the report. So, it had better be a good one and worth all the money you're putting into it. If you give me a report that just shows me what you broke, how you broke it, all the details on the CVE, or all the different ways that you broke it, and how you circumvented the control, well, then you wasted my time and money. You have to be able to show the client the ways to make it better, the ways to fix it. It's not about the breaking; they're paying for how to fix the flaws you found.

How do you ensure your program results are valuable to people who need a full narrative and context?

Always when I do an engagement (again, I do security awareness engagements) my goal is not just to break in and find an exploit or a vulnerability; my job is to teach the people while I'm there what happened and why it's bad, so my value is not so much in the report but in the education piece I bring to it. Once I've broken into a place, I will then leave for two minutes. I come back after that two minutes with an employee of the company who's trusted, and I explain to each person I compromised what I did that was bad. For example, if they let me in, I explain why that was a bad thing and how they can be more emboldened and encouraged to not let that happen again. I'm the inoculation. I make sure that they understand right then and there how to be more security conscious. That makes it valuable to them because they learned that lesson instead of just waiting until three months later, when the memo goes out to employees telling them, "Hey, something bad happened three months ago. This is what you all did wrong." I show them right then and there what the problem is.

How do you recommend security improvements other than pointing out where it's insufficient?

I think you showcase the security improvements. You do it by saying, "Here are the things that you are doing well, and here's what you can augment. Also, if you add these other components, it would be even better." It's about showing where you can actually advocate for them to do what's good, recognizing what they were doing well, and building on that to make it better. If you show that you're trying to build on something that they were already doing, even if not 100 percent correctly or effectively, you're not just kicking them when they're down.

What nontechnical skills or attitudes do you look for when recruiting and interviewing red team members?

Communication, communication, communication, and I don't mean between one technical person and another technical person. You need to find people who know how to communicate to executives, to regular users, to anyone. They need to know how to convey what they did and how they broke into something, and they need to be able to communicate that to people who don't have a clue what Nmap is, what Nessus is, or what a zero-day is. They need to be able to communicate how to resolve that issue in terms that everyone understands, because that is where the true value lies. I don't care how great you are at breaking something if you can't reliably communicate to your client how something was broken, why it needs to be fixed, and how to fix it. Otherwise, you're wasting the client's time. You have to provide that kind of value.

What differentiates good red teamers from the pack as far as approaching a problem differently?

Understanding what each client is looking for and giving them what they need, not what they just expected based on faulty expectations. You have to be able to understand what your client is requesting and what their needs are versus what they're expecting. You need to also make sure that they understand the difference. Give them value by giving them actionable information and actionable intelligence on how to remediate and mitigate potential threats. I think that's one of the biggest things that a good red team does. They manage the expectations of their clients, and they help them understand what their real-world adversaries are like. Most importantly, they help the client understand what they are trying to protect. You have to understand what makes them money and how to protect that. ■

Twitter: @christruncer

Chris Truncer

> "Call me an idealist, but I would like to believe that most companies today have the same general definition of red teaming, but it's in the details where we all likely differentiate."

Christopher Truncer is a cofounder and offensive security lead with FortyNorth Security. He is a cofounder and current developer of the Veil-Framework, a project that aims to bridge the gap between advanced red team and penetration testing toolsets along with other tools such as WMImplant and EyeWitness. Chris develops tools that are not only designed for the offensive community but can enhance the defensive community's ability to defend their network.

39

How did you get your start on a red team?
I believe the biggest thing that helped me get into offensive security, and then red teaming, was getting involved in CTFs. When I first was starting, I didn't really have any offensive security experience, but I practiced using the tools on my home computer and wanted to test what I knew in a CTF. I still remember the first CTF I was involved in at CarolinaCon. I met the staff there who ran it, and I really enjoyed the challenges that forced me to learn new things. I was lucky enough to win the CTF, and I put that on my résumé when I started applying for offensive security positions. Participating in the CTF and being able to speak to what I was learning on my own time helped demonstrate that I loved the work, and I believe it helped me to get my first job as a pentester and eventual red teamer.

What is the best way to get a red team job?
Show your passion for the industry in a way that works best for you. Do you enjoy coding different tools that automate something or developing scripts

to help make your job easier? Put it on GitHub or some other public code repository and link to it on your résumé. Do you like testing out tradecraft in a lab environment? Write a blog post about your experience, let me know what worked well and what was hard, and showcase your thought process. Link to your blog on your résumé. While these are just some examples, you can, and should, show whomever you are interviewing with that you are really interested in understanding the field. We can teach anyone to hack, but we can't teach people to care. If you can show your passion, you will put yourself leaps and bounds in front of others who don't have the same drive.

> "We can teach anyone to hack, but we can't teach people to care."

How can someone gain red team skills without getting in trouble with the law?

There are plenty of options now for anyone to learn new skills without breaking the law. You can start by building out a PC/server that can run multiple virtual machines and just test hacking your own systems. VulnHub is a community-built resource for people to download a virtual machine and attempt to solve the challenge that each system provides. There are also paid-for options that anyone can get involved with, such as RastaLab and Hack The Box. Finally, certain certifications can help give you the base skill set that you would use when red teaming, such as the OSCP.

Why can't we agree on what a red team is?

I think it partially comes down to education and the lack of having an industry-defined definition. From the education perspective, I get customers who come to me asking for a red team assessment without fully knowing what they are asking for. Usually, after some conversation discussing differences between a vulnerability assessment, a pentest, and a red team, the customer should have a better understanding of the differences and could very well recognize that they don't actually want or need a red team. On the other hand, without any central authority that the industry as a whole can point to and use their definition of industry terms, I think most companies will all have slightly different definitions. Call me an idealist, but I would like to believe that most companies today have the same general definition of red teaming, but it's in the details where we all likely differentiate.

What is one thing the rest of information security doesn't understand about being on a red team? What is the most toxic falsehood you have heard related to red, blue, or purple teams?

While I think it is starting to gain some traction, one falsehood that I've seen repeated is that blue teams need to stay perfect forever; otherwise, the bad guys/red teams will get in and win. While I can see where that thought originates, I believe it to be true only to a certain point. From an external perspective, blue teams do need to have their perimeter locked down or an attacker will gain unauthorized access into their environment. At that point, the scales tip in favor of the defenders. Attackers are now operating in another team's home turf (the blue team). Once internal to an organization, I believe that now the attackers need to remain perfect with their operation; otherwise, a single mistake can lead to the blue team detecting their presence and removing them from internal access.

When should you introduce a formal red team into an organization's security program?

I would only recommend that a company begin performing red team assessments after they have incident response practices in place and have already had an internal or external team conduct penetration tests. I believe that the team that will get the most value out of a red team assessment is the internal incident response team. A red team is the opportunity for an incident response team to test their detection capabilities and response procedures to identify strengths and weaknesses in their ability to detect and remove a determined actor. Without already having the procedures in place, or at least documented (if not tested), then your customer won't get the most value out of their test.

How do you explain the value of red teaming to a reluctant or nontechnical client or organization?

The way I found to be most effective to explain the value of a red team to my customers is by educating them on the differences between a vulnerability assessment, a penetration test, and a red team assessment. Each of these services provides different benefits to my customers, and highlighting their differences allows me to show how a red team can help them. For example, an internal IT team would likely get the most value out of a vulnerability assessment or a penetration test. Both of these will identify technical or configuration issues present within their environment and will offer different methods to help remediate the problems. An internal security team or incident response team will get the most value out of a red team. It allows the team to test their detection capabilities and remediation strategies against a determined attacker who is attempting to achieve a specific goal. When you work with your customer to find what it is they really want and break down the different benefits of each service, you can pair the two to explain the value to your customer.

What is the *least* bang-for-your-buck security control that you have seen implemented?

Data loss prevention (DLP) solutions. I've seen antivirus be more effective at blocking malicious applications than I have seen DLP products block sensitive data leaving a customer's network.

Have you ever recommended not doing a red team engagement?

All the time. I have had plenty of customers reach out to me, and the first thing that they request is a red team assessment. At this point, I'll normally begin asking a number of qualifying questions such as "Do you have a vulnerability management program?" or "When was your last penetration test?" or "Do you have an incident response team?" Plenty of times I have had customers only able to answer one of these questions, or even none of them. In those cases, I'll likely start to describe the benefits of having a penetration test done (or whatever it is that will help achieve their overall goals) to help prepare for a red team assessment.

What's the most important or easiest-to-implement control that can prevent you from compromising a system or network?

While it may not be the easiest to implement, especially if your workforce is used to having the rights themselves, a very low-cost control would be removing administrative rights from users on systems within their internal network.

This would require the internal staff to properly plan and ensure employees have what they currently need on their workstations, in addition to providing employees with a channel to request changes based on future needs. However, this shouldn't require any sort of additional technology purchase to perform. Rather, it just entails building out the work culture to support this.

"When performing offensive security work for your customer, the single item that makes the test legal is a rules of engagement document."

Why do you feel it is critical to stay within the rules of engagement?

When performing offensive security work for your customer, the single item that makes the test legal is a rules of engagement document. Beyond that, an intangible aspect to the relationship that will continue to keep a customer coming back to you is trust between the customer and you (or your company/organization). If you deviate from the rules of engagement, especially if an issue arises as a result of not adhering to the rules of engagement, then your customer is going to see this as a violation of their trust, something that they clearly laid out prior to beginning the assessment.

If you were ever busted on a penetration test or other engagement, how did you handle it?

While on an internal penetration test, I found a syste[...]
over HTTP that was protected with a password. Afte[...]
I was able to authenticate to the VNC server and had[...]
system. Once authenticated, the system showed a st[...]
negative of a photograph. There were odd colors and[...]
that I was unable to identify. After spending a small an[...]
understand what I was looking at, I saw that I could jus[...]
to the side and access the underlying computer (a Win[...]
exactly that, opened up a command prompt, did some[...]
and determined that the system wasn't going to expand[...]
disconnected from the machine.

A day later our point of contact came in to ask if we had compromised that system, and I said yes. The point of contact told us that that system was used to monitor the weather around the area and was broadcast on a TV in every single room within their organization (meaning every person could have seen me move the weather image to the side, open a command prompt, and start analyzing the system). Even with that much visibility, the point of contact said he was just informed about the weather image not showing on the TV, just about 24 hours later. After all of us having a small laugh, we helped to replace the weather application and return the system to its original status.

What is the biggest ethical quandary you experienced while on an assigned objective?

While not necessarily an ethical quandary, red teamers (or any pentester) can be put in awkward positions when reviewing the private data of an employee (in search of passwords or anything else of use for the assessment) while keylogging the keys employees are typing, taking screenshots of what an employee is doing, or other similar situations. Employees (correctly or not) are generally going to assume that the files on their system are private and the things that they type aren't going to be seen/recorded, so they may search for or download very personal data. Thankfully, I've not been put into a position where we've observed something so obscene that it required us to report the information up the chain to the appropriate individuals, but I have seen very private information that anyone would certainly want kept private. It comes down to your customer trusting you to do what's right. Unless the data needs to be reported, there's no reason to expose private data. I do my best to maintain my customer's privacy unless it's absolutely necessary not to.

How does the red team work together to get the job done?

I believe the team aspect of red teaming is paramount to the overall success of a red team. Generally speaking, a major reason to have a red team assessment done is to have your customer test their detection capabilities and incident response procedures against a persistent threat attempting to complete an objective. At the conclusion of the assessment (in addition to the assessment report), there should be a debrief between the red team and the blue team to deconflict (if not done during the assessment) and review the efficacy of their detection capabilities and incident response procedures. If you don't have an open-book discussion between the red and blue teams, the customer loses the learning opportunities that come from a red team engagement. The report itself should also provide enough detail that an internal red or blue teamer could re-create the attack path based on what's documented in the report. With that level of detail, your customer can fine-tune detection systems or tabletop incident response processes to help detect and prevent similar future attacks.

What is your approach to debriefing and supporting blue teams after an operation is complete?

Any debrief should be an absolute open-book session between the red and blue teams. You would be doing a disservice to your customer if there were vulnerabilities or attack paths that you observed but did not report to your customer for "future use." There also should not be any details left out of the report that the blue team could use to detect the actions of the red team. At the end of a red team assessment, the blue team should have multiple ideas of how to improve or scale their capabilities without any fear of not having all the data needed to do so.

> "Any debrief should be an absolute open-book session between the red and blue teams."

If you were to switch to the blue team, what would be your first step to better defend against attacks?

The first thing I would look to do is implement an application whitelisting policy/ solution and deploy it within my environment. Apex blue teams are doing this and are better protecting their environments than those who aren't. An application whitelist deployment offers multiple benefits. First, once properly configured, it can actually prevent custom malicious software from being detonated within your environment. When your blue team can show a blocked infection or an unsuccessful attack, it's a win that can be used to show the value of the program. Second, even if not fully blocking all malicious applications, an application whitelisting solution can help provide telemetry to defenders that can be ingested in a SIEM or manually reviewed to hunt for potentially malicious applications. I believe that an application whitelisting solution would provide significant value to an organization once deployed. I don't see this in most environments, likely because it can be a significant undertaking to do the up-front work. An internal team will have to thoroughly test their application whitelisting configuration against the needs of their company's workforce to ensure it does not prevent any business-critical application from running. With that said, I would love to find a company that has deployed application whitelisting internally but regrets doing so.

What is some practical advice on writing a good report?

This is a hard one for me because I believe that you should really differentiate yourself by writing a report that really impresses your customer. If they see your output and think it's lacking in content, you've done your customer a disservice. With that said, I think a good report should have at a minimum a couple of sections. Your executive summary should include high-level assessment information for any audience that is not going to be interested in the technical details. You should include assessment logistics, goals, high-level findings, and overall assessment analysis. Another section should include the assessment details, which I like to think of as the story of the assessment. The goal for this section should be to provide enough information that internal IT staff can re-create the steps you took and achieve the same results. It should contain all the information needed to make your work repeatable and allow your customer to also test fixes against your attack path. Finally (at a minimum), your report should contain a findings/recommendations section. This should include evidence-backed findings, a description of the finding, the level of impact, proof that the finding exists, and suggestions for remediating the issue. To help gather all of this data during the course of your assessment, I would strongly suggest that you report throughout the course of your assessment. It could be as simple as adding screenshots into your report template as you conduct important steps, or you could spend 30 minutes each day actually working on the report itself. This will ensure that you have all the screenshots or any other evidence needed to thoroughly document the work you performed.

How do you ensure your program results are valuable to people who need a full narrative and context?

I believe this comes down to how your reporting is done and ensuring you at least offer, if not always perform, an assessment out-brief with key stakeholders. Your report should essentially contain all the information that allows an internal blue team to follow the process that led you to perform certain attacks. Additionally, it should contain the technical details that would allow the blue team to re-create the attack path performed by the red team. By giving the context surrounding a red team's attack, you're not just saying their program or capabilities are deficient in a certain area. You're showing how an attacker could arrive at the same conclusion by providing the contextual details that guided you on your path. In this format, it's bigger than just you (the red teamer) "beating" a configuration or technology; it's helping to give all the information required that can help your customer change for the better and successfully defend their environment.

How do you recommend security improvements other than pointing out where it's insufficient?

I believe that this requires you to provide context to the findings discovered during your assessment and map your knowledge of your customer's environment with real-world attacker capabilities. If you just call your customer's baby ugly, your recommendations won't hold weight, and you also will likely lose a customer. You need to provide your customers with actionable output that they can use to help better protect themselves. Just saying something is inefficient won't elicit a positive response and possibly won't motivate them to fix an issue. However, if you can discuss observations you made during the course of your assessment and speak to how an attacker could theoretically abuse the current state of their environment, you are making the outcome bigger than just red team versus blue team. You should look to build a shared, communal interest in fixing what you've found to help make everything more secure. Doing so can help provide team buy-in and make these changes for the betterment of everyone versus just fixing a single misconfiguration.

> "If you just call your customer's baby ugly, your recommendations won't hold weight, and you also will likely lose a customer."

What nontechnical skills or attitudes do you look for when recruiting and interviewing red team members?

I like to look for three nontechnical skills when interviewing someone for a red team role: their passion, their ability to communicate with others, and their overall ability to work in a team. Passion is number one. You can teach anyone to be a successful pentester or red teamer, but you just can't teach or build that innate drive in someone that focuses them on understanding a new technique, solving a new problem, finishing a script, and so on. Without the passion to learn in an always updating industry, I believe it would be hard to be successful. Communication skills and ability to work in a team are tied for second because I think they are both equally important. I need someone to have the ability to speak with a customer in either a technical or nontechnical conversation and to communicate clearly and efficiently. Finally, it is called a red *team*, and as such everyone needs to be able to work together as a single team attempting to achieve a single goal. Not being able to work as a team can absolutely disrupt the flow of an assessment and prevent the team from succeeding.

What differentiates good red teamers from the pack as far as approaching a problem differently?

I think it comes down to passion and persistence, and these two can work hand in hand when applied to solving a problem. Without the passion or drive to go that extra mile and solve a problem, the individual may never achieve what they otherwise could. The persistence aspect is self-explanatory. I believe most problems anyone would encounter are solvable; it's just taking the time to understand the problem itself and test different theories until you discover a correct method of solving the current problem. Without the passion for the work, the persistence to take the extra time and not give up until you accomplish your goal just won't be there. ■

> "Smart people are smart people; they know how to write magical scripts that do amazing things, and blue teamers are probably even better at it than red teamers because they know their environments inside and out."

Twitter: @VYRU5

Carl Vincent

40

Carl has been a member of the professional information security industry for more than 10 years. His professional skill set spans a variety of disciplines that includes but is not limited to red cell operation, malware analysis, security infrastructure engineering, wireless assessment, and utility development for offensive security practices. As an ongoing participant in both the professional and nonprofessional hacker communities, he continues to work toward the advancement of both offensive and defensive security technologies by continuing to invest personal resources into research whenever he is able. Beyond the worlds of hacking and information security, Carl is a moderately accomplished musician, chef, craft spirit distiller, graphic artist, loving partner, and father.

How did you get your start on a red team?

As a security consultant at a small shop, I was partnered with two co-workers/longtime friends who wanted to get into the same full-spectrum work that I did. We ended up convincing our superiors to let us bid for a red team engagement at a major tech firm and won the bid. After heavily succeeding, we solicited approval from our superiors to pursue more of that type of work, but they were not interested as they were primarily a web shop and did not want to deviate from that core market. As a result, the three of us independently added that experience to our respective résumés and began soliciting work via the community. I ended up being the first one to be offered a position at a firm.

What is the best way to get a red team job?

The best way to get *any* job (including a red team one) is whatever way ends up working. Knock on all doors, follow all paths, all at the same time, until you land one. After that you can take your experience and find the shop that really sings to you.

How can someone gain red team skills without getting in trouble with the law?

- Military and or military contractor experience
- Working in any subset of offensive security at a shop that does red teaming and having other co-workers help you fill in experience gaps or, if possible, let you do "ride-a-longs"
- Not getting caught
- Homing in on the individual offensive security skills required of a red team operator (such as participating in CTFs and or competitions) and pursuing junior red team work
- Being a business-facing blue teamer so you get to interface with the red teams that run operations against your organization. Through the course of your job you will learn how they do theirs, and there is always the option to hit them up for drinks after the op for further networking

Why can't we agree on what a red team is?

Because actual red teaming is expensive, and by misusing the word we as an industry can sell generic offensive security services to more clients if we tell the client they are getting a "red team for cheap." Because by making the term obscure, industry sales teams can use the excuse "Pfft, that isn't a real red team" to move more product (even if they are correct in their assessment). Because at this point, the term has been misused long enough that there are professionals in the industry who think they have been doing red teamwork for several years, but in fact have not.

What is one thing the rest of information security doesn't understand about being on a red team? What is the most toxic falsehood you have heard related to red, blue, or purple teams?

Purple teams do not exist; the purpose of security is to assure business processes. To assure something, one identifies and remediates risk. There are operations that contribute to the assurance process by performing offensive security exercises (including but not limited to red team ops). There are other operations that contribute to the assurance process by performing defensive security exercises (aka blue team work). Doing both is called *security*, this "purple team" garbage is bullshit.

Color, such as red, blue, or purple, refers to an operation, not a person. *Hacker* and *information security professional* are identities; the classification of your last professional operation is not an identity.

The purpose of a red team is to find "unknown unknowns" in your security posture; scanning for known vulns with any level of transparency is not a red team op. A penetration test is not a red team op. A vulnerability assessment is not a red team op. Just because you used lockpicks and/or social engineering does not make your op a red team op (the phrase you are looking for is *blended threat assessment*). If the blue team knows who the adversary is, an adversarial simulation is not a red team op.

When should you introduce a formal red team into an organization's security program?

When your security team decides it is time to devote resources to uncovering unknown unknowns in its defense posture. (Note that I did *not* say after you have fixed all the small stuff. Once you get to the point where you think you know about all the small stuff, then you can put in detection at a bare minimum and get value from a red team telling you about new stuff you didn't have in your original defense model. Obviously whether that is financially sound or beneficial at that time is up to you.)

> "Rule number one at the red team shops I worked with was 'always speak to the threat model.'"

How do you explain the value of red teaming to a reluctant or nontechnical client or organization?

Rule number one at the red team shops I worked with was "always speak to the threat model." At the end of the day, every organization has leaders who know what keeps them up at night in terms of what they think the crown jewels are, and they are probably right. The goal of the red team is to prove just that—either through compromising a bunch of stuff that proves to "not matter all that much" in comparison to "the juice" or by compromising stuff that nobody thought mattered until you demonstrate the potential havoc had it been a malicious party. At the end of the day, as long as you're speaking to the core threat model of the organization and you're keeping focused on finding unknown unknowns that affect that, people are going to understand what you're talking about (in my experience anyway).

What is the *least* bang-for-your-buck security control that you see implemented?

WAFs. They don't stop web bugs from being present; they just make sure that they will be exploited only by attackers slightly more motivated than the bottom-feeders, and that when they are bypassed, the bugs exploited will be abhorrently prevalent throughout the ecosystem and a major disruption to remediate because "we didn't put energy into defending against that at X level because we have a WAF."

Have you ever recommended not doing a red team engagement?

Literally almost every time. The recommendations varied with the clients. The most common reason was they didn't do a threat model, so everything I told them was going to be an unknown unknown. In these situations, I would explain that they are literally throwing away money trying to "test" for things when what they needed to do was build an operational security model first, and then we could come back and hit them and show them what they didn't think about.

What's the most important or easiest-to-implement control that can prevent you from compromising a system or network?

2FA, a decent outbound proxy with actual coverage (don't neglect the VoIP network), and 802.1x. 802.1x is getting more and more irrelevant with the increasing prevalence of cloud-based resources, and VoIP networks are turning into company cell phone plans, which are both great things because it means replacing the last two things on that list with MDM or some equivalent, but 2FA is generally always a time-killer for the attacker.

Why do you feel it is critical to stay within the rules of engagement?

Well, the short answer is because by not doing so you are breaking your signed engagement agreement and by definition literally breaking the law. Even if you don't care about going to jail, it opens you up to lawsuits and makes your insurance provider unhappy.

The long answer is because then you aren't doing your job. If you insist on nmapping the substation and the station browns out, they lost more in business than you could have possibly provided by securing them with your services. Fuck with a production drug robot via a web app and add potassium to everybody's pills "because you can" and you just killed a bunch of people because that shit will kill them *way* before any medical staff can get to them. Zero-day a PLC in a nuclear reactor and, well, something something Stuxnet. Causing any of these problems does not make the organization safer, which is literally your one job.

If you were ever busted on a penetration test or other engagement, how did you handle it?

I got busted on a gig once where the business that shared a parking lot with the target called the cops (apparently a tall chunky black dude and a short skinny white dude in a rental car pulling into your parking lot to take a conference call is "suspicious"). The cops came, and since we were both flying a lot, we carried passports on us, so when the cops asked for ID, that's the one we both provided (something something about being a paranoid hacker and being able to hand a legal form of ID to a cop that doesn't have your address on it). Man, did they read us the riot act; we ended up giving the cops our cover story about being "third-party auditors" who were authorized by "another branch of the company" and were "on the phone checking in with our superiors as to why were denied entry" (which was technically true, since one of us had been shut down by the company across the lot calling the cops, and we were calling our air support to brainstorm about what to do next). They ended up buying it, but what was funny is that the cops never said anything to the target, so for all intents and purposes, we were still green. We ended up going back to the hotel and working on the implant side with our air support and getting in the following evening by leveraging some mad hax under some hilarious conditions, but that's another story (ask the internet about "black Santa").

What is the biggest ethical quandary you experienced while on an assigned objective?

I'm not really sure how to quantify "biggest" when they are all so different.

- Multiple times evidence of an active breach came to light, and the organizations in question flat out told me they weren't going to disclose; this includes major companies that own and/or control entire market segments of technology.
- I once did a web assessment where I discovered that the "notes field" of the app was being used to store all the sensitive data because the employees didn't want to deal with using the "secure" parts of the app. A guessed default cred from the open internet led me to a single screen filled with PII for everybody from Saudi princes to U.S. ex-presidents and Congress members. Beyond government, there were high-profile suspected criminals, major international celebrities, financial heavy hitters in the trade markets, you name it. The login was so easy that several hours after I started, I reported it as a possible backdoor account, and the site immediately went down, never to come back online again. To this day I have

no idea what ever happened to that site or its companion organization, but they paid in advance, so my boss never asked for any answers from me, and I never gave him any.

- I've done two ops for a company that provides a tracking service of sorts for individuals considered to be extreme risks to the organization if kidnapped or captured, and as a function of performing the test I had to prove I knew where they were when they claimed to be someplace else. In one instance, the individual was at a brothel well known to the high-up leadership of the org but (obviously) not his wife, and the other target was a gay woman whom I had to out in order to provide evidence. Not my best day.

- I've done one engagement ever where I found child pornography in an email account I breached. That was not a fun day.

- I've come across countless BDSM photos or accounts for Ashley Madison in `credentials.txt`-type documents discovered on breached systems.

- I hacked a company out of business once. The pen was on a target company that was owned by a company that was owned by a bigger company that was my actual client. I found some bugs in some critical software (that I found out later is used in more than 90 percent of the companies in that industry) manufactured by a third-party vendor, and the company two levels up from the target (aka my client) told me at the end of the first week of my two-week engagement that I could finish my report so that I had something to show my bosses on how I spent my time, but that after looking at my criticals, the company didn't generate enough revenue to be worth the potential liability risks of doing remediation on a third-party product and they were just going to fold the shop. I finished my work, and the target business closed literally 30 days later, but the entire time I had to walk around this office building with very nice people bringing me coffee and tea and homemade items for potluck lunches; it was hard.

- I reported a bug on a bank job once where they pulled a guy out of a cubicle and fired him on the spot in front of me, and he started crying, pulling pictures of his kids out of his wallet. Apparently he'd been there almost 30 years.

- I disclosed a bug in a third-party product to a shop where the shop decided not to bother telling their vendor about the bug and instead just switched products. A few years later, that vendor got bought by a defense contractor that sold the bug to a "government" that was later accused by the UN of human rights violations. I didn't find out till even later via a news article that the company that acquired them took all the bugs that company knew about and sold them to a party for the explicit purpose of tracking down activists and their family members within the country where that client operated and killing them...which they did.

- I've often wondered if I should turn in major executives to their respective boards for having serious drug problems.

- I had a woman in a board room slap, grab, and then hold onto my left ass cheek while looking me dead in the eye and smacking her lips once before starting a findings presentation. It was awkward, not so much for the event but because the entire rest of the meeting's participants were women, and none of them seemed to mind. They also spent a period making comments that seemed to be about me in a language I do not speak. On the upside, it's more attention than I usually get from women, so I guess I should be grateful?

- I'm currently aware (due to an engagement) of a bug that a manufacturer for a massively internationally distributed product is currently leveraging instead of fixing in order to sell the access to spy agencies via a number of technically legal data resellers. My NDA recently expired with that firm, but it's "gray" as to whether the client company itself could come after me if I said anything.

How does the red team work together to get the job done?

Effective red team operations happen because of teams that work together as opposed to individuals—period, zero exceptions. Whether it's somebody to answer the phone as "the CEO" or a lookout while you pick a lock or somebody to watch the compromised security cameras while you walk around the building or even just to get network coverage—teams make ops happen.

> "Effective red team operations happen because of teams that work together as opposed to individuals—period, zero exceptions."

Even doing generic penetration testing, I've never been at a shop that is any kind of effective without sharing tricks between consultants when stuck, and all the best and most effective teams I have been part of have shared constantly, almost compulsively. It's one of the reasons why the work is so rewarding; it's like sitting in a Slack with the smartest people you know from whatever con you frequent most five days a week, having them help you solve problems, and getting paid for it.

What is your approach to debriefing and supporting blue teams after an operation is completed?

Generally my rule of thumb is to just be flexible. At the end of the day, a red teamer's product is knowledge, so at heart you are being paid to teach, and a good teacher always bases their delivery and style on the student. I find that a great way to have awesome results is just to stay humble and remember that as a red teamer, I am a specialist; I am very good at one thing, which is not their thing, but they are an expert at their thing. By me going in with the goal to help them learn about my thing without telling them how to do their thing, we can all succeed in what we are there to do.

On a more general note, I always find it's better to be available to deliver data in a format that works best for the client. Why write a report if nobody is going to read it? Does a presentation work better for your team? Should we do a follow-up two-day, four-hour session? Maybe I just show up with some locks and a bunch of RFID gear and do a kind of workshop. At the end of the day, it can only mean I make more money because the target organization decides I can be of more help if they pay me for more hours, and hey, there is always something to be said for enlightened self-interest.

If you were to switch to the blue team, what would be your first step to better defend against attacks?

Well, in fact, as of a few weeks ago, I did just that. My plan is to remind myself to not be afraid to "get my hands dirty." As a red teamer, you build your own tools because what you're doing usually isn't the "approved use" of whatever technology you're abusing to accomplish your goal, so you spend a lot of time gluing stuff together. But blue teamers tend not to do that in my opinion, especially at shops where there is an established culture of "It will scale to the enterprise or it's not getting done." Obviously, there is nothing wrong with that approach if that is your business use case, but I think way too often the blue side of the house interprets that as "It must be a product or a very well-established open source, out-of-the-box solution," and I think that limits a lot of teams.

Smart people are smart people; they know how to write magical scripts that do amazing things, and blue teamers are probably even better at it than red teamers because they know their environments inside and out. My number-one goal going in is to keep my ears open and to not be afraid to write a few hundred lines of bash or PowerShell to keep us from spending another $2 million a year on some blinky box that solves half the problem because "Well, at least it will operate at scale."

What is some practical advice on writing a good report?
Don't rely on the boilerplate. One of the things I do before doing any reporting is look at my notes and boil down every bug into two descriptions: "What is the bug?" and "Why does it matter?" From there I do reporting, because at the end of the day that's what the readers of the report want, and if (in my experience) you do those things well, the "how to fix it" part is always an easy next step because you have already done the work to understand why it matters to the target.

Another thing (that even I still struggle with to this day) is to make sure you stop testing on time. Ours is a community that is typically passionate about its craft for a variety of reasons, and we often tempt ourselves to go beyond the deadline for trying to get that RCE to pop, feel anxious that we got a bunch of bugs but none of them are highs, or go after that extra site. In the end, the value is the report—take a full day to write it correctly. That value alone is worth more than you would have found in that extra day of testing "off the clock."

"Every offensive engagement I have ever done has ended with me asking if the client feels like they have enough of a deliverable to explain the findings to the stakeholders or if they feel like something else would be more effective."

How do you ensure your program results are valuable to people who need a full narrative and context?
Every offensive engagement I have ever done has ended with me asking if the client feels like they have enough of a deliverable to explain the findings to the stakeholders or if they feel like something else would be more effective. In the end, red teaming and/or consulting isn't different from any other business—you work with people, you ask them what they need, you tell them what you can provide, and the format is part of that conversation.

How do you recommend security improvements other than pointing out where it's insufficient?
You point out what's good, what slowed you down, and what mitigations you had to think your way past. I've written a lot of informational findings on red team reports based around cost or efficiency, such as areas where the target

organization is using four solutions where they could use one or where they are over-tooling with nine WAFs when they only need to add input sanitization in one app and save money on the other 15 boxes housing those 9 WAFs.

What nontechnical skills or attitudes do you look for when recruiting and interviewing red team members?

- Public speaking
- Professionalism
- I'm not really sure how to phrase it as a single word, but simply being prepared to give technical security advice. At the end of the day, as an offensive security practitioner, you are a specialist. People are coming to you because you are an expert in a subdiscipline and the really smart people who work at the target organization want to benefit from your expertise
- Definitely what I would call corporate self-sufficiency. Being a "kid" trying to "grow up" into the industry, I definitely learned that 9 times out of 10, the employee who turns in their expense reports on time, fills out their paperwork, and doesn't make their PM go running for their report are the employees who are going to be trusted with the cool projects. At the end of the day, if you make people's lives' harder, they aren't going to want you involved in things

What differentiates good red teamers from the pack as far as approaching a problem differently?

At the end of the day a good red teamer is just somebody who understands that beyond the technical nature of the craft, an information security professional is somebody who understands the value of information in a security context. Yes, we as humans use computers nowadays to sort and transmit that information around the world and into various categories, but if everybody stopped using computers tomorrow, information would still have value and would therefore need to be secure.

That being the case, a good red teamer is an information security professional who understands their core functionality—to use blended threat advisory simulation to locate unknown unknowns in the existing threat landscape of the target. That core drives all the other things—the urge to spend personal time expanding one's knowledge base, the drive to attend social events and learn from others, and the will to stay current on new technologies as they become prevalent in the industry.

One of the major things I count myself lucky to have been able to do as a consultant is learn from the clients I went after, especially in areas where they did well. We aren't blue teamers; we have defense advice, but that is not our specialty. The great thing about getting to see "under the hood" at everybody else's shop is that you get to see what they do right; the next time somebody asks you how to address a problem, you now have a tried and true, real-world, enterprise scaling solution to offer. ∎

> "One of the major things I count myself lucky to have been able to do as a consultant is learn from the clients I went after, especially in areas where they did well."

"Asset management is something we as an industry don't have down pat yet."

Georgia Weidman

41

Georgia Weidman is a serial entrepreneur, penetration tester, security researcher, speaker, trainer, and author. Her work in the field of smartphone exploitation has been featured internationally in print and on television. Georgia has presented or conducted training around the world, including at venues such as the NSA, West Point, and Black Hat. She was awarded a DARPA Cyber Fast Track grant to continue her work in mobile device security and is a Cybersecurity Policy Fellow at New America. Georgia is also the author of *Penetration Testing: A Hands-On Introduction to Hacking* from No Starch Press.

How did you get your start on a red team?
In college I competed in the Mid-Atlantic Collegiate Cyber Defense Competition. As part of the competition there was a red team whose job was seemingly just to make the students cry and vomit. By the end of the competition I knew I wanted to do what they did!

From there I started doing research, giving talks, and conducting training classes at security conferences and meetups. That eventually got me in front of the right people to get opportunities to participate in red team engagements.

What is the best way to get a red team job?
Unfortunately, for people like me who look for the nearest dustbin to dive into whenever I'm faced with having to talk to someone one on one, a lot of getting a job in any industry comes down to networking. At least for me I was able to

make up for what I lacked in social skills by being active in security research, presenting at conferences, and volunteering to give training classes at security meetups. This led to people with hiring power offering me jobs.

How can someone gain red team skills without getting in trouble with the law?

My book *Penetration Testing: A Hands-On Introduction to Hacking* is one resource for new people to learn about hacking in a controlled environment. The exercises are hands-on, but you complete them in a lab environment.

There are also competitions such as capture the flag (CTF) where you can hone your skills with permission to attack the targets. Many CTFs leave their problems up for you to work through later. For the physical side, there are lockpick villages at many hacker conferences. In general, as long as you are practicing on systems, applications, etc., that you own or have express permission to attack, you are learning ethically.

Why can't we agree on what a red team is?

I think it's mostly due to elitism in certain pockets of the hacker community. Some people brag that they only take engagements that are "no holds barred" and that anyone who does not is not a "real" red teamer. In the real world, that is just not realistic. Organizations that allow you to work without any rules of engagement are few and far between.

> "Some people brag that they only take engagements that are "no holds barred" and that anyone who does not is not a "real" red teamer. In the real world, that is just not realistic."

What is one thing the rest of information security doesn't understand about being on a red team? What is the most toxic falsehood you have heard related to red, blue, or purple teams?

I often hear, particularly from people who are in the business of making defensive security products, that security testing doesn't provide value. It's true that it can be a difficult sell because defensive products don't have metrics such as how many suspicious links were blocked or how many instances of potential malware were found. But attackers continue to get past as many security controls as we put in front of them. It's true that the goal of security testing is to secure the organization so that nothing happens, but, without real security testing, all the defense in the world will never be enough.

When should you introduce a formal red team into an organization's security program?

In my experience, many organizations bring in red teaming too soon and end up wasting their money. You shouldn't be paying red team prices to find missing patches, default passwords, and similar low-hanging fruit. Sign up to have your organization scanned for vulnerabilities first or, better yet, purchase a vulnerability scanner and scan your organization's IT assets regularly yourself as part of your security program.

You should engage a red team when you believe your organization's security posture is robust. Anyone can use a prepackaged tool to exploit a known remote code execution vulnerability. It takes a more sophisticated attacker to gain access to a more robust organization, and thus it takes more skill, time, and effort on the part of the security testers.

How do you explain the value of red teaming to a reluctant or nontechnical client or organization?

I've never been much of a salesman. My security testing clients are almost entirely inbound. Now that I have a mobile security testing product startup, I'm doubly faced with reluctance of many clients to do security testing combined with anxiety about bringing BYOD assets into a testing engagement. In general, testing is a more difficult sell since, ideally, after an engagement, nothing happens, and attackers do not break in. That's naturally a harder sell than "Our product stops 100 percent of security attacks" even though that's a logical fallacy.

> "While things are finally picking up steam with some of the more in-depth mobile threat defense products, some security companies have seemingly done little more than put the word *mobile* in front of the name of their Windows desktop antivirus products."

What is the *least* bang-for-your-buck security control that you see implemented?

While things are finally picking up steam with some of the more in-depth mobile threat defense products, some security companies have seemingly done little more than put the word *mobile* in front of the name of their Windows desktop antivirus products. As mobile devices have matured from the likes of iPhone OS 1, where everything including the browser ran as root, to among the most complex security models available, even basic tasks such as scanning the filesystem for malicious file signatures just don't work on mobile devices—nowadays mobile antivirus applications are typically restricted to their own sandboxes. In the extreme case, some mobile security apps simply periodically wake up and check if it is itself a virus before going back to sleep!

Have you ever recommended not doing a red team engagement?

This happens a lot. Many customers reach out to me looking for red teaming or penetration testing when really what they need to start is vulnerability scanning or help developing a basic security program. Even though it means less revenue for me, I always steer potential clients in the right direction for their needs. That honesty often makes them repeat customers down the road when they are ready for more rigorous, and better paying, testing.

What's the most important or easiest-to-implement control that can prevent you from compromising a system or network?

There is so much an organization can do with only a little budget. Certainly buying a vulnerability scanner can do wonders for finding the easy wins for attackers. Many of these are very affordable. They will help sort out missing patches, default passwords, and known vulnerabilities in commercial off-the-shelf software, etc., that are so often used as the initial foothold by attackers.

Additionally, an attack that gets me in nearly all the time is LLMNR poisoning, where I passively gather hashed credentials on the network. For this attack to work I have to be able to crack the captured password hashes and turn them back into their plaintext values so I can authenticate with systems. Certainly password complexity is not a problem we have managed to solve yet, but the IT department in an organization can download and run the same password cracking software and wordlists that security testers and attackers use. Feed the tool your domain credentials and require any user whose password is cracked in X hours to change it to something more robust.

Why do you feel it is critical to stay within the rules of engagement?

Naturally, given how so much of our society sees hackers—as criminal masterminds dead set on destroying the world just to show their rivals they can—many organizations have an understandable reluctance to

> "The rules of engagement that are decided before the testing begins can be as rigorous or liberal as the client is comfortable with."

allow security testers to attack their organization. The rules of engagement that are decided before the testing begins can be as rigorous or liberal as the client is comfortable with.

Breaking the rules of engagement, even if you think it makes the testing more real-world authentic, only feeds into the notion that ethical hackers are just malicious attackers with a cover job. We need organizations and society as a whole to be more comfortable with ethical hacking, not less. On a slightly less important note, if you want repeat business, you are unlikely to get it if you break scope, and you may even find yourself in breach of contract and not receiving payment for the work you did.

If you were ever busted on a penetration test or other engagement, how did you handle it?

I'm always happy when an organization catches me in the act. Of course, I use industry-standard methods to avoid detection and to bypass defensive technologies the organization has installed, but so many testers seem to be in it simply to show how elite they are. If an organization catches me, that means their security program is where it needs to be to catch real attackers.

It doesn't happen often, but, on one such occasion, I was performing an email-based phishing attack. The website was an off by one letter of a cloud service the organization used, it had an SSL certificate, and the email looked like emails the organization's users were used to receiving regularly. However, before all the phishing emails had even been sent out, a target had sent the email through the proper channels to be investigated as a phishing attack. Once it was verified, IT sent out a notification to everyone that it was a phishing attack. I simply praised them for their mature security posture around phishing.

What is the biggest ethical quandary you experienced while on an assigned objective?

While I've fortunately not had ethical quandaries during an engagement, I have been faced with ethical quandaries when choosing who I want to work with, as a subcontractor, a partnership, or even an acquisition for my mobile security testing product company.

Of course, the same skill sets that we use in our ethical hacking engagements can be used for evil, and the products we build to help with testing can be used by malicious attackers. For example, perhaps an entity hacks mobile devices without permission, but they only do it for governments, including foreign ones whose human rights policies don't match my own morals. In these situations, I have to make judgment calls about what makes sense for me.

How does the red team work together to get the job done?

The most valuable part of security testing is not getting domain admin but rather leaving the customer with a clear understanding of their security shortcomings and an actionable plan for how to fix them. Many automated tools will spit out remediation recommendations like "Disable the offending service" altogether, but that may not be possible for business reasons. Getting remediation and mitigation advice that is detailed and feasible is more valuable to a customer than the output of a tool they could have bought themselves for likely less than what they are paying you. There will always be some customers who just want to check the box that they did the bare minimum necessary, but many organizations' blue teams genuinely are invested in improving their security posture. For me it's important to not only clearly explain my results but also keep an open dialogue with the client blue team as they work through remediating the issues in case they have any questions. Additionally, I always offer a remediation validation to make sure the problems I found have been successfully mitigated.

What is your approach to debriefing and supporting blue teams after an operation is completed?

I recognize that me using testing as a way to feel elite for breaking in and accessing the keys to the kingdom doesn't provide value to the customer. The most important part of security testing is clearly explaining what I did and what the organization can do to fix it. There will always be some customers who just want to check the box that they did the bare minimum necessary, but many organizations genuinely are invested in improving their security posture. For me it's important not only to clearly explain my results but also keep an open dialogue with the client as they work through remediating the issues in case they have any questions. Additionally, I always offer a remediation validation to make sure the problems I found have been successfully mitigated.

> "I have so much respect for blue teams. On the offensive side we just have to find one weakness to break in. On the defensive side they have to secure everything."

If you were to switch to the blue team, what would be your first step to better defend against attacks?

I have so much respect for blue teams. On the offensive side we just have to find one weakness to break in. On the defensive side they have to secure everything.

I worked on an internal security team of a government agency at the beginning of my career, and aside from the sheer volume of devices, vulnerabilities, etc., in play, the most difficult part had to be getting buy-in from higher up the food chain to force employees to fix the remote code execution vulnerability, even though that patch will affect the functionality of an application.

On the offensive side, I'm called in when companies have a budget and are on board with what I am doing. On the defensive side, it was a constant battle even to be able to fix the printers that had security issues. Security was just a line item in the expense column on the budget, and the security team was seen as annoying people you hoped didn't show up in your office. We definitely need to see a cultural change around this for the sake of the defenders who are doing the hardest job in security.

If everything went bust for me and I found myself back in a blue teaming role, the first thing I would do is tackle the none too simple task of identifying all the IT assets in the organization. Asset management is something we as an industry don't have down pat yet. I can't count the number of times I've been on security testing engagements where I could tell a lot of time, money, and effort had been put into building a robust security posture. But it all came crashing down because there was an old box that was decommissioned ages ago, but no one actually turned it off, so it's been running in the back of a storage room for years. That system hasn't been under the scrutiny of the security team in a while and has vulnerabilities to match. It's particularly helpful if the box is an old domain controller and the domain administrator password on it is the same as the one on the updated, fully patched domain controller.

What nontechnical skills or attitudes do you look for when recruiting and interviewing red team members?

I don't shy away from social awkwardness, no pun intended, since I have the social skills of a rock myself. But I do look for the ability to communicate effectively both verbally and in writing to both a technical and nontechnical audience. I also look for passion for the field. I'm not looking for people who work their 9 to 5 and go home and play video games all night. I'm looking for the people who are doing security research and presenting it at conferences or via white papers or blog posts. I'm looking for the people who, if they know nothing about web application security despite their deep knowledge of network security, will seek out the resources and crackme apps they need to learn the skills in whatever they need to be proficient in.

What differentiates good red teamers from the pack as far as approaching a problem differently?

I believe the most important thing is insatiable curiosity and thinking outside the box. If you spend time in red teaming, you will eventually run into technology you aren't familiar with, that no one has done a security conference presentation or released a white paper about, and that there isn't a public exploit or even a CVE for.

Anybody can read the manual, watch a few videos, and click Go on an automated tool, but it takes dedication and passion to home in on ways a previously unknown technology might be used to undermine security and work out a successful attack on the fly while on an engagement. ■

"It has been said that the red team is the unwanted party guest that trashes the hotel, doesn't clean up, and blames everyone else."

Twitter: @asw_sec

Adam Willard

42

Adam Willard, at a young age, found out his passion was in computers. It started with building computers, graphic design, and digital photography. He spent the majority of his career writing software based on business requirements for customers, which led to many bruises from hitting his head on the keyboard. It was time to start something new, so he took an opportunity for a high-profile system as an application security analyst. Adam is now a senior penetration tester on multiple projects and is involved in several bug bounty programs. He is captivated by the industry and looks forward to growing with the next generation of security professionals.

How did you get your start on a red team?

It was a long road to where I am today. The start of my career was in software development, moving on to code reviews, to penetration tester, and today to working with a great team on the blue and red sides.

I was fortunate during my early days, between code review and penetration testing, to sit in the SOC, access all of their tools, and switch hats when needed. During the transition to penetration tester, I was allowed full access to the SIEM, Splunk, web application firewalls, and a few other items that let me see what was going on. This allowed me to ensure that my traffic was not obvious and was hard to track down.

That was the beginning of the red and blue teams as best defined where I am employed. I won't say we function at top capacity as red and blue teams; however, we have come a long way.

What is the best way to get a red team job?

Ask. We have had great success with all sorts of backgrounds on our team. Some have come, made their mark, and moved on, and some are still with us making a difference for our teams every day. We even steal them from our blue team.

How can someone gain red team skills without getting in trouble with the law?

There are programs out there that let you test your penetration testing skills, such as capture the flags or bug bounty programs. You can utilize bug bounty programs to ensure you are providing the best reports you can for the teams that may either mitigate or remediate your findings. There are other offerings by industry names that provide friendly competitions for teams to compete.

Why can't we agree on what a red team is?

I understand that it makes things easier to break into teams; you do this, and they do that. One of the pitfalls is that it makes us fail by putting each other into silos. One of the things that is the responsibility of our team members is to provide a solution if possible. While certain assets have specific protections in place, other systems may have a different set. Mitigation techniques, monitoring, and patches/fixes are items we can recommend to assist not only the defenders but the ones having to do the heavy lifting to fix the issues.

When it is a vendor that must provide a solution, we need to work with the teams to assist in mitigation. This may require reviewing their approach and retesting solutions until fixes can be deployed.

Because our work is to test the systems and protections other teams implement, being a red team is more than a penetration test. Our work on a red team doesn't stop after a report is submitted.

What is one thing the rest of information security doesn't understand about being on a red team? What is the most toxic falsehood you have heard related to red, blue, or purple teams?

It has been said the red team is the unwanted party guest that trashes the hotel, doesn't clean up, and blames everyone else. However, we are all on the same team working on a common goal. We are here to test what is in play. Occasionally we knock over a few lamps and leave doors unlocked; however, we are documenting our findings. Sometimes applications process our payloads in ways we did not expect, and we have no clue where things end up. It is important we document those issues when they occur.

> "Sometimes applications process our payloads in ways we did not expect, and we have no clue where things end up. It is important we document those issues when they occur."

What is the *least* bang-for-your-buck security control that you see implemented?

Automated scanners. I say this because no matter what the report states, it takes two teams at a minimum to implement the results: one to review the issues and then the staff to implement the fixes. If you just fire off a scanner and

"We all like to push our boundaries and break the rules, but that could cause many issues during an engagement."

never do anything with the results, it is a complete waste of time and money.

Reliance on automated scanners. While, yes, it baselines your scanning activities, it also causes unnecessary events in your blue team's tools. It takes time to weed those activities out and get rid of false positives. Automated scanners attack based on the known. As a red team, you aren't necessarily using known vulnerabilities.

Why do you feel it is critical to stay within the rules of engagement?
We all like to push our boundaries and break the rules, but that could cause many issues during an engagement. Many times, the component may be off limits due to who owns the software and the terms of service that the customer has signed. Even though we may see something that is exploitable, we don't have permission to attack. You can always write up in the report why something out of scope is a real issue.

How does the red team work together to get the job done?
The team I am so fortunate to work with has a broad range of talents and diverse work history. We all may be off hitting the systems, trying to find the next vulnerability to exploit, but when we reach a roadblock, we are all ready to jump in to help.

We are responsible for writing up our findings, but processes have come into place where we can utilize/reuse certain aspects of the issues. The team utilizes step-by-step procedures and videos, with audio as needed. Our lead views our reports, sends them back, or asks for clarifications, and then they are compiled for the business owner.

In regard to the blue team, part our team has been on that side of the fence. We utilize communication streams so that we are in contact throughout the day.

If you were to switch to the blue team, what would be your first step to better defend against attacks?
Shut down the datacenter and walk out the door.

At a point in my career I had access to the same tools the SOC used. While I was testing, I would monitor myself to make sure I wasn't being seen. Doing things like this allowed us to suggest other methods and indicators that would increase their chances of discovery.

One of the things I would suggest is for the blue team members to sit with the red team and discuss why and how they are going about certain activities. Just monitoring traffic doesn't allow the analyst insight as to why a technique may be used.

What is some practical advice on writing a good report?
A lot of work has been completed by the community at large. There are frameworks that assist with consistency and reusability. You can join the bug

bounty communities and practice finding bugs and writing reports. You need to submit quality reports if your bug is going to be accepted. Certain programs don't necessarily give the money to the person who first finds the bug but instead rewards the person with the best report for the bug.

I've noticed we get lazy with our reports when we use videos. Our videos show the step-by-step process, the annotation of why we did what we did, and more; however, that doesn't translate into the written report. When it comes time to retest, some of the critical components are missing in the text of the report, and it takes more time and effort to complete the task. Before turning in your report, ask yourself if you had never seen the finding, could you repeat it and does it make sense?

> "One of the things I would suggest is for the blue team members to sit with the red team and discuss why and how they are going about certain activities. Just monitoring traffic doesn't allow the analyst insight as to why a technique may be used."

How do you ensure your program results are valuable to people who need a full narrative and context?

We have a competent team lead that keeps us in check. Our lead works tirelessly with our team and the business owners. Our basic report findings have a set of well-defined common classifications and standard verbiage. We then specify at a high level why it is an issue for a particular issue. Then we walk step-by-step through their vulnerability.

How do you recommend security improvements other than pointing out where it's insufficient?

Staying up to date on current attack vectors. Whether these are human or cyber, knowing what is going on can improve security posture.

What nontechnical skills or attitudes do you look for when recruiting and interviewing red team members?

Attention to detail and the ability to communicate clearly. Communication, whether it is step-by-step instructions on how to exploit a vulnerability or just in a day-to-day conversation, allows each of us to learn about each other. Being able to adjust to a conversation and understand the other team members is critical. As a red team, we get to plunder and have a great time while the blue team is trying to figure out what we are doing. Communicating clearly after the fact or even during an engagement benefits everyone. ∎

Twitter: @MalwareJake

Jake Williams

43

InfoSec professional. Breaker of poorly written software. Incident responder. Digital defender. Business bilingual. Jake Williams treats InfoSec like the Hippocratic oath: first do no harm. By addressing realistic risks, Jake helps businesses create secure environments that actually function. He penetration tests organizations so they can find the weak spots before an attacker does. When an attacker does find a weak spot first, Jake works with the organization to remove the attacker, assess the damage, and remediate the vulnerabilities that allowed the attacker access in the first place. Jake is also a prolific conference speaker, an instructor, and an InfoSec mentor.

"When people started realizing that the red team model offers a different value than a penetration test, marketers jumped on this to differentiate and caused a lot of confusion."

How did you get your start on a red team?
I came from the government side, and they taught me how to hack nation-states. When I left government service, I looked for where I could best apply my skills. The answers were red team and incident response. The two fields are complementary since they both focus on adversary activities; only one is emulation, and the other is investigating their activities.

What is the best way to get a red team job?
Just like any other job—networking. Talk to red team members at conferences, show that you have the chops to think outside of the box (play capture-the-flag competitions, publish research, etc.), and you'll get noticed. The job offers will come quickly—you may never need to apply.

How can someone gain red team skills without getting in trouble with the law?

Join the military. I'm not joking here. This is a great way to get training and discipline on top of it. While this is a broad generalization, I find that those who are prior service members have much more discipline to color inside the lines than those who aren't. Of course, you can read books, play CTFs, etc., but those won't give you the same real-world knowledge a military tour in cybersecurity will.

Why can't we agree on what a red team is?

The answer is mostly marketing in my opinion. When people started realizing that the red team model offers a different value than a penetration test, marketers jumped on this to differentiate and caused a lot of confusion. Red teams do two things: threat emulation and adversary emulation, both with the intent of preserving operational security (not getting caught). A penetration test is a different animal—you still try to break in, but getting caught shouldn't matter since you're just exercising an exploit targeting a vulnerability. In my opinion, the emulation of specific threats is the biggest difference between a red team and a penetration test.

> "Red teams do two things: threat emulation and adversary emulation, both with the intent of preserving operational security (not getting caught)."

What is one thing the rest of information security doesn't understand about being on a red team? What is the most toxic falsehood you have heard related to red, blue, or purple teams?

People view the red team as mischief-makers, and they are often the outcasts of the security team. Sometimes this is well deserved (e.g., when they try to pretend they are better than the blue team). The most toxic falsehood is when someone claims that the red team walked all over the blue team. This doesn't help anyone. Security isn't a competition of red versus blue. If anything, it's a competition where red and blue face off together against adversaries. Any depiction of the red team that pits them against blue is horribly toxic.

When should you introduce a formal red team into an organization's security program?

It should definitely happen only after regular vulnerability scans have already been conducted and a patching/remediation program is in place. Red teams (like attackers) will typically use the least intrusive method to gain access and pivot throughout the organization. Without these programs already in place, attackers will exploit unpatched vulnerabilities and provide little value-add through the discovery of misconfigurations and weak security policies. Generally, you want a few penetration tests done, along with remediation, before involving a red team.

How do you explain the value of red teaming to a reluctant or nontechnical client or organization?

In most cases with a reluctant client, the red team is seen as an overpriced vulnerability scan or penetration test. Education is key to correcting this view, but before you can educate, you have to first get to the root cause of the misunderstanding. Once clients realize that a red team assessment can help them evaluate their controls against a simulated adversary that is in their threat model (as opposed to a hypothetical attacker), selling the red team is usually easy. It's really just a matter of educating.

What is the *least* bang-for-your-buck security control that you see implemented?

The least bang-for-the-buck security controls I've ever seen implemented are ridiculously complex passwords combined with quick password rotation requirements. Thankfully, password rotation requirements are falling out of favor, but many orgs continue to require passwords that are nearly impossible to remember. DoD required contractors to use 15 + characters with two unique characters in each character class that weren't adjacent, and the passwords couldn't have repeating characters. But people will find a way, and that way ends up being keyboard walks. In any sufficiently large environment, at least one person has the password !QAZ@WSX1qaz2wsx, and we regularly crack more than 70 percent of DoD contractor passwords just by using keyboard walk patterns. So this is a control that actually reduces security for many threat models.

"If you've never had a vulnerability scan or a penetration test, a red team is not a good use of resources."

Have you ever recommended not doing a red team engagement?

This happens all the time. If you've never had a vulnerability scan or a penetration test, a red team is not a good use of resources. However, there are times when the security team has been told to get a red team assessment specifically by executives or the board. In these cases, we work with the client to adapt the test parameters to provide maximum value, including vulnerability scanning the entire environment (something not typically done in a red team assessment) and being relatively noisy from the start to give them the best chance of detection.

What's the most important or easiest-to-implement control that can prevent you from compromising a system or network?

Probably the biggest one I can think of is randomizing local administrator passwords using a tool like LAPS. This won't stop the red team from compromising a single box, but it will stop them from laterally moving easily. A huge bonus is that as the attacker tries (and fails) to laterally move, they'll make a lot of noise (and we can easily detect that). Another easy control to implement is turning on the Windows Firewall and not allowing workstation-to-workstation communication over SMB. Provision a jump box in the server IP range that can still talk over SMB for administrative tasks, but don't let machines talk to one another. Also, disable LLMNR and NetBIOS.

Why do you feel it is critical to stay within the rules of engagement?

First and foremost, trust. Straying from the rules of engagement certainly erodes trust with the organization. Second, liability. When you stray from the terms of the engagement, you open yourself up to additional liability if something goes wrong. There are often reasons that certain scope limitations are put in place, and we don't always know what they are. Clearly communicating about the rules of engagement up front can save a lot of hassle during the engagement.

If you were ever busted on a penetration test or other engagement, how did you handle it?

I got busted trying to socially engineer my way onto a retail store's cash room (and server room), and security got involved immediately. The same ruse had worked at numerous other stores in the chain, but this location was having none of it. Despite me having an authorization letter, he wanted to call the police rather than my point of contact. I had to calmly explain that was a bad plan, that I'd have to bill for hours in police custody and dealing with the aftermath, and that it would reflect poorly on him to not at least make a phone call before going down that road. The entire time, I spoke calmly, listened to their concerns, and repeated back their concerns to them (to show I was listening). Physical testers should educate themselves on de-escalation procedures, which are a godsend in a situation like this.

What is the biggest ethical quandary you experienced while on an assigned objective?

It's when management wants the names of the people we've victimized during the red team assessment. Yes, I said victimized. Anyone who falls for one of our ruses is a victim. Most often, we agree at the beginning of a red team exercise to describe how we accomplished each step of our goal but to redact the identities of the victims. Management is usually fine with that going into the engagement but often changes its tune when they get the report. When this happens, we know they are planning to take retribution on employees, and that doesn't sit well with me. While we need to keep the environment safe, employees most often fall victim to attacks due to lack of training on specific scenarios. In other words, it's not really their fault in most circumstances.

How does the red team work together to get the job done?

We use a ticketing system to make sure that high-level tasks are accomplished and nothing gets missed. This is useful for standing up infrastructure and cleaning up in the network after ourselves on the way out. This is especially important when the test transitions to an incident response and the test goes on pause. We use Slack and another internally developed system to communicate. Every engagement has a lead, and that person is the team lead for that engagement regardless of their position in the organization. Just like in the military, position outweighs rank for tactical decisions.

What is your approach to debriefing and supporting blue teams after an operation is completed?

For starters, timestamp every step of the operation and keep meticulous notes. You want to be able to communicate to the blue team *exactly* when a particular task was performed so they can time-bound their analysis. This often allows the blue team to find logs that reflect our activity that neither red nor blue would have thought to look for in the first place. Next, we make sure to communicate why we chose a particular method to move through the network. Understanding why we chose one methodology over another helps them better predict the actions of real adversaries. Finally, we will suggest things they could have done to prevent our actions (or at least detect them). Having a blue team at Rendition that works closely with our red team makes this much easier. Most of our red team works with the blue team at various points, so they have that insight built in from the start.

If you were to switch to the blue team, what would be your first step to better defend against attacks?

I would implement a "device bounty." A KPI for blue team members should be the number of previously unknown devices they discover on the network.

Obviously, this works better in larger organizations (more devices overall equals more unknown devices). The premise of this is that you can't protect what you don't know about.

What is some practical advice on writing a good report?

Don't talk about your skills; the customer knows you have skills (that's why they hired you). Where possible, provide step-by-step instructions for replicating what you did to exploit a vulnerability. This is especially important if you did something particularly novel. Don't assume that the customer understands the impact. Make sure to communicate impact in terms that anyone in business can understand.

How do you ensure your program results are valuable to people who need a full narrative and context?

First, the report should never be about showcasing your skill set. It should be about identifying places where controls are not deployed in a way that is able to detect real adversaries. We always recommend performing adversary emulation for the first few red team exercises. This limits our available actions to those that a specific adversary would use, but it also allows us to explain the impact directly in terms of the same adversary. This helps to create a "ripped from the headlines" report narrative that is more specific to the customer while dispelling concerns that the impact is somehow overinflated.

How do you recommend security improvements other than pointing out where it's insufficient?

One of our approaches is to document the pros and cons of each recommendation. Every new security control implemented requires some level of effort and probably creates some level of friction in the environment. We like to communicate what a recommended control would have prevented/detected, the level of effort/resources to deploy that control, and the level of potential business disruption created with the control. Too many red teams skip the last two, to their customers' significant detriment.

What nontechnical skills or attitudes do you look for when recruiting and interviewing red team members?

I always ask for a writing sample. It doesn't have to be a report sample, but I want to see the way you describe an issue. I want to assess your writing style because it helps me assess how you think. It also tells me whether you can write a good report and whether I need to factor the cost of a dedicated editor into the salary I offer. That last part is only partly tongue in cheek. I'm likely to offer substantially higher salaries to those who obviously require less report QA.

What differentiates good red teamers from the pack as far as approaching a problem differently?

Good red teamers truly think outside the box and find ways to solve problems with what they have. I can't tell you how many red team "experts" I run into that claim to think outside the box but really just regurgitate the same few tricks that they've seen in classes or conferences. Expert red teamers are like the kid who buys a Lego set at a yard sale for 10 percent of the original MSRP—you know all the pieces aren't there, but you're going to make something cool out of those pieces anyway. It won't be what was on the box, but it's going to be darn cool anyway. I'm looking for that kid—all grown up and with systems administrator knowledge. ∎

> "Red teamers aren't out there to make the blue team look bad; everyone is on the same team, with the same goal of making an organization more secure."

Twitter: @rej_ex

Robert Willis

Robert Willis is a security consultant at 1337 Inc. with a BS in management and certifications in IT and security from Stanford University, USAF, DHS, CompTIA, EC-Council, ELS, and various other organizations. He began his journey into programming and hacking in the late '90s on AOL. Robert is also currently enlisted in the Texas State Guard, working in cybersecurity at Camp Mabry in Austin, Texas.

44

How did you get your start on a red team?
After working in tech for many years, I decided to pursue my dream job of becoming an ethical hacker. Ethical hacking wasn't really a known (mainstream) career field until recent times—in terms of companies actually hiring in-house employees or hiring third-party consultants to do red team activities to get an idea of how they appeared to a malicious actor or to meet/maintain required compliances (especially since many of the compliances we know today didn't exist before). I mention this because for the most part, organizations seem to only have a third party test their networks and products annually after they have been breached, or if they are forced to under the threat of losing or halting business.

I was an AOL hacker in the mid-late '90s, and as I got older, I was able to earn some formal security credentials, but at that point in time (to my knowledge) cybersecurity was usually a credential to add to a résumé for those pursuing a job in IT. Because of this, I worked in tech in various roles before red team jobs started to really pop up to a point where it seemed a feasible thing to pursue professionally.

To get my start in (private sector/civilian) red teaming, I made the decision to find a cybersecurity company and work for them with my current tech-based skill set, with the plan of being exposed to the industry and obtaining training and certs to move departments. After a year of full-time work in the industry, full-time at-home study that enabled me to pass certifications, and dozens of courses (and even more college credentials), I was able to prove my skills and move into the department I dreamed of. Already having a bachelor's degree and certifications in tech made it easier for the transition because I was able to get a job at a cybersecurity company (in a nonservices department) to learn the industry and gain skills while I worked to switch departments.

"Networking, proper planning, and obtaining the required skills are the way to get any job."

What is the best way to get a red team job?

Networking, proper planning, and obtaining the required skills are the way to get any job. I say networking first because I've found that when you're looking to get a job in any industry, who you know plays a major role. You want to be the best you can by obtaining the required skills to justify your hire (after your connections help you get an interview).

If you want to understand what skills jobs require, you should look at job postings and see what companies are looking for. Don't be discouraged by some of the postings because many times the people posting the jobs don't know what they want and post an unrealistic combination of skills and want you to have five years of experience in something that is one year old. Pay attention to the standard core skills that are across many job postings and begin planning on how to get them.

It's important to start with a basic and solid cybersecurity foundation before specializing as a red teamer. I recommend getting the Security+ (CompTIA) and then spending plenty of time in labs that end with certifications (Offensive Security, ELS). The EC-Council (CEH) is well loved by HR reps but made fun of on a regular basis by the hacker community. Does this mean you shouldn't get it? Not at all. You want to sell yourself to HR, not random people on the internet.

How can someone gain red team skills without getting in trouble with the law?

There are tons of websites that offer free (and paid) labs/CTFs where you can level up your skills by practicing on vulnerable machines. You can also create your own setup at home. I tell people looking to get into penetration testing to download Metasploitable and DVWA and check out walk-throughs online to begin to understand how to find vulnerabilities and exploit them at a basic level. If you've never done penetration testing and want a more hands-on walk-through, I strongly recommend eLearnSecurity's eJPT course.

Why can't we agree on what a red team is?

In InfoSec there are countless opinions by practitioners. I've done large amounts of training and can say that even different study materials/training can say conflicting things (no lie!). Some people may be on a red team for an organization that only does X and may not realize that there are other aspects outside of what they do.

What is one thing the rest of information security doesn't understand about being on a red team? What is the most toxic falsehood you have heard related to red, blue, or purple teams?

Red teamers aren't out there to make the blue team look bad; everyone is on the same team, with the same goal of making an organization more secure. Purple teamers can probably understand this the most. Some blue teamers dread seeing how you exploited systems they spent most of their lives on—and take it personally. Nobody should take anything personally! Nothing is 100 percent secure; anything can be broken into if the scope of work allows you to do whatever you want. Red teamers can also be toxic if they talk down to the blue teamers. Always be impeccable with your word, and never take things personally.

When should you introduce a formal red team into an organization's security program?

> "Security should be part of an organization starting at day one."

Security should be part of an organization starting at day one.

Everything should be built with security in mind and verified at minimum on a basic level by programmers and members of IT to make sure it abides by best practices (use the principle of least privilege, use safe coding subsets, validate data, don't use deprecated functions, use proper cryptographic practices, etc.). In my experience, the smaller companies will look to hire a third party to test prior to making a product release, or because they must comply with a larger organization's standards prior to being onboarded, or are looking to become compliant for a regulatory reason related to the industry they're in.

How do you explain the value of red teaming to a reluctant or nontechnical client or organization?

Business enablement is a huge factor for organizations because they care about things only when it makes (or loses) them money. Organizations need to be able to justify the spending that goes into anything cybersecurity related, which is why many organizations have a horrible security posture.

It's important to explain that, in today's world, to do business with large organizations, the smaller ones need to be able to pass vulnerability assessments and show that they have a good security posture. This usually helps to make the reality set in that they are hurting the expansion of their company by not taking security seriously, which in turn is losing them money by not getting the big deals they want. I usually mention that large organizations spend millions of dollars a year and aren't going to have all their investments into cybersecurity look pointless when a malicious actor compromises them through a vulnerable third party.

What is the *least* bang-for-your-buck security control that you see implemented?

Some large companies spend a ton of money on products that aren't set up properly or just never set up at all. That would fall under the category of least bang for your buck because it's a waste of money to pay for something that isn't actually being used.

Have you ever recommended not doing a red team engagement?

People who don't work in InfoSec have a hard time understanding it. Popular keywords like *penetration testing* are used by people often, but they don't really understand if they are ready to have one done. Without having an assessment, a security program, controls in place, or someone on staff able to remediate, it doesn't make sense to kick someone when they're already down. There have been customers who have wanted services that fall under the red team category who ended up getting completely different services done for them prior to a red team engagement.

> "Without having an assessment, a security program, controls in place, or someone on staff able to remediate, it doesn't make sense to kick someone when they're already down."

What's the most important or easiest-to-implement control that can prevent you from compromising a system or network?

The principle of least privilege is important. Disgruntled employees are known to be a large cause of headaches at small companies, so it's important to make sure that everyone has only the level of access that they need to perform their jobs—and nothing else.

Why do you feel it is critical to stay within the rules of engagement?

It's critical to stay within the rules of engagement because if you don't, you can be doing illegal activities without a "get-out-of-jail-free" card. It's also unprofessional not to follow the rules put forth by someone who is paying you and can damage your reputation.

If you were ever busted on a penetration test or other engagement, how did you handle it?

Once I didn't realize that I was in a honeypot, which was set up to totally mess with me (as many usually are). Things just weren't working, and it was done so well that I couldn't detect it as a honeypot at all. I must have tried everything I ever learned, and I'm sure the logs of everything I did probably looked insane. I held my cool, but it was frustrating; looking back I think it was really funny.

What is the biggest ethical quandary you experienced while on an assigned objective?

Some organizations really limit the scope of a test to the point where it really wouldn't be realistic in a real-world situation. When it's a large company and you're given a ridiculously small scope, I do think there are some ethical issues with the company just wanting to not be totally obliterated for reasons that may be unethical. If the scope is small enough, there can still be findings, but they can usually be remediated more quickly and more easily than they would be if the scope was appropriate for a real, malicious actor (who doesn't get given a scope at all). If these organizations agreed to have their scopes extended to cover more realistic scenarios of what a malicious actor would really do, their remediations may have been a mountain of things to do instead of a pebble, and that isn't fair to the people who have PII held by them.

How does the red team work together to get the job done?

During and after testing, as I create my report, I always keep in constant communication with my point of contact so they can be aware of findings (especially high ones). I let them know how to remediate the issues and give them the opportunity to. The findings will always be in my final report, but this gives the organization the opportunity to have them marked as "Resolved," which makes them look good, especially if they are able to resolve all the issues. You have to always remember that whether you are doing red team or blue team activities, you're all on the same team when it comes to better securing an organization.

What is your approach to debriefing and supporting blue teams after an operation is completed?

I always make myself available throughout a test and after the report is submitted for questions regarding remediations. My reports always have information on how to remediate findings, but if it's outside the skill set of the individual in charge of doing them at the organization, I always provide helpful information (within reason). A happy customer is a repeat customer, and it's important to understand that you weren't hired to show off your skills; you were hired for the organization to have a better security posture.

If you were to switch to the blue team, what would be your first step to better defend against attacks?

Employee security training is huge. It's important to provide everyone with proper training because employees are low-hanging fruit to get into an organization's systems, especially when a security program is in the process of being built formally for the first time. Part of this training would be on the organization's policies, so if they don't exist, the first thing to be done would be to create them as well.

> "It's important to provide everyone with proper training because employees are low-hanging fruit to get into an organization's systems, especially when a security program is in the process of being built formally for the first time."

What is some practical advice on writing a good report?

I always include a glossary at the top of a report, and the first thing readable is always a high-level executive summary that anyone (even the nontechnical) can understand, followed by a chart of specific findings with ratings (high to low) and if they were resolved or not by the time the report was handed in.

Afterward, for the more technical, I break down each finding with information identifying what asset was affected, the vulnerability, how I exploited it with screenshots showing/explaining what I did, references to the vulnerability (CVE, etc.), and remediation information. If anyone complains about a report like this, then they are the problem.

How do you ensure your program results are valuable to people who need a full narrative and context?

I let organizations know how remediating the results from my tests goes into bettering their overall security posture. I let them know how the current findings are standing in the way of realizing their goal of being as secure as possible and the ways in which it can affect their company. I usually only go into this much detail when an executive asks; I usually try to be thorough in the report's executive summary so they can understand what was done, how it was done, what was found, and if I believe the findings can be easily remediated.

How do you recommend security improvements other than pointing out where it's insufficient?

Sometimes something can be insufficient because the organization doesn't understand the big picture surrounding some controls. I give an overview of why their security needs to be better with specific scenarios and how it goes into what they are trying to accomplish—all while communicating with respect for them. Whenever you point anything out, you always have to remember that the person you are talking to has worked hard to get to where they are and you don't want to be rude. The whole reason you're there is because they knew that they may have issues; you don't want to come off as a jerk.

> "There are some people who just can't get along with others, who are rude, and who think they are always right. Nobody is always right, and if you think you are, you've probably missed learning many important things due to a closed mind."

What nontechnical skills or attitudes do you look for when recruiting and interviewing red team members?

It's important to be good at listening, working with others, and keeping an open mind. These are the best attributes for co-workers' personalities. There are some people who just can't get along with others, who are rude, and who think they are always right. Nobody is always right, and if you think you are, you've probably missed learning many important things due to a closed mind.

I have overheard disagreements where someone who thought they were always right was wrong and wouldn't give in. These people only hurt themselves. The truth is that negative people like this may have more skills in some areas than others early on, but when there is a positive person who is able to listen and always question what they know with an open mind, they will always beat out negative people (and eventually be better than them at their specialties) as time passes.

What differentiates good red teamers from the pack as far as approaching a problem differently?

I think approaching a problem differently doesn't just involve the ability to think outside the box, but also by having a solid foundation of knowledge by understanding how things work at a deep level so you can think realistically of what could actually work, even if it were to sound crazy to someone else. For this reason, I think good red teamers differentiate from the pack when they have an incredible foundation, can speak to many different aspects of systems and security, and are always staying updated on the newest published research and findings in cybersecurity. ∎

"In my opinion, as long as you scope a test correctly, it doesn't really matter what it is called."

Twitter: @digininja

Robin Wood

Hacker, coder, climber, runner. Robin is the cofounder of the UK conference SteelCon, as well as a freelance security tester. He is the author of many tools and is always trying to learn new things.

45

How did you get your start on a red team?
I should start by saying that red teaming is not my main job; I usually get brought into tests when the team needs specific skills, such as web security or tool development. So, my start was building up other skills and then being pulled into the world.

What is the best way to get a red team job?
I think there are two very different approaches; one, get skilled in one or two areas so you can be the person who goes into every team to do job X, and two, develop a rounded skill set so whatever is thrown at you, you can adapt and work with it. A good team needs both of these types of people. Which of these you go for depends on you and your abilities.

How can someone gain red team skills without getting in trouble with the law?
Without already being in a company that does this type of testing, it would be hard to cover all the skills used during a red team test. For example, phishing is hard to do outside a formal test. For general skills, CTFs and bug bounties are good for improving technical skills. Go for ones in areas where you are weak

to build them up rather than sticking to ones you are good at to always win or make money.

Also look outside standard security areas; learning about SCADA or IoT may give you skills that your next employer or team is looking for.

Why can't we agree on what a red team is?

For the same reason that we can't agree on whether pineapple should be allowed on pizza. Some people have very fixed views and are not prepared to change them. In my opinion, as long as you scope a test correctly, it doesn't really matter what it is called. A client may come in and ask for a red team test but actually just want a Nessus scan. During our time with the client we can gently try to explain that this type of test would usually be called a *vulnerability scan*, but if they go away still calling it a red team, you can't do much about it. Just make sure you document what has been done thoroughly enough so someone reviewing any reports generated can see beyond what the client labels it.

What is one thing the rest of information security doesn't understand about being on a red team? What is the most toxic falsehood you have heard related to red, blue, or purple teams?

Not quite answering the question, but resentment between red and blue when a test isn't handled well can cause a lot of problems: the blue thinking they've been picked on as red were dropped in without them knowing and then red boasting about successes at the end of the test without giving credit for all the things they tried but were unsuccessful. When done well, everyone should work together; when done badly, there can be a lot of friction.

When should you introduce a formal red team into an organization's security program?

When other types of tests, such as vulnerability scans and managed, collaborative tests (penetration tests?), come back clean every time and the blue team is able to detect and report on everything that was done during the tests. Doing a red team test when a company is not able to detect, and in some way defend against, basic scans and attacks is unlikely to give value for money.

How do you explain the value of red teaming to a reluctant or nontechnical client or organization?

Explain that by simulating real attacks in a controlled way, you are setting the company up for the day when they are attacked for real. Stress testing your systems, both human and automated, will get them ready to deal with whatever is thrown at them. A boxer who spends many hours in the ring trading punches with a willing sparring partner will be far better prepared for a fight than one who has only ever hit a punch bag.

> "Stress testing your systems, both human and automated, will get them ready to deal with whatever is thrown at them."

What is the *least* bang-for-your-buck security control that you see implemented?

Usually the latest blinky light box that is being sold by everyone at the last trade show. Immature technology, implemented by companies wanting a quick dollar and not fully understanding the sector, can give a false sense of security and can be a cash drain from other important areas.

Have you ever recommended not doing a red team engagement?
Regardless of what type of testing is being asked for, I'll usually take the scope along with the type of testing that I feel would be appropriate for the client and then try to work with them to come up with something that gives them what they need. In all instances so far, that has worked, and between us we have come to a compromise, which I think has given them the best value in both time and money.

If the client was not flexible and stuck to wanting something that I felt was not appropriate, I would probably walk away. I've found that clients who are hard to work with during the scoping phase become even harder once contracts are signed, and I'd rather work with nice clients.

> "If the client was not flexible and stuck to wanting something that I felt was not appropriate, I would probably walk away."

What's the most important or easiest-to-implement control that can prevent you from compromising a system or network?
Good whitelisting seems to work well. Locking down systems to only allow the bare minimum and regularly auditing the list to ensure it doesn't grow or end up out of date helps stop attackers by killing their tools, whether they are using imported ones or are trying to use built-in ones. If the whitelisting app also does reporting, then it is even better, as a report will be a good indicator that something bad is happening on a machine.

Why do you feel it is critical to stay within the rules of engagement?
The rules are there to keep the testers and the business safe. A rule may have been added that you don't fully understand the consequences of breaking, so don't risk it.

If you were ever busted on a penetration test or other engagement, how did you handle it?
First off, by congratulating whoever caught me; from there, it depends on the rules of the test. If capture means the stealthy part of the testing is over, I'm happy to carry on with the testing, leaving the blue team to keep watching and telling me what they see and if they catch me again. Working through different ways I could have done the task where I got caught may find holes that hadn't been expected.

I like the stealthy side of a test, but I also like it when I'm caught and can work with good defenders, as we can play off against each other in this style:

I'll try this; can you see it?

Yes.

OK, how about if I change this bit?

No, I'll update my checks; try again.

Done.

Caught you this time.

It can get really creative and lead to some fun sessions.

What is the biggest ethical quandary you experienced while on an assigned objective?
Staying within the scope of the test. Seeing what looks like it could be an easy win but having to ignore it.

How does the red team work together to get the job done?
As I usually get brought in as a specialist, my role in the team is to look at specific areas, usually web apps. The teams generally consist of some very good generalists and then the specialists who come in when needed.

Reporting and documentation always depend on other members of the team. I usually write up any issues as I find them and leave the bulk of the report to the main members to sort out.

For the debrief, if I find something, either I'll make sure I'm on a debrief call or email to discuss the finding with the client or I'll explain the issue to the client liaison so they can pass the details on. Whichever it is, it is important to be available if required, as there are often follow-up questions that come days or weeks down the line when things start getting worked on. This is where good notetaking really helps. Scratching your head trying to remember the path into a vulnerability is not going to help the client; being able to read it straight from the notes will.

> "Scratching your head trying to remember the path into a vulnerability is not going to help the client; being able to read it straight from the notes will."

What is your approach to debriefing and supporting blue teams after an operation is completed?
The key thing is to make sure the client fully understands each of the issues found, on both a technical and a business level. For example, a board won't care what SQLi is, but they will care that their client database can be stolen. The dev team, on the other hand, will want to know exactly what parameter in what query is vulnerable so they can reproduce the issue and fix it.

If you miss talking to the business, the dev team probably won't get the support they need to be able to fix the problem; if you don't talk to the dev team, the issue won't get fixed.

If you were to switch to the blue team, what would be your first step to better defend against attacks?
Improving awareness and training for other blue team members. The more the blue team knows about their network and the types of attacks it can come under, the better equipped they will be to defend it.

What is some practical advice on writing a good report?
Do it as you are going along. Write up your findings as you find them and, if you are giving a narrative, write that as it happens. It is much better to get to the end of a test and have the majority of the report already written than to start trying to write it and have to dig back through scribbled notes, shell histories, and screenshots to piece together what happened and in what order as you are bound to forget big chunks of it, especially the fun bits where the adrenaline is flowing.

How do you ensure your program results are valuable to people who need a full narrative and context?

You have to remember that the people on the other side are human and that you are there to help them improve the security of their company; you aren't there to show off how good you are. Issues should be covered in relation to the business, not just as standalone vulnerabilities.

Covering positives also really helps. Explaining what was done well and the areas in which you had difficulties, or were straight out caught, help the business understand their strengths and also helps to reduce any animosity from the defenders.

How do you recommend security improvements other than pointing out where it's insufficient?

It helps to think about the business as a whole and work out all the potential consequences of a failure that could be caused by not implementing the measure you are suggesting. You then need to deliver this in a way that doesn't use scare tactics but tries to frame the improvement as best you can. Having someone at the client on site really helps here, as they can often help to point out where the sensitive spots are, for example fear of regulatory fines or customer perception, which helps frame the advice.

You have to be careful here not to step over the line into fearmongering; if you are caught doing that your reputation is blown, and future suggestions are unlikely to go down well.

What nontechnical skills or attitudes do you look for when recruiting and interviewing red team members?

Being able to empathize with others. You have to be able to look at a test as a way to help the client, and in doing that, you have to understand their environment, limitations, and a whole host of other things. I've seen too many testers make comments like "Why don't they just do X?" without realizing that the client probably would do X if they were able.

What differentiates good red teamers from the pack as far as approaching a problem differently?

Being able to think around problems but also being able to work through them from start to end. There is a lot of testing work that isn't glamorous; looking through 200 network shares, most of which contain mundane, boring stuff, to find that one gem that unlocks everything is far from fun but often has to be done. The flip side to this is if you know you are looking for a specific item, coming up with a way to automate your search to save all that effort is also useful. ∎

> "There is a lot of testing work that isn't glamorous; looking through 200 network shares, most of which contain mundane, boring stuff, to find that one gem that unlocks everything is far from fun but often has to be done."

> "Penetration testers like myself are generally jacks-of-all-trades."

Twitter: @DHAhole

Wirefall

46

If you were given the opportunity to tell the world your story in 100 words or less, what would you say? Would you focus on the challenges you've overcome and highlight your accomplishments? Or, would you use the platform to advocate for a cause you support? This is the privilege I've been granted as a contributor to this book. My choice is to turn the mirror on you, the reader. How would you like your bio to read? Now be that person! If you still want to know my story, then DM me or engage with me in real life.

How did you get your start on a red team?

While I've been a hacker my entire life, I started performing security assessments professionally in 1995. My progression has been somewhat typical, transitioning from vulnerability assessments to pentesting to red teaming.

My origin story begins after separating from the Air Force in 1994. I had been stationed overseas, and upon returning stateside everyone was talking about the World Wide Web. The consensus was that it was going to be the next "big thing," so I signed up for a dial-up account through a local free-net. I had used computers to access bulletin boards as far back as 1982 and was excited to explore this newly connected world that had passed me by while I was in the military.

Having a hacker mind-set, I started poking around. I found that it was trivial to access almost anyone's computer connected to the same ISP. How could anyone think cyberspace was a good idea if this was the norm? I began researching how to secure myself. At that time there was a lack of good security resources. There were zines like Phrack and 2600, but we were still a couple of years from NMAP even being released.

In the end I was horribly wrong. The Web did become a big thing and very quickly, despite nothing about it or the underlying infrastructure being secure. Once the dot-com boom hit, if you could even say security—forget about spelling it—you were suddenly in high demand. I went from working a low-wage job at the county dump to earning ten times more as a security consultant all in about four years. That's not to say it didn't take effort. I took courses at my local community college and earned an AAS in computer network operations. I was also willing to relocate multiple times and in 1999 took a consulting position working with a major telecom supplier. I was sold as "one of the preeminent security resources in the field." This was ridiculous, of course; I'd only wanted to make sure nobody else could access my hard drive while online.

What is the best way to get a red team job?

I'm extremely active in my local security community and get asked this question rather frequently, but it's still difficult for me to answer. Duplicating my experience would require first inventing a time machine, as when I broke into the field there were scant security resources, whereas now there are full PhD programs. I was lucky! I prepared myself, I invested in myself, and I had people who believed in me even if I didn't myself. I was very lucky indeed.

My advice, for what it's worth, would be to learn as much as you can about as much as you can until you find that one thing you end up wanting to pour everything into. Penetration testers like myself are generally jacks-of-all-trades. The value of red teams is that they also include highly specialized resources. I strongly believe that this advice applies at a broader level as well. People should not be focused on getting *into* InfoSec; they should aspire to bring something *to* InfoSec. So, be an expert in databases or wireless or physical access systems or whatever. If you're just getting into the field, then focus on emerging technologies where there are fewer experts, areas like cloud security or software-defined networking.

Finally, network. The people kind, not the Cisco kind. I fought this for a long time. I believed in absolute meritocracy over cronyism. I discovered instead that success rarely aligned with either. Social media has made it easier for us introverts to network, but I would still advocate for venturing out into the real world and connecting with others who are doing what you want to do—others who share that passion because, let's be honest, if they didn't, they wouldn't be going out on a perfectly good afternoon or evening that could be spent at home.

How can someone gain red team skills without getting in trouble with the law?

Back in the day the internet was one of the few feasible testing grounds for the curious. Fortunately, things are very different now. With virtualization, containers, and so on, you can now spin up almost any environment in the cloud or even on your own laptop. There are also numerous educational resources available, from instructional videos to fully developed testing environments.

I would bring it back to specialization, though. Find something you're passionate about and learn everything you can. Research the tools and techniques used in your area of study and contribute to them.

Why can't we agree on what a red team is?

I'd like to blame marketing, but there's never been a standard definition for penetration testing either. Many companies will still run a vulnerability scanner and call it a pentest. That said, I see very clear delineations between vulnerability scanning, penetration testing, and red teaming.

The purpose of vulnerability scanning is to enumerate known security issues within an environment. These scans should be conducted with administrator or root credentials and be part of a vulnerability management program that includes metrics such as total number of vulnerabilities remediated and time to patch.

Penetration testing is meant to mimic an attacker within the environment, but they are also time/resource/scope-bounded. Exceptions in active defenses, such as IPSs or WAFs, are often requested as the assumption is that an attacker could take weeks, months, or even years to evade them, but the test itself must be completed in a much shorter time frame due to logistical or cost requirements.

The purpose of a red team is to test blue team capabilities. All defenses should remain in place, and the assessments should not be announced. Can the blue team effectively detect and respond to red team activities? Unlike a penetration test, which attempts to exploit as many weaknesses as possible, red teaming activities are typically scenario-driven. The red team tests the effectiveness of defenses against the current objective, for example assuming a third-party supplier has been compromised.

What is one thing the rest of information security doesn't understand about being on a red team? What is the most toxic falsehood you have heard related to red, blue, or purple teams?

The most harmful misunderstanding is that the red team is an adversary. This is wholly untrue. We are defenders—defenders who leverage a subset of attacker tools and methodologies to assess the effectiveness of the security investment an organization has made into its people, processes, and technologies. We still operate within the constraints of ethics and the law, which true adversaries do not. We won't deploy ransomware across the enterprise or do a smash-and-grab against the CEO's personal vehicle to get her corporate laptop. We may cause disruptions or inconvenience users and support personnel, but thoroughness is our mandate. Cleaning up after an actual adversary will always be exponentially more intensive. In the end, we're all on the same side!

When should you introduce a formal red team into an organization's security program?

The definition of red team that I've preferred is to test the effectiveness of the blue team. If an organization doesn't have a well-established blue team that is capable of detecting and responding to security incidents, then it shouldn't consider such an assessment.

Start with defining policy and getting inventory and patching down. Develop a vulnerability management program. Thoroughly test security controls through penetration testing while building out detection and response capabilities. If these programs are not in place, then the budget for a red team exercise would be better allocated elsewhere.

How do you explain the value of red teaming to a reluctant or nontechnical client or organization?

Asking questions. How much does the organization pay for its blue team: the people, processes, and technologies? How effective is that investment? What are their metrics, and how are they validated? This should get the conversation started. If they have answers, then they likely already understand the value of red teaming or are currently performing similar activities. If they don't know, then the discussion of a red team's value to the organization can focus on helping answer the question of blue team effectiveness.

What is the *least* bang-for-your-buck security control that you see implemented?

Honestly, most of them. The Achilles heel of so many organizations is access control. Depending on the scenario being tested, one of my goals during an assessment will often be to gain access to a single account, which in most environments is a trivial endeavor. As an "authorized user," I will typically be granted access to numerous shares, some of which may contain scripts with system or database credentials or even full database backups. An attacker doesn't need domain admin or root credentials if they have direct access to the data an organization is trying to protect.

Inventory is hard. Data classification and management are hard. Buying security software or blinking lights is easy. I would recommend focusing limited budgets on tools and training to make your people more effective, rather than on vendor solutions that claim to cure all that ails.

Have you ever recommended not doing a red team engagement?

My background is in penetration testing, and I am so tired of shooting fish in barrels. I'm frequently brought in to assess organizations that don't even have the most basic security controls in place. This is fine if the purpose of the pentest is to shock management and help loosen the purse strings, but it rarely provides any value outside of that context.

If a well-defined blue team doesn't exist, then there's nothing for the red team to test. In those cases, start with defining policy and getting inventory and patching down. Develop a vulnerability management program. Thoroughly test security controls through penetration testing while building out detection and response capabilities.

I recommend against red teaming more often than not. My goal is to build trust with my clients. When they are ready for the services that we can provide, then ideally we'll be considered a trusted advisor and they'll reengage us.

What's the most important or easiest-to-implement control that can prevent you from compromising a system or network?

First decrease the surface area of what requires protecting by minimizing the amount of sensitive data that is collected and stored in the first place. When data is no longer needed, expunge it.

Backup, backup, backup. Test your recovery strategy on a regular basis. Whether it's accidental or due to a ransomware attack, the loss of data can threaten the viability of small and medium businesses even more than large enterprises.

Finally, train your people. Train users to protect themselves at home. Encourage user groups and recognize champions within them. Train your support staff. As the adage goes, what if I train them and they leave? What if you don't and they stay?

Why do you feel it is critical to stay within the rules of engagement?

During the presales process, I lobby to create the conditions I believe will give the client the best value from their assessment, but at the end of the day I'm providing a contracted service. If I don't follow the rules of engagement, then there is no difference between me and the adversaries that I'm trying to protect the client from. Security is founded on trust, and trust is difficult to regain once violated. Be trustworthy!

If you were ever busted on a penetration test or other engagement, how did you handle it?

Unfortunately, these are rare occurrences. The following two examples demonstrate how an initial failure isn't necessarily final.

I was performing a physical penetration test for a client. The CIO found out about it and thought it wasn't fair so sent out an email to the entire organization that the assessment would be occurring over the next week. I was still able to breach three of my four targets without incident. On one site I even crashed an employee appreciation celebration and ended up in a picture that was included in the company newsletter. One of the successes came out of failure, though. I was directly challenged and produced my "get-out-of-jail-free" card. I then offered to provide an out-brief on what had been done correctly to apprehend me. I conducted the meeting, congratulated them on their success, and then left. They'd never verified who I was with anyone else in the organization, though. The credentials in my authorization letter were all forged. The next year I succeeded in compromising the one target that had previously stopped me. I leveraged the knowledge that they would be forewarned. I developed the following pretext: "Your site has been selected for the upcoming penetration test. You're going to have someone try to compromise your physical security within the next week, so corporate sent me to make sure that your defenses are up to par." My target gave me a full tour of the entire facility.

On another engagement I was assessing a pharmaceutical client. I was able to walk right by the front desk security the entire week. The company was in the middle of renovations, so it was easy to find an unused cube and claim it. By Friday I had obtained terabytes of highly sensitive information without ever having been challenged. It was time to get noisy. I launched a full vulnerability scan across the entire organization. The security team noticed that, but instead of tracking down the origin, they killed my port, so I knew I'd been detected. I packed up and left without ever being identified.

What is the biggest ethical quandary you experienced while on an assigned objective?

I was performing an assessment against a governmental agency. From the internet I was able to access the personally identifiable information of tens of millions of individuals including their names, addresses, phone numbers, driver's license numbers, and Social Security numbers. This was back when such information still had nontrivial monetary value. I could have retired to a nonextraditable country with the downloaded contents, but that's not why I do what I do. My moral compass never wavered. I discovered that this was a multiuse database, though. Unfortunately, I can't divulge what its other purpose was without giving away the client, but needless to say I found my name. I could have changed my status. Doing so wouldn't have affected anyone else, but it would have decreased certain "inconveniences" for me. The needle wavered but stayed true.

While I do bring a valuable skill set to the table, trust is the only thing that really matters in the end. Without that we are nothing.

How does the red team work together to get the job done?

This depends on a number of variables. Are the teams physically colocated or geographically dispersed? What is the size/makeup of the team? For example, is it mostly senior-level testers with one or two juniors, or is the core of the team already a cohesive unit but a new member has recently been added? Managing a red team is the same as managing any other group. I would recommend team dynamics training for all members, but at the least for the lead or project manager.

The chosen communication approaches should be what work best for the group as a whole. Red and blue teams have a greater need for highly secure communications channels. Invest in the infrastructure to support this. Members should never have to waste time figuring out how to securely share a document or, even worse, be standing up ad hoc solutions to solve the problem.

What is your approach to debriefing and supporting blue teams after an operation is completed?

The approach should always be tailored to your audience, but I like to provide all the documentation and supporting data up front and then give the recipients time to assimilate everything. I will schedule an initial follow-up with the technical team several days after the report is provided and let them know that the team is available to answer any questions in the interim. The initial follow-up should include time to review next steps and actions that can quickly enhance the organization's security posture. Prior to providing an executive out-brief, I will reengage the technical team so that any progress can be noted in the final presentation.

At the end of the engagement I'll reiterate that we're always available for follow-up questions. Scope creep is real and must be managed, but if something isn't clear, then I consider that a failure on our delivery and deal with it appropriately.

If you were to switch to the blue team, what would be your first step to better defend against attacks?

My first step would be to listen and learn. The next would be to start asking questions and continue learning. Why were red team activities not noticed or specific countermeasures not taken? In life I've found that what at first appears to be a stupid decision or action was made because of information or constraints that I wasn't even aware of. Given the full context, I find that I would likely do the same or similar.

What is some practical advice on writing a good report?

Optimally, a team should include a dedicated technical writer. If that isn't possible, then have the strongest writers QA the rest of the team's work. Develop style guides to help standardize the documentation process. Consider paying for and providing time for team members to take a technical writing course. This should be in addition to, not in lieu of, their technical training. It should never be seen as a punishment.

Collect feedback from your customers. What's the good, the bad, and the ugly? Is the information valuable but the format unusable? Are next steps clearly defined? We should never be lobbing thousand-page PDF bombs at our clients.

How do you ensure your program results are valuable to people who need a full narrative and context?

The goal of every assessment should be to provide as much value as possible within the scope of the engagement. The best way to do this is to talk to your clients. Get to know them. What are their pain points? What are their frustrations? How could you leverage the assessment and its results to address those areas of pain and frustration? Build rapport. Become a trusted advisor.

How do you recommend security improvements other than pointing out where it's insufficient?

I advocate for focusing on root-cause analysis. Listing a dozen findings is less useful than identifying the process that is producing them. Example scripts on an Apache web server and default credentials on a Jenkins instance are both examples of application hardening standards not being followed. Still provide references for remediating the findings, but also address the underlying cause.

Don't reinvent the wheel. I rely heavily on existing resources. OWASP, for example, has excellent guides on SQLi, XSS, and the proper deployment and use of SSL/TLS certificates. Make your clients aware of the resources at their disposal.

What nontechnical skills or attitudes do you look for when recruiting and interviewing red team members?

Passion, integrity, humility, and preparedness.

Passion: Tell me about your home lab. The size or investment doesn't particularly matter; it can be as simple as running virtual machines on a laptop. This is a great icebreaker, as a passionate candidate will be excited to talk about his or her setup.

How do you keep current? If it's podcasts, then which ones? If it's Twitter, then who do you follow? There isn't a right answer, but not being able to identify specific resources raises concerns about the candidate's commitment to continuous learning.

What security communities are you actively involved in? There is a place for well-qualified "lone wolf" testers, but I'm typically screening for a team environment. Community involvement is a good indicator that the candidate is passionate about the field and will be comfortable contributing within the group.

Integrity: You list tool X on your résumé; what are your preferred configurations/flags for it and why? I don't believe in gotcha questions, such as asking about esoteric tool settings, but if something is listed on your résumé, then you should at least know how you use it.

Have you ever been asked to do something that you felt was ethically questionable? If so, how did you respond? This is a situation many testers have encountered. Make sure that you're comfortable with the answer provided.

Humility: What's the biggest mistake you've made while performing an assessment? We're all human. We've all screwed up before. A follow-up to this would be asking if the candidate made any methodology changes to prevent similar errors.

Preparedness: Adding a new member has a significant impact on the team, so I take the responsibility of performing a technical interview seriously. If you're a candidate, then I can guarantee that I have thoroughly reviewed your résumé and performed some basic OSINT. I expect that you will have done at least the same amount of research.

What differentiates good red teamers from the pack as far as approaching a problem differently?

Red teamers, like hackers, exist in all walks of life. Often they are driven by pure curiosity; other times, it may be out of necessity. I attribute my success in the field to a completely different attribute: childishness. A security control is basically a way of saying you can't go there and I don't like being told what I can or cannot do! What I'm driving at is that we all have a different way of looking at things because of our varied backgrounds and drivers. There is such a thing as the hacker mind-set, though, and I believe it manifests itself when we embrace our differences instead of approaching challenges from the view of accepted norms. ∎

"We need to remember we are on the same team, and it's not us against them. When we all work together, we can accomplish amazing things."

Twitter: @PhillipWylie

Phillip Wylie

Phillip Wylie is a penetration tester with more than 21 years of experience in information technology and information security. He is an adjunct professor teaching ethical hacking and web app pentesting at Richland College in Dallas, Texas. Phillip is the founder and director of the Pwn School Project, an educational meetup group teaching pentesting and ethical hacking skills. He holds the following certifications: OSCP, GWAPT, and CISSP.

47

How did you get your start on a red team?

We were getting ready to go through layoffs at the company where I was working as an application security engineer. We were given advance notice before being laid off. My dream job was working as a pentester, and during my job search, I found an opening for a pentester working in consulting. I got the job and started my career as a pentester.

What is the best way to get a red team job?

Getting involved in the InfoSec community is the best way to get a red team job. This can be accomplished through networking by attending InfoSec meetings and conferences. My last two roles were through contacts I made through my local InfoSec community. Similarly, a member of our local community was hired by someone who saw his presentation at an InfoSec group meeting.

How can someone gain red team skills without getting in trouble with the law?

A few good ways to get experience hacking without breaking the law are to build a lab and to participate in bug bounties and capture the flags (CTFs). The first two methods, in my opinion, are more helpful. Labs can be constructed quickly by downloading purposely vulnerable VMs. Metasploitable 2 and 3 are great ones to start with. If your focus is more on web applications, then DVWA, bWAPP, Web Goat, and Juice Shop are great options. Owasp.org has a whole page dedicated to vulnerable VMs and apps. Bug bounties give you experience in real-world production environments, and you can even make some money in the process. CTFs can be useful; not all of the challenges are hacking related, but they can build other cybersecurity skills.

Why can't we agree on what a red team is?

I think we can't agree on what a red team is due to the term *red team* being used in two different ways. One way it is used is as a term for offensive security in general, much like the way *blue team* is being used for defensive security. The second way *red team* is used is for adversarial simulations where the blue team's capabilities and reactions are tested. I think most people use the first definition, but I agree with the second definition.

What is one thing the rest of information security doesn't understand about being on a red team?

I don't think they realize that we are ultimately on the same team. Our goal is to make our environments, applications, and devices secure. We like it when the vulnerabilities we discovered get remediated. Otherwise, it can feel like a waste of our time and efforts if they don't care enough to do their part and fix the vulnerabilities.

What is the most toxic falsehood you have heard related to red, blue, or purple teams?

It can be toxic when someone thinks their job is more important than others. All of our roles are equally important. These roles include security, IT, development, and business. We need to remember we are on the same team, and it's not us against them. When we all work together, we can accomplish amazing things.

How do you explain the value of red teaming to a reluctant or nontechnical client or organization?

What has proven effective in my experience is explaining that assessing security from an adversarial perspective is required to expose vulnerabilities that could be exploited by malicious threat actors.

Have you ever recommended not doing a red team engagement?

Yes, there was a time when I was doing a Wi-Fi pentest of a hospital, and the client was concerned that the pentest could adversely affect wirelessly connected medical devices. I recommended a security assessment instead of a pentest, which removed exploiting systems and doing a review of the security rules and settings for the wireless access point (AP) controller.

Why do you feel it is critical to stay within the rules of engagement?

One of the main reasons I feel it is critical to stay within the boundaries of the rules of engagement is for liability reasons. You don't want to risk outages and potential loss of business or risk lawsuit. You also don't want to lose your client's trust and confidence in you. If you find any reason to go beyond the rules of engagement or the scope, it is best to discuss with your client and your team first. If the client approves, then it is alright to proceed.

How does the red team work together to get the job done?

Most of my pentests have been solo, but I have worked on some team engagements or engagements where I was only doing network, wireless, or web app tests, but even on those occasions, we worked together writing reports. One of my favorite and most fun experiences was when I was working with three other pentesters on an internal network pentest. We had five days to complete as much as we could and try to remain undetected the first half of the first day. There was nothing special about the test really, but it was just fun working with the other team members. We all worked well together, which made it a big success.

What is your approach to debriefing and supporting blue teams after an operation is completed?

During debriefings, I like to share good practices and controls that I saw during the engagement. I let the blue team, IT, or development teams know that we are on the same side and I am working with them to secure the environment. I try to put myself in their shoes and understand their perspective. Having worked on a blue team and as a sysadmin gives me an understanding of their view, challenges, and concerns. It is their environment to support and defend. I keep this in mind as I test the environment to do my best to prevent outages or damage to operating systems or applications.

What is some practical advice on writing a good report?

The report is important and all you have to show for all of your hard work and effort. It serves as a report card on how well a client is doing with their security posture. You want your report to reflect the value of your security assessment. You should be thorough in your testing, as well as thoroughly documenting your findings with screenshots and detailed explanations. Be clear in your writing and make sure you use terms that nontechnical people can understand in the executive summary. Management and businesspeople will be most concerned with this part of the report. Use proper grammar and spelling and have it reviewed before submitting it to your client.

How do you ensure your program results are valuable to people who need a full narrative and context?

First, you need to make sure you focus on the goals of the pentest and strive to achieve those goals during the pentest. Second, make sure to provide sufficient detail and clarity for your findings. Third, in this type of scenario, put more effort into the remediation plan. Fourth, you can try to soften the blow by starting the executive summary with their strengths. Let them know what they are doing right. It will let them see that you are trying to be objective and not just trying to make them look bad.

What is one of the most beneficial nontechnical skills you use for red team activities?

Essential nontechnical skills are communication skills, both written and spoken. You need to be able to clearly communicate with clients to provide better value, and it can make the engagement run more smoothly.

What differentiates good red teamers from the pack as far as approaching a problem differently?

I think professionalism is a big differentiator. We are hackers at heart, but we are also supposed to behave professionally. Don't be rude; have patience. Communicate with the client, whether it be an external client or someone in your organization. Communicate with them along the way and don't get to a point where they have to ask you for things that you should be sharing with them. They will get frustrated, and it looks bad for you. Think of your interactions with excellent customer service in mind, and if you do this, they will request you when given a choice. A positive attitude goes a long way. ■

Epilogue

We know that not everyone will have the time to read through every single interview, so we condensed some commonly answered questions here and ranked them in order from least number of times mentioned to most number of times mentioned. We hope you learned as much about red teaming as we did!

What are some tips on writing a good report?

- Answer follow-up questions promptly. Gather feedback from your customers and make a note for your next report.
- Highlight areas where the customer performed well; compliment the client on as many positives as possible.
- Have someone double-check your spelling and grammar. Collaborate on the report with your peers and clients.
- Use a standard template for your reports and develop style guides. Remember to sanitize everything in the deck.
- Reframe your mind-set to view reporting as valuable. Use it as an opportunity to market yourself and set yourself apart.
- Stick to the facts. Tell the truth. Be brave and be willing to admit if you didn't find anything. It's okay to be embarrassed, but don't work past the contracted time just to see if you can finally "pop that shell."
- Put all technical data in the appendix. Have a "Findings" summary/glossary. Provide references to CVEs or technical guides.
- Make your report engaging, as if you're telling a story. Show how much work went into your engagement, and possibly inspire others to go into security.
- Take notes as you test; write/take screenshots as you move along. Don't worry about details and formatting until the end.
- Make your language succinct and nonambiguous. Concise writing prevents reader fatigue. Don't use jargon or flaunt your skills and technical know-how. You were hired for your expertise, so the customers already know that you're skilled.
- Give suggestions on how to prevent, detect, and remediate. Your findings should be actionable. Help build a case that funds remediation efforts. Provide a risk rating to prioritize remediation.
- Understand your objective, write the report to align with those objectives, and know your audience. High-level management should have a short report using third-grade reading level, whereas technical management and staff should have more detailed findings.
- Paint a picture of the attack path and give steps on how to re-create the same results. The results should be easily reproduced. Use charts, pictures, screenshots, and videos.

What nontechnical skills do you look for when recruiting a red teamer?
- Someone who doesn't complain about doing the "uncool" stuff
- Someone who can understand the big picture and not lose sight of the objective
- Someone who goes above and beyond and changes the industry for the better
- Someone with a diverse background in a different cybersecurity (or noncybersecurity) discipline
- Professionalism, punctuality, and preparedness
- Charisma, stage-acting ability, and a sense of humor
- Patience, persistence, resilience, and ability to handle difficult situations
- Eagerness and ability to work on a team
- Self-awareness, willingness to ask questions, willingness to admit they don't know everything, and introspective
- Trustworthiness, integrity, and accountability (internal locus of control)
- Empathy, sympathy, and humility
- Love for learning, willing to update skill set, teachable, "hacker mind-set," questions everything, creativity, curiosity
- Strong self-motivation, passionate
- Strong communication skills, ability to explain technical concepts to layperson, writing skills, listening skills

What differentiates good red teamers from the pack as far as approaching a problem differently?
- They are good communicators and confident in their abilities.
- They are cautious and test things in the lab environment before trying it live. They plan and strategize before going in.
- They understand the value their activities represent to organizations and understand their core function as a red teamer.
- They specialize in a specific area or have a niche skill. At the same time, they have a deep understanding of the foundations of systems and security.
- They are humble and don't assume they know how everything works. They are able to admit when they're wrong about something.
- They are patient and persistent.
- They can quickly evaluate an attack surface. Since they are highly sensitive to their environment, they don't need to flip every stone. They have situational awareness.
- They think, plan, and act like an attacker. They have an "attacker" or adversarial mind-set.
- They are thorough and detail oriented. They can focus for long periods of time.
- They love their craft and will never stop learning. They have a tenacious curiosity.
- They know where they fit into a team and how they can provide value. They're able to pool resources to create a cohesive and fluid team.
- They successfully approach problems in a high-pressure environment. They're able to think critically in the moment and are adaptable if their techniques aren't working as planned.
- They are able to think outside the box, approach problems with a creative mind-set. They question everything.